Refugee Roulette

Refugee Roulette

Disparities in Asylum Adjudication and Proposals for Reform

Jaya Ramji-Nogales,
Andrew I. Schoenholtz,
and Philip G. Schrag

Foreword by
Senator Edward M. Kennedy

NEW YORK UNIVERSITY PRESS

New York and London

NEW YORK UNIVERSITY PRESS
New York and London
www.nyupress.org

Library of Congress Cataloging-in-Publication Data

Refugee roulette : disparities in asylum adjudication and proposals
for reform / Jaya Ramji-Nogales, Andrew I. Schoenholtz, and
Philip G. Schrag ; foreword by Senator Edward M. Kennedy.
p. cm.
Includes index.
ISBN-13: 978–0–8147–4074–3 (cl : alk. paper)
ISBN-10: 0–8147–4074–x (cl : alk. paper)
1. Asylum, Right of—United States. 2. Administrative procedure—
United States 3. Political refugees—Legal status, laws, etc.—United
States. 4. Judicial statistics—United States I. Ramji-Nogales, Jaya.
II. Schoenholtz, Andrew Ian, 1951– III. Schrag, Philip G., 1943–
KF4836.R44   2009
342.7308′3—dc22   2009014685

New York University Press books are printed on acid-free paper, and their
binding materials are chosen for strength and durability. We strive to use
environmentally responsible suppliers and materials to the greatest extent
possible in publishing our books.

Manufactured in the United States of America
10 9 8 7 6 5 4 3 2 1

Contents

List of Figures

List of Tables

Foreword

THE UNITED STATES has long stood tall in the world in its commitment to the protection of refugees. In the Refugee Act of 1980, Congress and the administration reaffirmed our nation's commitment to refugees by striking the former discriminatory system that favored refugees from certain countries and discouraged others from seeking safe haven in the United States because of geographical or ideological considerations. The Refugee Act also established for the first time a uniform asylum program enabling refugees who are physically present in the United States to receive needed protection. Through these programs, millions of the world's persecuted have been given the opportunity to begin their lives anew in safety and dignity.

By protecting refugees from persecution, we honor our nation's finest traditions. But, as the information in this remarkable book makes clear, all is not well in the current asylum system. In a thoroughly researched study, the authors lay bare in painstaking detail the fact that many refugees are being turned away from protection in this country for reasons unrelated to the merits of their individual claims.

This important study demonstrates that in the current system, the decision whether to permit a refugee to remain in the United States to avoid persecution in his native land is strongly affected by the immigration judge's work experience, personal bias, gender, and lack of training; by the court to which the case is assigned; and by whether the refugee is fortunate enough to have effective legal representation. The authors describe, for example, how a woman fleeing persecution in Colombia would have an 88 percent chance of prevailing before one of the judges in the Department of Justice's Miami Immigration Court, but only a 5 percent chance before another judge in the same court. Similarly, one immigration judge in a New York Immigration Court was found to be nineteen times more likely to grant asylum to an Albanian applicant than another judge on the same court. Such "refugee roulette" is unacceptable in a system that makes life-or-death decisions for some for the world's most vulnerable persons.

The authors are deeply committed to ensuring that our institutions that rule on the merits of claims for refugee protection hold fast to basic principles of fundamental fairness. They give us an alarming portrait of the current system. It is imperative to restore justice and integrity to our critical refugee protection programs.

The determination whether to grant asylum to a person claiming a well-founded fear of religious or political persecution in his native country—be it China, Venezuela, Burma, Haiti, Iran, Sudan, Ethiopia, or any another country with a poor human rights record—should not rest on the random assignment of the case to a particular immigration judge, who may be predisposed to question the veracity of any asylum applicant or who may lack adequate knowledge of the applicant's country. There is far too much at stake in these cases.

As one prominent judge noted, "[E]ach time we wrongly deny a meritorious asylum application, concluding that an immigrant's story is fabricated when, in fact, it is real, we risk condemning an individual to persecution. . . . [W]e must always remember the toll that is paid if and when we err."[1]

Even if the Board of Immigration Appeals or a federal court of appeals remedies the immigration judge's error, a successful appeal—which can take years—still comes at great cost to the refugee. In many cases, the appeal process prolongs the refugee's detention in inappropriate conditions, with lack of access to adequate medical and mental health care, and uncertainty about the future of the refugee and the refugee's family as well.

Relying on the availability of appeal is highly risky for the refugee. As the authors confirm in this study, the likelihood of prevailing on an asylum claim in immigration court correlates significantly with whether the refugee is fortunate enough to be represented by counsel. Even if effective assistance of counsel is obtained, the streamlined review process of the Board of Immigration Appeals and the courts' highly deferential standard of review make it likely that the immigration judge's faulty decision will be affirmed, even though the immigration judge—giving in to the personal biases, attitudes, policies, or ideologies described in this study—rested his adverse credibility determination on misstatements, arbitrary rejection of testimony, unsupported conjecture, speculative conclusions, or inaccurate findings of fact. It is critical for the asylum officer and immigration judge, who have the first look at the application, to get it right by rigorously applying standardized norms. As the authors urge, the Department of Justice must provide far greater resources and training for immigration judges.

This book and its call for serious reform could not be more timely. In recent years, the federal courts have grown increasingly frustrated with the poor quality and arbitrary nature of decisions by immigration judges and the Board of Immigration Appeals. Courts across the country have expressed their discontent as well, emphasizing that "the adjudication of these cases at the administrative level has fallen below the minimum standards of legal justice"[2] and that some immigration judges have failed to demonstrate the necessary judicial temperament, neutrality, consistency, and professionalism.

In August 2006, Attorney General Alberto Gonzales proposed a number of reforms in the immigration courts and the Board of Immigration Appeals, and some progress has been made in their implementation. For example, Board members are now subject to performance appraisals, and procedural changes have somewhat reduced the harmful effects of streamlining. The attorney general's commitment to improving the resources and training of immigration judges, however, has not been fully realized, and the job performance of immigration judges is still not subject to periodic review.

Compounding these failures, as the inspector general of the Department of Justice reported in July 2008, the Department of Justice has politicized the process for selecting immigration judges. These judgeships are not, and have never been, political positions. Yet, high-level officials of the department bypassed the public competitive hiring process in favor of a process in which immigration judges are selected not for their individual qualifications and experience but for reasons of ideology and partisanship. Political affiliation trumped merit, with harsh consequences for immigrants and refugees whose lives hang in the balance in proceedings decided by these inexpert judges.

Immigration judges selected by the Bush administration for political reasons have been generally far less likely to grant asylum applications than judges chosen through the regular, politically neutral process.[3] As the authors properly suggest, strong consideration must be given to moving the immigration courts and the Board of Immigration Appeals out of the Department of Justice and granting them greater independence from political influence.

A mark of a great nation is how fairly it treats the most vulnerable. Refugees arriving on our shores, desperate to avoid a return to persecution, are among those who most deserve fair treatment under our immigration laws. For years, refugees have been arbitrarily denied asylum and returned to their native countries, at great risk to their lives and the lives of their families.

This indispensable study is a wake-up call that proposes well-supported, sensible changes in policies and operations to reduce the unacceptable disparities that tarnish the current asylum process. The new administration and new Congress in 2009 should take up the authors' recommendations and implement these needed reforms. Otherwise, the promise of the Refugee Act of 1980 will continue to go unfulfilled, and our nation's reputation as a beacon of hope for the persecuted will continue to decline. They, and America, deserve better.

Senator Edward M. Kennedy
Chair, Senate Subcommittee on Immigration
December 2008

1. Ming Shi Xue v. Bd. of Immig. Appeals, 439 F.3d 111, 113–14 (2d Cir. 2006) (Calabresi, J.).

2. Benslimane v. Gonzales, 430 F.3d 828, 830 (7th Cir. 2005) (Posner, J.).

3. *See* Charlie Savage, *Vetted Judges More Likely to Reject Asylum Bids*, N.Y. Times, Aug. 24, 2008.

Acknowledgments

THE AUTHORS THANK Dr. B. Lindsay Lowell, director of Policy Studies at the Institute for the Study of International Migration, for his wise counsel and statistical analyses of the data reported in this book, and Dean T. Alexander Aleinikoff, Associate Dean for Research Larry Gostin, and the Georgetown University Law Center for their generous funding of the cross-tabulations and regression analysis reported in chapter 3, as well as Temple University, Beasley School of Law, for support for this project. Many thanks go to Profs. Joshua Fischman, Jonathan M. Ladd, David Hoffman, and David Schrag, as well as Luis Carlos Ramji-Nogales and Kim Schoenholtz, for consulting with us about methods of presenting statistical findings. The authors also wish to thank their very able research assistants, Elizabeth Banaszak, Anaxet Jones, Kristin Ketelhut, Paulo Cesar DeFreitas Mamede, Daniel McLaughlin, Asa Piyaka, Jaclyn Sekula, and Zhi Yu for their outstanding help with compilation and organization of the data, as well as Josette Oakley for her dedicated assistance with administrative details. We are indebted to David Berten and I. V. Ashton, who obtained the immigration court data on which we draw heavily in chapter 3 of this book, and to Prof. David Law, who generously provided us with data he had previously compiled on asylum decision making in the Ninth Circuit. We also appreciate the cooperation of the Executive Office for Immigration Review in the Department of Justice and the Asylum Office of the Department of Homeland Security, which provided the databases that we analyzed in chapters 2 and 4. We also benefited enormously from suggestions by many scholars who read earlier drafts, including Stacy Caplow, Maryellen Fullerton, Lauren Gilbert, Kate Jastram, Stephen Knight, Audrey Macklin, David Martin, Susan Martin, Karen Musalo, Lori Nessel, John Palmer, Louis Michael Seidman, Robert Thomas, and Russell Wheeler. Special thanks are due to Hiroshi Motomura for allowing us to present this book as a work in progress at the 2006 immigration law professors' workshop, and to Deborah Gershenowitz, our outstanding editor at New York University Press. Special thanks go to Ariel Schrag and Zachary Schrag for their suggestions for the design of the book's cover.

An earlier version of portions of this book appeared in the *Stanford Law Review*, at volume 60, beginning at page 295. When possible and appropriate, please cite to the *Stanford Law Review* as well as to this book. The authors gratefully acknowledge the editorial assistance of the editors of that journal.

Introduction

WE AMERICANS LOVE the idea of "equal justice under law," the words inscribed above the main entrance to the Supreme Court building. We want similar cases to have similar outcomes. We publish tens of thousands of judicial decisions and have enshrined the concept of precedent in order to reduce the likelihood that Jane's case, adjudicated in December 2006, will come out very differently from Joe's very similar case adjudicated in January 2007. We have adopted sentencing guidelines in the hope that the punishment meted out to offenders depends on their offenses and prior records rather than on the whims, personalities, or ideologies of the sentencing judges. We use pattern jury instructions in both civil and criminal cases to guide lay adjudicators to apply the same law to similar disputes. When civil juries depart significantly from established norms, judges use remittitur to reduce awards, enter judgments that are at odds with the jury's verdict, or grant new trials.

Americans don't love consistent decision making merely because we think that fairness to the parties requires that similar cases should have similar outcomes. We also like the predictability that following precedent offers. Most disputes can be settled without all-out litigation when the results of formal adjudication can be predicted in advance with reasonable certainty. In addition, and perhaps most pertinent, we don't like the idea that litigants' lives, liberty, or property could be determined by the predilections or personal preferences of the individual men and women who happen to judge their cases. The very essence of the rule of law, embodied in the Due Process Clause of the Fifth Amendment, is that individual cases should be disposed of by reference to standardized norms rather than by arbitrary factors, particularly the personal biases, attitudes, policies, or ideologies of government adjudicators.

In recent years, however, the public and the press have become skeptical about the extent to which American judging reflects only the law and not the predilections of the adjudicators. Judges (and entire courts) are commonly referred to in the press as liberal or conservative, and many lawyers believe that although they cannot predict the outcome of a trial-level case on the day before it is filed, or the outcome of an appeal on the day before it is docketed, they can do so once they know which judge or judges have been assigned to decide it. In response to this public skepticism, Chief Judge Harry Edwards of the U.S. Court of Appeals for the D.C. Circuit wrote a noteworthy law review article defending the notion that "it is the law—and not the personal politics of individual judges—that controls judicial decision making."[1] His article spawned a series of rebuttals and counter-rebuttals. Professor Richard Revesz conducted a careful empirical study of decisions by the judges of Edwards's court in challenges to rules of the Environmental Protection Agency (EPA). He concluded that the political composition of three-judge panels often mattered a great deal.[2]

Judge Edwards wrote a surprisingly harsh critique of the Revesz "so-called 'empirical stud[y],'" claiming that its interpretations were "bogus."[3] Revesz then rebutted this critique,[4] and Edwards published a further article rejecting the "neo-realist arguments of scholars who claim that the personal ideologies [rather than law and collegiality] . . . are crucial determinants" of outcomes.[5]

Much of the Edwards-Revesz debate concerned relatively small differences in the voting patterns of the various judges. For example, in two of six periods of time reported, Democratic judges voted 44% of the time to sustain environmentalists' challenges to EPA rules, while Republican judges did so only 42% of the time (a 5% disparity). In another period, the Democratic-to-Republican ratio was 47% to 33%. In the other periods, Republican judges were more prone to sustain such challenges than Democratic judges. In some periods, a Democratic judge was perhaps 50% more likely to vote for an environmentalist challenge than a Republican judge, a difference that should perhaps be disturbing if we expect judges to leave their political leanings behind when they take the bench. The differences were somewhat more dramatic in the case of industry challenges to the EPA. Republican judges voted nearly twice as often as Democratic judges to sustain those challenges.[6] In other words, a judge might be nearly 100% more likely to vote for an industry-requested remand if the judge were Republican rather than Democratic—a statistic that may again suggest cause for concern. Those percentages are far larger than the 16% to 18% disparity (about five months) in the lengths of sentences meted out by federal judges in 1986–1987, before federal sentencing guidelines took effect, a disparity thought so great as to warrant a federal statute imposing those guidelines.[7]

But how about a situation in which one judge is 1,820% more likely to grant an application for important relief than another judge in the same courthouse?[8] Or one in which one U.S. court of appeals is 1,148% more likely to rule in favor of a petitioner than another U.S. court of appeals considering similar cases?[9]

Welcome to the world of asylum law.

Collectively, asylum officers, immigration judges, members of the Board of Immigration Appeals, and judges of U.S. courts of appeals render about seventy-nine thousand asylum decisions annually.[10] Almost all of them involve claims that an applicant for asylum reasonably fears imprisonment, torture, or death if forced to return to her home country. Given our national desire for equal treatment in adjudication, one would expect to find in this system for the mass production of justice many indicators demonstrating a strong degree of uniformity of decision making over place and time. Yet in the very large volume of adjudications involving foreign nationals' applications for protection from persecution and torture in their home countries, we see a great deal of statistical variation in the outcomes pronounced by decision makers. The statistics that we have collected and analyzed in this book suggest that in the world of asylum adjudication, there is remarkable variation in decision making from one official to the next, from one office to the next, from one region to the next, from one court of appeals to the next, and from one year to the next, even during periods when there has been no intervening change in the law. The variation is particularly striking when one controls for both the nationality and current area of residence of applicants and examines the asylum grant rates of the different asylum officers who work in the same regional building, or immigration judges who sit in adjacent courtrooms of the same immigration court. When an asylum seeker stands before an official or court who will decide whether she will be deported or may remain in the United States, the result may be determined as much or more by who that official is, or where the court is located, as by the facts and law of the case. The fact that the outcome of a case appears to be strongly influenced by the identity or attitude of the officer or judge to whom it is assigned is particularly discomfiting in asylum cases, because when a bona fide application is erroneously denied, the applicant is almost always ordered deported to a nation in which she will be in grave danger.[11]

We cannot prove that the variations in outcomes based on the locations or personalities of the adjudicators are greater in asylum cases than in criminal, civil, or other administrative adjudications. Only a few scholars, such as Revesz, have attempted to analyze similarities or differences in adjudication in a large database of cases that involve particular subject matters and were governed by a single body of law.[12] In this book, however, we report and analyze new statistical data that suggest to us that very significant differences from one decision maker to the next in the adjudication of asylum cases should be a matter of serious concern to federal policymakers.[13] The new statistics show disconcerting variability among individual adjudicators in the institutions for which adequate data are available for analysis.

Part 1 of this book reports our study of disparities in asylum adjudication. In chapter 1, we describe the systems through which asylum cases are adjudicated and the four institutions that decide them: the asylum offices, the immigration courts, the Board of Immigration Appeals, and the United States courts of appeals.

In chapter 2 we look at the first stage of decision making: adjudications by asylum officers. The Department of Homeland Security provided us with grant rate data for each of the 928 asylum officers who served during fiscal years 1999–2005.[14] For decisions on cases of applicants from eleven key countries that generate many valid asylum claims, the department also provided individual grant rates by nationality of the applicant. From these data, we measured changes in the rate at which asylum was granted by the department from region to region (holding constant the group of countries of greatest interest and, in some cases, limiting our study to a particular country) and variations from officer to officer within each of the department's eight regional asylum offices (again controlling for countries of the applicants).

Chapter 3 examines statistics in asylum cases decided by 247 immigration judges from fiscal years 2000–2004. We investigated disparities in grant rates between different immigration courts, but more important, we examined disparities in the grant rates of different judges within the largest courts. We were also able to correlate the grant rates of individual judges with biographical information about those judges and with additional information about the cases. Certain correlations surprised us and raise serious questions about whether the results of cases are excessively influenced by personal characteristics of the judges, such as their gender and their prior government service.

We would have liked to include an analysis of how individual members of the Board of Immigration Appeals resolve cases assigned to them, but the Department of Justice does not keep statistics on the dispositions of appeals by individual members of the Board,[15] and it does not make public the vast majority of its asylum decisions.[16] We were able to examine variations from year to year in the Board's treatment of asylum appeals. Our study included the period just before, during, and after FY 2002, when the Board was in great turmoil due to substantial personnel and procedural changes.[17] Although we could not compare individual Board members' grant rates because the Board lacks the relevant data, we were able to measure the effect of these changes on its overall rate of decisions favorable to asylum applicants. Chapter 4 describes and analyzes the data that the Board was able to provide to us.

Chapter 5 investigates variations in the treatment of asylum cases in the U.S. courts of appeals from one circuit to another. We examined the rate at which asylum denials by the Board of Immigration Appeals were remanded by courts in all of the circuits. We were able to compare these rates both for all cases and for cases from a group of fifteen countries that generate a particularly large number and high percentage of successful asylum cases. We were also able to compare the rates at which individual judges in two circuits voted to remand cases.

In chapter 6, we summarize and comment on our findings and suggest several steps that might be taken to advance the degree to which the outcomes in asylum cases could become somewhat more uniform. These reforms are largely aimed at making the immigration courts and the Board of Immigration Appeals into more independent and professional adjudicative bodies. We suggest that these agencies should be moved from the Department of Justice to a new, independent agency within the executive branch, insulated from political directives; that standards for hiring and training judges should be made more rigorous; that more staff resources should be given to the new agency; and that the attorney general should be denied the power to remove immigration judges or Board members (except for cause) and to alter asylum decisions. We also propose that the United States should provide legal representatives for indigent asylum seekers who are threatened with deportation to countries in which they face danger, just as it does for criminal defendants who may be incarcerated in our own country.

The findings that we report in chapters 2 through 5 were originally posted on the internet in May 2007 and reported in a law review in November of that year. In September 2008, the Government Accountability Office (GAO) published two studies that it conducted of the adjudication of asylum cases.[18] The GAO used slightly different counting methods and significantly different measures of disparity than we did, and its database of cases covered somewhat different time frames. Nevertheless, its data largely confirm our findings. Where appropriate, our end notes compare the results of our research with the results reported by the GAO.

Part 2 of the book consists of commentaries on implications of the data, and further suggestions for policy and administrative reform, by several experts from academic life, from the judiciary, and from other nations that also seek consistency in their asylum decisions. Bruce J. Einhorn, who served as an immigration judge for nearly seventeen years, offers his observations on why different judges come to quite different conclusions in different cases, focusing on the difficulty of assessing credibility and the preconceptions that immigration judges bring to this task. Professor Carrie Menkel-Meadow looks at one particular factor that correlates with different grant rates: the gender of the judge. She explores why male and female judges might have different reactions to similar groups of asylum applicants. Professors Margaret H. Taylor and Steven H. Legomsky examine the problem of disparities from the perspective of administrative law (the law governing the executive branch of government). Professor Taylor compares efforts to reform the immigration court system with similar efforts to improve the adjudication of Social Security claims, and Professor Legomsky explores possible reforms that might reduce unwanted disparities, suggesting that improvements are possible but that some cures would be worse than the disease. Professor Audrey Macklin of the University of Toronto and Robert Thomas of the University of Manchester provide international perspectives. Professor Macklin relates a series of experimental Canadian efforts to reduce disparities in asylum adjudication. Mr. Thomas describes the British experience in which selected cases, tried under special conditions, were used to guide court decisions involving similar facts. Finally, Judge M. Margaret McKeown and her former clerk Allegra McLeod explore another element that strongly affects the outcome of asylum decisions. They suggest that the 40.5% rate at which represented asylum seekers prevail in immigration court may mask vast differences in success rates that are associated with the quality of representation, and they suggest ways in which more competent representation might be encouraged.

The final section of the book consists of two appendices. The first is a methodological appendix, explaining in detail our processes and the decisions we made as we worked on the raw data provided by the U.S. government. The second applies our methodology to data collected by Prof. David Law, who looked at disparities in the adjudication of asylum cases by the U.S. Court of Appeals for the Ninth Circuit, the circuit with the nation's largest immigration docket.

Human judgment can never be eliminated from any system of justice. But we believe that the outcome of a refugee's quest for safety in America should be influenced more by law and less by a spin of the wheel of fate that assigns her case to a particular government official.[19]

NOTES

1. Harry T. Edwards, Public Misperceptions concerning the "Politics" of Judging: Dispelling Some Myths about the D.C. Circuit, 56 U. Colo. L. Rev. 619, 620 (1985).
2. Looking only at individual votes, Revesz found that
> (1) for industry challenges [to EPA rules on procedural grounds], Republicans had a higher reversal rate [that is, rate of reversing the EPA] than Democrats in all the periods [of time studied]; and (2) for environmental [group] challenges, Democrats had a higher reversal rate than Republicans in all the periods. . . . These relationships are consistent with the selective deference hypotheses (that judges' votes are determined by their preferences concerning the substance of environmental policy). . . . (Richard L. Revesz, Environmental Regulation, Ideology, and the D.C. Circuit, 83 Va. L. Rev. 1717, 1738–39 (1997))

Turning to the composition of three-judge panels, Revesz found that judges were significantly more likely to vote to invalidate an EPA rule when at least two of the three members of the panel had been appointed by a president whose party could be expected to disagree with the rule (i.e., when at least two Republicans considered an industry challenge or when at least two Democrats considered an environmentalist challenge). In other words, "the effects of panel composition are far greater than the effects of individual ideology." Id. at 1764. The effects were presumably greater because, on a three-judge appellate panel, when members who had been appointed by a party that was more likely to disagree with an EPA decision constituted a majority of the panel, they had the power to change it or at least to force the EPA to reconsider its decision.
3. Harry T. Edwards, Collegiality and Decision Making on the D.C. Circuit, 84 Va. L. Rev. 1335, 1335, 1368 (1998).

4. Richard L. Revesz, Ideology, Collegiality, and the D.C. Circuit: A Reply to Chief Judge Harry T. Edwards, 85 Va. L. Rev. 805 (1999).

5. Harry T. Edwards, The Effects of Collegiality on Judicial Decision Making, 151 U. Pa. L. Rev. 1639, 1640 (2003).

6. Revesz, *supra* n. 2, at 1750 tbl.8.

7. James M. Anderson, Jeffrey R. Kling & Kate Stith, Measuring Interjudge Sentencing Disparity: Before and after the Federal Sentencing Guidelines, 42 J.L. & Econ. 271, 303 (1999).

8. *See* chapter 3 *infra* (discussing the difference in grant rate of two New York immigration judges for Albanian applicants).

9. *See* chapter 5, *infra*, and accompanying text (discussing the difference in remand rates of the Fourth and Seventh Circuits when considering asylum claims from the same group of fifteen countries from which asylum is frequently granted).

10. In FY 2005, asylum officers rendered 28,305 merits decisions (grants, denials, referrals after interviews, and rejections after interviews based on failure to meet the statutory deadline) for applicants from all countries other than Mexico. E-mail from Ted Kim, Chief of Operations, U.S. Citizenship & Immigration Servs., to Philip Schrag (Aug. 23, 2006) (attaching "Refugees, Asylum, and Parole System: Grant Rates by Asylum Officer—FY99 through FY05 National Table (All Officers)," which contains the data) (on file with authors). In the same year, immigration judges made 30,903 decisions on the merits in asylum cases. U.S. Dep't of Justice, Immigration Courts, FY 2005 Asylum Statistics (2006), *available at* http://www.usdoj.gov/eoir/efoia/FY05AsyStats.pdf. During that year, the Board decided 16,762 asylum cases (this number excludes about two thousand cases that the Board is not able to characterize as favoring either party). Computer disk from Brett Endres, Executive Office of Immigration Review, to Andrew I. Schoenholtz (May 31, 2006) (on file with authors) (attaching Board of Immigration Appeals, "Crosstabulation for Decision Type by Attorney and Nationality per Year of Appeal"). Finally, during calendar year 2005, the U.S. courts of appeals decided 2,163 asylum cases, as described in chapter 5 of this book.

11. This book explores statistical disparities in asylum adjudication but does not attempt to convey the human suffering attendant on the denial of an application for asylum. One of us has recently coauthored, with an unsuccessful asylum applicant who had been tortured and nearly executed, a full account of the applicant's persecution and flight to the United States, and of the adjudication of his case. His application went through all of the stages of hearing and appeals that are described in this book. After his request for asylum was turned down by an asylum officer and denied by the immigration judge who had the lowest grant rate in her immigration court, his appeal was rejected by a single member of the Board of Immigration Appeals and then by the U.S. court of appeals in the circuit that had the lowest rate of remanding cases to the Board. Forced to return to Africa, he was nearly murdered once again. David Ngaruri Kenney & Philip G. Schrag, Asylum Denied: A Refugee's Struggle for Safety in America (Berkeley: University of California Press, 2008).

12. *See, e.g.,* John R. Allison & Mark A. Lemley, How Federal Circuit Judges Vote in Patent Validity Cases, 10 Fed. Cir. B.J. 435, 436 (2001) (finding that "[j]udges do not fit easily into pro-patent or anti-patent categories, or into affirmers and reversers"); Robert G. Dixon, Jr., The Welfare State and Mass Justice: A Warning from the Social Security Disability Program, 1972 Duke L.J. 681, 717 (showing that 153 of 252 Social Security disability hearing examiners reversed denials of benefits between 36% and 55% of the time, but nineteen examiners reversed 66% to 80% of the time, and twenty-six reversed 21% to 30% of the time, a "striking and disturbing" disparity); James Edward Maule, Instant Replay, Weak Teams, and Disputed Calls: An Empirical Study of

Alleged Tax Court Judge Bias, 66 Tenn. L. Rev. 351, 400 (1999) ("[W]eighted taxpayer prevalence scores demolish the assertions that Tax Court judges make decisions in congruity with their backgrounds."); Cass R. Sunstein, David Schkade & Lisa Michelle Ellman, Ideological Voting on Federal Courts of Appeals: A Preliminary Investigation, 90 Va. L. Rev. 301, 306, 353 (2004) (finding that although the political affiliation of the appointing president is not correlated with judicial votes on criminal appeals, takings, or federalism, in cases involving abortion and capital punishment, "judges vote their convictions").

13. A recent law journal article reviews some of the data relating to disparities in immigration courts (looking only at rates within the New York City immigration court and ranking disparity levels for twenty-eight immigration courts) and briefly examines reversal rates in the courts of appeals (looking only at the Seventh Circuit and the combined reversal data for all federal circuits). Sydenham B. Alexander III, A Political Response to Crisis in the Immigration Courts, 21 Geo. Immigr. L.J. 1 (2006). That article does not analyze the Asylum Office and Board of Immigration Appeals data that we obtained, and does not engage as comprehensively with the data on the immigration courts and courts of appeals. It instead focuses on the evidence it examines to advocate compellingly for a political solution to the immigration court crisis. The article notes that legal scholars "concerned about IJ inconsistency . . . have been slow to incorporate statistical analysis into their work." Id. at 21 n.125.

14. "The fiscal year is the accounting period for the federal government which begins on October 1 and ends on September 30. The fiscal year is designated by the calendar year in which it ends; for example, fiscal year 2006 begins on October 1, 2005 and ends on September 30, 2006." United States Senate, Glossary, http://www.senate.gov/reference/ glossary_term/fiscal_year.htm.

15. The Board claims that it does not track decisions by outcome, but there is some evidence to the contrary. See John R. B. Palmer, Stephen W. Yale-Loehr & Elizabeth Cronin, Why Are So Many People Challenging Board of Immigration Appeals Decisions in Federal Court? An Empirical Analysis of the Recent Surge in Petitions for Review, 20 Geo. Immigr. L.J. 1, 56 n.248 (2005). Even if the Board does track decisions by outcome, it apparently does not track them by member.

16. Confidentiality concerns could justify the Board's refusal to publish decisions that include identifying information about asylum applicants, as they or their relatives could suffer retaliation for reporting on their countries' human rights violations. However, the Board does not publish or otherwise make available even redacted copies of most of its asylum decisions.

17. See Dorsey & Whitney LLP, Board of Immigration Appeals: Procedural Reforms to Improve Case Management 19–25 (2003), available at http://www.dorsey.com/files/upload/DorseyStudyABA_8mgPDF.pdf.

18. Government Accountability Office, U.S. Asylum System, Significant Variation Existed in Asylum Outcomes across Immigration Courts and Judges, GAO-08-940 at 56 (2008), and Government Accountability Office, U.S. Asylum System: Agencies Have Taken Actions to Help Ensure Quality in the Asylum Adjudication Process, but Challenges Remain, GAO-08-935 (2008).

19. We agree with Stephen Legomsky that accuracy, consistency, and public acceptance are among the most important goals of any adjudicative system, and particularly one in which human life and liberty are at stake. See Stephen H. Legomsky, An Asylum Seeker's Bill of Rights in a Non-Utopian World, 14 Geo. Immigr. L.J. 619, 622 (2000).

PART I

Refugee Roulette

1   The Asylum Process

AS PART OF its commitment to human rights, the United States offers asylum to foreign nationals who flee to its shores and can prove that they are "refugees"—that is, that they have a well-founded fear of persecution in their own countries and that their race, religion, nationality, political opinion, or membership in a particular social group is at least one central reason for the threatened persecution.[1] A foreign national who seeks asylum in the United States may do so either affirmatively or defensively. An affirmative applicant is one who seeks asylum on her own initiative and voluntarily identifies herself to the Department of Homeland Security (DHS) through her application. An affirmative applicant may be either an individual who maintains a valid nonimmigrant visa (e.g., a tourist or student) or a person who either overstayed her visa or entered the United States without being formally processed by an immigration official. A defensive applicant is one who applies for asylum after having been apprehended by DHS and placed in removal proceedings in immigration court, a part of the Department of Justice (DOJ).[2] A successful applicant of either type is granted asylum and is not ordered removed.

The Department of Homeland Security (DHS) is the executive agency primarily responsible for overseeing immigration processes, including affirmative asylum applications. The department's Office of Citizenship and Immigration Services (USCIS) houses the asylum corps, comprised of asylum officers who evaluate asylum applications and interview the applicants. The department's Bureau of Immigration and Customs Enforcement includes the trial attorneys who oppose asylum claims before the immigration courts.

Asylum decisions, whether made by asylum officers or by immigration judges, involve both a judgment about whether the applicant's story, if true, would render the applicant eligible for asylum under American law and an assessment as to whether the applicant is telling the truth about his or her personal experiences of actual or threatened persecution. Among similar cases, we would expect some, but relatively little, variation from one experienced adjudicator to another in relationship to the legal assessment of a truthful applicant's legal eligibility. Assessments of credibility are more difficult and subjective, so we might expect somewhat greater variability from one adjudicator to another with respect to this component of the decision. Nevertheless, a system that endeavors to prevent arbitrary adjudication should attempt to keep even this aspect of variability within a relatively narrow range.

The adjudicators face a difficult task, as it is important not only to grant genuine claims but also to deny false claims. Successful false asylum claims undermine the integrity of the asylum system and reduce public support for the admission of genuine refugees.

A. The Regional Asylum Offices

Several weeks after filing a written application for asylum, an affirmative asylum seeker is interviewed by a trained asylum officer in one of the eight regional USCIS asylum offices. Within each regional office, cases are assigned randomly to particular asylum officers.[3] The interview is nonadversarial, with the asylum officer in an inquisitorial role. No representative for the government is assigned to oppose the grant of asylum, and asylum seekers may be represented by counsel at their own expense. The asylum officer can grant asylum, refer the asylum claim to immigration court, or, if the asylum seeker has valid immigration status in the United States, deny the asylum claim.[4] About 35% of adjudicated cases in most recent years are grants of asylum. Most asylum officer decisions, however, result in referrals to immigration court.

FIGURE I.I

The Affirmative Asylum Process

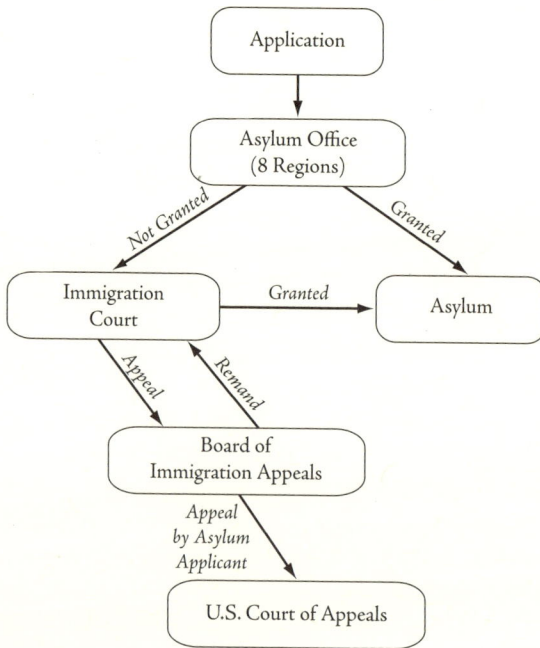

The Asylum Office keeps separate statistics on three different types of referrals, though all three result in removal hearings in immigration court. First, referrals without interviews occur when an asylum applicant does not appear for a scheduled interview. Because there is no interview or adjudication on the merits in these cases, we have excluded them entirely from our study of decisions by asylum officers, which is reported in chapter 2. Second, regular referrals occur when the asylum officer either (1) does not believe that the applicant has carried her burden of proving facts showing that she meets the statutory definition of a refugee or (2) accepts the proffered facts as true but does not believe that those facts qualify the applicant for asylum as a matter of law. The third type of referral, called a "rejection" for purposes of statistical record keeping, occurs when the asylum officer does not believe that the applicant applied for asylum within one year after last entering the United States, a deadline imposed by Congress in 1996, effective April 1, 1998.[5] An applicant who filed more than a year after entering the United States may be granted asylum if she can prove the existence of "changed circumstances" or "extraordinary circumstances" justifying late filing.[6] If she is not able to prove entry less than a year before application, or if her entry occurred more than a year before application and she is not able to show the existence of a qualifying excuse, she is "rejected" and referred to an immigration court hearing.

Decisions by asylum officers are reviewed by a supervisory asylum officer within the regional office before being released to the asylum applicant approximately two weeks after the interview takes place. In rare cases (e.g., if the case presents a novel issue of law as to which neither the Department of Homeland Security nor the attorney general has made a policy decision), the case may be referred to DHS national headquarters before a decision is rendered.

B. The Immigration Courts

When an asylum officer refers a case to immigration court, the Asylum Office serves the asylum applicant with a Notice to Appear in that court on a specific date.[7] The Notice to Appear is the equivalent of a summons in a civil case, and with service of this notice, the asylum applicant becomes a "respondent."

In most cases, the respondent has no basis for denying the government's charge of being present in the United States without authorization, so the bulk of the court proceeding, which can last for several hours, is devoted to a de novo hearing on her evidence of eligibility for asylum. If for some reason the respondent does not qualify for asylum (e.g., she missed the application deadline), she may be eligible for withholding of removal[8] or protection under the Convention against Torture.[9] The benefits awarded with those types of relief are far more limited. For example, an asylee may obtain asylum for her dependent spouse and minor children in the United States, or, if they are abroad, she may later bring those dependents to the United States as derivative beneficiaries of her asylum claim. After a year, asylees may apply to become permanent residents, and, after five years, to become American citizens. However, grants of withholding of removal or protection under the Convention against Torture do not lead to permanent residence or citizenship and do not provide derivative protection for dependents.[10]

The immigration court also hears defensive asylum cases. A defensive case is one that is presented by an applicant without valid immigration status who was apprehended by DHS before the individual filed an asylum application. Such an individual does not have an opportunity to present a claim to an asylum officer and may file an asylum application only in immigration court. Defensive applicants are usually detained (jailed) by DHS after apprehension. A small number are released on bond (or on their own recognizance) before their immigration court hearings, while most remain detained through their hearings and any subsequent appeal.

Both in affirmative cases that were referred by an asylum officer and in defensive cases, immigration court hearings are adversarial proceedings. A DHS attorney is assigned to cross-examine the asylum applicant and usually argues before the immigration judge that asylum is not warranted. Asylum seekers may be represented at their own expense, but indigent applicants are not provided with legal counsel even though nearly all unsuccessful applicants are ordered deported.

C. The Board of Immigration Appeals

An applicant who is denied asylum by an immigration judge may appeal to the Board of Immigration Appeals, another institutional component of the Department of Justice. Today the Board consists of eleven to fifteen members appointed by the attorney general of the United States. The Board was created by a directive of the attorney general, rather than by statute, and its members serve at the pleasure of the attorney general, exercising his delegated authority.[11]

D. The United States Courts of Appeals

An asylum applicant (and anyone else whose order of removal is sustained) may seek review of an adverse Board decision in a U.S. court of appeals.[12] The circuit courts may remand a case in which the Board rendered a decision contrary to the law or abused its discretion, but the courts grant a great deal of deference to the Board.[13] Except in rare instances, the courts of appeals can only remand a decision to the Board; they cannot grant asylum.[14]

E. The Supreme Court

In principle, a foreign national who has been ordered removed and whose removal has been sustained by a court of appeals could seek certiorari in the U.S. Supreme Court. However, as a practical matter, the court of appeals is the last stop; the Supreme Court receives about ten thousand requests to review cases each year, but accepts only about eighty cases for its docket. It has accepted review in only a handful of asylum cases since the Refugee Act authorized asylum in 1980.

The next four chapters of this book examine the outcomes of adjudication at each of the four stages of the asylum process. As we shall see, there is reason to believe that at every stage, factors other than the merits of the case strongly influence the outcome. It is not our contention that the strength or weakness of a case is irrelevant to the decision. The statistical evidence that we present, however, suggests that other factors, particularly whether the applicant had representation, the predispositions of the adjudicators, and perhaps the cultures of particular offices or courts, unduly influence whether the United States provides protection to an applicant or orders her deported to a country in which she claims that her life or freedom would be at risk.

NOTES

1. 8 U.S.C. §§ 1101(a)(42), 1158(b)(1) (2000).
2. DHS may have apprehended the individual in the interior of the country or at an airport, seaport, or land port of entry at which he arrived without a valid passport or visa. Individuals without proper documentation who voluntarily identify themselves to immigration officials at a port of entry as applicants for asylum are apprehended and detained just as if they were discovered by officials to have lacked such documentation.
3. Asylum Div., Office of Int'l Affairs, Dep't of Homeland Security, Affirmative Asylum Procedures Manual 13 (2003).
4. 8 C.F.R. §§ 1208.1(b), 1208.9, 1208.14(b)–(c) (2006). Because a person who has a valid status, such as a student visa, has a right to remain, at least temporarily, the asylum officer merely denies and does not make a referral to a judge for a removal (deportation) hearing. Denials comprise only a small fraction of asylum officer decisions, as only 7% of asylum seekers apply while they still have a lawful immigration status. See Dep't of Homeland Sec., 2004 Yearbook of Immigration Statistics 55–64 tbls.18 & 19 (2006).
5. 8 U.S.C. § 1158(a)(2)(B) (2000).
6. 8 U.S.C. § 1158(a)(2)(D) (2000); 8 CFR § 208.4(a)(4)–(5) (2007) (interpreting the statute); see Philip G. Schrag, A Well-Founded Fear: The Congressional Battle to Save Political Asylum in America (2000) (describing the history of the enactment of the deadline); Michele R. Pistone & Philip G. Schrag, The New Asylum Rule: Improved but Still Unfair, 16 Geo. Immigr. L.J. 1 (2001) (detailing the exceptions to the deadline and their limitations); Karen Musalo and Marcelle Rice, Center for Gender & Refugee Studies, The Implementation of the One-year Bar to Asylum (accounts of what the authors regard as unjust applications of the one-year bar to particular cases).

7. 8 C.F.R. §§ 1003.18(b), 1208.2(c)(3)(ii) (2007).

8. 8 U.S.C. § 1231(b)(3) (2000). An important distinction between asylum and withholding is that to win asylum, an applicant must demonstrate only well-founded fear, perhaps only a 10% chance, of persecution. INS v. Cardoza-Fonseca, 480 U.S. 421, 431 (1987). By contrast, to obtain withholding of removal, an applicant must prove that persecution is more likely than not (that is, more than a 50% chance). INS v. Stevic, 467 U.S. 407, 423–24 (1984).

9. 8 C.F.R. §§ 1208.16-.18 (2007).

10. 8 C.F.R. §§ 1208.21, 1209.2 (2007).

11. Charles Gordon et al., Immigration Law and Procedure § 3.05[2] (2007).

12. The Board acts for the attorney general and the attorney general's decisions bind the Department of Homeland Security, so the department does not appeal adverse decisions of the Board. John R. B. Palmer, Stephen W. Yale-Loehr & Elizabeth Cronin, Why Are So Many People Challenging Board of Immigration Appeals Decisions in Federal Court? An Empirical Analysis of the Recent Surge in Petitions for Review, 20 Geo. Immigr. L.J. 1 at 38 n.203.

13. The standard of deference that courts should grant to the Board varied among circuits for several years before Congress codified the standard in 1996. See Stephen M. Knight, Shielded from Review: The Questionable Birth and Development of the Asylum Standard of Review under Elias-Zacarias, 20 Geo. Immigr. L.J. 133 (2005). The current uniform standard requires that the circuits uphold findings of fact unless "any reasonable adjudicator would be compelled to conclude to the contrary." 8 U.S.C. § 1252(b)(4)(B) (2000). Credibility determinations must be sustained unless they are not supported by specific, cogent, and relevant reasoning. See, e.g., Gjerazi v. Gonzales, 435 F.3d 800 (7th Cir. 2006); Camara v. Ashcroft, 378 F.3d 361 (4th Cir. 2004). In actual practice, however, the federal circuits appear to vary dramatically in the way they apply those standards. See infra chapter 5.

14. INS v. Ventura, 537 U.S. 12 (2002).

2 The Regional Asylum Offices

THE ASYLUM OFFICE, part of the Department of Homeland Security, makes decisions in the first instance when asylum seekers come forward on their own to assert claims. These individuals provide voluminous information about themselves, including their identities and addresses, to the U.S. government. They thereby begin a process that will result in their being placed into removal proceedings if they are not successful and are among the 93% of applicants who have no lawful immigration status in the United States. These "affirmative" claims, assessed at eight regional asylum offices, constitute the vast majority of first-instance asylum cases.[1]

Asylum officers receive training, and their decisions are subject to intensive quality control. Every new asylum officer completes an intensive five-week basic training course that includes testing.[2] Each week, every regional office conducts four hours of training on new legal issues, country conditions, procedures, and other relevant matters.[3] A supervisory asylum officer reviews every decision proposed by an asylum officer. Supervisory asylum officers must complete an intensive two-week training course on substantive law, also with testing. At least one quality-assurance or training officer in each regional office regularly reviews supervisory sign-offs on cases in order to report to the regional office director on possible inconsistencies in the application of the law and to identify training needs.[4]

To support these regional officers, the Asylum Office headquarters maintains staff dedicated to quality assurance, training, and country-conditions research to provide support to the field. Every month, quality-assurance/training officers in each regional office hold a conference call with headquarters office quality-assurance staff and country-conditions researchers to address common issues or concerns, new cases, emerging patterns of claims, and training ideas. The quality-assurance team reviews cases involving novel or complex legal issues. This team also closely monitors the implementation of new laws. For example, in implementing the one-year filing deadline, this staff reviewed all referrals based on the deadline to ensure consistent application of the new law. In addition to asylum quality-assurance staff, each regional office has fraud-prevention coordinators and immigration officers with the Fraud Detection and National Security Division of USCIS, whose responsibilities include identification of fraud indicators, provision of training, and assistance to asylum officers and supervisory asylum officers.[5]

Nationals from well over one hundred countries applied for asylum in recent years.[6] Asylum officers in the eight regions have different nationality caseloads because applicants from various countries are concentrated to different degrees in certain regions. In order to account for nationality differences in caseloads, we based comparisons of grant rates only on cases of nationals from countries that we call Asylee Producing Countries (APCs). The countries on this list had at least five hundred asylum claims before the asylum offices or immigration courts in FY 2004, and a national grant rate of at least 30% before either the Asylum Office or the immigration court. The minimum-claim criterion ensures that the database includes a significant number of applicants and grantees. The minimum-grant-rate requirement ensures that asylum officers or immigration judges have reached a reasonable degree of consensus in concluding that many applicants from these countries are bona fide refugees.

Fifteen countries met these criteria: Albania, Armenia, Cameroon, China, Colombia, Ethiopia, Guinea, Haiti, India, Liberia, Mauritania, Pakistan, Russia, Togo, and Venezuela. Countries with low grant rates, such as El Salvador and Guatemala, are not on our APC list. We also excluded Mexicans from our database since the vast majority entered the affirmative asylum system for purposes other than to obtain asylum.[7] We first examined the data from eleven countries[8] that offered sufficient data on individual asylum officers for us to compare certain nationalities fairly.

The Asylum Office provided us with data on decision making by 928 asylum officers from all eight regional offices over a period of seven years, from 1999 to 2005.[9] For security and privacy reasons, the Asylum Office provided these data without identifying either the individual officers or the regional office by name. Rather, each officer was assigned a number, and each regional office a letter (Regions A through H). We studied the grant rates of only the 527 officers who decided at least fifty APC cases.

We also established a standard to measure disparities among individual adjudicators in the same office. For this book, we created a very tolerant standard of consistency, regarding an adjudicator as deviating significantly only if her grant rate for the population in question was higher or lower by more than 50% than the overall grant rate for the same population in the decision maker's own regional asylum office.[10] Some might argue that this measure tolerates too much deviation within an office, but even with this benchmark, there is a great deal of disparity in asylum adjudication in some of the eight regions.

A. Grant-Rate Disparities for Asylee Producing Countries among Individual Asylum Officers

Figure 2.1, like many of the bar graphs in this book, shows the spread of grant rates among adjudicators in a particular office. Each bar represents a different adjudicator's grant rate. Bar graphs like these offer a way of viewing the degree of con-

FIGURE 2.1

Individual Asylum Officer Grant Rates for APC Cases—Regions A & H

Region A

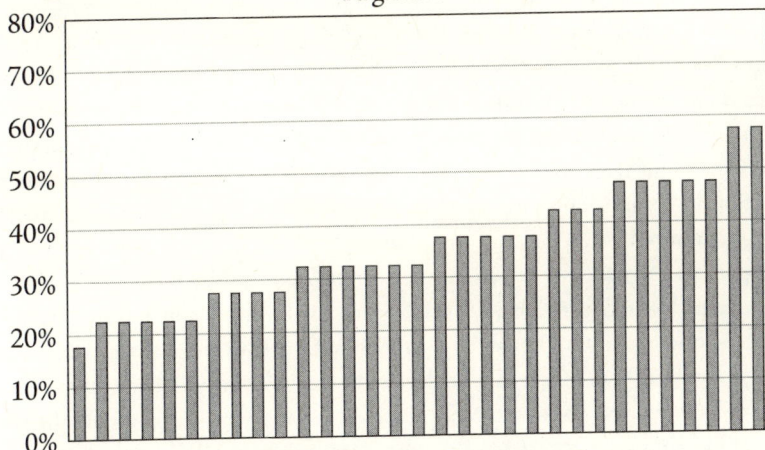

Note: Data are shown for all officers deciding at least 50 APC cases; the mean grant rate for APC cases in Region A was 35%.

Region H

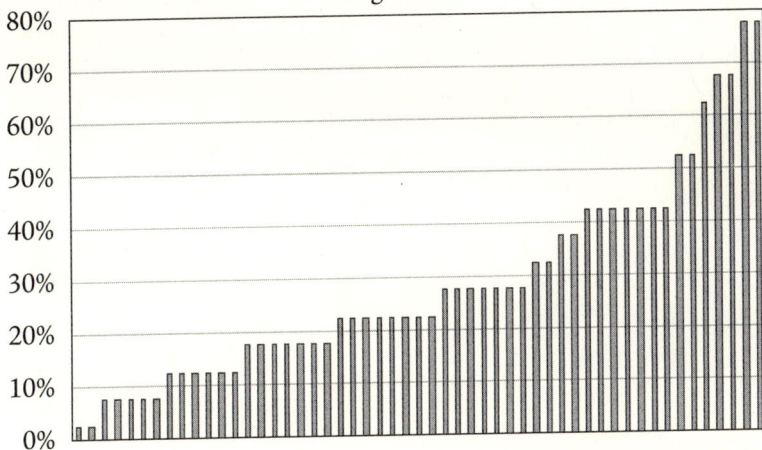

Note: As above, data are shown for all officers deciding at least 50 APC cases; the mean grant rate for APC cases in Region H was 26%.

sistency within an office: the flatter the slope of a line connecting the tops of the bars, the more consistent the decision making within the office. Figure 2.1 shows the grant rates of individual officers in APC cases in two asylum office regions.

In principle, since clerks in the asylum offices assign cases to asylum officers randomly,[11] the graphs of grant rates for asylum officers deciding similar cases within a particular regional office should be quite flat. Indeed, the graph for Region A is relatively flat. Most of the officers grant asylum to nationals of APC countries at a rate of between 25% and 50%. But Region H shows a much steeper slope and therefore much less consistency among its asylum officers.

We thought it would be useful to compare these individual officers' APC grant rates either to the mean regional office or to the national APC grant rate. Since there are significant differences in the mix of countries of origin of those making APC claims in the various regional offices, we concluded that comparing individual grant rates to the mean national APC grant rate would not take that variation in composition into account. We therefore used regional mean grant rates for comparison purposes.

Figure 2.2 and the other deviation graphs in this book display the degree to which each officer deviated from the mean APC grant rate for the region in question. Figure 2.2 shows exceptional consistency in Region D as measured by this standard. Only one of sixty-four officers deviated from the Region D mean by more than 50%.

Similarly, in Region A, shown in figure 2.3, only two of thirty-one officers deviated by more than 50% from the regional office mean APC grant rate.

But not all regional offices show that extraordinary degree of consistency. In Region H, more than half of the officers deviated by more than 50% (figure 2.4). In fact, five officers deviated as much as 130–190%.

FIGURE 2.2
Individual Officers' Deviations from the Regional Office Mean Grant Rate in APC Cases—Region D

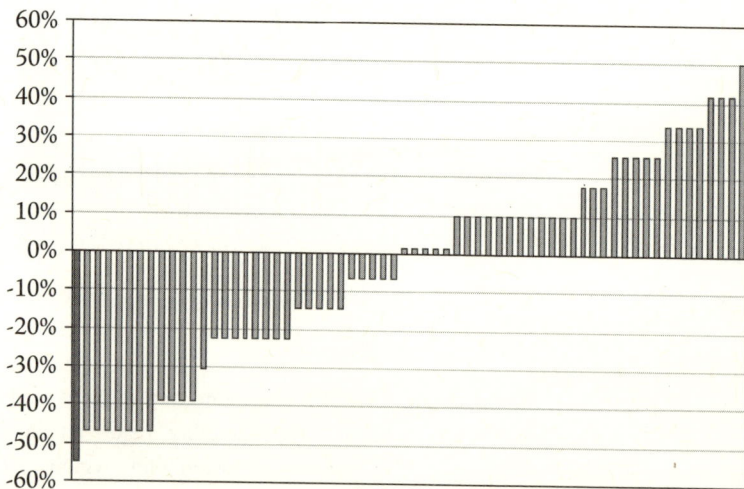

Note: Data are shown for all Region D officers who decided at least 50 APC cases (64 officers). The mean grant rate for APC cases decided by these officers was 62%. One officer, shown in black, deviated by more than 50%.

FIGURE 2.3

Individual Officers' Deviations from the Regional Office Mean Grant Rate for APC Cases—Region A

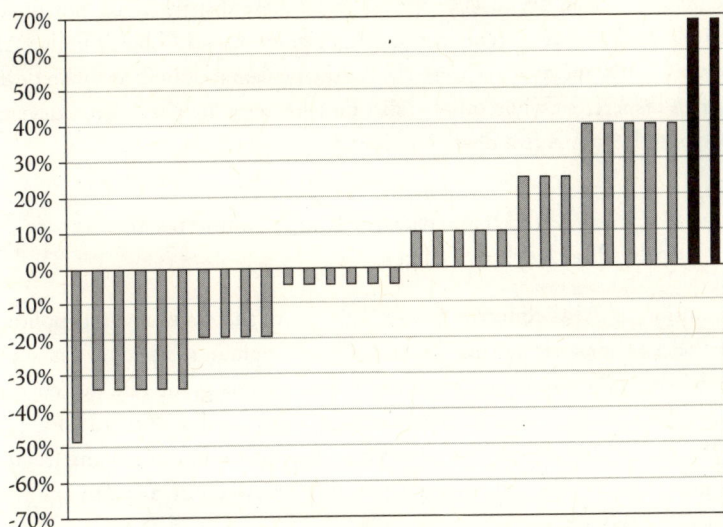

Note: Data are shown for all Region A officers who decided at least 50 APC cases (31 officers). The mean grant rate for APC cases decided by these officers was 35%. *See supra* Figure 2.1. Two officers, shown in black, deviated by more than 50%.

FIGURE 2.4

Individual Officers' Deviations from the Regional Office Mean Grant Rate in APC Cases—Region H

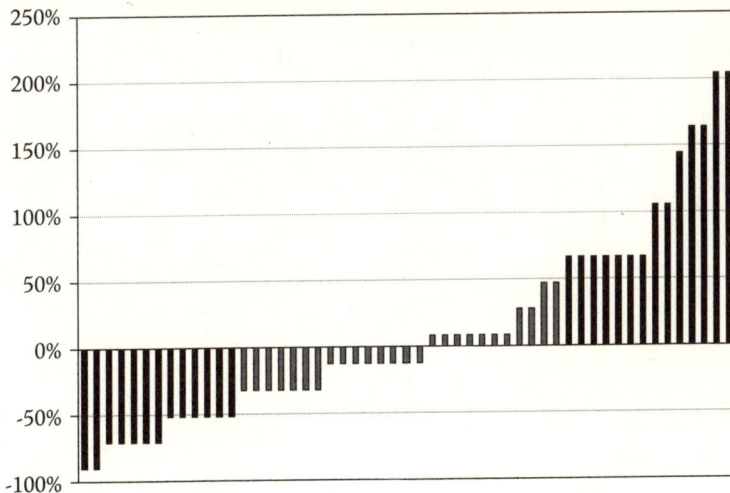

Note: Data are shown for all Region H officers who decided at least 50 APC cases (53 officers); the mean grant rate for APC cases decided by these officers was 26%. *See supra* Figure 2.1. Twenty-seven officers, shown in black, deviated by more than 50%.

When we compare the grant and deviation rates for all of the asylum offices, we see significant variation. As table 2.1 shows, the regional deviation rates vary tremendously—from 2% to 51%. Interestingly, these disparities do not depend exclusively on the grant rate. For example, Regions A and G have similar APC grant rates—35% and 38%, respectively. Yet the percentage of officers who deviate from their respective asylum office is six times greater in Region G (35% deviation rate) than in Region A (6% deviation rate).[12]

B. Grant Rate Disparities for Single Countries among Individual Asylum Officers

By definition, all APC countries have a high rate of successful asylum applicants. Nevertheless, the particular mix of countries of origin in the pool of cases adjudicated in a particular region may affect that region's grant rate, which could explain at least some of the disparity between offices with respect to APC grant rates that we see in table 2.1.[13] We therefore decided to look at whether regional office grant rates continued to vary when we narrowed our focus to applicants from a single country.

Our first analysis examines cases from China. Figure 2.5 shows the grant rates of 290 asylum officers nationwide who decided at least one hundred Chinese cases from FY 1999 to FY 2005. This graph shows that asylum officers nationally have not reached any consensus regarding Chinese cases. The disparities are striking, from a low grant rate of 0% to a high of more than 90% and almost every possibility in between.

TABLE 2.1
Grant and Deviation Rates for All Regional Offices

Region	APC Grant Rate	Percentage of Officers Deviating from Regional APC Grant Rate by over 50%
D	62%	2%
A	35%	6%
C	56%	9%
B	39%	11%
E	26%	18%
F	52%	22%
G	38%	35%
H	26%	51%

Note: This table is based on 126,504 cases decided by the 527 asylum officers who had decided at least fifty APC cases.

FIGURE 2.5
Individual Officer Grant Rates in Chinese Cases—All Regions

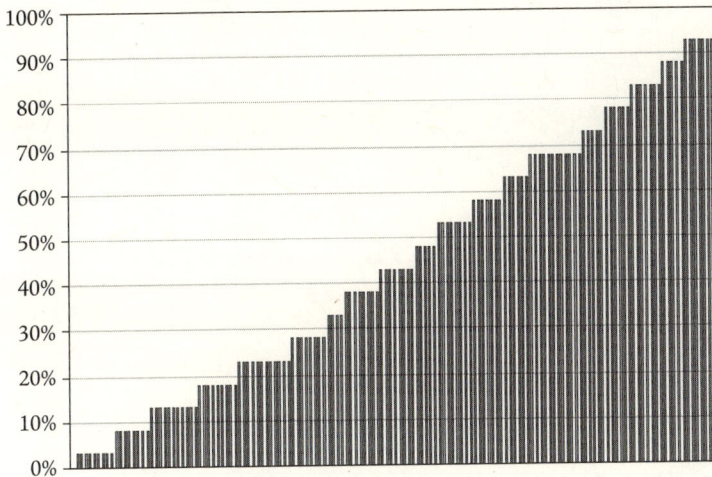

FIGURE 2.6
Individual Officer Grant Rates in Chinese Cases—Region C

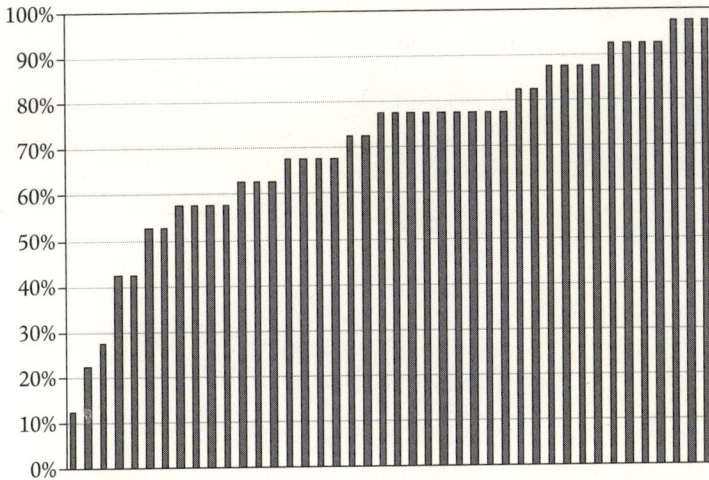

Note: Data are shown for all Region C officers with at least 25 Chinese cases (42 officers); the mean grant rate for Chinese cases decided by these officers was 72%.

We also examined asylum officers' grant rates in Chinese cases by region. To ensure sufficient data within each region, however, we had to reduce to twenty-five the minimum number of cases decided by an officer before that officer would be included in our study. Some regions show high consistency among asylum officers deciding Chinese cases. In Region C, for example, grant rates were pretty consistent (figure 2.6).

FIGURE 2.7
Individual Officers' Deviations from the Regional Office Mean Grant Rate in Chinese Cases—Region C

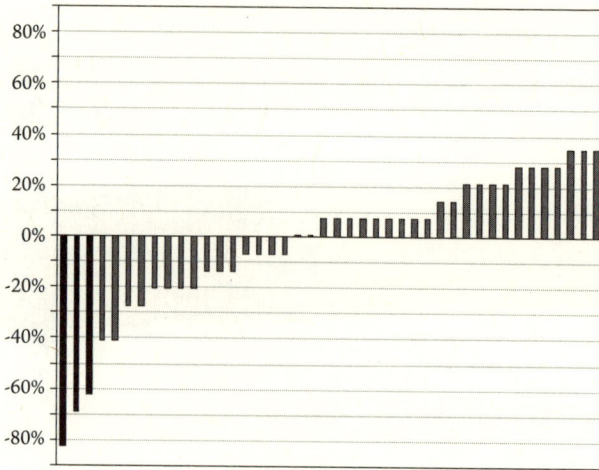

Note: Data are the same as in Figure 2.6. Two asylum officers had grant rates at exactly the mean; their data points have been jittered so as to appear visible on the graph. Three officers, shown in black, deviated by more than 50%.

FIGURE 2.8
Individual Officer Grant Rates in Chinese Cases—Region E

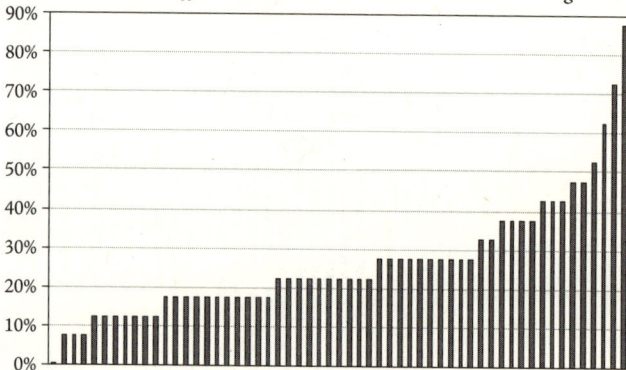

Note: Data are shown for all Region E officers who decided at least 25 Chinese cases (57 officers); the mean grant rate for Chinese cases decided by these officers was 24%. One officer granted no cases; that data point is jittered so as to appear visible on the graph.

As figure 2.7 shows, only three of forty-two officers deviated from the Region C China mean by more than 50%.

However, in Region E, there is considerably less consistency (figure 2.8). As figure 2.9 shows, seventeen of fifty-seven asylum officers, or about 30%, deviated from the regional China mean by more than 50%. This graph also shows extreme

FIGURE 2.9
Individual Officers' Deviations from the Regional Office
Mean Grant Rate in Chinese Cases—Region E

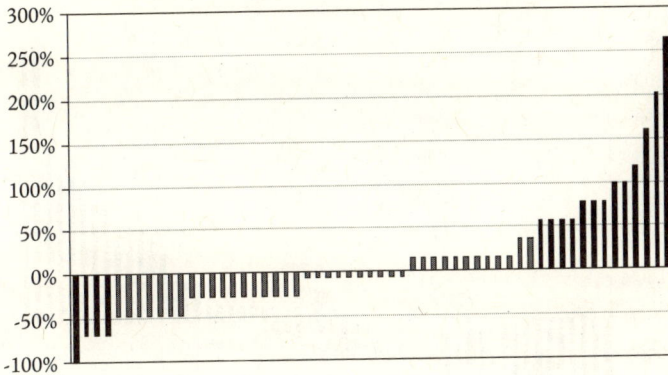

Note: Data are same as in Figure 2.8 Seventeen officers, shown in black, deviated by more than 50%.

FIGURE 2.10
Individual Officer Grant Rates in Chinese Cases—Region H

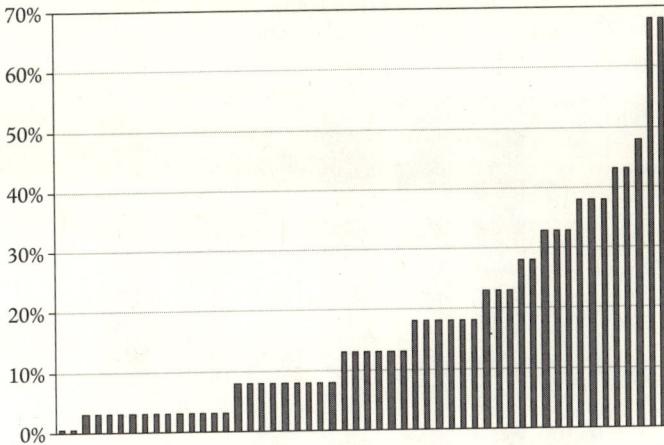

Note: Data are shown for all Region H officers who decided at least 25 Chinese cases (52 officers); the mean grant rate for Chinese cases decided by these officers was 15%. Two officers granted 0% of their cases; their data points have been jittered so as to appear visible on the graph.

rates of deviation from the mean, with several officers deviating 100% or more and one officer over 250% deviant.

Some regions are even less consistent than this, despite the fact that the officers are deciding essentially the same pool of cases. In Region H, the grant rates vary between 0% and 68% (figure 2.10). In this region, thirty-one of fifty-two officers, or 60%, who decided more than twenty-five China cases deviated from the regional

FIGURE 2.11

Individual Officers' Deviations from the Regional Office
Mean Grant Rate in Chinese Cases—Region H

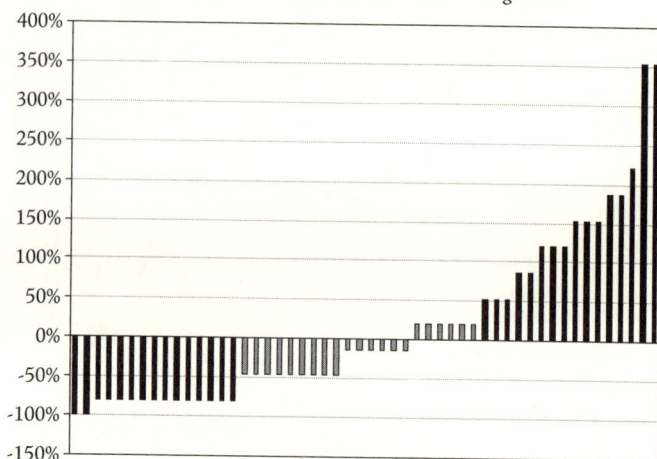

Note: Data are the same as in Figure 2.10 Thirty-one officers, shown in black, deviated by more than 50%.

FIGURE 2.12

Mean Grant Rates in Chinese Cases By Region

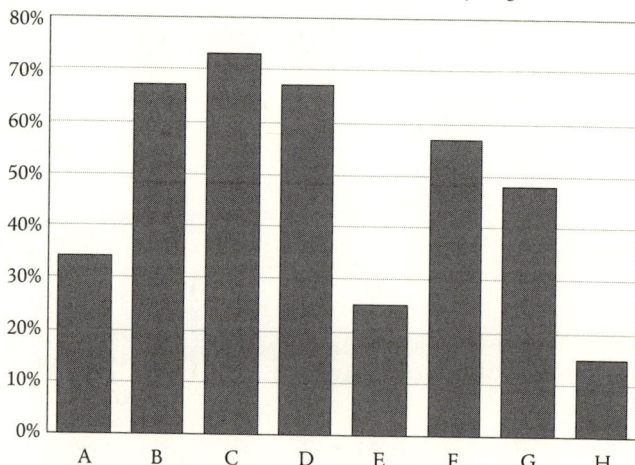

Note: Data show the mean grant rate for all officers in Chinese cases (total of 38,748 cases in all regions).

China mean by more than 50% (see figure 2.11). Two officers granted asylum in none of their cases. One of them (identified to us by the Asylum Office only as Officer 343) decided 273 Chinese cases, but did not grant a single asylum claim.

Figure 2.12 provides the same information broken down into mean grant rates by regional office. The range is very significant: while Region H grants at a 15%

FIGURE 2.13
Percentage of Officers Who Are Outliers in Chinese Cases by Region

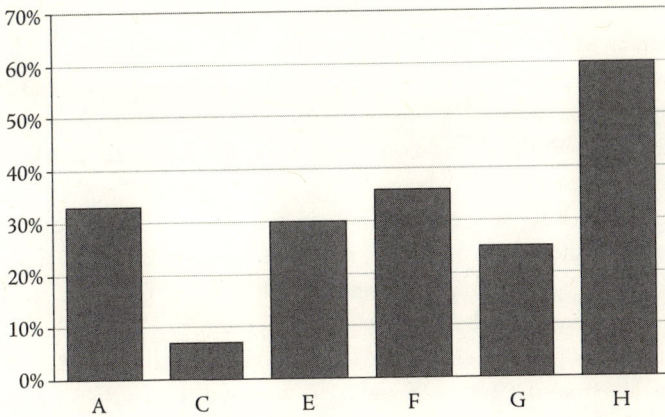

Note: Officers are considered outliers if their grant rates deviated by more than 50% from the regional office mean grant rate. Data are shown for officers deciding at least 25 Chinese cases. There were no such officers in Region B and only two such officers in Region D, so they are omitted from this chart.

rate, Region C grants asylum to people from the same country at a 72% rate. What could account for this? It is possible that migrants from certain regions within China (or traffickers who assist them) choose to go to particular regions of the United States before applying for asylum, and that fraud is more prevalent among migrants from some of those regions than among migrants from other regions. Perhaps, therefore, migration patterns cause Region H to receive a much higher proportion than Region C of Chinese applicants who have false claims for asylum. While in principle these migration patterns could explain some degree of disparity among the U.S. regional asylum offices, we doubt that it could account for a five-fold difference in grant rates from one office to another. Furthermore, there are significant differences in mean grant rates from region to region even when we examine the rates for applicants from countries much smaller than China. For example, the regional mean grant rates for Armenian claims in Regions C, F, and G were, respectively, 57%, 37%, and 23%.[14] We can think of no reason why Armenians with strong asylum claims would flee to one region of the United States while Armenians with weak claims would escape to a different region, so we believe that these differences reveal something about the asylum offices, rather than about the Armenian population. Moreover, differences in the destinations of various types of refugees from China, Armenia, or other countries could not possibly explain the differences in grant rates from officer to officer within regional asylum offices.

Figure 2.13 compares the degree of deviation from the regional mean China grant rate in the six regional offices that had many asylum officers who decided twenty-five or more China cases. The deviation rate is extraordinary, varying from about 7% in Region C to about 60% in Region H.

The last graphs in this chapter examine the degree of consistency within a regional office with respect to single countries other than China. Region D decides many Ethiopian cases, and figures 2.14 and 2.15 show that it does so with a good deal of consistency.

Figure 2.14 shows that many asylum officers in this region seem to grant at similar rates in these cases.

In fact, *no* officer deviates from the mean by more than 50% (figure 2.15).

By contrast, in Region C, the grant rates for Indian cases range considerably, from 3% to 88% (figure 2.16). In Region C, fifteen of thirty-nine officers deviate from the mean Indian grant rate by more than 50% (figure 2.17). We find this of particular interest because only one in eleven asylum officers in Region C deviated more than 50% from the mean regional APC grant rate. Given Region C's high degree of consistency in its adjudications of APC cases generally, perhaps the significant degree of inconsistency in Indian cases reflects particular disagreements among officers about the extent of persecution within India, or about the extent of fraud committed by Indian applicants.

But what explains the tremendous range from very little to quite significant degrees of inconsistency at the eight Asylum Offices? The training, supervisory review, and quality-assurance mechanisms described at the beginning of this

FIGURE 2.14

Individual Officer Grant Rates in Ethiopian Cases—Region D

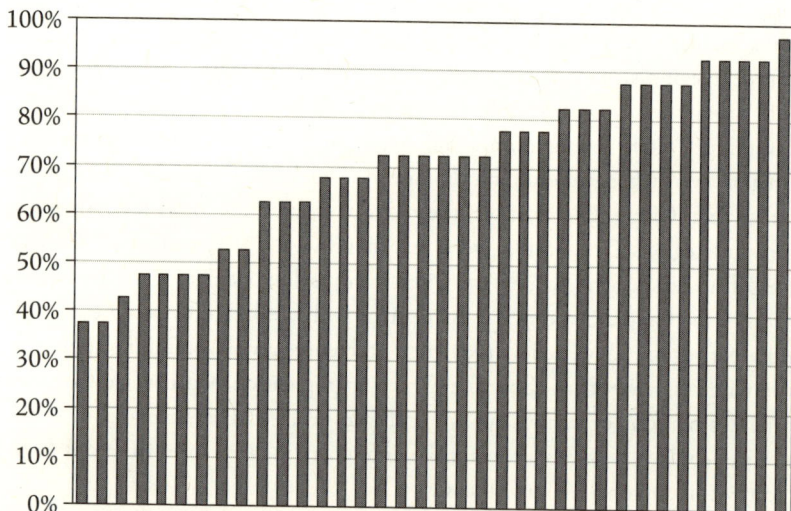

Note: Data are shown for all Region D officers who decided at least 50 Ethiopian cases; the mean grant rate for Ethiopian cases decided by these officers was 72%.

FIGURE 2.15
Individual Officers' Deviations from the Regional Office Mean Grant Rate in Ethiopian Cases—Region D

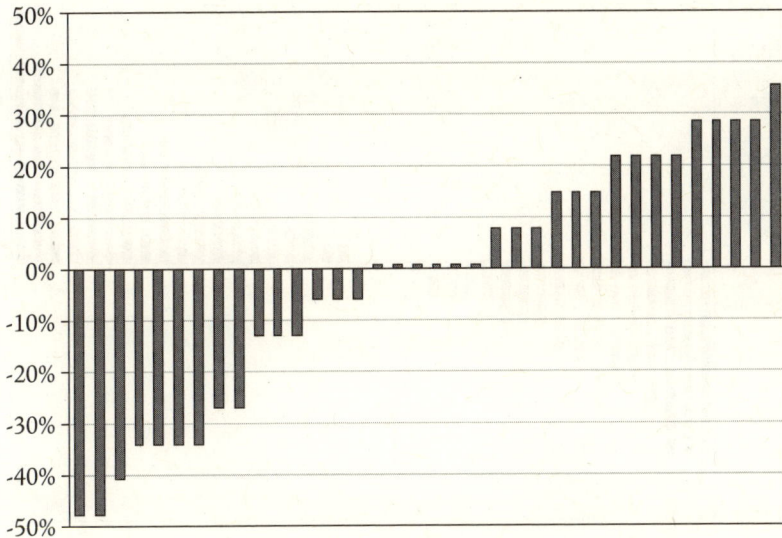

Note: Shows percentage deviation from the mean grant rate in Region D for Ethiopian cases, which was 72%.

FIGURE 2.16
Individual Officer Grant Rates in Indian Cases—Region C

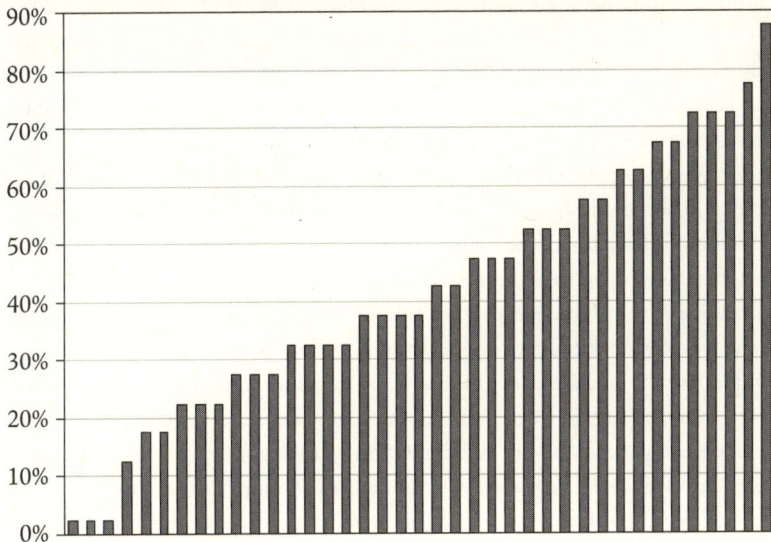

Note: Data are shown for all Region C officers who decided at least 50 Indian cases; the mean grant rate for Indian cases decided by these officers was 39%.

FIGURE 2.17
*Individual Officers' Deviations from the Regional Office
Mean Grant Rate in Indian Cases—Region C*

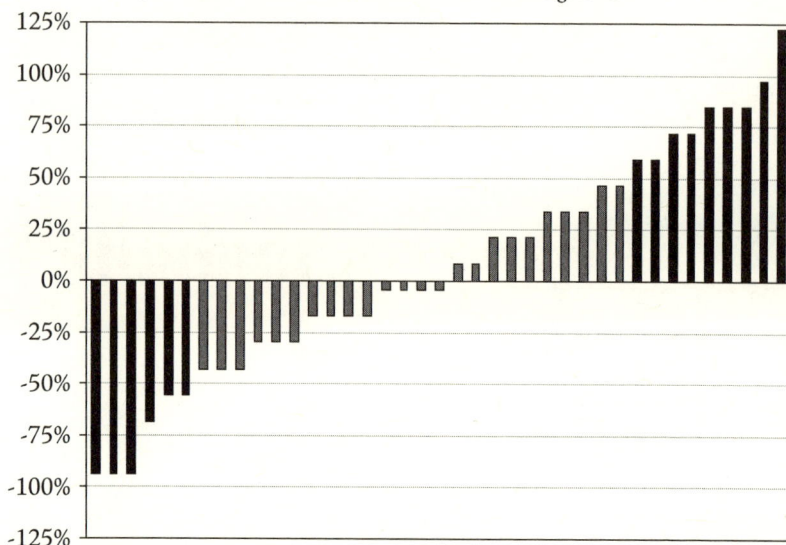

Note: Deviations are from the mean grant rate of 39%. The darker shaded bars show deviations of greater than 50%.

chapter could well account for the high degree of consistency that exists in several offices. Group training provides everyone with the same legal and country-condition information and puts them through the same exercises to apply what they've learned. Each supervisory asylum officer reviews the decisions of many asylum officers, raising the same questions and asserting the same adjudicative approach to each officer on every case. The national headquarters and regional office quality-assurance staff also participate in regular training activities. While these highly professional efforts have contributed to a significant degree of consistency in some offices, these mechanisms have not yet created a just system in all regional offices for those whom America wants to protect. New approaches need to be developed to achieve such a result.

If adjudicators whose every decision is reviewed by a supervisor and who receive significant initial and ongoing training are inconsistent, how do immigration judges who preside over adversarial proceedings fare? The judges receive far less training, and their work is subjected to very little quality control other than the appellate process, a very different kind of review that is much less interactive than review by a supervisory official. Do the more formal litigation procedures followed by immigration judges result in a greater degree of consistency? Does formal review by the Board of Immigration Appeals contribute to such an outcome? Or do other various factors such as the lack of ongoing training and the widely varying prior work experiences of the judge lead to at least as much inconsistency, or more, in the decisions of the adjudicators at this next stage of the adjudicative process?

NOTES

1. *See* Office of Planning, Analysis, and Tech., U.S. Dep't of Justice, FY 2005 Stat. Y.B. I1 (showing 35,049 affirmative cases and 15,551 defensive ones), *available at* http://www.usdoj.gov/ eoir/ statspub/fy05syb.pdf. On the different stages of the asylum process, *see generally* U.S. Citizenship and Immigration Servs., Obtaining Asylum in the United States: Two Paths to Asylum, *available at* http://uscis.gov/graphics/services/asylum/paths.htm. The eight regional asylum offices are located in Arlington (VA), Chicago, Houston, Los Angeles, Miami, Newark (NJ), New York City, and San Francisco. Previous research suggested a significantly lower rate of granting asylum both nationally and regionally, particularly at two offices, following the terrorist attacks on September 11, 2001. Andrew I. Schoenholtz, Refugee Protection in the United States Post-September 11, 36 Colum. Hum. Rts. L. Rev. 323, 340–44 (2005) (showing the significant decline in grant rates at the Houston and Los Angeles offices). To understand what factors might account for such variation, we asked the Asylum Office for raw data on nationality, representation, the eight regional offices, and individual decision makers over time. The Asylum Office provided us with very useful data on each of these factors associated with grant rates for fiscal years 1999–2005. The Methodological Appendix to this book includes a complete explanation of these measurements.

2. E-mail from Joanna Ruppel, Deputy Dir., Asylum Div., U.S. Citizenship and Immigration Servs., Dep't of Homeland Sec., to Andrew I. Schoenholtz (Dec. 18, 2006) (on file with authors).

3. While the regular training that asylum officers receive is substantial and far exceeds the training given to immigration judges, 88% of asylum officers told the Government Accountability Office that the opportunity to observe skilled interviewers, which they are not given, would improve their interviewing skills. Government Accountability Office, U.S. Asylum System: Agencies Have Taken Action to Help Ensure Quality in the Asylum Adjudication Process, but Challenges Remain, GAO-08-935 at 5 (2008).

4. Local quality-assurance officers are supposed to observe some of the interviews conducted by each asylum officer, and they are supposed to review a sample of the decisions that the officers write. But in three of the eight regions, they do not routinely review a sample of decisions, and in none of the three regional offices visited by the Government Accountability Office did the quality-assurance personnel observe Asylum Office interviews. Government Accountability Office, *supra* n.3, at 6 (2008).

5. Ruppel e-mail, *supra* n.2.

6. Dep't of Homeland Sec., Yearbook of Immigration Statistics: 2006, table 17 (2007), http:// www.dhs.gov/xlibrary/ assets/statistics/yearbook/2006/Table17D.xls.

7. According to the Asylum Office, Mexicans voluntarily entered the affirmative asylum system in large numbers during this period principally in order to be placed into immigration court proceedings where they could seek relief other than asylum. Since they are generally not seeking asylum, they are not included in our analysis. *See* Schoenholtz, *supra* n.1, at 338 n.62 (explaining this behavior).

8. There was not sufficient data on asylum officer decisions to compare four APC nationalities fairly, so the individual decision-making analysis that follows does not include data on Guinea, Mauritania, Togo, and Venezuela. *See* Methodological Appendix, part 2.

9. The Methodological Appendix includes the terms and definitions established by the Asylum Office for this data set, along with other relevant materials. This data is *available at* http://www.law.georgetown.edu/humanrightsinstitute/refugeeroulette.htm.

10. Our rationale for adopting this measure of consistency is explained in more detail in the Methodological Appendix. *See* Methodological Appendix.

11. Asylum Div., Office of Int'l Affairs, Dep't of Homeland Security, Affirmative Asylum Procedures Manual 13 (2003).

12. Perhaps there is some relationship between the offices with high disparities and the offices in which quality-assurance personnel do not routinely review officers' decisions. *See supra* n.4. However, because we do not know which offices are designated by which letters, or which offices the Government Accountability Office found to have quality-assurance officers who did not review decisions, we are unable to test this hypothesis.

13. Differences in the mix would not, however, explain the differences in rates of consistency.

14. The data for Armenia are derived from the country-by-country statistics for individual asylum officers supplied to the authors by the Department of Homeland Security, Oct. 23, 2006, in E-mail from Ted Kim, Operations Branch Chief, Asylum Division, USCIS, Dept. of Homeland Security, to Andrew Schoenholtz (Oct. 24, 2006), *amended by* E-mail from Trina Zwicker, Program Manager, Operations Branch, Asylum Division, USCIS, Dept. of Homeland Security, to Philip Schrag (Jan. 23, 2007) (stating that the headings for Armenia and Cameroon in the October 23, 2006 data set should be reversed).

3 The Immigration Courts

AS EXPLAINED IN chapter 1, immigration courts are the "trial-level" administrative bodies responsible for conducting removal hearings—hearings to determine whether noncitizens may remain in the United States.[1] For represented asylum seekers, these hearings are generally conducted like other court hearings. The immigration judge hears testimony from the asylum seeker and from any other witnesses who are available, documentary evidence is introduced formally (and is subject to objections), and closing statements may be made by each side. However, because the immigration judges are actually Justice Department officials rather than federal district judges, neither the Federal Rules of Civil Procedure nor the Federal Rules of Evidence apply.[2] Immigration court hearings are adversarial proceedings, but for several reasons, approximately one-third of asylum seekers in immigration court are unrepresented.[3] When an applicant has no representative, the immigration judge must play a particularly active role in questioning the applicant and building the factual record.

Until 1983, immigration courts were part of the Immigration and Naturalization Service (INS), which was also responsible for enforcement of immigration laws and housed the INS trial attorneys who opposed asylum claims in court.[4] In January of that year, the Executive Office for Immigration Review (EOIR) was created, placing the immigration courts in a separate agency within the Department of Justice.[5] In 2003, when the Department of Homeland Security was created, the trial attorneys became part of that agency, but the courts remained in the Department of Justice.

There are fifty-three immigration courts located in twenty-four states, and more than two hundred immigration judges sit on these courts.[6] An asylum case is assigned to the immigration court that has jurisdiction over the geographic region in which the asylum seeker resides.[7] The administrators in each immigration court assign cases to immigration judges to distribute the workload evenly among them, and without regard to the merits of the cases or the strength of defenses to removal that may be asserted by the respondents.[8]

For the approximately 65% of asylum seekers whose cases are referred by asylum officers to immigration court, the removal hearing allows them to present their claims anew; the immigration judge is not bound by the asylum officer's decision not to grant asylum.[9] The immigration court presents the last good opportunity for these asylum seekers to prevail. The immigration court also hears claims from individuals who raise an asylum claim after being placed in removal proceedings. For such individuals, the immigration court hearing is the only opportunity they will have to present evidence in support of their case. It is therefore of the utmost importance that immigration court proceedings be predictable and fair, as a loss in immigration court will probably result in an order of removal—a possible death sentence for some asylum seekers whose cases are wrongly denied.

We were fortunate to have access to vast amounts of data relating to asylum decision making in immigration court from January 2000 through August 2004. Our analysis takes three prior reports on disparities in the asylum process as a jumping-off point,[10] analyzing the available data in two new ways. First, we examined the grant rates across and within courts, looking at 78,459 decisions in the aggregate for APCs as well as cases involving asylum seekers from individual countries.[11] Second, we used immigration judges' biographical information and a database of 66,443 cases to run a descriptive cross-tabulation analysis that showed us how characteristics such as age, gender, and prior employment experience correlated with their decisions in asylum cases.[12] This analysis also looked at individual characteristics of asylum seekers, such as number of dependents and legal representation, revealing interesting insights into how these factors play into immigration judges' decisions. We also ran three regression analyses to confirm the results of the bivariate cross-tabulations.[13] The methodological challenges we faced and choices we made are described in part 3 of the Methodological Appendix.

A. Disparities between Courts

Figure 3.1 shows, for each APC, the grant rate in the high-volume immigration courts with the highest and lowest grant rate for nationals of that country, as well as the average grant rate for all high-volume immigration courts. The graph reveals that even for asylum seekers from countries that produce a relatively high percentage of successful asylees, there are serious disparities among immigration courts in the rates at which they grant asylum to nationals of five of these countries. As explained further in the Methodological Appendix, we are primarily concerned with court-wide grant rates that deviate by more than 50% from the national average grant rate for any of these countries.[14]

We found serious disparities in decision making with respect to applicants from six of the fifteen APCs. Asylum seekers from three of these countries faced a grant rate in at least one court that was more than 50% below the national average, and applicants from four of these countries enjoyed a grant rate in at least one court that was more than 50% above the national average. For one of these countries, China, the high grant rate and the low grant rate deviated by more than 50% from the national average.

FIGURE 3.1

High, Low, and Average Grant Rates for Nationals of APCs in
High-Volume Immigration Courts

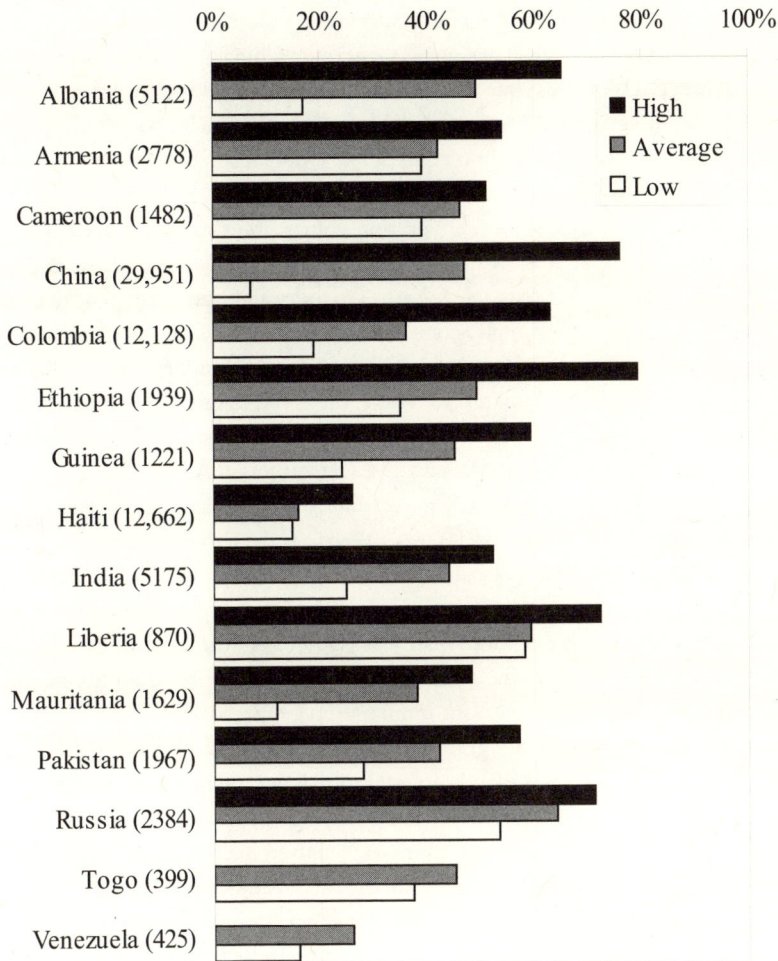

Note: The "High" and "Low" bars represent the highest and lowest grant rates from high-volume immigration courts deciding at least 100 cases involving nationals from a particular country. The "Average" bar denotes the average grant rate across all immigration courts for such cases. Togo and Venezuela have only "Low" and "Average" bars because only one immigration court heard more than 100 cases from those countries. The numbers in parentheses denote the number of asylum cases from that country decided by high-volume immigration courts during the time frame studied.

This means that a Chinese asylum seeker unlucky enough to have her case heard before the Atlanta Immigration Court had a 7% chance of success on her asylum claim, as compared to 47% nationwide.[15] Moreover, if this same asylum seeker had presented her claim four hundred miles to the south, before the Orlando Immigration Court, she would have had a 76% chance of winning asylum, over ten times the Atlanta grant rate. Colombian asylum seekers also faced major disparities: those who appeared before the Orlando Immigration Court had a 63% grant rate, while those heard by the Atlanta Immigration Court faced a grant rate of 19%. The average national grant rate for Colombian asylum seekers is 36%. Why is an individual fleeing persecution in China 986% more likely to win her asylum claim in one venue than in another? Why is the average national grant rate for Chinese asylum claims 571% higher than the Atlanta court's grant rate? And why are Colombian asylum seekers 232% more likely to win their claims in Orlando than they are in Atlanta?

One answer is that some immigration courts grant asylum cases from the aggregate of *all* APCs at a rate much lower (e.g., Atlanta, Detroit, Miami, and San Diego) or much higher (e.g., New York, Orlando, and San Francisco) than the national average.[16] For example, grant rates at least 50% below the national average rate were awarded in Atlanta for Chinese cases and in Detroit for Albanian and Mauritanian cases. As figure 3.2 shows, the average grant rate in high-volume immigration courts for APCs was 40% between January 2000 and August 2004, but the average grant rates in Atlanta and Detroit for all APCs, at 12% and 19%, respectively, were more than 50% lower than the national average. The Miami court's average grant rate for APCs was 42% below the national average, at 23%.

There were also upward disparities in the high-granting courts, although these were not as extreme. The San Francisco Immigration Court, which granted asylum to Ethiopians at a rate more than 50% greater than the national average rate, had an average grant rate for all APCs that was 35% greater than the national average. In addition, the New York Immigration Court, which had the high grant rate for Haiti, had an average grant rate for APCs that was 30% greater than the national average, and the Orlando Immigration Court, which had the high grant rate for both China and Colombia, had an average APC grant rate that was 23% higher than the nationwide mean. One explanation for the differences between the courts could be simply cultural, for lack of a better term—some courts are more likely to grant asylum claims while other courts, despite being components of a single national Executive Office for Immigration Review, are especially tough on all asylum seekers. We explore below the individual characteristics that might incline judges to grant or deny asylum claims; perhaps courts composed of a group of judges in which certain of these characteristics predominate are more likely to adopt one culture or the other.

It seems possible that, to some extent, the differences across courts (and from one region of the Asylum Office to another) may be due to differences in the composition of the APC asylum-seeker population in different geographic locations. That is, although Togo and Armenia are both Asylee Producing Countries, the APC population may have relatively more applicants from Togo (with

FIGURE 3.2
Average Grant Rates for All APCs in High-Volume Immigration Courts

Court	Grant Rate
Arlington (1349)	37%
Atlanta (687)	12%
Baltimore (2304)	41%
Boston (1440)	40%
Chicago (1663)	38%
Dallas (560)	37%
Detroit (1462)	19%
Houston (796)	37%
Los Angeles (6819)	41%
Memphis (1049)	40%
Miami (19,402)	23%
New York (27,942)	52%
Newark (2392)	42%
Orlando (2974)	49%
Philadelphia (1512)	39%
San Diego (449)	30%
San Francisco (5659)	54%
TOTAL (78,459)	40%

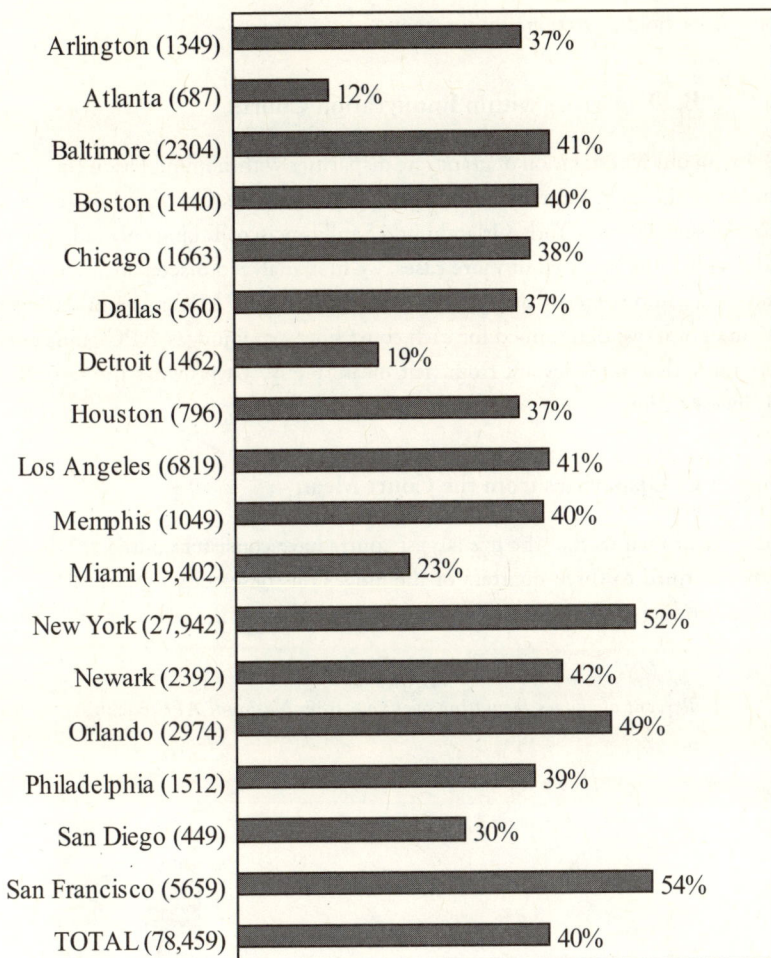

Note: The numbers in parentheses after the court name indicate the number of cases from all APCs decided by the court in question.

a higher or lower success rate than Armenians) in one region of the United States than another. However, we know of no reason why Orlando should attract a much higher proportion of bona fide asylum applicants from APCs than nearby Atlanta.[17] Within a court, however, no such geographic variable should exist, as nearly all cases are assigned randomly to the judges.[18] As explained below, our research found tremendous differences in the asylum grant rates of immigration judges on the same court, even with respect to applicants from a particular country. To further investigate discrepancies among decision makers within the high-volume immigration courts, we examined the grant rates of individual immigration judges, holding nationality constant.

B. Disparities within Immigration Courts

We began our investigation of grant rate disparities within immigration courts by looking at the eight largest courts by volume: Baltimore, Chicago, Los Angeles, Miami, Newark, New York, Orlando, and San Francisco. Taking only judges who had decided one hundred or more cases, we first analyzed discrepancies in grant rates for asylum seekers from APCs.[19] With the national APC mean of 40% as a starting point, we determined for each court how many judges' APC grant rates were more than 50% deviant from that mean. Figure 3.3 provides the results of this investigation.

C. Disparities from the Court Mean

The statistics tell us that the five largest courts have consistent outliers;[20] that is, from one-third to three-quarters of the judges on these courts grant asylum in Asylee Producing Countries cases at rates more than 50% greater or more than

FIGURE 3.3
Percent of Judges Deviating over 50% from National APC Mean

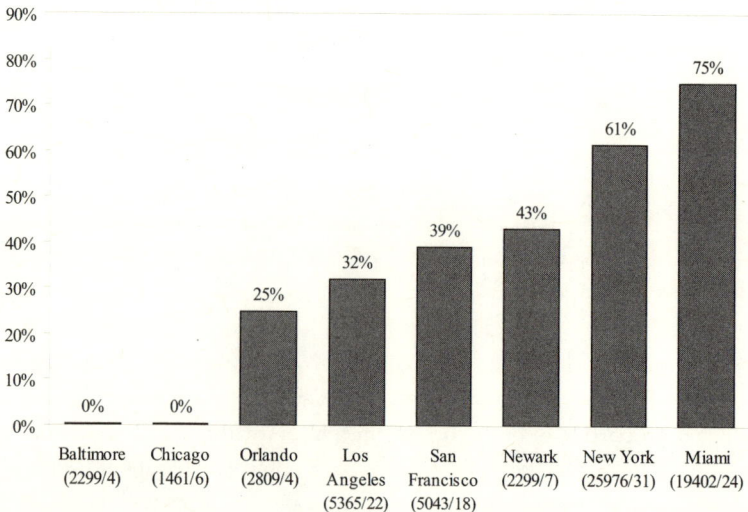

Note: The x-axis shows city (number of cases decided/number of judges). As noted *supra* note 19, the number of cases decided includes only cases heard by judges hearing 100 or more APC cases on each court, and the number of judges includes only judges who decided 100 or more APC cases on each court.

FIGURE 3.4
Grant Rates for Judges Who Are Outliers in APC Cases—New York (9 of 31 judges)

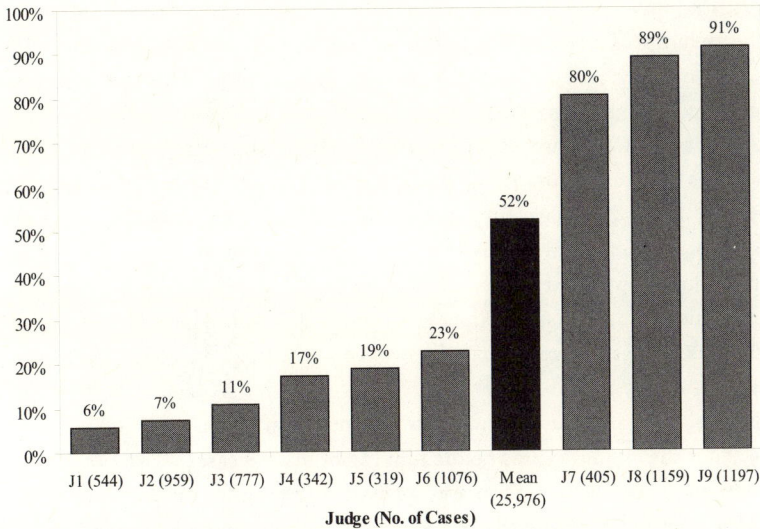

Note: This graph and the two graphs that follow show grant rates for judges deciding at least 100 APC cases who deviated by more than 50% from their court's mean in APC cases.

50% less than the national average. Why would it be that there are such discrepancies in grant rates between judges on the same court? One obvious response to this finding is that there may be different geographic populations of asylum seekers in different regions; for example, it may be that in Chicago, the Chinese asylum seekers all come from a certain region or ethnic group and have similarly viable asylum claims, while in Miami, the Chinese asylum-seeker population is more diverse, resulting in greater disparities in claim viability. As a result of these differences in Chinese claims, individual judges in Miami might produce grant rates more discrepant in APC cases than judges in Chicago.

We tested this concern by limiting geographic variability, looking only at individual judges' discrepancies from *their own court's* average grant rate for asylum seekers from APCs.[21] We focused on the four largest courts:[22] San Francisco, Miami, New York, and Los Angeles, with eighteen, twenty-one, twenty-six, and twenty-seven judges, respectively.[23] We discovered that in the three largest courts, more than a quarter of the judges were markedly out of step with the other judges in their own courthouse.[24]

As figure 3.4 shows, in New York, one judge granted only 6% of the APC asylum cases before him, and another pulled in just behind him, having granted 7% of asylum cases he heard. A New York judge who was transferred to the Miami court in September 2003 granted asylum in 11% of the APC cases he heard in

New York (as compared to 6% in Miami). Three more judges granted less than a quarter of the cases that came before them, at rates of 17%, 19%, and 23%. The New York Immigration Court also had three judges who awarded asylum to most of the asylum seekers before them, at rates of 80%, 89%, and 91%. This means that 29% of New York judges decided APC cases at rates more than 50% discrepant from the court's mean of 52%.

As illustrated in figure 3.5, in Los Angeles, one judge granted asylum to only 10% of the applicants from APCs who came before him; another judge approved only 16% of the APC asylum cases she heard; and three judges granted only 17% of the APC asylum claims in their courts. Against these five, the highest-granting judge approved 83% of the asylum cases from APCs in his court, and another judge granted 64% of the cases from APCs before him. In the end, 32% of the Los Angeles judges deviated more than 50% from the court's APC mean of 41%.

Figure 3.6 shows that the numbers are similar in Miami: one judge granted only 3% of the asylum claims before him (27 of his 958 cases). Two other judges eked in just ahead of him, with average asylum grant rates for APCs of 5% and 6%. The next judge in line granted 8% of the asylum cases he saw, and another granted 9%. In contrast, three judges granted asylum at rates more than 50% above the Miami average: 75%, 61%, and 38%. In sum, 33% of the Miami judges decided APC asylum cases at rates more than 50% deviant from the court's mean of 23%.

In total, in the Los Angeles, Miami, and New York immigration courts, we found eight judges whose average grant rates for all asylum seekers from APCs during the period studied were more than 50% above their court's mean and sixteen judges whose rates were more than 50% below their court's mean. From a pool of approximately seventy-four judges, 32% decided asylum cases from APCs at rates significantly discrepant from their court's average grant rate.[25]

D. Disparities from the Court Mean, Holding Nationality Constant

Even when one examines disparities from each court's mean, thus correcting for any geographical differences in populations of asylum seekers, there are serious discrepancies in the grant rates of individual immigration judges on the same court. To delve more deeply into the causes of these disparities, we again limited the variables and examined individual grant rates for asylum seekers of only one nationality for immigration judges in each of the four largest courts.[26]

Figures 3.7 through 3.10 show, for each of the four largest courts, the grant rate for each judge when he or she decided cases involving nationals of one of the two

FIGURE 3.5
Grant Rates for Judges Who Are Outliers in APC Cases—
Los Angeles (7 of 22 judges)

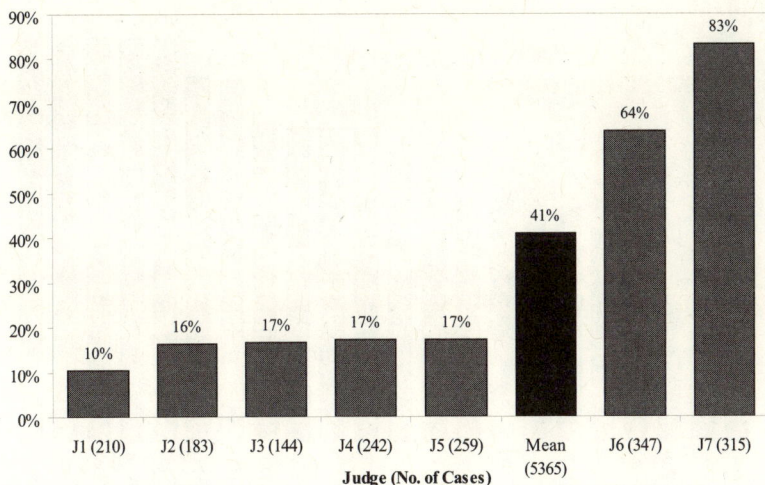

FIGURE 3.6
Grant Rates for Judges Who Are Outliers in APC Cases—Miami (8 of 24 judges)

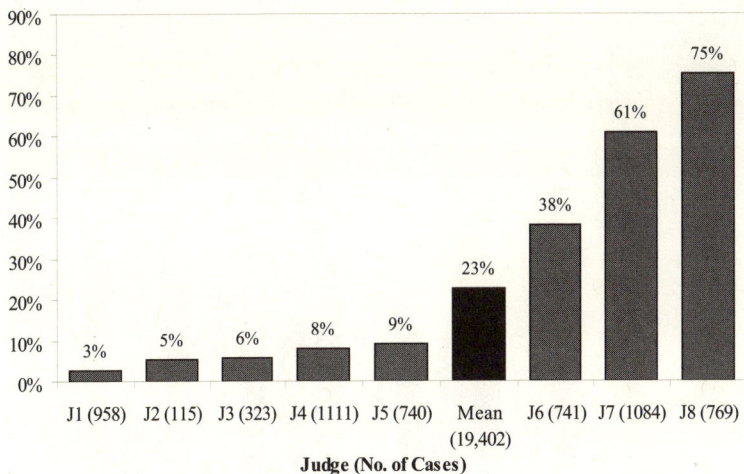

countries from which the largest number of asylum cases were filed in that court. In each chart, the black bar marked "Mean" shows the mean grant rate for that country's applicants in that court. In New York, for example, three judges decided Albanian cases at a rate more than 50% below the court average—meaning that 14% of the judges ruled at a rate considerably at odds with the court's mean of 67%.

FIGURE 3.7
Judges' Grant Rates in Albanian Cases—New York

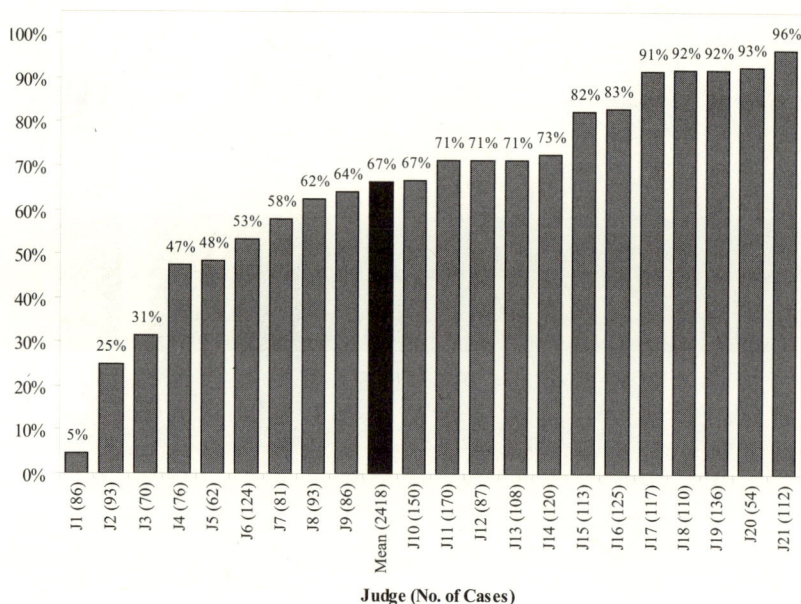

Note: See note 26.

FIGURE 3.8
Judges' Grant Rates in Indian Cases—San Francisco

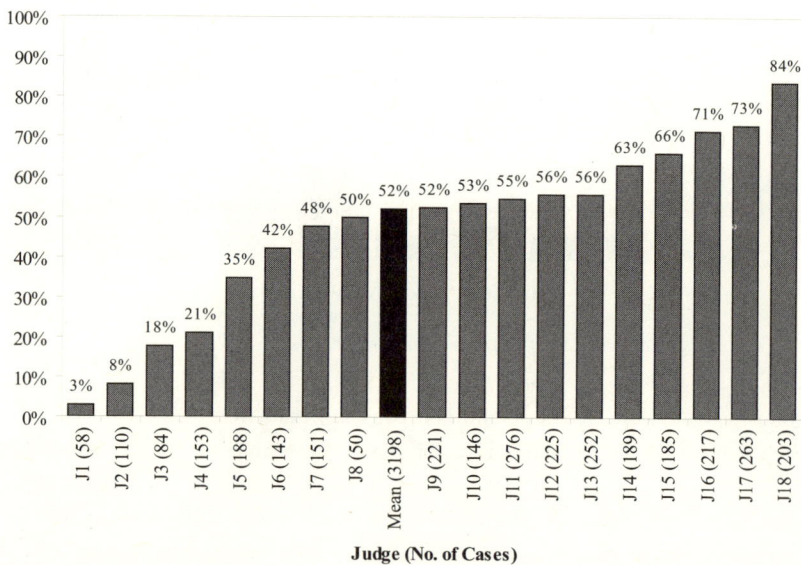

FIGURE 3.9

Judges' Grant Rates in Chinese Cases—Los Angeles

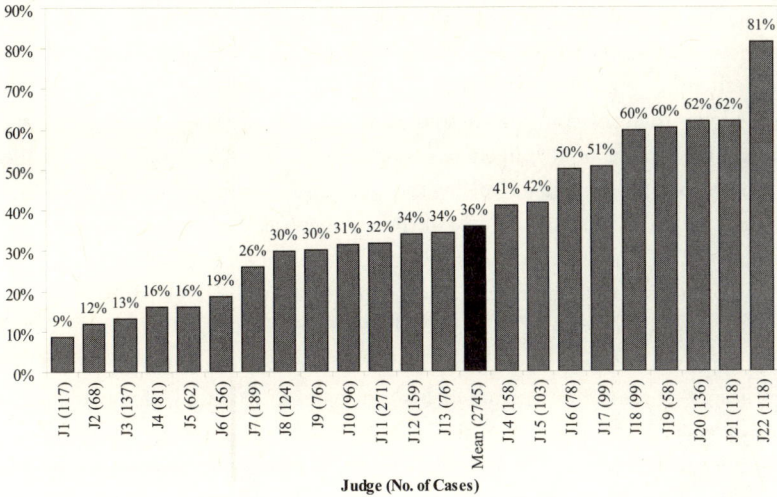

Judge (No. of Cases)

FIGURE 3.10

Judges' Grant Rates in Colombian Cases—Miami

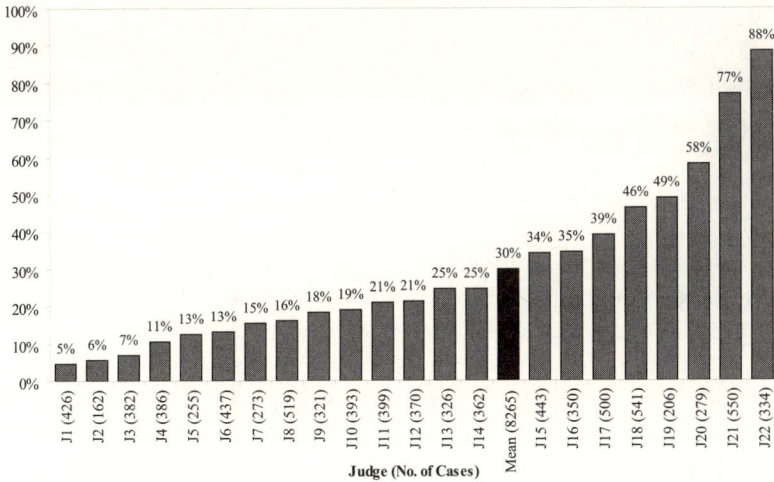

Judge (No. of Cases)

And in San Francisco, four judges decided Indian cases at rates more than 50% below and one judge at a rate more than 50% above that court's mean; 28% of the judges deviated by more than 50% from the court's average of 52%. The situation was even worse in Los Angeles for Chinese cases, where five judges granted at a rate more than 50% lower than and five judges granted at a rate more than 50% higher than the court mean, so that 45% of the judges were out of step with the court's average of 36% in these cases. Similarly, in Miami six judges decided Colombian cases at rates 50% below the mean and five judges decided these cases at rates 50% above the mean; 50% of these judges decided asylum cases at a rate that varied by more than 50% from the court's average of 30%.

The differences in grant rates among the judges in the larger courts are large. In Los Angeles, one judge granted asylum to 9% of the 117 Chinese applicants who appeared before him, whereas another granted asylum to 81% of 118 Chinese applicants—nine times the rate of his colleague. In Miami, Colombians before one judge were granted asylum at a rate of 5%, while those who appeared before another judge, with an 88% grant rate, were almost eighteen times more likely to win asylum. The same story is repeated in New York, with one judge granting asylum to 5% of the Albanians whose cases he heard, and another granting asylum to 96% of the Albanians in her court. The second judge worked in the same suite of offices as the first judge but was nineteen times more likely to grant asylum. And the case in San Francisco is even more dramatic; one judge granted 84% of Indian asylum cases, a rate twenty-eight times that of another judge in the same courthouse who granted 3% of these cases.[27] What could possibly account for such dramatic variations within the same court in grant rates to asylum seekers from the same country?

E. Variables Impacting Judges' Decisions

We also performed a descriptive analysis, using cross-tabulation, of the decisions of the judges during the time frame discussed above. We examined the following variables to determine their impact on the judges' grant rates: whether the asylum seeker was represented, the number of dependents the asylum seeker had, the gender of the judge, and the prior work experience of the judge.[28] The last category was broken out into experience working in the following fields: for the Immigration and Naturalization Service or the Department of Homeland Security, for the government (except the INS or DHS), in the military, for a non-governmental organization, in private practice, and in academia. The relationship between grant rates and each of these variables was statistically significant to a 99% probability (this is, the relationships did not occur by chance). We confirmed the statistical significance of the cross-tabulation analysis with chi-square

FIGURE 3.11
Relationship between Representation and Grant Rates

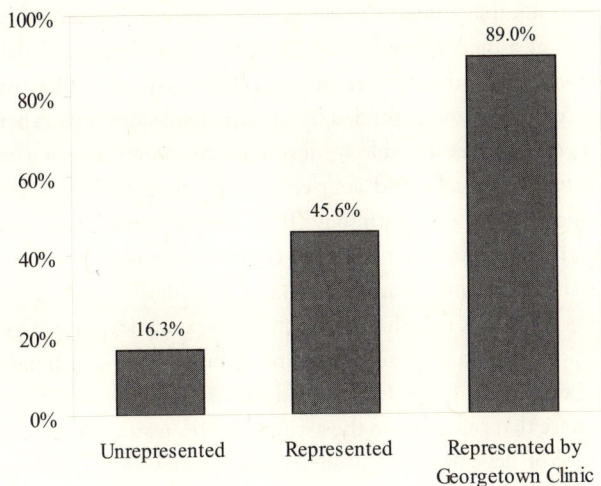

and performed two logistic regression analyses and one hierarchical linear regression to ensure that the results of the cross-tabulation analysis would remain consistent with all other variables held constant.[29]

The results of the cross-tabulation analysis confirm earlier studies showing that whether an asylum seeker is represented in court is the single most important factor affecting the outcome of her case.[30] Represented asylum seekers were granted asylum at a rate of 45.6%, almost three times as high as the 16.3% grant rate for those without legal counsel.[31] The regression analyses confirmed that, with all other variables in the study held constant, represented asylum seekers were substantially more likely to win their case than those without representation.[32]

Given the complexity of the asylum process and increasingly stringent corroboration requirements in immigration court, it is not surprising that legal assistance plays an enormous role in determining whether an asylum seeker wins her case. While there could be a selection effect in play—that is, legal representatives might take on only viable asylum cases, thus weeding out weak claims—the power of the representation variable makes it unlikely that this is the only causal factor. Moreover, the data do not take into account the quality of representation. Asylum seekers represented by Georgetown University's clinical program from January 2000 through August 2004 were granted asylum at a rate of 89% in immigration court.[33]

Other law school asylum clinics have had comparable success rates.[34] Similarly, asylum applicants represented pro bono by large law firms cooperating with Human

Rights First (formerly the Lawyers Committee for Human Rights) had a success rate of about 96% in the 479 cases they handled to conclusion in that same period.[35]

We do not think that students in law school clinics and lawyers in large firms win these cases at a higher rate because they are more skilled at legal research or oral argument than other lawyers who represent asylum applicants. Rather, because their representation is funded by tuition or subsidized by other firm clients, these representatives are able to devote much more time (and money for international telephone calls and courier services) to obtaining documents to corroborate their clients' oral testimony. They are also more likely to search for experts who will file affidavits or testify in court about a country's human rights violations or the applicant's mental or physical condition. It is not unusual for representatives who work in a clinic, a nonprofit organization, or a large law firm to work for months on a case and to file three hundred to five hundred pages of supporting evidence.[36] Fully documented claims are easier for adjudicators to decide than those that rely only on the asylum seeker's testimony.

The number of dependents that an asylum seeker brought with her to the United States played a surprisingly large role in increasing the chance of an asylum grant. According to the cross-tabulation analysis, while asylum seekers with no dependents have a 42.3% grant rate, having one dependent increases the grant rate to 48.2%.[37] It could be that asylum seekers who bring children or a spouse appear more credible, or that immigration judges are more sympathetic to asylum seekers who have nuclear family members to protect. In any case, the regression analyses confirm that this factor affected judges' determination whether to grant an asylum claim.

FIGURE 3.12
Relationship between Asylee's Dependents and Grant Rates

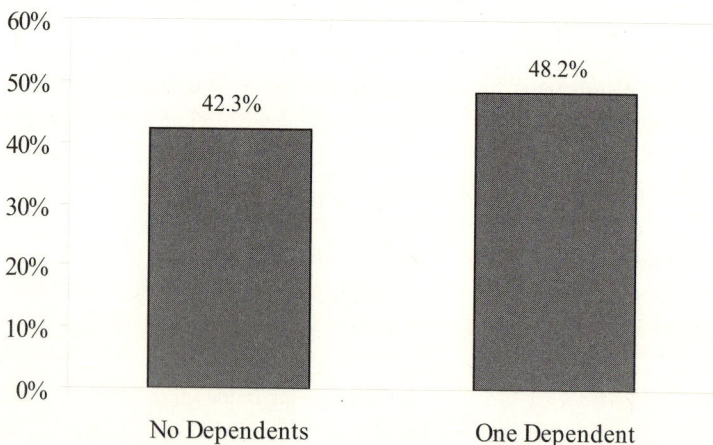

FIGURE 3.13
Relationship between Judge's Gender and Grant Rates

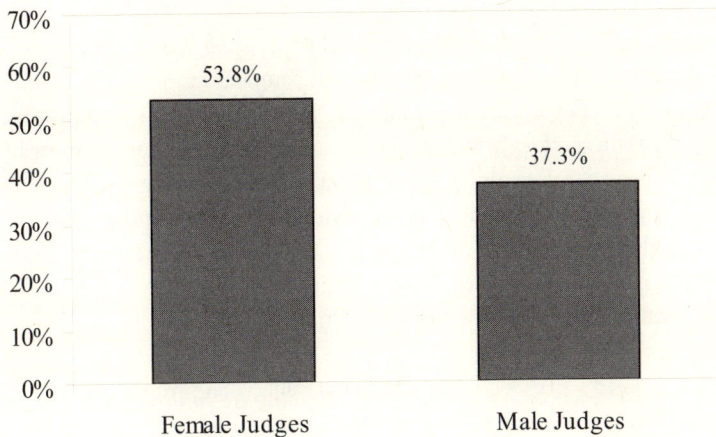

We also looked at characteristics of the judges that impacted the asylum decision. Perhaps the most interesting result of our cross-tabulation study was that the gender of the judge had a significant impact on the likelihood that asylum would be granted. Female immigration judges granted asylum at a rate of 53.8%, while male judges granted asylum at a rate of 37.3%.[38] An asylum applicant assigned by chance to a female judge therefore had a 44% better chance of prevailing than an applicant assigned to a male judge.[39] In contrast, no appreciable difference existed in the grant rates of male and female asylum officers. Our study of the grant rates of 264 male and 257 female officers who decided fifty or more APC cases from FY 1999 through FY 2005 shows only a 7% difference, with male officers granting asylum at a rate of 44% and female officers granting at a rate of 41%.

Several political scientists have studied the effect of gender on judicial decision making in federal and state courts. Our cross-tabulation analysis, which analyzes over sixty thousand decisions by seventy-eight female immigration judges and 169 male immigration judges, includes significantly greater numbers of both female judges and decisions than any of the prior studies.[40] The literature in this area offers several possible reasons for gender differentials in judicial decision making.[41] One survey of federal judges found that while 81% of female judges had experienced sex discrimination, only 18.5% of men on the bench had experienced race or class discrimination.[42] This experience may have an impact in the courtroom: it might make female judges more sympathetic to stories of persecution, as well as more conscious in eliminating their own biases from the decision-making process. Carrie Menkel-Meadow has noted that some women lawyers would prefer that trials take the form of "conversations with fact-finders—rather than persuasive intimidation."[43] It is possible that female immigration judges are inclined to a nonadversarial proceeding in their courtrooms, an approach more likely to solicit a coherent and complete story from a traumatized asylum seeker.[44] Finally, Judith Resnik has argued that feminist approaches to judging focus on caretaking and an understanding of connections to those before them.[45] This may lead feminist immigration judges to empathize more with the plight of asylum seekers, and to decide asylum cases from a perspective of connection with, rather than distance from, the applicant. In the end, we cannot be sure of the cause of this difference, or whether women or men are more likely to decide asylum cases "correctly," but this statistical outcome points to issues ripe for future study.

We wondered whether some of the "gender effect" on asylum decision making was related to the different prior work experience of male and female judges. We found that the two groups—male judges and female judges—had distinctly different work experience prior to appointment to the bench.[46] Of seventy-eight female judges studied, 29% had previously worked for nongovernmental organizations, defending the rights of immigrants or indigent populations. But of 169 male judges studied, only 9% had worked for NGOs. In contrast, 56% of male judges had previously worked for the INS or DHS, and 83% of male judges had worked for the government in some capacity (excluding work for INS or DHS) before their appointment to the bench. Only 51% of female judges had prior work experience with INS or DHS, although 72% of women had previous government experience.

As figure 3.14 illustrates, this differential in previous INS or DHS experience becomes even more striking with time; while 32% of female judges and 44% of male judges had over five years of INS/DHS experience, 10% of females and 17% of males had worked for INS/DHS for more than ten years, 1% of females and 8% of males had over fifteen years INS/DHS experience, and 1% of females but 4% of the males had over twenty years INS/DHS experience. While women had more prior experience in occupations likely to make them sympathetic to asylum seekers, men had substantially more and longer experience in positions adversarial to asylum seekers.

We also found that prior work experience of all types had a significant impact on a judge's grant rate (figure 3.15). Judges with prior government experience (excluding work for INS or DHS) granted asylum at a rate of 39.6%, contrasted with a grant rate of 47.1% for those with no prior government experience, a difference of 19%.[48] Judges with prior INS or DHS experience granted 38.9% of the asylum claims before them, in contrast to judges without DHS/INS experience, who granted at a rate of 48.2%, a difference of 24%. Judges with military experience

FIGURE 3.14
Judges' INS/DHS Experience by Gender47

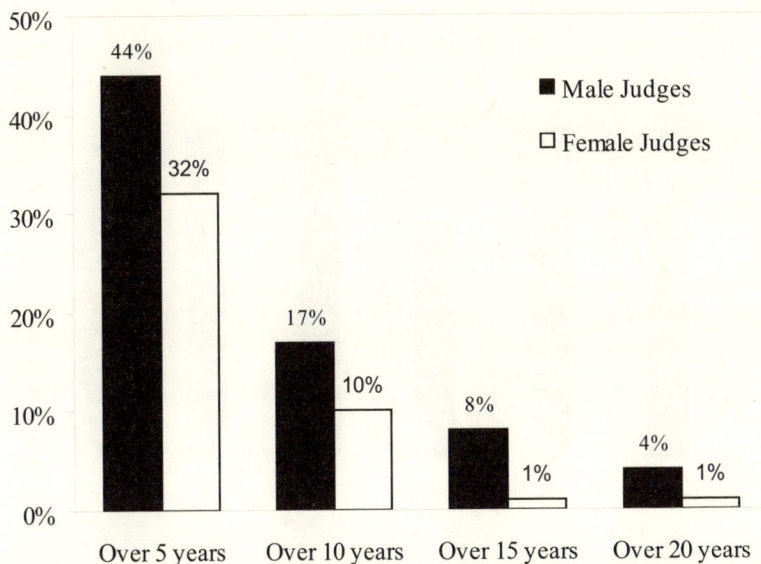

granted asylum at a rate of 37.4%, compared with a rate of 44.2% for those without military experience, a difference of 18%. On the other end of the spectrum, judges who had worked for nonprofits granted asylum at a rate of 55.4%, compared with a rate of 41.1% for those without such experience, a difference of 35%.[49] And judges with prior experience in academia granted asylum at a rate of 52.3%, in contrast to a rate of 43.2% for those without such experience, a disparity of 21%. Finally, judges who had worked in private practice granted asylum at a rate of 46.3%, compared to 39.5% for judges without experience in a private firm, a difference of 17%.

As further detailed below, despite our initial hypothesis that male judges had lower grant rates because they had more prior work experience of the type that leads judges to be skeptical of applicants' claims, we found, once again, that gender had an impact on grant rates independent of prior work experience. When we considered only the grant rates of judges with no prior work experience in government, or no such experience in INS or DHS, or no such experience in nonprofit organizations, the chance of winning with a female judge was in each instance at least 37% greater than the chance of winning with a male judge.[50]

Setting the gender findings aside for a moment, we explored further the finding that work experience in an enforcement capacity with the former Immigration and Naturalization Service or the current Department of Homeland Security made judges less likely to grant asylum. This effect became more pronounced

FIGURE 3.15
Grant Rates by Different Types of Prior Work Experience

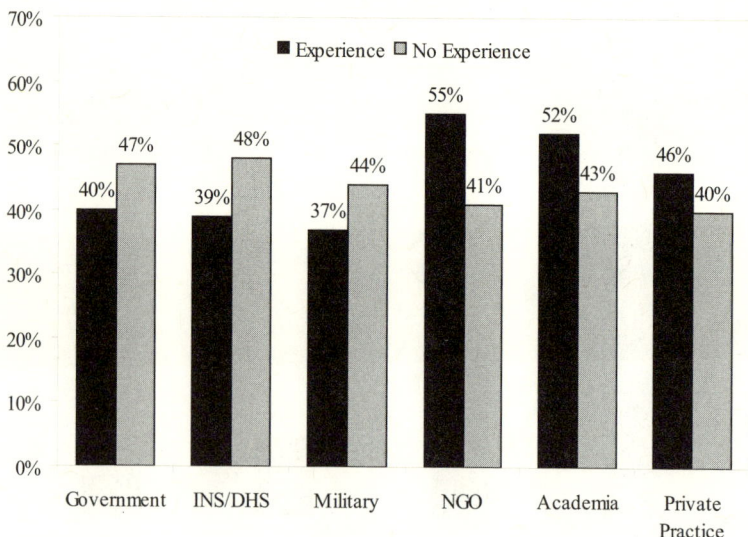

with years of service. The cross-tabulation analysis tells us that judges who had not worked for the INS or DHS had a grant rate of 48.2%, while judges who had worked there for one to five years granted asylum at a rate of 42.9% (figure 3.16). Moreover, judges with six to ten years of INS or DHS experience granted asylum at a rate of 40.2%, and those with eleven or more years in the INS or DHS granted asylum to only 31.3% of the asylum seekers before them. Perhaps people who spend many years enforcing the immigration law carry some of the culture or ideology of their agencies with them when they are appointed to the bench.[51]

We next explored a combination of independent variables—namely, gender and work experience—and learned that gender has an effect on grant rate even among judges with similar prior work experience or without a certain type of work experience.[52] As figure 3.17 shows, female judges still grant asylum at consistently higher rates than male judges regardless of the type of prior work experience. For example, when we look only at judges with no work experience for the INS or DHS, we find that women grant at a rate of 59.4%, which is 50% higher than the male judges' rate of 39.6%. In the group of judges with no prior government work experience (excluding INS or DHS), female judges granted 56.8% of the asylum cases they heard, a rate 40% higher than male judges, who granted 40.5% of the asylum cases before them. And when we look at judges without experience working for NGOs, the grant rate for female judges is 49.9%, a rate 37% higher than the 36.5% grant rate awarded by male judges.[53]

FIGURE 3.16
Grant Rates by Judges' INS/DHS Experience[54]

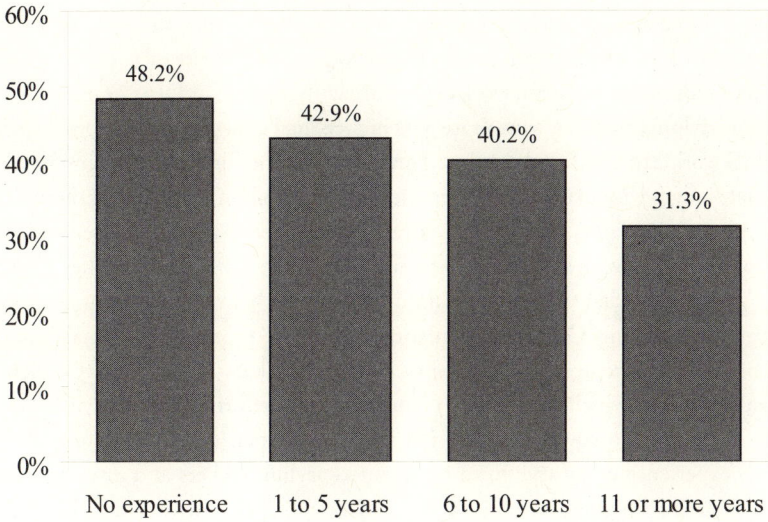

48.2%	42.9%	40.2%	31.3%
No experience	1 to 5 years	6 to 10 years	11 or more years

FIGURE 3.17
Grant Rates by Gender and Work Experience

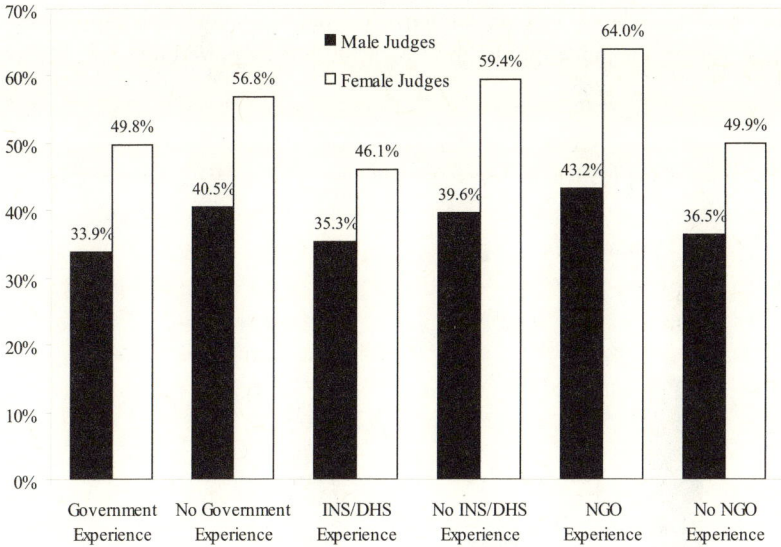

■ Male Judges
□ Female Judges

	Government Experience	No Government Experience	INS/DHS Experience	No INS/DHS Experience	NGO Experience	No NGO Experience
Male	33.9%	40.5%	35.3%	39.6%	43.2%	36.5%
Female	49.8%	56.8%	46.1%	59.4%	64.0%	49.9%

When we examine gender and *contrasting* prior work experience, the disparities in grant rates increase. Female judges with no prior government work experience granted asylum at a rate of 56.8%, a rate 68% higher than that of male judges with prior government work experience, who granted at a rate of 33.9%. Similarly, female judges without prior work experience with the INS or DHS granted 59.4% of the asylum cases they saw, a rate 68% higher than male judges with prior INS/DHS work experience, who granted only 35.3% of the cases before them. Finally, female judges with prior work experience at a nonprofit organization granted 64% of the asylum claims before them, a rate 75% higher than male judges with no prior nonprofit work experience, who granted only 36.5% of the cases they heard.

When we added the representation factor into the mix, the disparities were even more striking. Our cross-tabulation analysis determined that female judges grant asylum to represented asylum seekers at a rate of 55.6%, a rate 289% higher than the rate at which male judges granted asylum to unrepresented asylum seekers, or 14.3%. Moreover, as figure 3.18 illustrates, female judges with no DHS/INS experience grant asylum to represented asylum seekers at a rate of 60.6%, which is 324% higher than the 14.3% grant rate of male judges with DHS/INS experience hearing the cases of unrepresented asylum seekers.

We imagine the reader will find these results surprising, if not shocking. While our findings concerning representation serve to buttress prior studies and the outcomes relating to prior employment might comport with expectations, the gender of the judge appears to be an astonishingly powerful factor in deter-

FIGURE 3.18
Grant Rates by Gender, Representation, and DHS/INS Work Experience

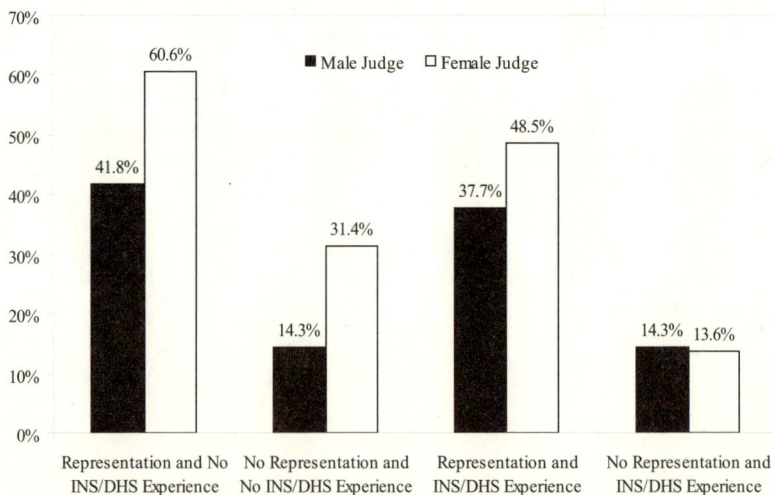

mining grant rates. In view of these disturbing disparities at the Asylum Office and immigration court levels of the process, one would hope and expect that the process in the Board of Immigration Appeals and the federal courts of appeals would be so transparent and accurate as to give asylum applicants and scholars strong confidence that adjudication errors were being fully corrected at higher levels. In the next two chapters, we will see that the statistical evidence does not provide the level of confidence that would be desirable.

NOTES

1. 8 C.F.R. § 1240.1(a)(1)(i) (2007). For further information on removal hearings, *see supra* chapter 1.

2. The Federal Rules of Civil Procedure "govern . . . civil actions and proceedings in the United States District Courts." Federal Rule of Civil Procedure 1. The Federal Rules of Evidence govern proceedings in all federal courts, including bankruptcy courts and courts of appeals. Federal Rule of Evidence 101. Immigration courts are administrative bodies, not federal courts. Instead, the immigration courts' procedures are governed by relevant provisions of the United States Code. 8 U.S.C. § 1229a(b)(1) (2000) ("The immigration judge shall . . . interrogate, examine, and cross-examine the alien and any witnesses.").

3. Andrew I. Schoenholtz & Jonathan Jacobs, The State of Asylum Representation: Ideas for Change, 16 Geo. Immigr. L.J. 739, 742 (2002). Asylum applicants face numerous barriers to obtaining quality representation, including the "dearth of attorneys qualified to practice asylum law," the cost of representation (especially given that asylum seekers are not granted work authorization until 180 days after their application is filed), language barriers, and cultural and societal disorientation. *See id.* at 747.

4. Indeed, before 1956, "special inquiry officers," who were the predecessors to immigration judges, held hearings as only part of a range of responsibilities that included enforcing immigration laws. These officials were retitled "immigration judges" in 1973. T. Alexander Aleinikoff & David A. Martin, Immigration: Process and Policy 107–9 (2d ed. 1991).

5. *See* Board of Immigration Appeals, 48 Fed. Reg. 8038 (Feb. 25, 1983) (to be codified at 8 C.F.R. pts. 1, 3, 100).

6. Executive Office of Immigration Review, U.S. Dep't of Justice, Office of the Chief Immigration Judge, *available at* http://www.usdoj.gov/eoir/ocijinfo.htm.

7. Asylum cases are assigned to the court with jurisdiction over the asylum seeker's residence when the Notice to Appear is issued. 8 C.F.R. §§ 1003.14(a), 1003.20(a) (2007). *See supra* chapter 1 for discussion of the Notice to Appear. An asylum seeker may move to change venue "for good cause." 8 C.F.R. § 1003.20(b) (2007).

8. The only exception is that in some courts, a particular judge may be designated to hear cases initiated against unaccompanied minors, which are referred from the Office of Special Investigations, and attorney discipline cases. The percentage of such cases is very small, in the low single digits. E-mail from the Executive Office for Immigration Review to Andrew Schoenholtz (Feb. 1, 2007) (on file with authors); *see also* U.S. Gov't Accountability Office, Executive Office for Immigration Review: Caseload Performance Reporting Needs Improvement 17 (2006) ("Within each immigration court, newly filed cases are generally assigned to immigration judges through an automated process; however, some flexibility exists. . . . [T]he court administrator may manually schedule some cases to correct inequities that occurred in the number and type of cases that were assigned to a

judge by the automated system. Also, cases that are re-entering the immigration court system are generally manually assigned to the immigration judge who had initially adjudicated the case. Further, if a judge already has a heavy caseload, . . . the [delegate of the] Chief Immigration Judge . . . may decide to exclude a judge from assignment of newly filed cases through the automated system." (footnote omitted))

9. In legal parlance, the hearings are considered "de novo." The legal term "de novo" (literally, "anew") means that the record from the Asylum Office is not used in the immigration court hearing, so it is an entirely new trial. However, the DHS trial attorney may use any inconsistencies between the documents that the applicant originally filed with the asylum office and the testimony and documents presented to the immigration court to challenge the applicant's credibility. The judge may disbelieve the applicant's testimony due to such inconsistencies "without regard to whether an inconsistency . . . goes to the heart of the applicant's claim" 8 U.S.C. Sec. 1229a(c)(4)(C) (2007).

10. Our analysis of disparities in decision making in the asylum process follows three reports: Frederick Tulsky's article in the *San Jose Mercury News* detailing the results of his Freedom of Information Act (FOIA) request to the Immigration and Naturalization Service, Frederick N. Tulsky, *Asylum Seekers Face Capricious Legal System*, San Jose Mercury News, Oct. 18, 2000, at 1A; the asylumlaw.org website, which provides data received in response to asylum.org's FOIA request to the Department of Homeland Security, Asylumlaw.org, U.S. Immigration Judge Decisions in Asylum Cases, Jan. 2000 to Aug. 2004, http://www.asylumlaw.org/ legal_tools/ index.cfm?fuseaction=showJudges2004; and the Transactional Records Access Clearinghouse (TRAC) website, which analyzes the data from the first two requests and provides extensive biographical information for many of the immigration judges, Trac Immigration Report, Immigration Judges, http://trac.syr.edu/immigration/ reports/judgereports. We are indebted to Tulsky, asylumlaw.org, and TRAC for obtaining and sharing these data. Moreover, the United States Committee on International Religious Freedom conducted a statistical analysis of immigration judge rulings on claims of asylum seekers in expedited removal from FY 2000 to FY 2003. Patrick Baier, *Selected Statistical Analyses of Immigration Judge Rulings on Asylum Applications, FY 2000–2003*, in II Report on Asylum Seekers in Expedited Removal 674 (2005), *available at* http:// www.uscirf.gov/countries/global/asylum_refugees/2005/february/index.html.

11. For the criteria by which these "Asylee Producing Countries" were selected, *see supra* chapter 2. As further explained in the Methodological Appendix, this data includes defensive asylum claims but eliminates detained asylum cases as thoroughly as possible. Approximately 30% of the asylum claims in the database were defensive, and approximately 7% were detained. *See* E-mail from Executive Office of Immigration Review to Andrew Schoenholtz (Jan. 25, 2007) (on file with authors); *infra* Methodological Appendix part 3.

12. We eliminated defensive asylum seekers from this database, thus minimizing the number of detained cases. According to information provided by the Executive Office for Immigration Review, only 996 detained cases remain in the data after elimination of defensive cases. *See* E-mail from Executive Office of Immigration Review to Andrew Schoenholtz (Feb. 6, 2007) (on file with authors); *see also* Methodological Appendix part 3.

13. The regression analyses included several independent variables for which we did not report cross-tabulations. These additional variables are discussed further in part 3 of the Methodological Appendix.

14. As further explained in part 3 of the Methodological Appendix, the "national average" is limited to cases from APCs decided in "high-volume immigration courts," terms defined in the Methodological Appendix. *See infra* Methodological Appendix part 3.

15. The following chart identifies the immigration courts in which high and low grant rates were awarded by country of asylum seeker. We examined only courts that decided one hundred or more cases from the country in question. Only one immigration court (Baltimore) decided one hundred or more cases from Togo, and only one immigration court (Miami) decided one hundred or more cases from Venezuela; as a result, both these countries have only a low grant rate and not a high grant rate in table 3.1

TABLE 3.1
Immigration Courts with High and Low Rates for Each Asylee-Producing Country

Country	High Grant Rate (%)	Low Grant Rate (%)
Albania	New York (65%)	Detroit (17%)
Armenia	San Francisco (54%)	Los Angeles (39%)
Cameroon	Houston (51%)	Baltimore (39%)
China	Orlando (76%)	Atlanta (7%)
Colombia	Orlando (63%)	Atlanta (19%)
Ethiopia	San Francisco (79%)	Arlington (35%)
Guinea	New York (60%)	Baltimore (24%)
Haiti	New York (27%)	Miami (15%)
India	Los Angeles (52%)	Newark (25%)
Liberia	Newark & New York (72%)	Philadelphia (58%)
Mauritania	New York (49%)	Detroit (12%)
Pakistan	Philadelphia (57%)	Houston (28%)
Russia	San Francisco (71%)	Newark (53%)
Togo	N/A	Baltimore (37%)
Venezuela	N/A	Miami (16%)

16. The study by the Government Accountability Office, which looked at twenty rather than fifteen Asylee Producing Countries (but only nineteen immigration courts) and covered a longer period of time (Oct. 1, 1994, through April 30, 2007) than we did (January 2000 through August 2004) reached similar conclusions. It found that

> the likelihood of being granted asylum . . . varied depending on the immigration court in which the case was heard" and that "affirmative applicants in the San Francisco immigration court were 12 times more likely to be granted asylum than affirmative applicants in the Atlanta immigration court, even after we controlled for the statistically significant effects of applicants' nationality, time period of the decision, representation, filing within 1 year of entry, and claiming dependents.

Government Accountability Office (GAO), U.S. Asylum System, Significant Variation Existed in Asylum Outcomes across Immigration Courts and Judges, GAO-08-940 at 4, 7, 23 (2008).
17. The Government Accountability Office similarly noted "large differences" between immigration courts that were physically near each other (Atlanta and Orlando, and New York and Newark). It reported that "12 percent of Chinese affirmative asylum seekers were granted asylum in Atlanta, while 75% were granted asylum in Orlando" and that "the grant rate for affirmative

applicants from Colombia, Indonesia and Peru was more than 2.5 times higher in New York than in nearby Newark." GAO, *supra* n.16 at 24.

18. *See supra* n.8 and accompanying text.

19. The number of cases decided by judges hearing one hundred or more APC cases on each court as well as the number of judges hearing one hundred or more APC cases are indicated in parentheses after the name of the court on each graph in this subpart.

20. It is important at this juncture to clarify that these judges' decisions are not necessarily inaccurate simply because their grant rates are discrepant with the national average or their court's average. It could be, for example, that a judge with an unusually high grant rate is deciding cases as fairly as possible, and that the average grant rate is inaccurate because of a plethora of low-granting judges who are not deciding cases as fairly as the high-granting "outlier" judge. We note only that these discrepant grant rates indicate the need for further investigation to determine whether any inappropriate personal biases are coming into play. To be clear, we are *not* advocating that these judges be disciplined or otherwise sanctioned solely on the basis of discrepant grant rates, but instead that the data may be a jumping-off point for a more thorough examination of performance and professionalism in the courtroom.

21. To determine disparities, we looked only at judges hearing one hundred or more APC cases. The number of APC cases decided by each judge is noted in parentheses along the x-axis of each chart. We looked at all APC cases decided by each court (in other words, we did not limit this calculation to cases decided by judges hearing one hundred or more APC cases) to determine the court APC mean. The number of APC cases decided by all judges on each court is noted in parentheses next to the "Court Mean" label.

22. In the four other courts examined in figure 3.3, the percentages of judges deviating from *their own court's* APC mean by 50% or more were Baltimore: 0% (0 of 4 judges; 41% mean); Chicago: 17% (1 of 6 judges; 38% mean); Newark: 29% (2 of 7 judges; 42% mean); and Orlando: 0% (0 of 4 judges; 49% mean).

23. The numbers of judges per court were current in July 2004. As further explained in part 3 of the Methodological Appendix, the Miami court numbers exclude judges at Krome Detention Center, and the New York court numbers exclude judges at the Varick Street court, as these judges hear predominantly detainee cases.

24. Only three of eighteen, or 17%, of San Francisco judges deviated by more than 50% from that court's mean APC grant rate of 54%.

25. The Government Accountability Office also found that

> even within immigration courts, there were pronounced differences in grant rates across immigration judges. . . . For example, grant rates for affirmative cases ranged between 19 percent and 61 percent in Arlington, Va., 8 percent and 55 percent in Boston, 2 percent and 72 percent in Miami, and 3 percent and 93 percent in New York City. The variation across immigration judges in many of the remaining courts was similarly large.

(GAO, *supra* n.16, at 33)

26. We excluded from depiction in the chart judges who had decided fewer than fifty asylum cases from the country in question as well as immigration judges detailed to the court in question. *See* part 3 of the Methodological Appendix for further explanation of the concept of "detailing" immigration judges. The data by court includes judges who retired or were hired during the January 2000 to August 2004 time frame. We included the following numbers in parentheses: after each judge's number, the number of cases that judge heard from the country in question; and after the word "Mean," the total number of cases from the country in question heard by judges on that court, including judges who heard fewer than fifty asylum cases from that country (but still excluding judges detailed to the court in question). For each court, we have provided a chart showing grant rates for one of the top two nationalities by volume heard in that court. For both Los Angeles and New York, China was the top nationality by volume. To avoid repetition of nationality, we provided grant rates in New York for Albania, which was the second nationality by volume in New York. Moreover, Haiti was the top nationality by volume in Miami; because the grant rate for Haitians in immigration court was substantially lower than that for all other APCs, we provided grant rates for Colombia, which was the second nationality by volume in Miami. India was the top nationality by volume in San Francisco.

27. The study by the Government Accountability Office, using a larger database, reached similar results. It concluded that "the likelihood of being granted asylum differed considerably across immigration judges within the same immigration court even after we statistically controlled simultaneously for the effects of applicants' nationality, [representation, and other variables]." GAO, *supra* n.17, at 33. For example, in the New York immigration court, the likelihood of an affirmative applicant being granted asylum was 420 times greater if the applicant's case were handled by the immigration judge who had the highest likelihood of granting asylum than if the applicant's case were handled by the immigration judge who had the lowest likelihood of granting asylum in that immigration court. Even when the third-highest and third-lowest judges are compared, the likelihood remained thirty-five times higher with one judge than with the other. *Id.* at 34. The GAO found that "in 14 of 19 immigration courts for affirmative cases . . . the likelihood of being granted asylum was at least 4 times as great for applicants whose cases were decided by the immigration judge with the highest versus lowest grant rate in the immigration court." *Id.*

28. We ran cross-tabulation analyses for several other independent variables, which we do not report here. We did include these variables in the regression analyses to increase the accuracy of our models. The cross-tabulation and regression results for these variables can be found at http://www.law.georgetown.edu/humanrightsinstitute/refugeeroulette.htm. First, we did not report here the age of the judge, the size of the judge's caseload, the size of the court's caseload, or the weekly earnings in the state in which the judge's court sits because both the cross-tabulation analysis and the regression analyses found that these variables did not have much impact on grant rates. Second, we did not report years that a judge served on the bench because the cross-tabulation analysis did not reveal a clear pattern relating to grant rates. Third, we did not report the national freedom index of the asylum seeker's country of origin because this variable, as expected, related inversely to grant rate (less freedom, higher grant rate), and was largely included to increase the accuracy of the regression models. Finally, we did not report results for political party of the president whose attorney general appointed the judge because important results were not statistically significant to a 95% probability.

29. The full results of the cross-tabulation analysis as well as the regression analyses confirming these results can be found at http://www.law.georgetown.edu/humanrightsinstitute/refugeeroulette.htm. An explanation of the methods we used can be found in part 3 of the Methodological Appendix.

30. See Donald Kerwin, *Revisiting the Need for Appointed Counsel, in* Insight, at 1 (Migration Policy Inst., No. 4, 2005), *available at* http://www.migrationpolicy.org/insight/ Insight_Kerwin. pdf; Charles H. Kuck, *Legal Assistance for Asylum Seekers in Expedited Removal: A Survey of Alternative Practices, in* II Report on Asylum Seekers in Expedited Removal 232, 239 (2005), *available at* http://www.uscirf.gov/countries/global/asylum_refugees/2005/february/index. html; Schoenholtz & Jacobs, The State of Asylum Representation: Ideas for Change, 16 Geo. Immigr. L.J. 739, 740 (2002).

31. The GAO study, using its different database, reached similar results and concluded that in affirmative cases, the grant rate for unrepresented asylum seekers was 12%, while for represented asylum seekers it was 39%. GAO, *supra* n.16 at 30.

32. The bivariate cross-tabulation analysis does not control for other variables, while the multivariate regression analyses do control for other variables. These analyses exclude all Mexican cases and defensive cases; *see* part 3 of the Methodological Appendix for our method and reasoning.

33. Because two of the authors of the book have selected cases for the Georgetown asylum clinic, they can verify that these cases are not selected solely due to the likelihood of success—that is, the clinic does not select only those cases most likely to win. There is, of course, some selection bias, as the clinic's standard for acceptance of asylum clients is that they present a genuine, nonfrivolous claim, but this is a low bar. Indeed, the clinic often chooses particularly complex and difficult cases so that students will have challenging educational experiences. The main selection principle is that the case has to be one that will have a hearing in April or November, when our students, who arrive in August and January, will be fully trained.

The Georgetown asylum clinic, known as the Center for Applied Legal Studies (CALS), represents refugees seeking political asylum in the United States. Students in CALS assume primary responsibility for the representation of these refugees, working in pairs on at least one major case during the semester. The students interview the client; research the human rights record of the country of origin; develop documentary and testimonial records; locate and prepare witnesses; and represent the client at a hearing before an immigration judge. CALS's professors and fellows help students prepare for their cases through weekly classes, simulation exercises, tutorial meetings, and mock hearings. For more information, *see* http://www.law.georgetown.edu/clinics/cals/.

34. For example, between 2005 and the completion of this chapter in September 2008, the asylum clinic at Hofstra University Law School lost no cases. Interview with Prof. Lauris Wren, Hofstra University Law School, by Philip Schrag, Sept. 24, 2008.

35. Human Rights First (HRF) refers cases to large law firms in New York and Washington, DC. The HRF data refers to cases accepted from January 2000 through December 2004 and adjudicated during that period. The 96% success rate (94% grants of asylum, 2% grants of withholding of removal) refers not only to adjudications in immigration court but also to cases that HRF cooperating lawyers handled in the Asylum Office, the Board of Immigration Appeals, and in federal court, because HRF is unable to separate its final adjudication data by forum. However, only final outcomes are reported, so no case was counted twice. E-mail from Anwen Hughes, Human Rights First, to Philip Schrag (April 27, 2007) (on file with authors).

36. For a detailed example of what students in a law school clinic typically do to corroborate a client's asylum claim, *see* chapters 4 and 5 of David Ngaruri Kenney & Philip G. Schrag, Asylum Denied: A Refugee's Struggle for Safety in America (2008).

37. The GAO study also found a significant relationship here. In its database, the 43% of affirmative applicants who claimed dependents won asylum, compared with 36% of those who did not. GAO, *supra* n.16 at 31. The GAO speculated that perhaps "those who came to their hearings with a spouse or dependent children may have appeared to adjudicators to have more sympathetic cases than applicants who appeared alone," but this explanation assumes that the dependents attended the hearing. Immigration court rules forbid bringing the children into the courtroom unless they are testifying, so while a judge might be aware of their existence, the children would probably not be present at the asylum hearing. Department of Justice, Immigration Court Practice Manual Rule 4.12 (c) (iii) (2008).

38. Our regression analyses confirm that with all other variables held equal, female gender of the judge is correlated with higher grant rates. *See* http://www.law.georgetown.edu/ humanrightsinstitute/refugeeroulette.htm.

39. The study included seventy-eight female judges and 169 male judges. The GAO study also found a marked judge-gender disparity. It concluded that "male immigration judges were [only] about 60% as likely as female immigration judges to grant asylum...." GAO, *supra* n.16 at 36.

40. Most of these studies have found that a gender differential exists, but there has been great variation in findings about the types of cases that are impacted by the gender of the decision maker. *See, e.g.,* David W. Allen & Diane E. Wall, Role Orientations and Women State Supreme Court Justices, 77 Judicature 156, 159, 165 (1993) (finding that twenty-four female state supreme court justices in the 1970s and 1980s voted differently from male justices in cases involving women's issues, but not in those involving criminal rights and economic liberties, with some variation due to political party); Sue Davis, Susan Haire & Donald R. Songer, Voting Behavior and Gender on the U.S. Courts of Appeals, 77 Judicature 129, 131–32 tbls. 2–4 (1993) (finding that female judges on the federal courts of appeals from 1981 to 1990 voted differently from male judges in employment discrimination and search and seizure cases, women being 36.9% more likely to vote in favor of the plaintiff in the former and 62.4% more likely to cast a liberal vote in the latter, but finding no significant gender differential in obscenity cases; examining votes of fifteen female and 237 male judges in search and seizure cases and sixteen female and 188 male judges in discrimination cases); Elaine Martin & Barry Pyle, Gender, Race, and Partisanship on the Michigan Supreme Court, 63 Alb. L. Rev. 1205, 1224–25, 1227 tbl.1 (2000) (finding differences in the voting patterns of twelve male and female justices on the Michigan Supreme Court from 1985 through 1998 in thirty-six divorce cases, in which women were 32.9% more likely to cast a liberal vote, and in forty discrimination cases, in which men were 36.5% more likely to vote liberally, but finding no statistically significant gender disparity in twenty-one feminist-issues cases); Jennifer A. Segal, The Decision Making of Clinton's Nontraditional Judicial Appointees, 80 Judicature 279, 279 (1997) (finding differences in the voting patterns of male and female judges appointed by President Clinton to the federal district courts through July 1996 in sixty-two cases involving race issues decided by twenty judges, in which women were 74.8% more likely to vote in favor of the minority position, but finding no gender disparity in twenty-four cases involving women's issues decided by sixteen judges). *But see* Orley Ashenfelter, Theodore Eisenberg & Stewart J. Schwab, Politics and the Judiciary: The Influences of Judicial Background on Case Outcomes, 24 J. Legal Stud. 257, 265, 275 (1995) (finding that gender and other variables did not affect outcomes in 2,258 federal civil rights and prisoner cases filed in three federal districts and decided by forty-seven district judges in FY 1981; the number of female judges in this study was so small that the authors caution that these results cannot be a basis for inferential statistics beyond the sample); Jon Gottschall, Carter's Judicial Appointments: The Influence of Affirmative Action and Merit Selection on Voting on the U.S. Courts of Appeals, 67 Judicature 165, 167–68, 172 (1984) (finding no statistically significant differences between the 121 female and male judges sitting on four federal courts of appeals from July 1979 to June 1981 in 765 cases involving criminal procedure, race discrimination, and sex discrimination).

41. *See, e.g.,* Martin & Pyle, *supra* n.40, at 1214–20 (discussing three groups of studies of gender differences, namely, tokenist, feminist jurisprudence, and "different voice" judicial studies); Carrie Menkel-Meadow, *Feminization of the Legal Profession: The Comparative Sociology of Women Lawyers,* in Lawyers in Society: An Overview 221, 222 (Richard L. Abel & Philip S. C. Lewis eds., 1995) (arguing that female lawyers will bring a different perspective to the profession); Suzanna Sherry, Civic Virtue and the Feminine Voice in Constitutional Adjudication, 72 Va. L. Rev. 543, 543 (1986) (finding a different, feminine jurisprudence in Justice O'Connor's constitutional opinions); *see also* Judith Resnik, On the Bias: Feminist Reconsiderations of the Aspirations for Our

Judges, 61 S. Cal. L. Rev. 1877, 1906–28 (1988) (discussing implications of feminist theories for the judiciary). These studies all reference Carol Gilligan, In a Different Voice (1982), which, though not a legal study, remains perhaps the most influential book in prompting academics to examine the question whether men and women reason differently.

42. Elaine Martin, Men and Women on the Bench: Vive la Différence?, 73 Judicature 204, 207 (1990).

43. Carrie Menkel-Meadow, The Comparative Sociology of Women Lawyers: The "Feminization" of the Legal Profession, 24 Osgoode Hall L.J. 897, 915 (1986). In chapter 10 of this volume Menkel-Meadow expands on these ideas and others discussed in this section.

44. *See* Physicians for Human Rights, Examining Asylum Seekers: A Health Professional's Guide to Medical and Psychological Evaluations of Torture 23–25 (2001), *available at* http://physiciansforhumanrights.org/ library/documents/reports/ examining-asylum-seekers-a.pdf (describing these results in physical and psychological examinations).

45. Resnik, supra note 41, at 1921, 1927.

46. Of course, the regression analyses demonstrate that gender has a significant impact on grant rate even with work experience held constant. *See* http://www.law.georgetown.edu/ human-rightsinstitute/refugeeroulette.htm.

47. The GAO study of its somewhat different database found that judges with prior government experience granted asylum at a rate of 32%, while those with no prior government experience granted asylum at a rate of 42%. However, when the GAO adjusted this statistic in a multivariate analysis to adjust for other characteristics of the case, such as representation and whether the claimant had dependents, the difference was not regarded as statistically significant. GAO, *supra* n.16, at 120, table 19.

48. Unlike the other figures in this section, this figure demonstrates the relationship between two independent variables (gender and INS/DHS experience) but does not include the effect of either on the dependent variable (grant rate).

49. The GAO found that judges with prior nonprofit experience granted asylum in 53% of their cases, compared with only 33% for judges with no prior nonprofit experience. But as in the case of prior government experience, it concluded that when this statistic was adjusted to take other variables into account, the difference was not statistically significant. GAO, *supra* n.16, at 120, table 19. On the other hand, the GAO did a find statistically significant outcome for a variable for which our cross-tabulation analysis did not reveal a clear pattern relating to grant rates: the length of the judge's service on the bench before rendering the decision in question. The GAO found that those with 3.5 to ten years experience granted asylum at a statistically significantly higher rate than those on the bench for less than 3.5 years.

50. *See infra* figure 3.17 and preceding text.

51. The GAO study, *supra* n.16, did not test for the effects of prior service with INS or DHS.

52. Of course, it was not possible to use regression analyses to confirm the results of these cross-tabulations that combined independent variables.

53. Similarly, when we examine grant rates of judges with INS or DHS experience, female judges grant 46.1% of the asylum cases before them, a rate 31% higher than male judges, who grant only 35.3% of asylum cases they hear. As for judges with government experience, female judges grant at a rate of 49.8%, 47% higher than the male grant rate of 33.9%. And women with NGO experience had a grant rate of 64%, 48% higher than men, who had a grant rate of 43.2%.

54. We did not confirm this relationship in the regression analyses, as we ran INS/DHS experience by number of years of experience, but not broken down by the ranges laid out in this graph. The regression analyses did confirm that years of INS/DHS experience correlated negatively with grant rates.

4 The Board of Immigration Appeals

A. Background

Any party may appeal an adverse immigration court decision to the Board of Immigration Appeals (BIA). As one of us has argued elsewhere, the BIA has been the single most important decision maker in the asylum adjudication system.[1] It reviews cases nationwide and sets precedents that immigration judges and asylum officers must follow. Given that the Supreme Court issues very few asylum law decisions,[2] the BIA essentially interprets immigration law for the country. While a U.S. court of appeals may disagree with a Board interpretation, the BIA must follow that court's jurisprudence only for appeals from immigration courts in the court's own jurisdiction. Moreover, Congress has directed the federal courts to show extreme deference to the BIA.[3]

The attorney general established the BIA by regulation and has the power to overrule its decisions, change its adjudicatory procedures, and appoint and remove Board members who disagree with his or her political ideology.[4] During the 1990s, Attorney General Janet Reno increased the size of the BIA to address a growing caseload. She added members who had served as INS trial attorneys or Office of Immigration Litigation attorneys at the Department of Justice, a senior congressional staffer who had served the Republican chair of the House Immigration Subcommittee, and several lawyers from private practice, advocacy, and academia.[5] The latter appointments balanced somewhat the predominant government experience of existing members and of her appointees who had prior law enforcement experience. The caseload, however, continued to increase, resulting in a large backlog. To address this, the attorney general authorized major changes in the adjudicatory process.

Throughout the first half-century of operations, the Board issued its decisions in two ways. Most decisions consisted of reasoned explanations for affirming or reversing an immigration judge's order, and nearly all of them resulted from three-member reviews of a case. In a limited number of cases, the Board issued en banc decisions (decisions reached by the entire Board). In October 1999, the attorney general authorized a new procedure to enable the Board to address the large backlog of cases. She gave individual BIA members the authority in certain circumstances to issue summary affirmances—decisions without any written analysis.[6] Instead of having all appeals decided by three-member panels or en banc, the BIA began to issue individual-member summary affirmances in certain limited categories of cases where

> the result reached in the decision under review was correct; . . . any errors in the decision under review were harmless or nonmaterial; and . . . (A) the issue on appeal is squarely controlled by existing Board or federal court precedent and does not involve the application of precedent to a novel fact situation; or (B) the factual and legal questions raised on appeal are so insubstantial that three-member review is not warranted.[7]

The Board issued its first summary affirmances in September 2000.[8] The BIA chairman did not authorize affirmances without opinion at that time in any asylum, withholding, or CAT cases.

In December 2001, an independent audit determined that this limited use of the summary affirmance procedure was an unqualified success. First, the Board completed 53% more cases using summary affirmances in a circumscribed manner during its implementation period from September 2000 to August 2001, as compared to the previous twelve-month period. Second, for the first time in a number of years, the Board completed more cases than it received.[9]

Despite this demonstration that a more efficient Board could address its caseload over time, as well as agreement "with the fundamental assessment that the Board's [initial] use of the [summary affirmance] process has been successful,"[10] Attorney General John Ashcroft authorized new policies that he referred to as "streamlining." These new policies fundamentally changed the nature of the BIA's review function. In addition, he radically changed the composition of the Board. Although he cloaked his policy changes in the language of administrative efficiencies that would be required to eliminate a backlog of cases that remained substantial, his alterations limited the BIA's function as a reviewing body and its political orientation, as explained below and in chapter 6.

The February 2002 proposed rule became final in August 2002. It made single-member decision making the "dominant method of adjudication for the large majority of cases" and single-member summary affirmances commonplace.[11] In March 2002, even before the proposed rule became final, Acting Chairman Lori Scialabba authorized the expansion of affirmances without opinion to several new types of cases, including asylum, withholding of deportation, and Convention against Torture claims.[12] The final rule also authorized single members to issue short orders affirming immigration judge decisions or dismissing appeals on procedural grounds.[13] The regulatory language appeared to establish a streamlining hierarchy, stating that, "[i]f the Board member to whom an appeal is assigned determines, upon consideration of the merits, that the decision is not appropriate for affirmance without opinion, the Board member shall issue a brief order affirming, modifying, or remanding the decision under review, unless the Board member designates the case for decision by a three-member panel."[14] As the second major streamlining tool, these single-member short orders are more similar in kind to affirmances without opinion than to the more fully reasoned panel decisions that the Board regularly issued until 2002.[15] As analyzed more fully below, the streamlining swiftly shifted BIA decision making 180 degrees away from the traditional panel opinions, undercutting the important review role that reasoned decisions had provided to the parties, the federal courts above, and the immigration judges below since the Board had first begun its work decades earlier.

The new rule also reduced the membership of the Board from twenty-three to eleven authorized positions. By downsizing, Attorney General Ashcroft removed from the Board five members who had been appointed during the Clinton administration, and a sixth resigned when she saw that she would not be retained. The members he removed were not those with the least seniority. The attorney general observed in the final streamlining rule that "the ability of individuals to reach consensus on legal issues" was a justification for the reduction in size,[16] but those removed from the Board were the members who most disagreed with him ideologically. He did retain some members who had been appointed by his Democratic predecessor, but the members he removed were those who had come from the practice of immigration law, advocacy, and law teaching, while those who were retained had experience primarily in federal government service.[17]

Finally, during the downsizing transition, the attorney general required BIA members to clear their current backlog of fifty-five thousand cases within 180 days.[18] Human Rights First pointed out that to do so, each Board member "would have to decide 32 cases every work day, or one every 15 minutes."[19]

Prof. David Martin, a keen observer of reform as well as a major contributor to the successful INS reforms implemented in 1995,[20] perceptively diagnosed the Ashcroft approach to the backlogs and the constitution of the Board:

> At the time, the BIA had a serious case backlog. . . . But rather than hashing out possible solutions with the board's career attorneys and professionals (who had already made real headway on the backlog with well-designed changes adopted in 1999), Ashcroft assigned the reform job to a small, tight-knit circle in his inner office. And those people rarely consulted with anyone who actually decided immigration cases, [resulting in] reforms of dubious merit. . . . [The downsizing of the Board was a] bizarre directive [that] made sense only if Ashcroft wanted to target certain BIA members for removal. (A reduction in force is a classic tactic to mask such a motive.) . . . All of the [BIA members who resigned under pressure or were transferred] would probably be characterized as liberals. . . . A noticeable shift in the board's orientation was thus achieved under the guise of an efficiency package. And the changes left all EOIR decision makers wondering whether they too might be reassigned if they ruled too often or too visibly for the immigrant alien.[21]

To say the least, the 2002 streamlining changes were controversial. An independent study concluded that the Board's remand rate declined significantly,[22] and the Board's chairman responded that the data on which the study was based were outdated and "unsubstantiated."[23]

Various studies focused as well on the significant, increased caseload at the federal courts of appeals reportedly resulting from the 2002 streamlining changes. The leading scholars of this development, Professor Steven Yale-Loehr, Second Circuit director of legal affairs Elizabeth Cronin, and Second Circuit staff member John Palmer concluded as follows:

> [O]ur data support the hypothesis that [the] appeal rate has increased as a result of a surge in BIA decisions that leave non-detained aliens with final expulsion orders and a fundamental shift in behavior among lawyers and their clients, causing them to focus their litigation in the courts of appeals for the first time. We think this fundamental shift was triggered by the high volume of final expulsion orders that began to be issued starting in March 2002 and a general dissatisfaction with the BIA's review.[24]

B. Data Request and the Limitations of Board Record Keeping

To measure the effects of streamlining on appeals involving asylum, we requested data from the Board regarding asylum determinations for fiscal years 1998–2005. We specifically asked for statistics that would enable us to examine individual member decision making on the merits of asylum claims. We also requested data regarding the mode of decision making (i.e., panel, single-member short opinions, or affirmances without opinion). Finally, we asked for information on the nationality of noncitizens whose cases were appealed and whether they were represented in the appellate process.[25]

The Board provided us with data on nationality and representation, as well as on mode of decision making. Two important problems surfaced with regard to the data that the Board collects and the way it does so. First, the Board knows the period of service of every Board member, and it knows the outcome of each Board decision, but it does not keep statistical records from which it can ascertain which members made or participated in which decisions, or from which it could calculate the rate at which individual members rendered decisions (grants or remands) that benefited asylum applicants. Therefore, we were not able to determine the existence or extent of disparities in the decisions from one member to the next, as we were able to do for asylum officers and immigration judges. Nor could we explore the possible effect of the genders or prior experiences of the adjudicators. Second, for fiscal years 2001 and 2002, the precise period during which the attorney general radically altered its procedures, the Board did not have reliable data on the mode of decision making—whether particular decisions were rendered by a single member or by a three-member panel. The coding of the decision modes changed during that period. Unfortunately, the very helpful EOIR staff currently responsible for statistical reports did not have the information needed to decipher the meaning of the codes used in 2001 and 2002.

Accordingly, the analysis that we present below is limited by these factors. Unlike our analyses of Asylum Office and immigration court decision making, our study of the Board cannot address the degree to which disparities exist among individual decision makers. That in itself is an important finding. In order to ensure consistency in the application of the law and for its own quality-control purposes, the Board should reform its data system so that it can collect and analyze individual member decision making.[26]

C. Findings

In examining the BIA data,[27] we looked to see what we could learn about the impact of the major 2002 streamlining changes ordered by Attorney General Ashcroft. The first impact has been widely reported by the Palmer, Yale-Loehr, and Cronin study described above: significantly increased caseloads at the federal courts of appeals.[28]

In February 2002, the month before Attorney General Ashcroft and Acting Board Chair Scialabba changed the procedures,[29] two hundred cases were appealed to the courts each month. One year later, nine hundred cases a month were appealed, and by April 2004, more than one thousand cases per month were being appealed.[30] This increase is graphically represented in figure 4.1, which also demonstrates that grant and remand rates declined significantly as the number of panel decisions dramatically dropped.

The decline in remand rates of all Board decisions was mirrored in its asylum decisions.[31] To understand the factors that might account for the drop, we examined the different types of Board decisions. We began by looking only at panel decisions (for the six years with reliable data). As figure 4.2 demonstrates, following the 2002 streamlining, these three-member decisions increasingly favored asylum applicants. During fiscal years 1998–2000, that is, when asylum decisions were made only by three-member panels or en banc,[32] panel decisions regarding all applicants from APCs favored the government about two-thirds of the time. During fiscal years 2003–2005, after the implementation of the Ashcroft changes, almost the exact opposite occurred in panel decisions: 64% of the panel adjudications favored asylum applicants.

FIGURE 4.1
All Immigration Cases Appealed from BIA to Courts of Appeals

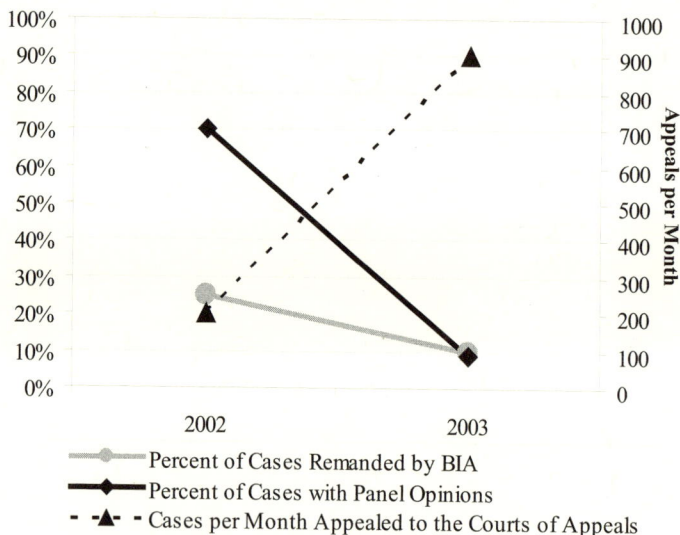

FIGURE 4.1
All Immigration Cases Appealed from BIA to Courts of Appeals

━━━ Percent of Cases Remanded by BIA
━◆━ Percent of Cases with Panel Opinions
━ ▲ ━ Cases per Month Appealed to the Courts of Appeals

FIGURE 4.2
Grant and Remand Rates in Panel Asylum Decisions (FYs 1998–2000, 2003–2005)

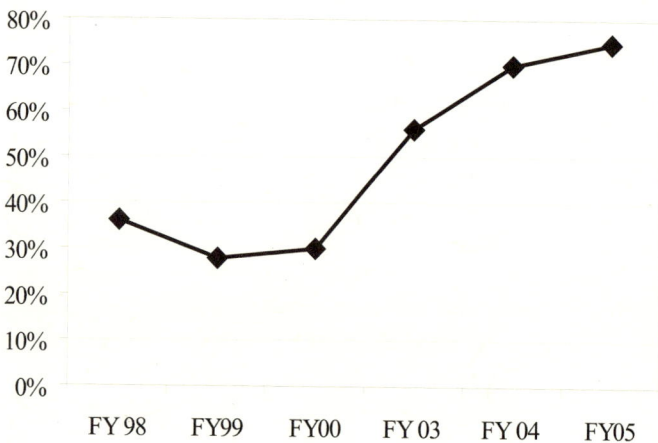

But as figure 4.3 shows, the number of panel decisions decreased significantly, from about nine thousand in FY 1998 to eleven hundred in FY 2005. The number of affirmances without opinions rose to over ten thousand in FY 2003, as did the number of single-member short opinions in FY 2005. Initially following the Ashcroft changes, the affirmances without opinion dominated Board decision

FIGURE 4.3

Number of Decisions by Year and Type (FYs 1998-2000, 2003-2005)

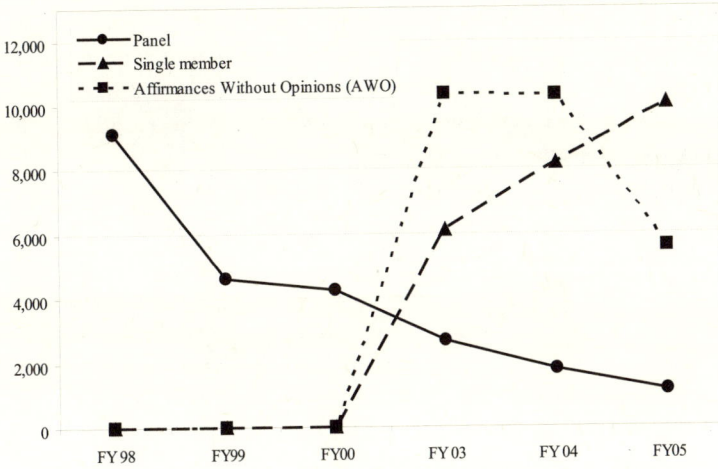

FIGURE 4.4
Number of Decisions Issued by Panels and Single Members

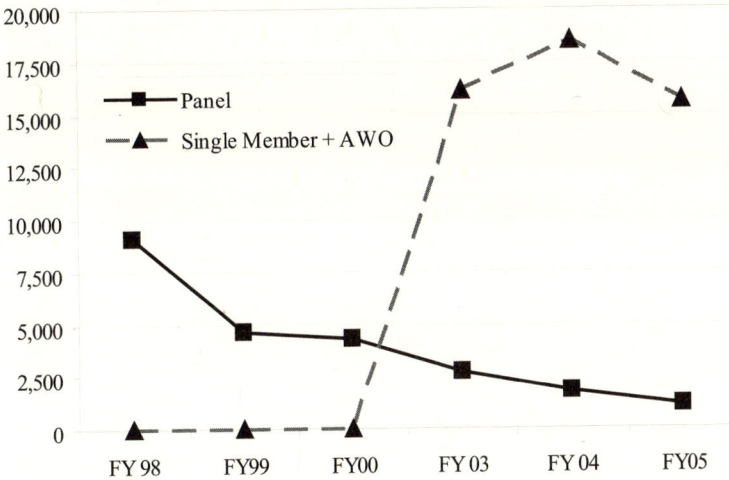

making. That changed in FY 2005, when single-member short opinions began to dominate.

As figure 4.4 illustrates, by FY 2005, single-member decisions (affirmances without opinions and short opinions combined) totaled some sixteen thousand compared to the eleven hundred panel decisions. With this major change in the mode of decision making, what happened to the outcomes in these cases?

Figure 4.5 shows a steep drop in remand rates favorable to asylum applicants. During fiscal years 1998–2000, asylum applicants received favorable decisions in over 30% of the cases. For fiscal years 2003–2005, the rate dropped by more than half. Affirmances without opinion favored asylum applicants in about 3% of cases. The single-member short opinions favored asylum seekers 25% of the time in FY 2003, but as they increased in dominance, asylum applicants found favor through short opinions less than 10% of the time.[33]

When the asylum grant and remand rates are viewed as a simple bar graph, we see in figure 4.6 that the success rate for all asylum applicants fell from 37% in FY 2001 to 11% in FY 2005, a drop of 70%.[34]

We also wanted to understand the degree to which representation affected outcomes as the Board changed its mode of decision making. Figure 4.7 shows that the change in outcomes following the Ashcroft changes—the sudden and lasting decline in the rate of success by asylum applicants—occurred whether or not the applicant was represented by counsel. As figure 4.7 shows, the success rate of represented asylum applicants fell from 43% in FY 2001 to 13% in FY 2005, a decrease of 70%. Unrepresented applicants were hit even harder: during the same time frame, the success rate of unrepresented applicants fell from 26% to 6%, a decrease of 77%.[35]

FIGURE 4.5
Remand Rates in Asylum Cases

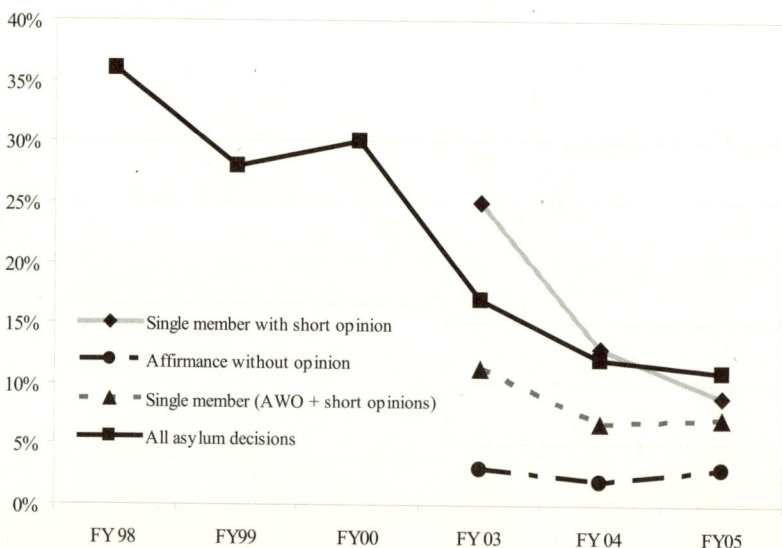

Note: In order to present an understandable graph, we did not include a separate line for panel decisions. Because those decisions are included in the line for "All asylum decisions," the line ends in FY 2005 at a point higher than the end point for the other lines. This reflects the higher grant and remand rate in panel decisions as set forth in Figure 4.2.

FIGURE 4.6
Asylum Grant and Remand Rates

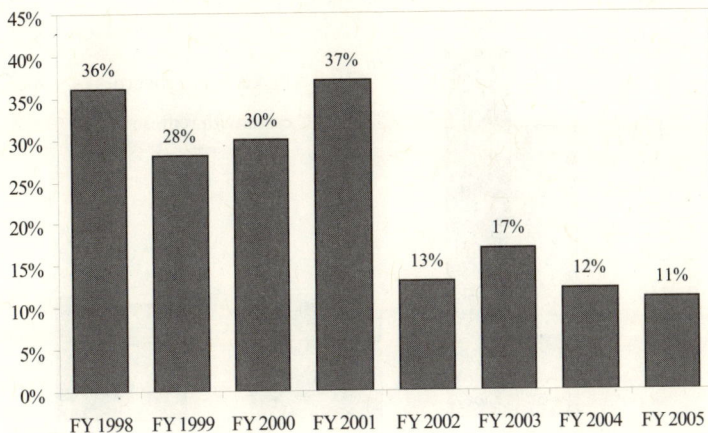

FIGURE 4.7
Asylum Grant and Remand Rates, including Representation

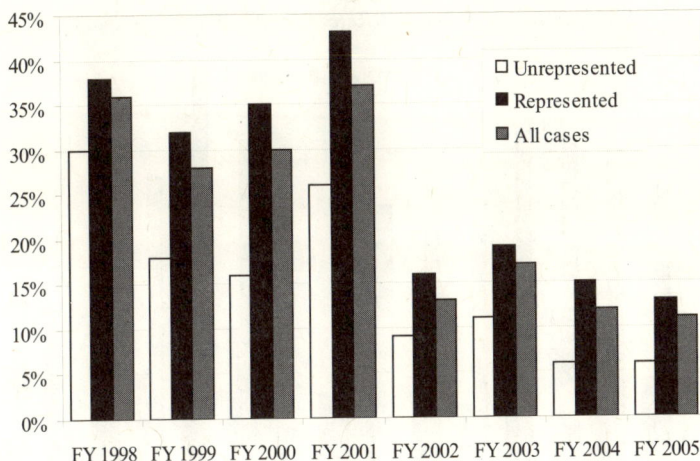

Note: Based on 84,191 appeals.

Even when only cases from APCs are considered, an extraordinary decline occurred.[36] As figure 4.8 demonstrates, the success of all APC asylum applicants declined from 35% in FY 2001 to 14% in FY 2005. The decline for represented APC asylum applicants was even greater: from 44% in FY 2001 to 15% in FY 2005, a 66% drop. The greatest decline occurred with regards to pro se asylum applicants from non-APC countries, from a 31% success rate in FY 2001 to a 5% success rate in FY 2005, or a decline of 84%.

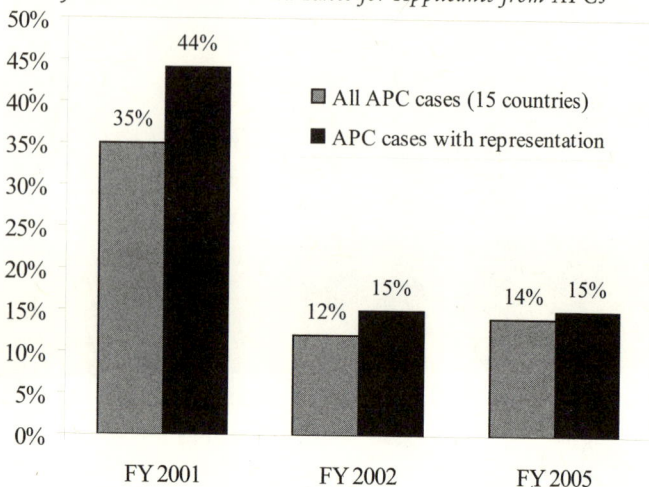

FIGURE 4.8
Asylum Grant and Remand Rates for Applicants from APCs

All APC cases (15 countries)
APC cases with representation

FY 2001: 35%, 44%
FY 2002: 12%, 15%
FY 2005: 14%, 15%

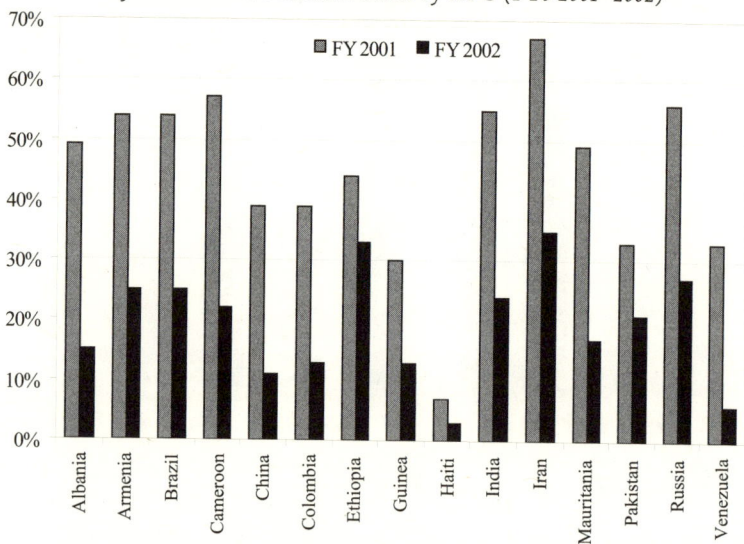

FIGURE 4.9
Asylum Grant and Remand Rates by APC (FYs 2001–2002)

FY 2001   FY 2002

Albania, Armenia, Brazil, Cameroon, China, Colombia, Ethiopia, Guinea, Haiti, India, Iran, Mauritania, Pakistan, Russia, Venezuela

Finally, as figure 4.9 shows, the success rates of asylum seekers from each of the fifteen APC countries declined significantly and immediately once the Ashcroft changes occurred. The drops from FY 2001 to FY 2002 ranged from 25% (Ethiopia) to 82% (Venezuela). Asylum seekers from eleven of the fifteen APC countries faced a decline in grant rates of more than 50%.

The steep decline in remand rates favorable to asylum applicants, then, correlates precisely with the radical streamlining ordered by Attorney General Ashcroft. The combination of affirmances without opinion and the political removal of Board members resulted in a major and disturbing shift in outcomes. In the name of efficiency and "cohesiveness,"[37] the Board simply no longer played its traditional role of carefully reviewing Immigration Court decisions. We do not know whether the dramatic drop in the percentage of decisions favorable to asylum applicants was primarily due to the removal of the Clinton administration's appointees or to the lesser degree of consideration afforded by single members who no longer had to confer with colleagues or address the contentions of the appellants, since both changes occurred simultaneously. Either explanation—political meddling or casual disregard for careful appellate review in life or death cases—is troubling.

Some might argue that the steep and apparently permanent decline in the Board's rate of ruling in favor of asylum applicants was caused neither by the purge of Clinton administration appointees with higher rates of decisions in favor of immigrants nor by the streamlined procedures that the attorney general imposed. This criticism of our conclusions might take two forms. First, skeptics might note that although the steep declines illustrated by figures 4.6, 4.8, and 4.9 occurred between FY 2001 and FY 2002, the member who resigned did so partway through FY 2002, and the five members who were removed by the attorney general did not leave until the end of FY 2002. Therefore, it might be said, the decline should have occurred between FY 2002 and FY 2003. This argument overlooks the fact that the attorney general announced in February, 2002, that he would be removing five members from the Board.[38]

Many or all of the members, perhaps concerned about job security, appear at that point to have reduced the rate at which they ruled in favor of asylum applicants. As Prof. Stephen Legomsky put it, "during that transition period, BIA members were predictably reticent to render decisions in favor of noncitizens and against the government. [Peter] Levinson's empirical data show that, to no one's surprise, several BIA members began to rule in favor of noncitizens much less frequently than those same members had before the original announcement."[39]

The second argument against our conclusion might claim that the rate of grants of asylum by the Board and of remands in favor of asylum applicants was artificially inflated in the period FY 1998–2001 because of certain changes in the substantive law of asylum made by Congress in 1996, 1997, and 1998. In most respects, the 1996 immigration law made asylum more difficult to achieve,[40] but in one respect, eligibility standards were relaxed. Specifically, a person who had been forced to abort a pregnancy or undergo involuntary sterilization was deemed to have been persecuted on account of political opinion.[41] This provision made asylum a possibility for many Chinese applicants. In 1997, Congress provided that a

Soviet-bloc national who had entered the United States before Dec. 31, 1990, and applied for asylum before Dec. 31, 1991, and had not yet received a final decision could apply to become a permanent resident.[42] And in 1998, Congress allowed Haitians who had filed asylum claims before Dec. 31, 1995, to apply for permanent resident status.[43] The asylum remand statistics in figures 4.6 and 4.8 include cases filed by residents of Albania, Armenia, China, Haiti, and Russia. Therefore, if the Board in FY 1998–2001 was so backlogged that it was still remanding, for consideration under the new laws, many cases of Chinese who had applied for asylum before 1996, Soviet-bloc nationals who had applied before 1992, and Haitians who had applied before 1996, *and* if the Board substantially eliminated that backlog of aging asylum cases during those three years, the FY 1998–2001 remand rate might be higher for that reason than the rate in subsequent years.

The Board has not published a breakdown showing the fraction of asylum remands in the period FY 1998–2001 that were decisions remanding cases to immigration judges because of disagreements with those judges on the merits, as opposed to those that were pro forma reversals based on the enactment of these three new laws. Therefore, we have not been able to analyze fully the extent to which the sudden-backlog-reduction theory might account for the drop in the grant rate. However, we have reason to suspect that it does not account significantly for the sudden, permanent decline in the remand rate. First, figure 4.9 shows a sudden drop in the grant rate, from FY 2001 to FY 2002, for each country separately. It shows a sudden, significant decline for the applicants from all fifteen countries, including the ten that were unaffected by the legal changes. Second, we also examined the change in the remand rate, in the years in question, for the aggregate of all APC countries *other than* the five affected by legal changes. This database consisted of 944 cases in FY 2001 and 2,474 cases in FY 2002.[44] In FY 2001, the Board's rate of decisions favorable to those appealing asylum denials from these countries was 48.4%. In FY 2002, it was 19.5%, a decline of nearly 60% from the FY 2001 level that cannot be attributed to changes in the law.

The Board's new streamlining rule and the contemporaneous change in its membership appears to have resulted in a significant reduction in the percentage of its votes in favor of asylum applicants. It had another effect as well. Attorney General Ashcroft required cases assigned to individual Board members to be decided within ninety days.[45] The Board did in fact decide most cases that rapidly. But the combination of rapid adjudication and the distrust of immigrants and their lawyers in the accuracy of the new system resulted in an inundation at the next level up, forcing appellate judges who sit just below the Supreme Court to review many more immigration court oral opinions or summary BIA decisions. Did the federal appellate courts provide any greater degree of consistency than the adjudicators they reviewed?

1. Andrew I. Schoenholtz, Refugee Protection in the United States Post-September 11, 36 Colum. Hum. Rts. L. Rev. 323 (2005), at 352–53.

2. The U.S. Supreme Court largely determines which cases to hear, selects a very small number of cases every year, and has infrequently selected asylum law cases since the 1980 Refugee Act established the modern asylum law regime. A total of eight to ten thousand litigants seek Supreme Court review each year, but "the number of cases taken by the Court has been declining in recent years, from about 150 merits cases per year in the mid-1980s down to about 80 a few years ago and this year's historic low of 68." November 2, 2007, http://www.law.harvard.edu/news/2007/11/02_solicitor.php. For a graph showing the relationship between applications for Supreme Court review and cases accepted, see Laura Castro, Supreme Persuasion, www.utexas.edu/features/2007/supreme/ (visited Sept. 27, 2008) (in 2005, the Supreme Court heard seventy-eight cases from among the 8,517 cases in which review was requested).

3. An unusually extreme degree of deference is required by 8 U.S.C. § 1252(b)(4)(B) (2000), specifying that "the administrative findings of fact [of the BIA or of an immigration judge whose findings are not rejected by the BIA] are conclusive unless any reasonable adjudicator would be compelled to conclude to the contrary."

4. The Board was created by the attorney general in 1940, after a transfer of functions from the Department of Labor. See Reorganization Plan No. V, 3 C.F.R. 1940 Supp. 336 (1941). The Board is not a statutory body; it was created wholly by the attorney general from the transferred functions. Delegation of Powers and Definition of Duties, 5 Fed. Reg. 2454 (July 1, 1940); see In re L——, 1 I & N Dec. 1, 2 n.1 (B.I.A. 1940).

5. See Executive Office for Immigration Review, U.S. Dep't of Justice, Fact Sheet (Dec. 2006), http://www.usdoj.gov/eoir/fs/ biabios.htm (describing the biographical information of Board members Juan P. Osuna, Gerald S. Hurwitz, Patricia A. Cole, Lauri S. Filppu, Edward R. Grant, Frederick D. Hess, David B. Holmes, Neil P. Miller, and Roger Pauley); Executive Office for Immigration Review, U.S. Dep't of Justice, Fact Sheet (June 2005), http://www.usdoj.gov/eoir/fs/ogcbio.htm (describing the biographical information of former Board members Gustavo D. Villageliu and Cecelia M. Espenoza); see also Peter J. Levinson, The Facade of Quasi-Judicial Independence in Immigration Appellate Adjudications, 9 Bender's Immigr. Bull. 1154, 1159 (2004) (describing Paul W. Schmidt, Noel A. Brennan, and John W. Guendelsberger).

6. See Board of Immigration Appeals: Streamlining, 64 Fed. Reg. 56,135, 56,135–42 (Oct. 18, 1999).

7. 8 C.F.R. § 3.1(a)(7)(i)–(ii) (2000). Even this relatively modest regulatory change allowing some cases to be decided without opinions drew criticism from the bar. Most of the twenty-three commenters on the proposed rule objected that allowing a single Board member to decide appeals on the merits "would compromise consistency and thereby devalue the guidance that the Board provides," but the Department of Justice rejected those comments because three-member review "is extremely time and labor intensive and is of significantly less value in routine cases." Board of Immigration Appeals: Streamlining, 64 Fed. Reg. 56,135, 56,139 (Oct. 18, 1999); see also Philip G. Schrag, The Summary Affirmance Proposal of the Board of Immigration Appeals, 12 Geo. Immigr. L.J. 531 (1998).

8. See Memorandum from Paul Schmidt, Chairman, Bd. of Immigration Appeals, to Board Members, Streamlining Implementation—Phase III (Aug. 28, 2000), available at http://www.usdoj.gov/eoir/vll/genifo/streamimplem.pdf.

9. To be precise, the Board completed four thousand more cases than it received. See Arthur Andersen & Co., Board of Immigration Appeals (BIA): Streamlining Pilot Project Assessment

Report 5, 6 (2001), *reprinted in* Dorsey & Whitney LLP, Board of Immigration Appeals: Procedural Reforms to Improve Case Management 19–25 (2003), *available at* http://www.dorsey.com/files/upload/ DorseyStudyABA_8mgPDF.pdf app. 21; Executive Office for Immigration Review, U.S Dep't of Justice, Statistical YearBook: 2002, at S2 (2003), *available at* http://www.usdoj.gov/eoir/statspub/fy02syb.pdf.

10. Board of Immigration Appeals: Procedural Reforms to Improve Case Management, 67 Fed. Reg. 54,878, 54,879 (Aug. 26, 2002).

11. *Id.* Under the new regulation, all cases are adjudicated by a single Board member unless they fall into one of six specified categories, which are handled by a panel of three Board members. Those six categories are where there is a need to (1) settle inconsistencies between the rulings of different immigration judges; (2) establish precedent construing the meaning of ambiguous laws, regulations, and procedures; (3) review a decision by an immigration judge or DHS that is not in conformity with the law or applicable precedents; (4) resolve a case or controversy of major national import; (5) review a clearly erroneous factual determination by an immigration judge; or (6) reverse the decision of an immigration judge or DHS, other than reversal under 8 C.F.R. § 1003.1(e)(5). 8 C.F.R. § 1003.1(e)(6) (2007). The new rule also largely stripped the Board of its de novo review authority. *See* Board of Immigration Appeals: Procedural Reforms to Improve Case Management, 67 Fed. Reg. 54,878, 54,888–91 (Aug. 26, 2002).

12. Memorandum from Lori Scialabba, Acting Chairman, Bd. of Immigration Appeals, to Board Members, Use of Summary Affirmance Orders in Asylum and Cancellation Cases (Mar. 15, 2002), *available at* http://www.usdoj.gov/eoir/vll/genifo/slo31502.pdf. In May, Scialabba authorized summary affirmances in all cases. Memorandum from Lori Scialabba, Acting Chairman, Bd. of Immigration Appeals, to Board Members, Expanded Use of Summary Affirmance for Immigration Judge and Immigration and Naturalization Service Decisions (May 3, 2002), *available at* http://www.usdoj.gov/eoir/vll/genifo/sto50302.pdf.

13. Board of Immigration Appeals: Procedural Reforms to Improve Case Management, 67 Fed. Reg. 54,878, 54,880 (Aug. 26, 2002).

14. 8 C.F.R. § 1003.1(e)(5) (2007).

15. For examples of more fully reasoned panel decisions, *see* Deborah E. Anker, The Law of Asylum in the United States: A Guide to Administrative Practice and Case Law app. VI (2d ed. 1991).

16. Board of Immigration Appeals: Procedural Reforms to Improve Case Management, 67 Fed. Reg. 54,878, 54,893 (Aug. 26, 2002). The attorney general observed in full:

> The Department has determined that 11 Board members is the appropriate size for the Board based on judgments made about the historic capacity of appellate courts and administrative appellate bodies to adjudicate the law in a cohesive manner, the ability of individuals to reach consensus on legal issues, and the requirements of the existing and projected caseload. The Board is expected to function with two three-member panels and five Board members acting individually in deciding cases. The Department believes that this is a realistic evaluation of the resource needs, capacities and resources of the Board in adjudicating immigration issues. The Attorney General may reevaluate the staffing requirements of the Board in light of changing caseloads and legal requirements following implementation of the final rule. (*Id.*)

17. *See* Peter J. Levinson, The Facade of Quasi-Judicial Independence in Immigration Appellate Adjudications, 9 Bender's Immigr. Bull. 1154, 1159 (2004), at 1155–56.

18. Board of Immigration Appeals: Procedural Reforms to Improve Case Management, 67 Fed. Reg. 54,878, 54,903 (Aug. 26, 2002).

19. Press Release, Human Rights First, New Regulations Threaten to Turn Board of Immigration Appeals into Rubber Stamp: Justice Department Rules Place Speed above Justice for Refugees Seeking Asylum in the United States (Aug. 28, 2002), *available at* http://www.humanrightsfirst.org/media/2002_alerts/0828.htm.

20. INS Commissioner Doris Meissner engaged Prof. Martin as a consultant to help develop reforms to address the backlog of over 425,000 asylum cases. For a detailed treatment of the history and the reform regulations, *see* David A. Martin, Making Asylum Policy: The 1994 Reforms, 70 Wash. L. Rev. 725 (1995).

21. David A. Martin, *Another Second-Class Citizen: How the Justice Department Has Been Debasing Immigration Courts for Years*, Legal Times, August 11, 2008, p. 2.

22. Dorsey & Whitney, *supra* n.9, at 39–40.

23. Letter from Lori Scialabba, Chairman, Bd. of Immigration Appeals, to the Comm'n on Immigration Policy, Practice, and Pro Bono, Am. Bar Ass'n (Dec. 22, 2003), *available at* http://www.usdoj.gov/eoir/press/03/ABA.pdf.

24. John R. B. Palmer, Stephen W. Yale-Loehr & Elizabeth Cronin, Why Are So Many People Challenging Board of Immigration Appeals Decisions in Federal Court? An Empirical Analysis of the Recent Surge in Petitions for Review, 20 Geo. Immigr. L.J. 1 (2005), at 94.

25. *See* Letter from Andrew Schoenholtz to Lori Scialabba, Chairman, Bd. of Immigration Appeals (Jan. 30, 2006) (on file with authors).

26. With appropriate resources, EOIR has proven that it is capable of improving its data systems with regards to the immigration court. Improved reporting based on these data systems, such as EOIR's Statistical Year Books, has made it possible for government and independent researchers to examine trends and help policymakers understand just how well, for example, the immigration courts are working. EOIR should do the same for the BIA.

27. Part 4 of the Methodological Appendix, *infra*, more fully describes the data set and the decisions on the merits at the Board.

28. Palmer et al., *supra* n.24, at 3.

29. The pertinent procedures were actually changed several months before the regulation requiring those changes became effective in August 2002. *See* sources cited *supra* n.12.

30. Palmer et al., *supra* n.24, at 3; Dorsey & Whitney, *supra* n.9, at 40. These monthly caseload numbers include both asylum and other immigration law appeals.

31. *See infra* figure 4.5.

32. Affirmances without opinion were first issued in September 2000, right at the end of the fiscal year, but none was issued in asylum cases until the Ashcroft changes were implemented.

33. Using somewhat different counting techniques and including FY 2006 statistics, the Government Accountability Office reached the same conclusion: in 2004–2006, decisions by single BIA members were favorable to asylum applicants only 7% of the time. Government Accountability Office, U.S. Asylum System, Significant Variation Existed in Asylum Outcomes across Immigration Courts and Judges, GAO-08-940 at 56 (2008).

34. The Government Accountability Office's study produced somewhat different percentages of decisions favorable to applicants in both the pre-streamlining (21%) and post-streamlining (10%) periods. GAO, *supra* n.33 at 52. Both methods of computation show a sudden, dramatic drop in the percentage of decisions favorable to asylum applicants.

35. The study by the Government Accountability Office found that success rates of represented applicants at the BIA declined, as a result of streamlining, from 23% to 13% in affirmative cases and from 26% to 9% in defensive cases. GAO, *supra* n.33, at 55.

36. Chapter 2 includes an explanation and list of the Asylee Producing Countries and the criteria by which we selected them. See also Methodological Appendix at p. 310.

37. Board of Immigration Appeals: Procedural Reforms to Improve Case Management, 67 Fed. Reg. 54,878, 54,894 (Aug. 26, 2002).

38. Board of Immigration Appeals: Procedural Reforms to Improve Case Management, 67 Fed. Reg. 7309, 7310 (proposed Feb. 19, 2002).

39. Stephen H. Legomsky, "Deportation and the War on Independence," 91 Cornell L. Rev. 369, 376 (2006).

40. Philip G. Schrag, A Well-founded Fear: The Congressional Battle to Save Political Asylum in America (New York: Routledge, 2000).

41. Illegal Immigration Reform and Immigrant Responsibility Act, P.L. 104–208, Sec. 601 (1996), codified at 8 U.S.C. Sec. 1101(a)(42).

42. Nicaraguan Adjustment and Central American Relief Act (NACARA), P.L. 105–100 (1997). This law also provided similar rights to Nicaraguan, Guatemalan, and Salvadoran asylum applicants, who were in fact, by volume, its principal beneficiaries. But Nicaragua, Guatemala, and El Salvador are not APC countries, so decisions in most NACARA cases did not enter the statistical data sets reported in figures 4.8 or 4.9.

43. FY 1999 Omnibus Consolidated and Emergency Supplemental Appropriations Act, P.L. 105–277 (1998).

44. As in our other studies of Board decisions, the database excluded decisions coded by the Board as those in which it was impossible to determine which party was favored.

45. Id. at 54,903.

5 The United States Courts of Appeals

AS A PRACTICAL matter, the last chance for an unsuccessful asylum applicant is to appeal an adverse Board decision to a U.S. court of appeals.[1] Appeals can be taken only to the circuit in which the immigration judge decided the underlying asylum case.[2] Since the location of the immigration court that decides a case is determined by the state of residence of the foreign national when removal proceedings are initiated a year or two before the appeal, the venue for the appeal depends on where the asylum applicant lived at that time. It is therefore not possible for an applicant who has been ordered deported to "shop" for a particularly sympathetic circuit.

A court of appeals may sustain a Board decision, or it may remand the case for further consideration by the Board.[3] We do not think that the likelihood of success (that is, of obtaining a remand) should depend on the state in which the applicant happened to have settled, and one might think that federal courts would be sensitive to any significant disparity in remand rates from one circuit to another. We therefore investigated whether any such disparity existed.[4] Table 5.1 and figure 5.1 show the results of our data compilation. They demonstrate a surprising degree of variation among circuits.

The table and graph show that an asylum applicant who lives in the Fourth Circuit, known generally among lawyers as the most conservative circuit,[5] has only a 1.9% chance of winning a remand, whereas in the Seventh Circuit, about 36.1% of asylum cases are remanded to the Board. We know of no rational reason why a person living in Illinois, Indiana, or Wisconsin should have a 1,800% greater chance of winning her asylum appeal than a person living in Virginia, Maryland, West Virginia, and the Carolinas. We hypothesized that the federal judges' remand rate might be much higher in the Seventh Circuit than in the Fourth Circuit if the *immigration judges* in the Seventh Circuit had been inappropriately reluctant to grant asylum, compared to the immigration judges in the Fourth Circuit. However, the only immigration court in the Seventh Circuit (Chicago) does not seem to be less inclined to grant asylum than its counterparts in the Fourth Circuit. It grants asylum to applicants from all countries at a rate of 34% and to applicants from APCs at a rate of 38%. This is about the same rate as the two immigration courts in the Fourth Circuit (Arlington, where the corresponding rates are 31% and 37%, and Baltimore, where the rates are 38% and 41%). We believe that to a large extent, the statistics shown in the

TABLE 5.1
Asylum and Related Appellate Decisions by Circuit (Calendar Years 2004 and 2005)

Circuit	2004			2005			2004–2005		
	Number of merits decisions	Number of cases remanded	Percentage of cases remanded	Number of merits decisions	Number of cases remanded	Percentage of cases remanded	Number of merits decisions	Number of cases remanded	Percentage of cases remanded
1st	39	4	10.3%	55	8	14.5%	94	12	12.8%
2d	30	3	10.0%	421	74	17.6%	451	77	17.1%
3d	156	12	7.7%	174	27	15.5%	330	39	11.8%
4th	143	2	1.4%	126	3	2.4%	269	5	1.9%
5th	94	4	4.3%	78	3	3.8%	172	7	4.1%
6th	104	9	8.7%	109	18	16.5%	213	27	12.7%
7th	56	19	33.9%	77	29	37.7%	133	48	36.1%
8th	85	12	14.1%	57	4	7.0%	142	16	11.3%
9th	1220	225	18.3%	877	183	20.9%	2097	408	19.5%
10th	34	3	8.8%	32	3	9.4%	66	6	9.1%
11th	91	4	4.4%	156	4	2.6%	247	8	3.2%
ALL	2052	296	14.4%	2163	354	16.4%	4215	650	15.4%

Notes: There are no immigration courts in the District of Columbia, and therefore the D.C. Circuit hears no appeals from denials of relief from removal. "Related" decisions are those involving withholding of removal and Convention against Torture protection.

FIGURE 5.1
Remand Rates in Asylum and Related Cases, 2004–2005, by Circuit

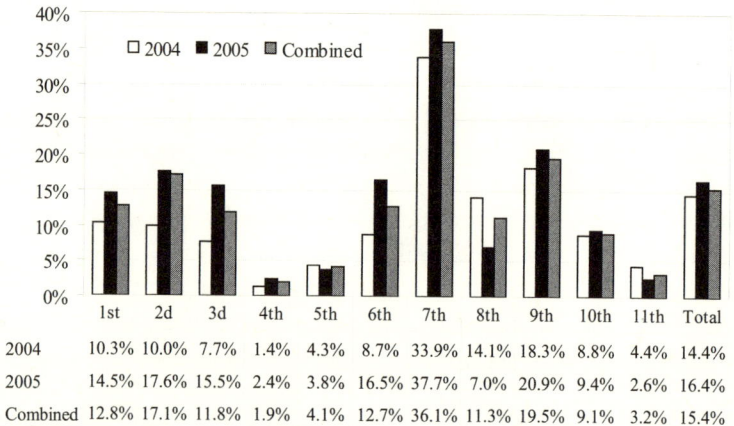

	1st	2d	3d	4th	5th	6th	7th	8th	9th	10th	11th	Total
2004	10.3%	10.0%	7.7%	1.4%	4.3%	8.7%	33.9%	14.1%	18.3%	8.8%	4.4%	14.4%
2005	14.5%	17.6%	15.5%	2.4%	3.8%	16.5%	37.7%	7.0%	20.9%	9.4%	2.6%	16.4%
Combined	12.8%	17.1%	11.8%	1.9%	4.1%	12.7%	36.1%	11.3%	19.5%	9.1%	3.2%	15.4%

table reflect not the relative merits of the cases or the differential grant rates of the immigration judges, but rather the differing attitudes that the judges in these circuits have, in the aggregate, with respect to asylum seekers' claims, or at least the differing degrees of their skepticism about the adequacy of Board and immigration judge decision making.[6] The fact that the three circuits with the lowest grant rates are the three southern circuits reinforces our surmise that the variation is somehow linked to regional culture, which apparently affects federal appellate judges as well as other citizens, rather than differing characteristics of these asylum cases.

Commenting on an earlier draft of this book, Judge Richard Posner of the Seventh Circuit Court of Appeals termed the differences between the remand rates from one circuit to another "extraordinary." He added that

> the inference one draws from that is that given the uncertainties in the law, the difficulties in the facts, [and] the seemingly arbitrary variance among the immigration judges, the court of appeals judges are also going to be falling back on kind of personal reactions, intuitions, values and so on. That's pretty unsatisfactory. This is supposed to be a uniform body of federal law, not something turning on the luck of who you draw for an immigration judge or what circuit you happen to be in for the appeal. So this is a system of adjudication that is clearly very unsatisfactory. This is a pathological picture that I am painting.[7]

We note, incidentally, that variations among circuits in their remand rates in asylum cases are much greater than variations in their rates of remanding or reversing civil cases. Figure 5.2, making this comparison, shows that in FY 2005, ten of the eleven circuits in our study had a rate of overturning district courts in civil cases that was between 10% and 20%. In asylum cases the spread from circuit to circuit was much greater.[8]

It may be objected that the comparison across circuits shown in figure 5.2 is not very meaningful because the Fourth, Fifth, and Eleventh Circuits, which have the lowest remand rates, may receive many more appeals from Mexicans or Central Americans with relatively weak asylum claims, whereas the Seventh Circuit may receive most of its appeals from asylum seekers from countries such as Cameroon that have had worse human rights records in recent years. To control the sample to the extent possible, we also calculated the remand rate for decisions rendered during calendar years 2004 and 2005 in appeals from the Board by nationals of the fifteen nations that we denominated as APCs. Neither Mexico nor any Central American countries are among the fifteen APC countries.

Figure 5.3 shows the remand rates for asylum, withholding, and Convention against Torture cases filed by APC nationals and decided during calendar years 2004 and 2005:

FIGURE 5.2
Asylum Remand Rates (Calendar 2005)
and Civil Reversal Rates (FY 2005) Compared

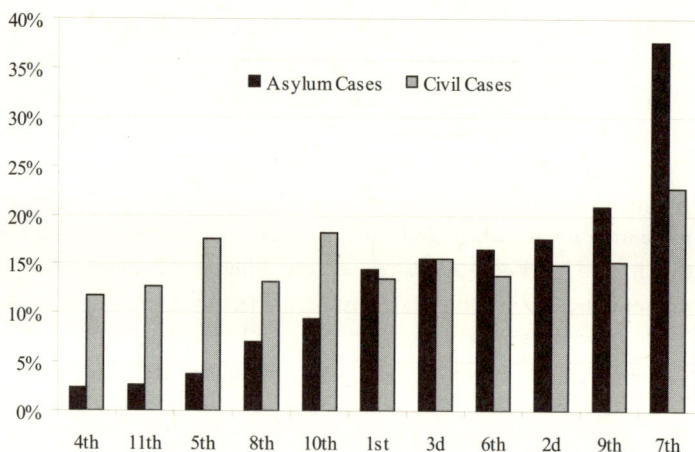

Note: The data are displayed in order of increasing grant rate in asylum cases. Civil cases exclude prisoner cases; reversals and remands are both counted as reversals, because both are decisions favorable to the appellant.

FIGURE 5.3
Percentage of APC Cases Remanded, 2004–2005, by Circuit

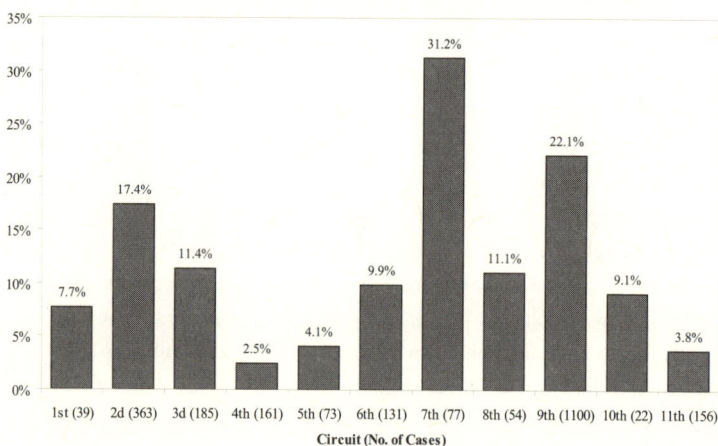

Nationals of the fifteen APC countries account for almost half of all asylum appeals to the U.S. courts of appeals. We expected that because all of these cases come from countries with poor human rights records (as measured by a high grant rate at lower levels of the system), we would find a significantly lower level of disparity among circuits than that revealed by table 5.1. However, the level of disparity in remand rate from one circuit to another is reduced only very slightly. There are still significant differences among circuits, with the three southern circuits granting remands in a negligible fraction of cases, five circuits (the First, Third, Sixth, Eighth, and Tenth) granting remands in a range between about 8% and about 12% of their cases, and another three circuits (the Second, Seventh, and Ninth) remanding in a range between 17% and 31% of their cases. The Seventh Circuit continues to top the list, so that an asylum applicant from an APC who appeals to that circuit has a 721% greater chance of obtaining a remand than one who must appeal from the removal order of an immigration judge in Miami to the Eleventh Circuit, and a 1,148% greater chance than one whose order of deportation was rendered by an immigration judge in Arlington or Baltimore in the Fourth Circuit.

Although the number of cases is much smaller, we can also compare the results obtained by applicants from China, the single APC with the largest number of asylum cases. In order to increase the number of cases considered, we have included in table 5.2 all asylum cases decided in three years (2003, 2004, and 2005), rather than only two years, as in the previous analysis.[9]

This table suggests that even for a set of cases that are likely to be the most similar, because they all involve claims of persecution by the same country, there is wide variation in the remand rate from circuit to circuit.[10] In three circuits, the remand rate was in single digits or lower (the Fourth Circuit remanded none of its twenty-eight Chinese cases), while in six circuits, the remand rate was 20% or more.

TABLE 5.2

Remand Rates for Asylum and Related Cases by Nationals of China (2003–2005)

Circuit	Number of Merits decisions	Number of cases remanded	Percentage of cases remanded
1	13	1	7.7%
2	307	47	15.3%
3	114	16	14.0%
4	28	0	0%
5	22	5	22.7%
6	10	2	20%
7	27	8	29.6%
8	9	2	22.2%
9	211	78	37.0%
10	4	1	25.0%
11	26	1	3.8%
Total	771	161	20.9%

We could not compare the individual rates of votes to remand in some circuits (such as the Fourth, Fifth, and Eleventh Circuits) because there were not
enough votes to remand to make such a study statistically meaningful; few of
these judges cast any votes to remand. At the other extreme, the Ninth Circuit
decided so many cases that we lacked the resources to count individual judges'
votes.[11] However, we did examine the individual votes to remand in two circuits, in each of which the judges collectively cast more than six hundred votes
on asylum cases during 2004 and 2005.[12] In the Third Circuit, sixteen judges
voted in twenty-five or more asylum cases. Figures 5.4 and 5.5 show their grant
rates and their rates of deviation from the 12.1% circuit mean.[13] These figures
show considerable consistency. Only one judge deviated from the circuit mean
by more than 50%.

We also investigated whether there was any relationship between the voting
pattern of the Third Circuit judges and the political parties of the presidents who
appointed them. We found no relationship: as a group, appointees of presidents
of each party voted to remand at the same 12% rate. In figure 5.6, each bar represents the vote-to-remand rate of a judge who voted on at least twenty-five asylum or asylum-related cases in 2004 and 2005. Black lines represent Republican
appointees and gray lines represent Democratic appointees.[14]

The remand rate in the Sixth Circuit was nearly identical to that of the Third
Circuit (12.7% vs. 11.8%),[15] but a close investigation of voting shows a much more
scattered pattern. Figure 5.7 and figure 5.8 show the grant rates, and the rates of
deviation from the circuit mean, respectively, of the thirteen judges who voted in
twenty-three or more asylum and asylum-related cases.[16]

FIGURE 5.4
Remand Rates of Third Circuit Judges, 2004–2005

Note: Includes judges with at least 25 cases; judges' names are omitted.

FIGURE 5.5
Third Circuit Judges' Deviation from Circuit Mean

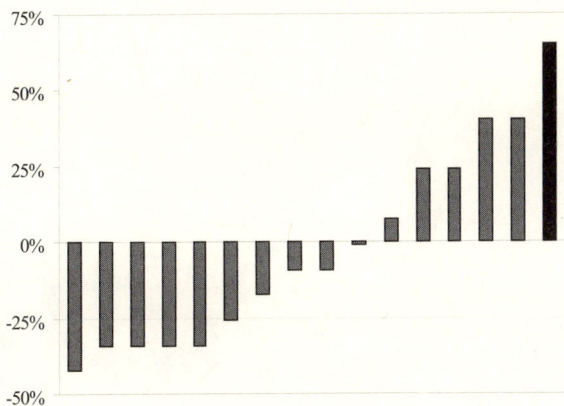

FIGURE 5.5
Third Circuit Judges' Deviation from Circuit Mean

Note: Only one judge (shaded black) deviated more than 50% from the mean.

FIGURE 5.6
Third Circuit Remand Vote Rates by Party of Appointing President

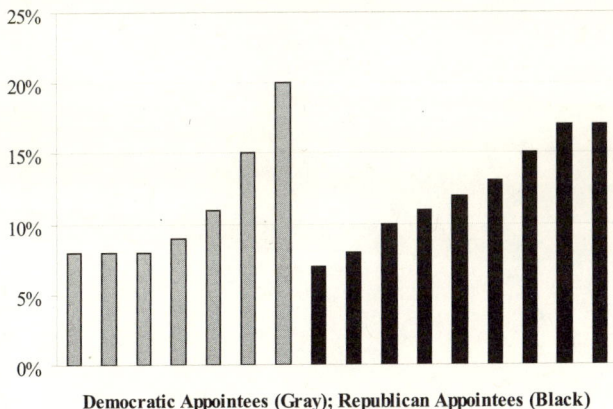

Democratic Appointees (Gray); Republican Appointees (Black)

Votes on the Sixth Circuit showed much greater disparity than in the Third Circuit. Seven of the thirteen judges who voted in at least twenty-three cases deviated from the circuit mean by more than 50%.

Furthermore, in the Sixth Circuit, unlike the Third Circuit, there appears to be a significant difference in the voting patterns of judges appointed by presidents of different parties. The judges appointed by Republican presidents had a weighted mean grant rate of 9.3%, while those appointed by Democratic presidents had a weighted mean rate of 14.6%. In other words, the Democratic presidents' appointees voted to remand at a rate 57% higher than that of the appoin-

FIGURE 5.7

Remand Rates of Sixth Circuit Judges, 2004–2005

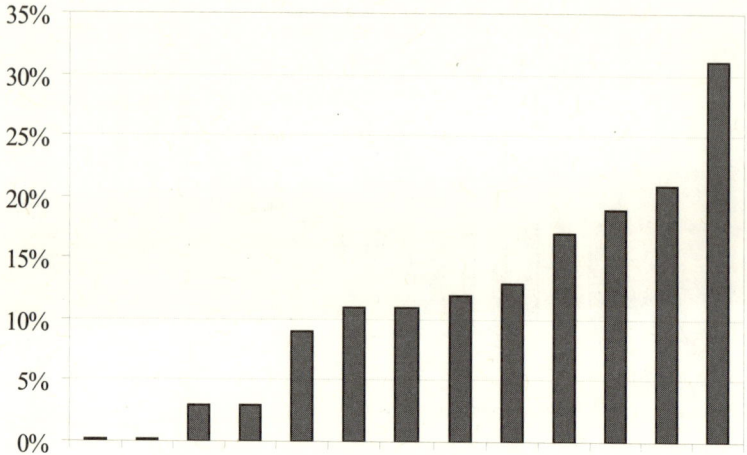

Note: Two judges, whose bars are jittered so as to be visible in the graph, voted to remand in 0% of their cases.

FIGURE 5.8

Sixth Circuit Judges' Deviation from Circuit Mean

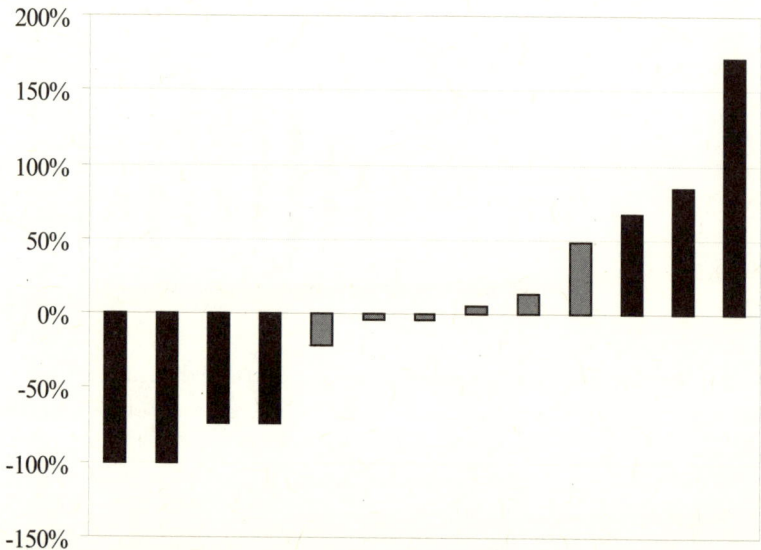

Note: Seven of thirteen judges, shaded in black, deviated by more than 50% from the mean.

FIGURE 5.9
Sixth Circuit Remand Vote Rates by Party of Appointing President

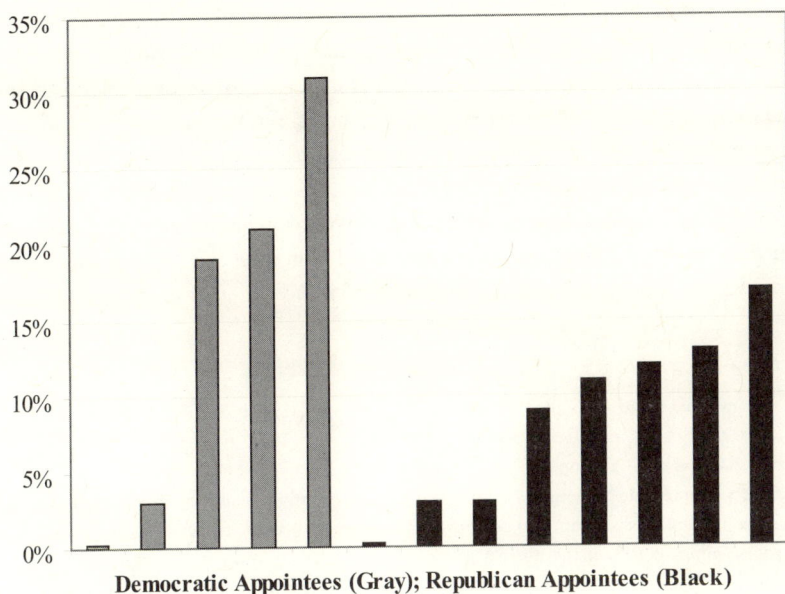

Democratic Appointees (Gray); Republican Appointees (Black)

Note: Two judges, whose bars are jittered so as to be visible in the graph, voted to remand in 0% of their cases.

tees of Republican presidents. Figure 5.9 compares individual vote-to-remand rates on the Sixth Circuit.

The samples are smaller than those in most of our other investigations, but the results suggest that at least in some courts, political ideology may play a role in decision making in these asylum cases. We hope that in the future we or others will be able to conduct a more exhaustive study, with a larger database, of the influence of political party affiliation on the appellate courts' adjudication of asylum cases.[17] Asylum decisions are a particularly good database for studies of judicial decision making because a very large volume of decisions is available for study and the cases are sufficiently similar so that one could reasonably expect that individual variations from case to case will wash out if one examines large numbers of decisions by trial or appellate judges to whom cases are randomly assigned.

This chapter completes our report on the data that we collected and analyzed. These data suggest that to a significant degree, the outcome of asylum cases is determined by the identities, characteristics, and backgrounds of the decision makers, and they also confirm earlier studies showing a huge difference in outcome depending on whether or not an asylum applicant can find and afford competent representation. Outcomes will be affected by the identities of the adjudicators and advocates in any system in which there is more than one decision maker, and in which lawyers are not provided for indigents, so some degree of disparity is inevitable. But the magnitude of the disparities in the asylum system are troublingly large. In addition, the consequences of these disparities can mean that an unsuccessful applicant for asylum is deported to her death while in the adjacent courtroom, another applicant with an essentially similar case is put on a path that will lead in a few years to American citizenship. As a result, the disparities that we have documented should be of great concern to policymakers and to people concerned with human rights. Accordingly, in the next chapter we summarize our findings and then recommend structural and policy changes that could reduce the degree of randomness in the adjudication of asylum cases.

NOTES

1. As explained in chapter 1, the government does not appeal decisions rendered by the Board, because the Board speaks for the attorney general.

2. 8 U.S.C. § 1252(b)(2) (2000).

3. The Supreme Court has instructed courts of appeals that they should ordinarily remand an erroneous Board decision and not grant asylum themselves, because even if an individual is legally eligible for asylum, the attorney general has discretionary authority to grant or refuse to grant asylum. *INS v. Ventura*, 537 U.S. 12, 16 (2002). Since withholding of removal is not a discretionary form of relief, courts of appeals may in principle grant that form of relief. But since the standard of proof for obtaining withholding of removal is much higher than the standard of proof for asylum, the courts almost always either sustain the board or remand the case.

4. *See* the Methodological Appendix for our case identification criteria and search methods.

5. The Fourth Circuit often writes opinions that "lead the way [to the right], issuing groundbreaking rulings in the hope that the Supreme Court will ratify them as the law of the land." Brooke A. Masters, *4th Circuit Pushing to Right: Federal Court Tests Supreme Intentions*, Wash. Post, Dec. 19, 1999, at C1; *see also* Tony Mauro, *4th Circuit Seen to Be the "Right" Place, as a Rule*, USA Today, Mar. 9, 1999, at 11A; Laura Sullivan, *4th Circuit's Reputation Is Polite, Conservative: Bush Administration Steers Sensitive Cases to Friendly Panel of Judges*, Balt. Sun, Nov. 18, 2003, at 1A.

6. The Seventh Circuit's skepticism is plain from the first paragraph of Benslimane v. Gonzales, 430 F.3d 828 (7th Cir. 2005). Judge Posner wrote,

> Our criticisms of the Board and of the immigration judges have frequently been severe. E.g., *Dawoud v. Gonzales*, 424 F.3d 608, 610 (7th Cir. 2005) ("the [immigration judge's] opinion is riddled with inappropriate and extraneous comments"); *Ssali v. Gonzales*, 424 F.3d 556, 563 (7th Cir. 2005) ("this very significant mistake suggests that the Board was not aware of the most basic facts of [the petitioner's] case"); *Sosnovskaia v. Gonzales*, 421 F.3d 589, 594 (7th Cir. 2005) ("the procedure that the [immigration judge] employed in this case is an affront to [petitioner's] right to be heard"); *Soumahoro v. Gonzales*, 415 F.3d 732, 738 (7th Cir. 2005) (per curiam) (the immigration judge's factual conclusion is "totally unsupported by the record"); *Grupee v. Gonzales*, 400 F.3d 1026, 1028 (7th Cir. 2005) (the immigration judge's unexplained conclusion is "hard to take seriously"); *Kourski v. Ashcroft*, 355 F.3d 1038, 1039 (7th Cir. 2004) ("there is a gaping hole in the reasoning of the

board and the immigration judge"); *Niam v. Ashcroft*, 354 F.3d 652, 654 (7th Cir. 2003) ("the elementary principles of administrative law, the rules of logic, and common sense seem to have eluded the Board in this as in other cases"). Other circuits have been as critical. See *Wang v. Attorney General*, 423 F.3d 260, 269 (3d Cir. 2005) ("the tone, the tenor, the disparagement, and the sarcasm of the [immigration judge] seem more appropriate to a court television show than a federal court proceeding"); *Chen v. U.S. Dep't of Justice*, 426 F.3d 104, 115 (2d Cir. 2005) (the immigration judge's finding is "grounded solely on speculation and conjecture"); *Fiadjoe v. Attorney General*, 411 F.3d 135, 154–55 (3d Cir. 2005) (the immigration judge's "hostile" and "extraordinarily abusive" conduct toward petitioner "by itself would require a rejection of his credibility finding"); *Lopez-Umanzor v. Gonzales*, 405 F.3d 1049, 1054 (9th Cir. 2005) ("the [immigration judge's] assessment of Petitioner's credibility was skewed by prejudgment, personal speculation, bias, and conjecture"); *Korytnyuk v. Ashcroft*, 396 F.3d 272, 292 (3d Cir. 2005) ("it is the [immigration judge's] conclusion, not [the petitioner's] testimony, that 'strains credulity'"). (*Id.* at 829)

7. Judge Richard Posner, Speech before the Chicago Bar Association, at 5 (Apr. 21, 2008), *available at* http://38.105.88.161/search/basic.asp?ResultStart=1&ResultCount=10&BasicQueryText=Posner.

8. The civil case rate was determined by dividing the number of remands and reversals in all nonprisoner civil cases (those civil cases that included the United States as a party and those that were entirely private cases) by the number of all such cases terminated on the merits. *See* Admin. Office of the U.S. Courts, 2005 Ann. Rep. Dir. app. tbl. B-5, *available at* http://www.uscourts.gov/judbus2005/appendices/b5.pdf. Although the spreads are very different, the means for the two sets of rates were comparable: 16.4% for asylum cases and 15.2% for civil cases.

9. We did not have the resources to conduct this type of examination for cases from all countries for a three-year period. *See* part 5 of the Methodological Appendix for further discussion of our search method. Although the number of cases in the table is relatively small, we did not need to compute whether sampling error might account for the disparities between circuits, because we did not sample; we looked at every case from China for the three-year period reported by the table.

10. The difference between the 0% rate in the Fourth Circuit and the 30% rate in the Seventh Circuit cannot be explained by the possibility that *immigration judges* in the Fourth Circuit were overly generous to Chinese applicants, compared to their counterparts in the Seventh Circuit. The grant rates in Chinese cases in the Fourth Circuit's immigration courts (Arlington and Baltimore) from 2000 through August 2004 were 30% and 38%, respectively, while the grant rate for such cases in Chicago was 31%.

11. Although we were unable to study the more than six thousand asylum votes cast by Ninth Circuit judges during the period 2004–2005, a period after Attorney General Ashcroft's changes in BIA procedure sharply escalated appeals to that circuit, a study by Prof. David Law did code, by judge, the nearly six thousand Ninth Circuit asylum votes that were cast between 1992 and 2001. We apply our methodology to his data in the Ninth Circuit Appendix.

12. *See infra* Methodological Appendix part 5 (explaining further our methodology in choosing to examine the Third and Sixth Circuits).

13. There is usually a small difference between the mean rate at which a court, through its panels, votes to remand, and the mean rate at which individual judges vote to remand. Figures 5.4 and 5.7 show deviations from the mean in vote-to-remand rate of judges who have heard at least twenty-five cases (Third Circuit) or twenty-three cases (Sixth Circuit). In the Third Circuit, this

rate was 12.1%, and in the Sixth Circuit it was 11.4%. The mean vote-to-remand rate was computed by dividing the total number of votes in favor of remanding asylum cases that were cast by the judges who voted at least twenty-five or twenty-three times by the total number of votes in such cases cast by these judges.

14. The 12% vote-to-remand rate for each party's appointees is the mean rate for all twenty-two judges of the party in question, not only the sixteen judges who met the threshold number of votes for display in the diagram.

15. The political composition of the circuits was also similar during the time period of this study. The Third Circuit had nine Republican and seven Democratic appointees who voted in at least twenty-three asylum and asylum-related cases (in fact, the minimum number of votes cast by any of these sixteen judges was twenty-eight), while the Sixth Circuit had eight Republican and five Democratic appointees who cast at least twenty-three votes.

16. We lowered our usual minimum threshold slightly to capture more data. Eleven of these thirteen judges voted in at least twenty-five asylum cases. The two others voted in twenty-three and twenty-four cases, respectively.

17. In the Ninth Circuit, there appears to be a strong relationship between the rate at which a judge votes in favor of asylum applicants and the political party of the appointing president. *See infra* Ninth Circuit Appendix (describing an empirical study by Professor Law).

6   Conclusions and Policy Recommendations

A. Conclusions

In 1940, Attorney General Robert H. Jackson wrote to Congress that "[i]t is obviously repugnant to one's sense of justice that the judgment meted out . . . should depend in large part on a purely fortuitous circumstance; namely the personality of the particular judge before whom the case happens to come for disposition."[1] We assume that Attorney General Jackson recognized that the personal histories and personalities of judges would inevitably have *some* effect on their judgments in cases and that what he meant was that the effect of these individual characteristics should not be very large. With that understanding, we agree with his view. We are therefore quite troubled by the large degree to which the grant rates of asylum adjudicators in certain regional asylum offices, large immigration courts, and courts of appeals diverge from those of other adjudicators in the same offices and from courts deciding cases from nationals of the same country or group of countries in the same time frame.[2]

1. Disparities within Particular Asylum Offices, Immigration Courts, and Federal Appeals Courts

We adopted what we considered a very forgiving standard for assessing the degree to which adjudicators vary from the norm. We accepted the possibility that even within the subset of refugees who come from the small group of APCs that produce the highest rates of successful asylum seekers, variations in the refugee populations who migrate to particular regions might justifiably account for at least some region-to-region variation. Therefore, except in a few instances in which we explicitly compared one region with another, we measured adjudicators' deviations from the mean by comparing individual grant or remand rates not with national norms but with the norms for those adjudicators' own local offices. We also decided, for purposes of this book, to count an adjudicator as an "outlier" from the norm only if the adjudicator's grant or remand rate was more than 50% higher or lower than the local mean.

Even by this standard, officers who adjudicate asylum applications in some of the eight regional offices of the Department of Homeland Security's Asylum Office appear to have grant rates that reflect personal outlooks rather than an office consensus. Over the course of a seven-year period, more than 20% of the asylum officers in three of these regional offices had grant rates for applicants from APCs that deviated from the regional norm by more than 50%. In all but three offices, at least 10% of the asylum officers had grant rates that deviated from the regional norm by more than 50%. In one office, there was so little consensus that most of the officers deviated from the office norm by more than 50%.

Even when our analysis is confined to applications by nationals of a single country, asylum officers in some regions appear to issue grants at very different rates from each other. Six of the eight regional asylum offices adjudicate large numbers of applications from China. One of those offices (Region C) shows great consistency among officers in their rates of granting asylum to these applicants. In that region, only 7% of the officers deviate from the regional office's mean grant rate for Chinese cases by more than 50%. In four other regions, the percentage of officers who deviate by more than 50% ranges between 25% and 35%. And in one office, thirty-one of the fifty-two officers deviated by more than 50% from the mean. In that office, two officers did not grant asylum to any Chinese applicants (one of those officers turned down 273 applications), while two other officers granted asylum in 68% of their cases (one of them had 150 such cases).[3] Some individual officers deviated by much more than 50%. For example, in Region F, in which the mean grant rate for Chinese applicants is 57%, four of the officers granted asylum in fewer than 5% of their 364 Chinese cases, while twelve other officers granted asylum in more than 90% of their 1,145 Chinese cases.

Judges of the immigration courts with large numbers of cases also appear to adjudicate asylum cases inconsistently. In the three largest immigration courts, more than 25% of the judges have asylum grant rates in cases from APCs that deviate from their own court's mean rate for such cases by more than 50%. The degree of deviation is dramatic even when the analysis is confined to nationals of one country. For example, half the judges (eleven of twenty-two) in the Miami Immigration Court who adjudicated at least fifty cases over a period of nearly five years have grant rates for Colombian asylum seekers that deviate from that court's Colombian mean grant rate by more than 50%. A Colombian asylum seeker might be assigned to a judge who granted asylum in 5% of his 426 cases during the period of our study or to another who granted asylum in 88% of the judge's 334 cases.[4]

We would have liked to have been able to analyze the internal consistency of decision making within the Board of Immigration Appeals, and we were very surprised to learn that although the Board keeps voluminous statistics on its work, it does not keep statistical records from which it could discern the pattern of individual members' votes. This gap in the statistical record is especially troubling in view of the decisions of Attorney General Ashcroft and Board Chair

Lori Scialabba to direct individual members of the Board, rather than panels, to make most of the Board's decisions in asylum cases. A single individual now makes the life-altering decision to affirm, remand, or grant asylum in these cases, but the Board keeps no statistical records of what the members are doing in these cases, making its own quality control very challenging and rendering public accountability virtually impossible. One member could be remanding only 1% of appellate cases to correct immigration judges' errors, while a member in the next office is remanding 10% of similar cases. Yet the Board would never know that the assignment of a case to a particular member had such a great impact on the applicant's odds of obtaining a remand or an eventual grant of asylum.

We also analyzed asylum decisions of the U.S. courts of appeals, though our investigation of asylum cases in the federal courts is necessarily incomplete. Because the court system does not keep separate statistics on its asylum cases, we had to examine individually thousands of unpublished decisions to determine which ones were in fact appeals from the BIA of denials of asylum, withholding of removal, or protection under the Convention against Torture. In the period we examined, calendar years 2004 and 2005, most circuits had too few cases to enable us to compare the rates at which individual judges voted to remand cases. (The Ninth Circuit, by contrast, had too many cases for us to undertake this analysis, although Professor David Law's collection of Ninth Circuit decisions from the 1990s, reported in the Ninth Circuit Appendix, suggests a large degree of disparity in that court.) We did analyze the decisions of the Third and Sixth Circuits, however, and we found that the results were quite different in those two circuits. The Third Circuit showed a remarkable degree of consistency from judge to judge, while in the Sixth Circuit, seven of the thirteen judges who cast twenty-three or more votes in asylum cases deviated from the circuit's mean rate of votes to remand by more than 50%. In addition, we could find no significant pattern in the Third Circuit relating remand votes to the political party of the president who appointed the judge, while in the Sixth Circuit, judges appointed by Democratic presidents voted to remand cases at about twice the rate of judges appointed by Republican presidents.

2. Disparities from Region to Region

Although we focused principally on deviations within local adjudicative bodies (asylum offices, regions, cities, or circuits), our data also showed some dramatic differences across geographic territory. Among regional asylum offices, overall grant rates for applications from nationals of eleven APCs varied between 26% in one region to 62% in another region.[5] This disparity could be simply the result of differences in nationalities (and therefore appreciable differences in degrees of threatened persecution) in the mix of cases in the different regional offices. We have reason to be skeptical of this explanation, however. First, there is a very large disparity in grant rates among regional offices even when we examine decisions involving a single small country, such as Armenia.[6] The officers in one regional Asylum Office (Region C) granted asylum to Armenian applicants at a rate 148% higher than those in another office (Region G).[7] Also, even if the Asylum Office with the lowest rate had a caseload entirely composed of cases from the APC country with the lowest grant rate and the Asylum Office with the highest rate had a caseload composed entirely of cases from the country with the highest grant rate, the difference between the offices would be only 84%, not the observed 138%.[8]

Among immigration courts, there is some consistency from city to city. In cases from the APCs, nearly all of the immigration courts grant asylum at a rate of between 37% and 54%. No courts granted asylum in these cases at a rate higher than 54% during the time period studied. However, four immigration courts— in Atlanta, Miami, Detroit, and San Diego—grant asylum at rates significantly lower than 37%.

We also compared the remand rates of the circuits in cases involving nationals of fifteen APCs (once again excluding all countries whose nationals are not in large measure successful at the lower levels of the asylum process). Five of the eleven circuits that hear asylum appeals have remand rates of between 8% and 11%, and two other circuits had remand rates between 12% and 22%. But the Seventh Circuit's remand rate was significantly higher (31%), and the Fourth, Fifth, and Eleventh Circuits all had remand rates under 5%. It may not be surprising that all three of those circuits are in the American South, which is often considered more conservative than other parts of the country. Nevertheless, all of these circuits are applying the same national asylum law,[9] and it seems odd to us that the rights of refugees seeking asylum in the United States should turn significantly on the region of the United States in which they happen to file their applications.

3. Possible Causes of Disparities among Immigration Judges

Thanks to sophisticated statistical software and to the fact that the Executive Office for Immigration Review publishes biographical information on immigration judges, we were able to present a descriptive analysis correlating judges' grant rates with personal and biographical information, as well as with certain other information about the immigration court cases. We confirmed the findings of prior studies showing that represented clients win their cases at a rate that is about three times higher than the rate for unrepresented clients. This difference could reflect the reluctance of lawyers to accept weak cases, but to a significant extent it probably also reflects the difficulty of winning an asylum case without the assistance of a professional advocate. Such advocates are able to collect affidavits from lay and expert witnesses and other corroborating documents; are familiar with the Immigration and Nationality Act, the voluminous regulations promulgated under that law, and the volumes of case law interpreting it; understand the court's exacting standards for the corroboration of testimony and authentication of documents; know the court's timetables and formal requirements for filing papers; are aware of the procedures for pleading and motions; and know how to conduct direct and cross-examination of witnesses and make closing statements that tie together the facts and law.

Our other discoveries resulting from our study of immigration court decisions were more surprising. We found that applicants had a significantly greater chance of winning if their applications included a request for protection of a spouse or minor child in the United States. Perhaps family applications are more persuasive, because judges don't believe that married applicants would flee from danger and leave a spouse or child behind, or because the judges feel additional sympathy for spouses and children, or because they suspect that unmarried applicants are more likely to commit fraud or be terrorists. The reasons for the increased odds of prevailing if one has dependents in the United States merit further study.

Perhaps the most interesting result of our study is that the chance of winning an asylum case varies significantly according to the gender of the immigration judge. Female judges grant asylum at a rate that is 44% higher than that of their male colleagues. The work experience of the judge before joining the bench also matters: the grant rate of judges who once worked for the Department of Homeland Security (or its predecessor, the Immigration and Naturalization Service) drops largely in proportion to the length of such prior service. By contrast, an asylum applicant is considerably advantaged, on a statistical basis, if her judge once practiced immigration law in a private firm, served on the staff of a nonprofit organization, or had experience as a full-time law teacher.

4. The Erosion of Appellate Review by the Board of Immigration Appeals

If adjudication by the Asylum Office and the immigration courts has become something of a random process, one might expect reform to have been initiated by appellate review. Unfortunately, in recent years the Board focused primarily on reducing its own backlog (which it accomplished by rapidly affirming the vast majority of removal orders) rather than providing effective appellate oversight.

Even though we were unable to evaluate the consistency of decision making from one Board member to another, the statistical information that the Board provided enabled us to confirm and expand upon a previously reported change in the Board's work over time. As the law firm of Dorsey & Whitney discovered in 2003, the "reforms" mandated by Attorney General Ashcroft—firing five Clinton appointees and encouraging others to leave, requiring most decisions to be decided by summary affirmances or very short opinions, and replacing three-member panel decision making with single-member affirmances for most asylum cases—were accompanied by a sudden and drastic reduction in the rate at which the Board rendered decisions favorable to asylum applicants.[10] The statistical information available to Dorsey & Whitney included all Board cases, not just asylum cases, but our study shows that its conclusions are equally valid when the cases under study are limited to those involving asylum. Although the BIA was rendering decisions favorable to asylum applicants in 37% of asylum appeals in FY 2001, before the attorney general announced his intention to fire several appointees and before most asylum cases were assigned to a single judge who could affirm summarily, that rate dropped precipitously to 13% the following year, and by FY 2005 it was only 11%. Some might argue that from FY 1998 through FY 2001, the Board was being too generous to asylum applicants and that a rate such as 11% is more appropriate, or that fewer meritorious appeals came to the Board for decision after FY 2001. We have no way of knowing which rate is a more accurate reflection of justice. But we are troubled by the facts that the rate drop was sudden and persistent, that it was associated temporally with a purge of certain members appointed by a prior administration and with increased fear of foreign nationals after the 9/11 attacks, and that it also coincided with the institution of new procedures that provided less scrutiny of immigration judges' decisions. These factors cause us to suspect that in many asylum cases, the BIA has ceased to function as an effective appellate body.

B. Policy Recommendations

We think that the degree of disparity we have observed in certain asylum offices and in all large immigration courts reflects a fundamental lack of due process that must be addressed. Whether an asylum applicant is able to live safely in the United States or is deported to a country in which she claims to fear persecution is at present very seriously influenced by a spin of the wheel of chance—that is, by a clerk's random assignment of an applicant's case to one asylum officer rather than another, or one immigration judge rather than another. We think that an adjudicator's deviation by more than 50% from the mean rate for similar cases in that adjudicator's own office raises serious questions about whether the adjudicator is imposing his or her own philosophical attitude (or personal level of skepticism about applicants' testimony) to the cases under consideration. The outcome of a life-or-death case should not depend to such a great extent on the identity of an adjudicator to whom a case is assigned by chance.

Similarly, at the appellate levels, we are troubled by the fact that factors unrelated to the merits of cases so significantly affect an appellant's chance of obtaining a remand. These extraneous factors include, at the Board of Immigration Appeals, a Republican attorney general's 2002 decision to purge the Board of many members selected by his Democratic predecessor, and to require cursory opinions, at best, rather than careful analyses of appellants' contentions.[11] At the U.S. court of appeals level, the most obvious extraneous factor affecting the outcomes of cases is the region of the country in which the asylum applicant happened to settle before filing her application.[12]

But before we offer policy prescriptions to remedy this problem, we pause to note three possible arguments against any effort to reform the system, and in particular to revise the decision-making process in the immigration courts.

1. Arguments against Reform

First, some may suggest that immigration judges should have absolute independence. On this view, independence is so central to impartiality that it trumps all controls, and we should be willing to tolerate very wide disparities in outcome rather than try to achieve greater consistency through hiring, training, appellate review, or structural reforms. Advocates of this strong pro-independence stance may analogize immigration judges to federal judges, particularly Supreme Court justices, who have total independence and make little apparent effort to harmonize their philosophies.

We reject this analogy. The federal courts are much more professionalized and transparent than the immigration courts. The federal courts of appeals sit in panels of three (or occasionally in still larger groupings), and the Supreme Court decides cases as a body of nine; the immigration judges, by contrast, hear and decide cases individually, without having to try to justify their decisions to colleagues. And they do so in secret; unlike federal court decisions, asylum decisions are generally oral decisions delivered at the end of a merits hearing and are never published, so only the parties and their representatives know the result or the judge's reasoning. Because the immigration courts lack the professionalization of the federal courts, independence by itself does not lead to the same impartiality that we see on the federal bench.

Second, some may argue that it is simply impossible to design an asylum adjudication system in which there is much more consistency. Professor Legomsky comes close to this claim when he says,

> In asylum cases, the unavoidable abstractness, complexity and dynamism of the relevant legal language make it inevitable that the human adjudicators will bring their diverse emotions and personal values to bear on their decisions. Under these

circumstances, we should not expect anything but the sorts of disparate outcomes that [this book] has documented.[13]

The experience of at least some regional asylum offices suggests that a good deal of consistency is in fact possible. In half of the eight regions, fewer than 12% of the asylum officers deviated from their regional grant rate by more than 50%. In Region A, thirty-one officers each adjudicated at least fifty APC cases during the period we studied. In total, these officers adjudicated 4211 such cases. Yet only two of the thirty-one officers deviated from the Region A grant rate by more than 50%. In Region D, sixty-four officers made decisions in at least fifty APC cases, adjudicating 11,547 cases during the period under consideration. Only one officer of the sixty-four deviated from the grant rate for the office as a whole by more than 50%.

We also doubt that Prof. Legomsky really accepts the status quo as much as the passage that we have quoted would suggest. He goes on to say that "there are ways to reduce the inconsistencies at the margins"[14] and to offer prescriptions similar to those in this chapter. His reduction of inconsistency at "the margins" may mean, in the end, significantly reducing the percentage of adjudicators whose grant rates are more than 50% out of line with the average, a step that we also would applaud. While we agree that some disparity is an acceptable, and indeed inevitable, result of our adjudication process, the extreme differences in grant rate that we found in our study reflect a failing system, rather than harmless human variation in decision making.

Finally, we have spoken with some refugee advocates who would support greater consistency as a desirable goal but believe that no attempt to reduce disparities should be made because politicians who oppose more immigration and those who agree with them within the federal executive branch would be likely to convert a project seeking more consistency into one that imposes uniformly lower grant rates on the adjudicators. We acknowledge that anti-immigrant feeling in some quarters runs high, and that it is often impossible to predict the outcome of legislative or other political processes. We are very troubled, however, by the central finding of our study, and we think that the potential gains of reform outweigh the risk that efforts to make the asylum system more fair will in fact lead to a system that is less just.

2. Three Wrong Approaches to Reform

A. QUOTAS

The most obvious way to end disparities among adjudicators is simply to order consistency. For example, the Department of Homeland Security could require each asylum officer to approve no less than 35% and no more than 40% of all asylum applications, and the attorney general could order each immigration judge to grant asylum to between 40% and 50% of applicants.

Despite our misgivings about the random factors affecting the current system, we think that the cure of a quota system would be worse than the disease of random adjudication. First, there is no way to know what the right percentage would be for any quota. The mean rate for a particular nationality in a particular adjudicating office could be too low or too high. The fact that it is the mean does not make it self-evidently the correct rate. Second, nothing in our study dictates what the correct range or tolerance should be for a quota system. We selected a 50% test as our measure of deviation, but this range actually seems to us extremely tolerant of variation by individual adjudicators. On the other hand, a range of plus-or-minus 10% or even 20% from the mean seems to us to allow too little tolerance for individual variation based on the normal scatter of valid or doubtful asylum cases. Third, we fear that any quota system imposed by political authorities would become ossified, reflecting historical national or regional grant rates but not changing quickly enough to reflect alterations in human rights conditions that may occur within persecuting countries. Also, while approximately fifteen countries produce enough cases to generate reliable mean grant rates, most countries—even many with bad human rights records—have fewer nationals who flee to the United States, so the statistical record of grant rates from those countries would not be a good basis for a quota system, even within a limited time frame. Finally, the imposition of quotas would permit even greater and more overt political influence on asylum adjudication than the present system tolerates. In periods when public anti-immigrant sentiment was on the rise, candidates might even campaign on pledges to reduce the quotas, with little regard for the rights of (nonvoting) asylum applicants under domestic or international law.

B. MORE "SUPERVISION" OF IMMIGRATION JUDGES

In 2008, the Government Accountability Office advised the Executive Office of Immigration Review (EOIR), the Justice Department agency that houses the immigration courts and the Board of Immigration Appeals, to address the problem of outlier immigration judges by "redeploying some ACIJs (Assistant Chief Immigration Judges) from headquarters to local immigration courts" so that they could more "effectively supervise" immigration judges.[15] At the time that the GAO made this recommendation, "supervision" was undefined, either by the EOIR or by the GAO. EOIR already used ten of its eleven ACIJs as supervisors of immigration judges, but EOIR had "not provided them with guidance on how to carry out their supervisory roles."[16]

If supervision means that judges will be counseled on how to perform their adjudication functions more professionally, we can hardly quarrel with the idea, but we think that it will fail; for the most part, the immigration judges already try to do the best they can with the resources they have, but we think that the problems run much deeper than a lack of supervision. As we indicate below, they are rooted in flawed hiring processes, a lack of resources (including a sufficient number of judges), insufficient ongoing training, and the ever-present threat of political oversight by Justice Department officials who disagree with decisions of the immigration judges or of the Board of Immigration Appeals. Furthermore, we fear that undefined or badly defined "supervision" could usher in a quota system through the back door, with supervisors subtly directing outlying immigration judges to grant or deny more asylum cases simply to make the disparity statistics less of an embarrassment to EOIR, rather than providing the resources necessary so that judges can take the time they need to make thoughtful, professional judgments in each case.

C. CODIFICATION

We also do not recommend a more detailed codification of the substantive rules governing asylum. Some of the legal rules governing eligibility for asylum are expressed in broad terms that are not elaborated in the Code of Federal Regulations or in precedent cases. For example, there has never been a succinct, definitive definition of "persecution," because the nature of persecution and our understanding of it keep changing. But while a more detailed codification could theoretically reduce disparity in decision making, we know of no study suggesting that this factor accounts significantly for the disparities that we have documented.

In addition, our experience practicing asylum law, as well as discussions with adjudicators over many years, suggests that disagreements among adjudicators about the meaning of the law accounts for little of the difference in grant rates among adjudicators. A few asylum cases do turn on the interpretation of legal terms; for example, for nearly a decade there has been disagreement about the conditions under which victims of domestic violence may be characterized as a "social group" entitled to protection.[17] But only a small number of decisions by the BIA and the courts of appeals interpret the legal standards. Moreover, such an analysis cannot possibly account for the extraordinary degree of inconsistency with respect to decisions even within particular immigration courts or asylum offices regarding, for example, Chinese asylum seekers who assert claims based on coercive population control. In these cases, Congress has already determined statutorily that such claims are on account of political opinion. Accordingly, we believe that two other factors account for the differences among adjudicators to a much larger extent than disagreement about the law.

First, asylum officers and judges must often engage in the process of applying clearly understood legal standards to the facts before them. The most challenging of these applications of law to fact involve the question of causation: is the persecution with which the applicant is threatened "on account of" one of the five grounds recognized by U.S. law and the Refugee Convention?[18] Some of the difficulties result from the adjudicators having to guess at the motives of a persecuting government or group. Some arise when persecutors have mixed motives for persecuting their victims (such as the desire both to punish them for their beliefs and to seize their property for personal enrichment). Many others emerge because cases do not fit neatly into the statutory pigeonholes. For example, if government security forces had beaten and threatened to kill an applicant to frighten him out of testifying to a political murder that he had seen one of the members of the force commit, is that a threat on account of the applicant's political opinion, or for the purposes of protecting the murderer? Particular asylum officers or immigration judges faced repeatedly with borderline cases such as these may tend to tilt, consistently, either in favor of applicants or against them, and this could account for some of the disparities that we have noted.

We suspect, however, that most of the disparities are related to the second factor: judgments about the credibility of the applicant.[19] In every asylum case, however straightforward as a legal matter, the asylum officer or immigration judge must ascertain whether the applicant is telling the truth, and unfortunately, some people do commit fraud to try to gain asylum. Some applicants may invent threatened persecution; others may borrow and memorize the stories of friends or relatives who have won asylum. Because even bona fide asylum applicants are often unable to obtain corroborating documentation from their home countries without jeopardizing the safety of associates or family members who remain abroad (and sometimes because no records of threats or of past persecution exist), adjudicators cannot expect the kind of corroboration that often exists in civil or criminal cases. They must judge credibility, as best they can, on the consistency and level of detail provided by applicants from one retelling to the next,[20] and in direct and cross-examination during court proceedings.[21] In many cases, perhaps a majority, applicants testify inconsistently about at least one or two small details of their experience, or are unable to remember some detail about an experience that took place many years earlier. Even truthful applicants who present their histories to asylum officers are likely to remember new details as they prepare for court hearings, or to realize that in their prior testimony they were mistaken about some of the facts (especially dates).[22] The question, then, is how the adjudicator evaluates those lapses: as the normal, expected difficulties that anyone (particularly a victim of torture or other trauma) would have in recalling the past, or as evidence of fabrication.[23]

We suspect, but cannot prove, that much of the disparity among adjudicators results from differences among them in the degree of skepticism that they bring to the task of judging credibility based on an applicant's imperfect recollection or inconsistent retellings of personal history.[24] Our data on the strong correlations between adjudicators' grant rates and their prior work experience suggests that as a result of their particular personal histories, backgrounds, and philosophies, different officers and judges may bring to their task quite different presuppositions about the degree to which inconsistencies or lapses in the telling or retelling of a personal history prove that an applicant is committing fraud.[25] Prof. Robert Thomas notes that in Britain, a government official

> recently concluded from a sample of asylum decisions that a significant number of applicants' accounts are disbelieved because apparently western assumptions had been used to judge claimants' actions and that there were indications of a tendency to disbelieve. . . . While the decision-maker's own background values should be down-played, they are likely to be unarticulated and implicit and therefore so deeply ensconced within the decision-maker's own personal psychology and social upbringing that they simply cannot be left [out] of the decision-making function.[26]

Neither differences in the way adjudicators try to fit unique cases into the statutory pigeonholes nor differences in the way they assess the truthfulness of testimony can be reduced by additional codification of substantive rules, because they are rarely the result of ambiguity about the rules themselves. In fact, there is a huge body of asylum law resulting from thousands of published U.S. courts of appeals decisions in asylum cases,[27] but because every case is unique, the statistical disparities reported in our study persist. We do believe, however, that worthwhile steps can be taken to improve decision making. Some of our recommendations are very modest, while others would require statutory restructuring. We offer suggestions for depoliticizing the immigration court and the Board of Immigration Appeals and for increasing the professionalism of the adjudicators. We also have more modest recommendations for improving consistency among asylum officers and reducing the influence of regional cultures on the decisions of the U.S. courts of appeals.

3. Depoliticize the Immigration Courts and the Board of Immigration Appeals

A combination of events in 2002 and 2006 reveals just how much a presidential administration is able to manipulate Board membership to serve partisan political ends and to control the Board's decision making. As noted in chapter 4, in 2002, Attorney General John Ashcroft decided that a Board of only eleven members was appropriate, "based on judgments made about the historic capacity of appellate courts and administrative appellate bodies to adjudicate the law in a cohesive manner, the ability of individuals to reach consensus on legal issues, and the requirements of the existing and projected caseload."[28] To achieve the desired efficiency, he removed five members appointed by the previous Democratic administration. The members he removed were those with the highest rate of voting in favor of immigrants.[29] Legomsky notes that in the months between Ashcroft's announcement that he would reduce the size of the Board and his actual removal of five members, the Board's rate of voting in favor of immigrants declined,[30] which should not be surprising in view of the natural human tendency to take threats to one's livelihood seriously.

Fewer than five years later, when the Board had only nine members (as a result of the downsizing and two retirements), the Bush administration decided that the correct size of the Board was fifteen rather than eleven.[31] The administration did not reappoint any of the seven members whom Attorney General Ashcroft had removed from the Board or encouraged to resign. The net effect of the downsizing and upsizing actions, therefore, was to provide the Bush administration with the opportunity to replace seven appointees of a Democratic administration with five to seven appointees of a Republican administration.[32]

When Attorney General Ashcroft removed from the Board the members most likely to vote in favor of immigrants, he also subtly threatened to punish immigration judges who did not rule the way he wanted them to rule. In the course of rewriting the standards for Board members, replacing a statement that they should use "independent judgment" with a direction that they should act as his delegates, Ashcroft asserted that "all attorneys in the Department are excepted employees, subject to removal by the Attorney General."[33] Immigration judges, like BIA members, are attorneys employed by the Justice Department. It seems likely that at least some of them read Attorney General Ashcroft's statement, together with his removal of five Board members who had experience in academia or representing immigrants, as a warning that they, too, might be removed if they rendered decisions that met with the attorney general's disapproval.

While Attorney General Ashcroft only implied that he might politicize the lower-level immigration judges by removing those who did not vote his way, the Department of Justice under his successor, Alberto Gonzales, actually did extend partisan politics to the immigration courts, though it used the hiring rather than the firing process. Senior Justice Department officials did so despite civil service laws and Justice Department policy prohibiting discrimination in hiring immigration judges.[34] The "normal" procedure for selecting immigration judges is supposedly a task for the Office of the Chief Immigration Judge, who advertises for candidates and screens them on a nonpolitical basis:

> Unless the Attorney General elects to make a direct appointment, . . . [a vacancy announcement is sent] to various sources (DOJ postings, Internet sites, bar associations, law journals, etc.). . . . [The Office of the Chief Immigration Judge looks for] experience in at least three of the following areas: knowledge of immigration laws and procedures; substantial litigation experience, preferably in a high-volume context; experience handling complex legal issues; experience conducting administrative hearings; or knowledge of judicial practices and procedures. After reviewing the written applications, OCIJ selects applicants for an interview when appropriate.[35]

Under Attorney General Alberto Gonzales, the "unless" clause swallowed the rest of the procedure. From October 2004 through the year 2006, the Justice Department filled immigration judge positions through direct selection by the attorney general, bypassing the public competition process.[36] The actual vetting was done by Jan Williams, the Justice Department's White House liaison, and her successor, Monica Goodling. Goodling subsequently admitted that she had taken political considerations into account in selecting immigration judges. Acting under directions from the White House, these two officials prevented the Chief Immigration Judge from using the normal methods for recruiting and screening judges. They hand-picked the appointees, and the only persons they selected were Republican lawyers.[37] Furthermore, only candidates whose names were submitted by the White House Office of Political Affairs, the White House Presidential Personnel Office, the Counsel to the President, Republican members of Congress, and Republican political appointees in the Department of Justice were considered.[38] The screening process for these candidates included database searches to determine whether they had contributed money to political parties. By using political factors to select and screen immigration judge candidates, these Justice Department officials, along with Kyle Sampson, Attorney General Gonzales's chief of staff, systematically violated federal law.[39]

Using political standards to hire and fire immigration judges and Board of Immigration Appeals members may have been a conscious effort "to pack the court with judges who would always give the government's deportation arguments every benefit of the doubt."[40] Indeed, the Bush administration's appointment of thirty-one judges whom it selected on the basis of their political party affiliations and campaign contributions has lowered the immigration court's rate of granting asylum cases; the politically selected judges rule in favor of asylum cases at a rate significantly lower than the average rates of the courts on which they sit.[41] But even if an administration's intention is only to reward political cronies and not consciously to alter the overall rate at which asylum is granted, the use of political or ideological tests to select immigration judges, when practiced by one or both political parties, is likely to result in significant disparities in adjudication, probably with Democratic appointees having higher rates of decisions favorable to applicants than Republican appointees, as seems to be the pattern in at least the U.S. Courts of Appeals for the Sixth and Ninth Circuits. In other words, although judicial independence and consistency might at first blush seem at odds with each other, because more control from political officials could increase consistency in the short run, we believe that the ideological leanings of judges appointed by different administrations on the basis of party loyalty rather than competence would tend to increase disparities in grant rates in the long run.

Senior Justice Department official have so discredited the legitimacy of the adjudication process that the structure of the system must be changed.[42] The perversion of the selection system cannot be dismissed as merely an unlawful practice committed by three Bush administration officials who have since left public office. The director of EOIR and his deputy, both of whom were career Justice Department officials, knew that the normal hiring mechanisms had been bypassed and knew or had reason to know that immigration judges were being selected on the basis of Republican party credentials. They "should have brought these issues to the attention of other senior Department officials, such as senior career officials in the Office of the Deputy Attorney General, or the Office of the Inspector General or the Office of Professional Responsibility."[43] Neither of them did so, perhaps because they feared the kind of demotions that the attorney general had administered to several Board of Immigration Appeals members just a few years earlier. And another Department of Justice employee, who himself had been selected because of his Republican affiliations,[44] was active in recommending another immigration judge to become chief immigration judge in part because of his "loyalty to the Bush Admnistration."[45] The Justice Department later elevated this former DOJ employee to membership on the Board of Immigration Appeals.[46]

The Board and the immigration judges should be moved out of the Department of Justice.[47] Congress should create an independent Immigration Court and Immigration Court of Appeals in an executive branch agency that is not part of any department. This "Article I" court should have no function other than to decide immigration cases in accordance with the Constitution and the applicable statutes and regulations; it should not conceive of itself as a policy arm of whatever administration happens to be in office, and it should have no role in rule making, which should be left to the political branches, primarily the Department of Homeland Security.[48] Judges of the Immigration Court of Appeals, successor to the Board of Immigration Appeals, should be appointed for substantial, fixed terms (e.g., fifteen years) by the president with the advice and consent of the Senate. This procedure would increase their stature and visibility, attracting the most qualified candidates to the office. Senate confirmation would help protect the court from being filled with judges who hold extreme positions on immigration issues, and the tenure rules, permitting firing a judge only for malfeasance, would also increase their independence from political control.

It is not feasible to provide for presidential appointment and Senate confirmation of the hundreds of immigration judges who will serve in the Immigration Court, so they should be selected by a special advisory panel using rigorous hiring standards described below.[49] We suggest that with the advice and consent of the Senate, the president should appoint the chief immigration judge to head up the Immigration Court for a fixed term and that Congress should require the chief immigration judge to appoint an advisory committee to interview, screen, and recommend candidates for appointment (by the chief immigration judge) as immigration judges. The committee should consist of well-respected immigration judges, members of the appellate immigration court, and leading experts from outside of the government. The inclusion of outside experts on the committee will help to make the process more transparent and to prevent the selection of persons who are unqualified for the office.[50] The role of such a panel is to further professionalize and raise the stature of this important adjudicatory function, while insulating appointments as much as possible from political considerations.

Our suggestion to remove the immigration court and the Board of Immigration Appeals from the Department of Justice and to place these bodies in an independent agency is neither new nor radical, though it has new urgency in view of the recent political hiring of immigration judges and removal of Board members. The United States Commission on Immigration Reform recommended in 1997 that "administrative review of all immigration-related decisions" should be vested in a "newly-created independent agency . . . within the Executive Branch."[51] The commission added presciently that EOIR's location within the Department of Justice "injects into a quasi-judicial appellate process the possibility of intervention by the highest ranking law enforcement official in the land, and, generally, can undermine the BIA's autonomy and stature."[52] Moreover, our call for independence has been echoed by Judge Dana Leigh Marks, the president of the National Association of Immigration Judges.[53]

A desirable by-product of moving the Board out of the Department of Justice is that such a reorganization would end the ability of the attorney general to reverse a Board decision, substituting his own policy decisions whenever he disagrees with the Board.[54] (The Department of Homeland Security, which is the party adverse to the asylum seeker in immigration court, may seek this review by the attorney general, but the asylum applicant has no such opportunity pursuant to current regulations.)[55] Personal review of individual adjudications by a political officer of the government is yet another way in which asylum decisions can be politicized. Even though the attorney general has not used this power often, observers have found that it makes our immigration courts appear unfair, hinders the independence of the administrative courts, and increases the potential for conflicts of interests of the immigration judges and the Board.[56] The very possibility of such review may affect the thinking of Board members and immigration judges in many cases. The regulation permitting it should be repealed whether or not the Board is moved out of the department.

4. Create a More Professional Culture in the Reconstituted Court

In addition to being subject to political influence, the immigration court suffers from poor working conditions, crippling its ability to create as professional a culture as one might expect from a federal tribunal entrusted with life-and-death decisions protecting rights laid out in a federal law that implements an important international human rights treaty. For a forthcoming book exploring the problems of the immigration courts, Anna O. Law interviewed eight judges and three senior staff members of the U.S. Court of Appeals for the Ninth Circuit, promising anonymity to the respondents. They summarized, in equally blunt terms, the criticism of the immigration courts and the Board that are also voiced in such decisions as the Seventh Circuit's *Benslimane* case, quoted in one of the notes to chapter 5,[57] and in opinions in other circuits as well.[58] "Every judge and staff member that I interviewed was keenly aware of the shortcomings of the immigration system," she reported. "[One judge] summed up the sentiments of many of her colleagues . . . when she [stated], 'the system is a disgrace.'"[59] On the record, the courts of appeals have avoided the word "disgrace," but many stinging opinions in recent years suggest their frustration with the quality of immigration court decisions.[60]

Research by Dr. Stuart L. Lustig and his colleagues suggests that from the perspective of the immigration judges, a systemic institutional failure, rather than the incompetence or lack of professionalism of particular adjudicators, is responsible for the low regard in which the U.S. courts of appeals hold the immigration courts.[61] The institutional failure is the result of years of underfunding and understaffing the immigration court, as well as the absence of regular training. With the cooperation of the National Association of Immigration Judges, Lustig administered two survey measures, the Secondary Traumatic Stress Scale and the Copenhagen Burnout Inventory (CBI), to all 212 immigration judges. Ninety-six judges responded, and fifty-nine of them submitted narratives to supplement the coded responses. The immigration judges "reported more burnout than any other professional group to whom the CBI has been administered, including prison wardens and physicians in busy hospitals." The "typical" narratives reported by Lustig revealed judges who feel unable to render thoughtful decisions given their high caseloads, lack of support staff, and pressure from managers:

> We are told to keep producing—to get the cases done, without regard to the fact that we have insufficient support staff, insufficient time to deliberate and to complete cases, and out-dated equipment.
>
> [We can't do our jobs properly because of] lack of research resources, slow computers. . . . , no support, unfilled IJ positions, meaningless completion goals, [DHS] transferring aliens to detention facilities hundreds of miles from their attorneys and families simply to satisfy their numbers games, incompetent DHS attorneys and deportation officers, telephonic interpreters and hearings, faulty outdated recording equipment (for YEARS!)
>
> In my office the lack of competence among the staffers is a glaring shortcoming. Our court administrator appears interested in everything but competence and professionalism.

In view of the criticism leveled by the courts of appeals, a major effort should be made to turn the immigration court into a body that comports with the highest standards of fairness and due process. The federal government should adopt more rigorous hiring standards for judges, increase the number of immigration judges, provide them with more staff and better equipment, require written decisions in merits cases, institute regular on-the-job training (including measures specifically to address the statistical disparities without imposing quotas), and provide counsel to represent indigent respondents, at least in cases in which they seek asylum or protection under the Convention against Torture.

A. ADOPT MORE RIGOROUS HIRING STANDARDS FOR IMMIGRATION JUDGES

First, we suggest that EOIR implement more rigorous hiring standards. At present, immigration judges may be appointed by the Department of Justice even if they have no experience with adjudication, litigation, or people from other cultures, or any knowledge of immigration or human rights law.[62] In our view, however, to be selected as an immigration judge, a candidate should be able to produce well-reasoned written decisions that take into account all of the evidence and legal arguments presented by the parties, treat all parties respectfully, and manage a large docket without becoming impatient. A candidate should also be predisposed to be very careful in judging the credibility of people who claim to be victims of trauma or torture, sensitive to cultural differences, and knowledgeable about foreign cultures and immigration or human rights law. Their selection process should be rigorous because of the consequences of the judges' decisions and because the high caseloads make appellate review particularly challenging.

On paper, at least, the Canadian immigration adjudication system provides an instructive model of hiring standards.[63] Persons appointed to be adjudicators in the refugee protection division of the Canadian Immigration and Refugee Board must meet certain criteria of education, knowledge, and experience[64] and must also demonstrate nine "key behavioral competencies," which are tested in a written test and in a "behavioral event interview" with a panel of three trained members of the Selection Advisory Board. The nine competencies include reasoning ability, research and communication skills, and organizational talent, but they also include several more subtle interpersonal skills that are important in presiding over hearings involving people from other cultures. One requirement, for example, is "self-control," defined as "the ability to keep one's emotions under control and restrain negative actions when provoked in order to preserve impartiality." Another requirement, "cultural competence," is

> the ability to take into account the social and cultural conditions, norms and beliefs prevailing in claimants' milieu of origin in assessing the credibility or

plausibility of their actions. This involves the ability to question one's own cultural assumptions, a willingness to understand a perspective other than one's own, and a commitment to recognize diversity both between and within cultural groups.[65]

In the United States, when a position as an immigration judge must be filled, the position should be advertised widely, and not only to persons already working for the federal government.[66] Information about the position should be posted on an appropriate website and sent to asylum officers, immigration practitioners, the American Immigration Lawyers Association, law school deans, and career services offices. They should also be advertised in *Interpreter Releases*, a weekly publication read by many immigration lawyers. Candidates' analytical and writing skills should be assessed through a written test. The test should provide fact patterns and require candidates to identify issues, to show how the law applies to the stated facts, and to discuss what further facts should be adduced to resolve the legal issues. Then, as in Canada, a candidate for the position of immigration judge should also be assessed in terms of what the American Bar Association characterizes as the judicial temperament that should be possessed by federal judges: "compassion, decisiveness, open-mindedness, sensitivity, courtesy, patience, freedom from bias and commitment to equal justice under the law."[67]

To assess these qualities, and particularly to judge how a candidate would exhibit them in the context of a real hearing with someone from another culture, the selection board should require the prospective judge to preside over one or two simulated asylum hearings in which the asylum applicant is played by a professional actor or (even better) a previously successful asylum applicant who would relate some version or variant of his actual case. The hearing should be conducted in a foreign language, with interpretation, just as in many actual immigration court hearings.[68] The respondent should be unrepresented by counsel, because a majority of immigration court respondents are unrepresented.[69] These simulated hearings should include events that often characterize real hearings: misunderstandings resulting from faulty memory of the applicant and imperfect language interpretation; minor inconsistencies (particularly inconsistencies about the dates of past events such as demonstrations and arrests) between the applicant's testimony and previous statements that the applicant has made to the government; claimed inability by the applicant to obtain documents to corroborate every aspect of the narrative; and ambiguous nonverbal behavior, such as a failure to look the judge in the eye (which in some cultures is a sign of respect) or critical testimony that sounds rehearsed. The candidate might be told in advance that many nationals from the applicant's country have been known to commit immigration fraud, to see whether the candidate allows stereotyping to enter his or her assessment. Following the role plays, the candidate should be required to render written decisions including credibility assessments of the persons in the role of applicants.

B. INCREASE THE NUMBER OF JUDGES

The number of judges in the immigration court probably needs to be doubled. In 2006, about 215 judges were deciding more than 328,000 cases per year. Thus each judge decided, on average, about 1,500 cases, or about six cases a day.[70] John Walker, the chief judge of the U.S. Court of Appeals for the Second Circuit, explained to Congress that such a high number is not consistent with a deliberative process:

> The 215 Immigration Judges are required to cope with filings of over 300,000 cases a year. With only 215 Judges, a single Judge has to dispose of . . . more than five each business day, simply to stay abreast of his docket. I fail to see how Immigration Judges can be expected to make thorough and competent findings of fact and conclusions of law under these circumstances. This is especially true given the unique nature of immigration hearings. Aliens frequently do not speak English, so the Immigration Judge must work with a translator, and the Immigration Judge normally must go over particular testimony several times before he can be confident that he is getting an accurate answer from the alien. Hearings, particularly in asylum cases, are highly fact intensive and depend upon the presentation and consideration of numerous details and documents to determine issues of credibility and to reach factual conclusions. This can take no small amount of time depending on the nature of the alien's testimony.[71]

The immigration judges apparently agree with Judge Walker's assessment.[72] As one of them told Dr. Lustig, in comments echoed by others, "It is very frustrating to cope with such a large caseload. IJs should not be pressured to do more than two cases a day. Can headquarters understand that we are dealing with issues that affect real people, that we are deciding their fate?"[73]

Social psychology research supports the idea that judges with heavy dockets are more likely to make inaccurate decisions. Chris Guthrie and his colleagues note that judges with overwhelming caseloads are more likely to decide intuitively, rather than deductively, on the bench—that is, these judges are more likely to make decisions based on instinct or a gut feeling rather than carefully processing the information presented. While intuitive decision making on the bench may be beneficial in limited circumstances, it is likely to lead to inaccurate choices and allows bias and undesirable influences to enter the decision-making process.[74] With respect to the state trial court judges studied in their article, the authors recommend that judges be provided more time to make decisions, and that this time should be created by hiring more judges.[75]

Responding to criticisms such as these, Attorney General Gonzales announced in 2006 that the Justice Department would seek budget increases to hire more immigration judges. DOJ made that request, but matters got worse. Congress did not appropriate the funds for new positions,[76] and because Justice Department officials could find only a limited number of politically connected Republicans who were interested in filling vacancies, the number of sitting judges actually declined while Gonzales was attorney general.[77] At the same time, the budget for the trial attorneys who prosecute cases in immigration court increased by 62%, and the number of attorneys in the Office of Immigration Litigation, which represents the government in removal cases in federal court, nearly doubled, from 123 in July 2006 to 245 in July 2008.[78] It is no surprise that the GAO found in its October 2008 report that "[t]he growth in the number of immigration judges has not kept pace with the growth in their overall caseload and case completions."[79] Yet in its budget submission to Congress for FY 2009, the Justice Department did not renew its request for the additional immigration judges.[80]

C. PROVIDE MORE STAFF AND EQUIPMENT FOR IMMIGRATION JUDGES

An increase in the number of judges is only a start on improving resources. In stark contrast with federal judges, who generally work with four law clerks each, there is only one law clerk for every four immigration judges.[81] In fact, at least fourteen immigration courts have no law clerks assigned to them at all.[82] There are no court stenographers; judges record their hearings on tape recorders, and where cassette recorders are still used, they are personally responsible for changing the cassettes whenever they run out. Court interpreters are of mixed ability. Every immigration judge should be assigned a law clerk, and the quality of interpreters should be improved. In addition, the Department of Justice should complete its project of replacing outdated recording equipment with digital tape recorders.[83]

The department, however, cut funds (approximately $13 million) for hiring, courtrooms, staff, digital tape recorders, and training in connection with departmental appropriation cuts in 2008, and these funding cuts were expected to continue into the following fiscal year.[84] With respect to digital tape recorders, for example, this initiative "has been years in coming and will not be fully implemented nationwide for some time."[85] It seems to us that DOJ is heading in exactly the wrong direction, and should instead be expediting these crucial initiatives.

D. PROVIDE BETTER AND MORE FREQUENT TRAINING FOR IMMIGRATION JUDGES

We also believe that more training is in order, with particular attention to exercises and lessons that will properly promote greater consistency. Training should focus on all aspects of adjudication: conducting hearings, writing opinions, developments in the law, intercultural communication, human rights conditions, the effects of trauma and torture, understanding one's own biases, and managing dockets.

Immigration judges receive little if any periodic training. As one judge explained to Dr. Lustig, regular periods of training are necessary because "there is insufficient time in our schedules to provide for self education and development in this complex area of law." The only training that judges receive is at a national conference, supposedly held annually. In 2006, however, Immigration Judge Denise Slavin, president of the National Association of Immigration Judges, complained, "We have had no training conferences in person for the last three years. . . . We used to have [a] training conference every year but because of funding cuts we have not."[86] In January 2007, EOIR announced that it would expand and improve training for all immigration judges,[87] and the annual training conferences were in fact reinstated in 2006 and 2007. But the 2008 conference was canceled when the Justice Department refused to provide the funds.[88] Instead, EOIR provided judges with a "virtual" training conference in their own offices, which "included recorded presentations" and "interactive computer-based training."[89]

In practice, the 2008 "virtual" conference was, according to one immigration judge who went through it, "ludicrous." EOIR sent audio CDs and PowerPoint slides to each judge to load into his or her own office computer. The judges in each office were encouraged but not required to listen to these CDs and look at the PowerPoint slides together. One of the two days set aside for this training was devoted to asylum. The training consisted of looking at eight hypothetical fact patterns written on the PowerPoint slides, each accompanied by five questions for discussion. The extent to which these questions were actually discussed collaboratively depended on the assistant court administrator in each court. The questions were "very difficult legal questions and it would have been very hard to discuss all 40 questions in a single day." There was no training on the difficult matter of judging credibility, which appears to be at the heart of the asylum adjudication problem. In addition, the judges were encouraged to read and discuss short summaries of several articles on disparities in adjudication, including a five-page summary of the 120-page article written by the principal authors of this book.[90] Only 15% of the immigration judges thought that the "virtual" conference even moderately enhanced their ability to adjudicate asylum cases.[91]

Periodic in-person training should be required for immigration judges, as it is for asylum officers. While occasional national conferences are desirable, and the interaction among judges from different regions might reduce regional disparities in grant rates, such conferences are expensive and of necessity very limited in duration. Therefore, the training should be conducted primarily through monthly or quarterly meetings on a local or regional basis. This will reduce costs and enable judges to focus on the issues posed in hearings by immigrants in their own particular regions.[92]

Regular training in human rights conditions is, in the words of Judge Richard Posner, crucial to ensure that "immigration judges hav[e] the knowledge they need to make credible determinations."[93] Without training, it's unlikely that judges will become aware of patterns of persecution in countries around the globe, particularly where such abuse takes unexpected forms and targets. Moreover, country-conditions education will help judges to understand the challenges faced by asylum applicants seeking documentation of persecution from countries with very different record-keeping practices from the United States. Immigration judges would also benefit from learning about differences in demeanor and attitude that might arise from cultural norms and cannot be assumed to be indicators of truthfulness.[94]

Training for immigration judges should include units on judicial temperament.[95] For example, immigration lawyers have sometimes complained that after an immigration judge is lied to several times by nationals of a particular country, the judge tends to suspect that all nationals of that country are liars. The training could include counseling on impartiality, avoiding stereotyping, and not taking personally the misconduct that the judges sometimes encounter from people who are desperate to remain in the United States. Moreover, judges should be trained in deliberative, rather than intuitive, decision making on the bench. As Guthrie explains, judges should be taught to understand the extent to which they rely on intuition, to identify when it is risky to do so, and to learn to interrupt intuition on these occasions.[96] Notably, Guthrie and his colleagues suggest the use of peer review to institute this process.[97]

Peer-to-peer training should also be used to directly address the statistical disparities. Judges within each regional Asylum Office and Immigration Court should be informed periodically of each other's grant rates so that the disparities are apparent to them (as they already are to readers of this book).[98] Within each office or court, adjudicators with particularly high and particularly low grant rates should sit together with judges who had near-median rates, as panels of three, to hear and decide jointly a certain number of cases. If the members of these panels do not initially agree on the outcome, they should confer with each other and try to ascertain the cause of this phenomenon. For example, they should try to determine whether they had different views of how the law applied to the facts, or different judgments about whether the respondent was telling the truth. If the differences are based on ideologies or preconceptions of the adjudicators, these should be discussed with the chief immigration judge or one of his deputies. Merely discovering the origins of statistical disparities or hearing other judges' views of the same cases could help to reduce some of the largest differences in grant rates that this study observed.[99] Moreover, this is an inexpensive and simple solution that could give rise to positive externalities such as increased collegiality on the bench.

Some of the comments that immigration judges made to Dr. Lustig suggest a wide attitudinal gulf that might be addressed by assignments to panels. Compare these two observations by different judges, for example, which represent very different preconceptions about asylum applicants:

> While it is emotionally very difficult to listen to the testimony of individuals who have experienced persecution and even torture[,] consider it a great privilege to have been given the authority to extend the protection of the U.S. government to such individuals.

> My frustration with the system is not due to the fact that I believe the claims and am troubled by what I hear. On the contrary, it is due to the rampant fraud.

In contrast to immigration judges, asylum officers currently receive much more initial and ongoing training. The tenure of every asylum officer begins with a five-week basic training course (including testing). In addition, on a continuing basis, four hours a week are set aside for training officers on new legal issues and country conditions. The trainers themselves participate in monthly conference calls with the national headquarters to address new issues, emerging patterns of claims, and ideas for training techniques.[100] During some periods, in at least some of the regional asylum offices, the weekly training has included work on interviewing techniques and intercultural communication. Perhaps this serious commitment to initial and then regular training contributes significantly to the high degree of consistency in certain asylum offices. In any case, resources would be well spent in developing serious training programs for immigration judges.

E. REQUIRE IMMIGRATION JUDGES TO ISSUE WRITTEN DECISIONS AFTER MERITS HEARINGS

With the increased resources and training we recommend, immigration judges should be required to issue written decisions. As noted above, federal appellate judges have strongly criticized the ill-reasoned oral decisions that immigration judges, trying to meet caseload requirements, often render immediately after they hear testimony.[101] Asylum cases often involve hundreds of pages of written testimony, and judges who make decisions and dictate opinions at the end of a long day of oral testimony should be able to go back over the written record, compare it to the oral testimony, and consider documentary evidence that might fill in gaps in the testimony. This is particularly important for the asylum applicant who is not represented by counsel, or whose representative has done a cursory, rushed job of advocacy.

Both our federal courts and the Board of Immigration Appeals should expect well-reasoned decisions by immigration judges, but it is rather unfair to expect written decisions in all asylum cases unless the government provides the resources that will allow the judges to have time to review the evidence, deliberate, and write. We diminish both justice and efficiency by failing to hire and train competent immigration judges and give them the time and resources necessary for them to analyze cases and issue thoughtful decisions. Written opinions will be of great benefit to the adjudicatory system as a whole—both to the adjudicators who review immigration judge decisions and the parties who must determine whether any grounds for appeal are worth pursuing.

F. PROVIDE APPOINTED COUNSEL FOR UNREPRESENTED INDIGENT ASYLUM APPLICANTS

We suggest that the government provide competent appointed counsel for any indigent asylum applicant who must defend himself in a removal proceeding in immigration court. A system that claims to provide procedural due process requires some degree of fair representation; few Americans would think it fair to pit an experienced government lawyer against an unrepresented, indigent asylum seeker in a fairly formal trial before a robed judge. Yet that is what happens every day in the immigration courts, where only 48% of respondents are represented, and not all of them competently.[102] Federal judges, BIA members, and immigration judges alike have expressed serious concerns about bad lawyering in removal cases.[103]

The constitutional requirement of free counsel for indigent criminal defendants has been extended to certain types of civil proceedings, but not yet to asylum applicants or others in removal proceedings. The Sixth Amendment's promise of a right to appointed counsel, for a person who is not able to afford a lawyer, applies only to criminal cases and juvenile proceedings that can result in death or a lengthy incarceration.[104] The courts indulge in the fiction that deportation is not a similarly punitive outcome,[105] and they repeatedly hold that indigent immigration court respondents have no Sixth Amendment right to be represented,[106] despite the fact that an erroneous deportation of someone who has fled from persecution may result in the death or extended imprisonment of the applicant after a forced return.

People trying to prove that they are refugees within the meaning of federal law should not be required to compile supporting affidavits and make highly technical legal arguments without the assistance of capable professional advocates, when the consequence of losing may be deportation to countries in which they face imprisonment, torture, and death. Some of the gap between the unrepresented affirmative asylum applicants in immigration court who win at a rate of 16% and the represented applicants who win at a rate of 46% may be explained by lawyers' refusals to accept cases that appear very weak, but we suspect that if the currently unrepresented applicants had counsel, the gap would close appreciably.

The problem of the lack of counsel could be solved either by the courts or by Congress. The conclusion that the Sixth Amendment does not apply to deportation should be reexamined. As one scholar has noted,

> Expulsion, which the [Supreme] Court has characterized [even in a case *not* involving possible persecution] as a "great hardship" that "may result in the loss of all that makes life worth living," is a serious deprivation of liberty more analogous to incarceration than to a mere fine. . . . [Therefore] appointment of counsel would be required. This would impose a significant expense on the government; however, as the Court has recognized, the United States Constitution requires such protection "regardless of the cost."[107]

Alternatively, Congress could create a program for supplying counsel to indigent asylum seekers, or at least those who, after a fair screening process, seemed likely to have meritorious cases. Donald Kerwin, executive director of the Catholic Legal Immigration Network, has published a well-reasoned article describing several affordable options for publicly funded legal support for indigent respondents in immigration court.[108]

Either of these approaches would be consistent with the more general movement toward a regime of "civil *Gideon*." The American Bar Association, for example, has urged that the government should provide counsel for indigents in proceedings in which "basic human needs are at stake, such as those involving shelter, sustenance, *safety*, health, or child custody." The ABA specifically supports the provision of counsel at government expense to all those in removal proceedings.[109] Of course, providing counsel to indigent asylum applicants has fiscal implications, but to some extent, the cost of providing counsel will be offset because hearings will take less time.[110] Lawyers make proceedings more efficient by screening out irrelevant testimony, focusing the factual and legal issues for the judge, and reducing the number of postponements of a case.[111]

G. REFORM THE PROCEDURES OF THE BOARD OF IMMIGRATION APPEALS

Whether or not the Board is reconstituted as an independent immigration court of appeals outside of the Department of Justice, it should reform its procedures.[112] To begin with, the Board should catch up to the Asylum Office and the immigration courts by keeping and publishing statistics on the decisions of individual members, at least in asylum cases. If one member is granting asylum or remanding asylum cases at ten times the rate of another member, the Board itself, and the public, should at least be aware of this fact. The Board already maintains statistics showing the number of its dispositions that favor immigrants or the government, so all it has to do is to collect the relevant information and add a code showing which Board member or members decided the case.[113]

Second, the Board's operating regulations should be amended to prohibit it from assigning asylum and Convention against Torture cases to a single member for decision. Given the apparently huge differences of opinion among adjudicators about who deserves asylum, more than one member should review each case, and the reviewers should discuss the reasons for any differences of opinion.

Finally, Board decisions in asylum cases that are briefed by the appellant should no longer be decided by summary affirmances or even by two- or three-sentence conclusory opinions. At least in asylum cases, the Board should respond in writing to each of the contentions of counsel or pro se appellants, just as federal district court opinions systematically address the contentions of the losing party.[114] This process is an essential element if losing parties, and their counsel, are to believe that they were at least heard and understood.[115] If the Board addressed the contentions of counsel, the rate of appeals to federal court might come down, and even if it did not, the courts of appeals would have a clear and complete statement of views from the Board, which would place them in a better position to decide whether to affirm or remand the Board's decision.

These suggestions—requiring multimember decisions in asylum cases, and addressing the contentions of counsel—would require an increase in resources for the Board, but in our view, such an increase is well justified by the important role that the Board could once again play as a reviewing body in life-or-death cases.[116] Its cost would be offset, at least in part, by decreased costs currently borne by the federal courts of appeals and by the Justice Department, which must prepare briefs and arguments in many more cases than it did before 2002.[117]

In 2006, the attorney general seemed to agree that the streamlining "reforms" of 2002 went too far in the direction of allowing single members to make so many decisions, although the Department of Justice concluded that "it is neither necessary nor feasible to return to three-member review of all cases." The attorney general determined that "[s]ome adjustments to streamlining, however, are appropriate" and stated that new rules will "allow the limited use of three-member written opinions—as opposed to one-member written opinions—to provide greater legal analysis in a small class of particularly complex cases."[118] This vague and apparently very limited reform does not go nearly far enough, unless the Department of Justice ultimately adopts our view that all asylum cases in which an appealing respondent contends that an immigration judge has erred are, in view of the many factual and legal issues present in each such proceeding, "particularly complex."

Also, the Department of Justice proposed a new rule on June 18, 2008, that would provide more flexibility to the Board to issue single-member written opinions instead of affirmances without opinion. The rule will give "single Board members . . . discretion to decide whether to issue an AWO [affirmance without opinion] or to issue a written opinion with an explanation of the reasons for the decision."[119] This rule, like the proposal to permit three-member panels, does not go far enough. It does not *require* opinions with explanations, and it does not require that any explanations address the contentions of the appellant. As we and others have suggested,[120] the Board should in the very least return to the 1999 streamlining rule concept that asylum claims could only be decided on the merits by panels, and it should reinstitute, as a formal requirement, the practice of addressing the losing party's contentions.[121]

5. Reduce Disparities within Regional Offices of the DHS Asylum Office and the Severe Geographic Disparities in Asylum Decisions by the U.S. Courts of Appeals

A. ASYLUM OFFICES

One of our prescriptions for immigration courts is equally valid for asylum offices, such as Region H, with substantial internal disparities: asylum officers with significantly different rates should sit for a while as panels to attempt to understand the source of the differences. The asylum offices need not become independent of a government department, because they do not have the final word on denying asylum and ordering the deportation of an applicant. And some regional offices have shown that they are capable of largely eliminating the disparities among officers deciding similar cases. But further training, particularly including collaborative decision making by three-member panels in a relatively small number of cases, may help to reduce disparities in regions that have large numbers of officers who deviate significantly from the norm.

In addition, a recent report suggests that asylum officers, like immigration judges, are too rushed to make careful decisions in all cases. Asylum officers are expected to put no more than four hours into each case, including a one- to two-hour interview with the applicant. But 92% of them stated that having more time to probe in an interview would "moderately or greatly help them elicit better information during the interview to properly evaluate the claim," and the same percentage said that having more time to read the documents submitted before the hearing would have helped them to elicit better information during the interview.[122] The four-hour-per-case standard was established without any empirical basis in 1999.[123] We believe that with ten years of experience under this productivity standard, the Department of Homeland Security should review it, possibly giving asylum officers five or six hours to work on each case.

Finally, we noted in chapter 2 that in some regional offices, quality-assurance officers do not appear to be reviewing decisions as they do in other regions. We assume that the department will address this problem soon if it has not already done so.

B. THE U.S. COURTS OF APPEALS

The U.S. courts of appeals should set an example for the lower bodies in the asylum-adjudication process by reducing the disparities in their own remand rates. We do not know why the Seventh Circuit consistently remands cases at a rate 700% or 800% higher than any of the three southern circuits, but if the answer is simply that the South is more conservative than the Upper Midwest, that is cold comfort to asylum seekers who arrive in the United States unaware that regional cultural differences in our country may determine the course of their lives if they need to appeal orders of removal.

We suggest that the Federal Judicial Center convene a national conference of appellate judges to discuss immigration in general and asylum in particular.[124] The conference agenda should include panels of experts on the work of the immigration courts and the BIA, and on persecution around the world. More importantly, the conference should offer ample opportunity for informal discussion among judges from different circuits. The conference format should include small-group discussions among judges who rarely vote to remand and those who often vote to remand, in an effort to reach a better national consensus on the standard for review of the Board's decisions and on the application of that standard.

These recommendations are far more modest than the proposal, made by former Senate Majority Leader Bill Frist, to confine all judicial review of the Board of Immigration Appeals to the Court of Appeals for the Federal Circuit.[125] That consolidation proposal would, by definition, have ended geographical disparities in the adjudication of asylum cases at the court of appeals level. But it had many drawbacks, including creating incentives for presidents to appoint judges based on their expected votes in immigration cases; depriving the judges in question of the perspective of generalists who decide many different kinds of cases; risking "capture" of the court by the Department of Justice, which would appear before it in virtually every case; and overwhelming a court that now decides intellectual property and a few other types of cases.[126]

The courts, too, should refrain from affirming removal orders without any opinion when an asylum applicant has made substantial contentions challenging a decision of the Board. Applicants for asylum are neither citizens nor permanent residents of the United States. Nevertheless, their claims are extremely serious, as errors of adjudication can deliver them into the hands of their persecutors. Rejections of their claims on appeal therefore warrant explanations from the court as well as from the Board.

6. Amend the Standard for Judicial Review of Board Decisions

In view of the results of this study, Congress should also amend the judicial review provision of the Immigration and Nationality Act to restore a more normal role for the federal courts in their review of asylum decisions. Currently, the federal courts defer excessively, especially in the southern circuits, to decisions of immigration courts and the Board of Immigration Appeals, even though those decisions appear to depend to a large extent on the identity, personal characteristics, and prior work experience of the adjudicator, as well as on whether or not the asylum applicant had representation or dependents in the United States.[127]

As amended in 1996, the law directs that on review, "the administrative findings of fact [of the BIA or of an immigration judge whose findings are not rejected by the BIA] are conclusive unless any reasonable adjudicator would be compelled to conclude to the contrary."[128] This extreme standard should be replaced with the more usual rule requiring deference only to findings that are supported by substantial evidence.[129] Meanwhile, the courts should interpret the review statute narrowly, deferring strongly only to formal findings of fact, and not to applications of law to fact (such as whether a certain number of beatings constitute "persecution," or whether an asylum applicant's reason to fear persecution was so great as to be "well-founded"). Perhaps some courts are already following our suggestion; differences in the circuits' willingness to defer to these applications of law to fact may account for the immense differences in their remand rates that we discovered in this study.[130]

Accuracy, consistency, and public acceptance are among the most important goals of any adjudicative system.[131] This study shows that disparities are deeply ingrained in the U.S. asylum system, and that the government must now take significant steps to achieve greater consistency in decision making. We believe that the recommendations discussed above are crucial to the government's efforts to achieve such a result.

NOTES

1. 1940 Att'y Gen. Ann. Rep. 5–6, *quoted in* James M. Anderson, Jeffrey R. Kling & Kate Stith, Measuring Interjudge Sentencing Disparity: Before and after the Federal Sentencing Guidelines, 42 J.L. & Econ. 271 (1999) at 275. The attorney general was referring to criminal sentencing.
2. The U.S. Supreme Court discussed disparities in punitive damage awards in its recent *Exxon* decision, noting that the unpredictability of such awards was problematic because "[c]ourts of law are concerned with fairness as consistency." Exxon Shipping Co., et al. v. Baker, 128 S.Ct. 2605, 2625 (2008). The Court focused on the spread between high and low awards as problematic, and seems to presume that great disparities are improper, unless scholarly work shows that inconsistency is based on reasonable differences. *Id.* at 2625–26.

3. In each of these regions, the officers whose grant rates are reported here adjudicated at least twenty-five cases from FY 1999 through FY 2005.

4. Our immigration court data set ends in August 2004, but the Transactional Records Access Clearinghouse (TRAC) continues to monitor the grant rates (which it expresses as denial rates) of individual immigration judges. *See* trac.syr.edu/immigration/ reports/judgereports. However, TRAC's data does not analyze rates in databases of APC cases, and TRAC does not attempt to show the degree to which particular judges deviate from their courts' norms. In 2007, based on an examination of cases from FY 2001 through FY 2006, TRAC concluded that "asylum disparities persist, regardless of court location and nationality." Transactional Records Access Clearinghouse, Asylum Disparities Persist, Regardless of Court Location and Nationality, http://www.trac.syr.edu/immigration/reports/183/ (2007).

5. *See* chapter 2, table 2.1.

6. It is possible that different groups of Chinese refugees, from different regions of China and with differing degrees of meritorious claims, might arrive at different U.S. coasts and therefore have their claims adjudicated by different regions of the Asylum Office. However, there are no empirical studies to support this speculation. Furthermore, it seems less likely that asylum seekers from smaller countries such as Armenia are composed of groups with particular characteristics that flee to different U.S. cities.

7. *See supra* chapter 2.

8. This conclusion is based on an examination of the disparity between the highest and lowest grant rates nationally among the five APCs (Armenia, China, Colombia, Ethiopia, and Haiti) that accounted for 78% of all cases from the eleven APC countries. Of these five APCs, the grant rate for the country (Ethiopia) with the highest grant rate (59% in FY 2003 and 2004 combined) is only 84% higher than the grant rate for the country (China) with the lowest grant rate (32% in FY 2003 and 2004). The percentages in this note are derived from Dep't of Homeland Sec., 2004 Y.B. Immigr. Stat. 55 tbl.18 and Dep't of Homeland Sec., 2003 Y.B. Immigr. Stat. 60 tbl.18. Unfortunately, DHS is no longer including in its annual statistical yearbooks detailed statistical information on the number of cases that it grants, denies, refers, and rejects. *Compare id., with* Dep't of Homeland Sec., 2005 Y.B. Immigr. Stat. 44 tbl.17. Both books are *available at* http://www.dhs.gov/ximgtn/ statistics/publications/yearbook.shtm. The discontinuance of detailed statistical reporting makes it much more difficult for researchers to analyze trends in asylum adjudication by DHS unless they make informal arrangements, as we did, to receive data sets directly. Fortunately, the department has been willing to share those data sets with scholars without requiring them to go through the often lengthy processes triggered by formal requests under the Freedom of Information Act.

9. There are, of course, minor differences in statutory interpretation from circuit to circuit. But very few asylum appeals turn on statutory interpretation. Most focus on whether the immigration court and the Board drew proper inferences and conclusions from the testimony and documentary evidence in the case. The leading treatises, such as Deborah Anker, The Law of Asylum in the United States: Administrative Decisions and Analysis (3d ed. 1994), cite circuits interchangeably to support their descriptions of the law because statutory interpretation is in fact so uniform nationally (although by dint of its larger asylum docket, the Ninth Circuit has had to reach and decide more legal issues than most others).

10. *See* Dorsey & Whitney LLP, Board of Immigration Appeals: Procedural Reforms to Improve Case Management 39–40 (2003), *available at* http://www.dorsey.com/files/upload/ DorseyStudyABA_8mgPDF.pdf.39-40.

11. *See* David A. Martin, *Another Second-Class Citizen: How the Justice Department Has Been Debasing Immigration Courts for Years*, Legal Times, Aug. 11, 2008.

12. The vast majority of asylum applicants are not permitted to work while their applications are pending. The authors know from personal experience that clients of the asylum clinic at Georgetown University have settled in the Baltimore/Washington area primarily because that is where they have friends or family members who can support them for several months until their cases have been decided. They know nothing about regional differences in immigration court grant rates, much less the statistical likelihood of winning appeals in various circuits.

13. Stephen H. Legomsky, *Learning to Live with Unequal Justice: Asylum and the Limits of Consistency*, chapter 12 of this volume, at 280.

14. *Id.*

15. Government Accountability Office (GAO), U.S. Asylum System: Significant Variation Existed in Asylum Outcomes across Immigration Courts and Judges, GAO-08-940 at 61 (2008).

16. GAO, *supra* n.15, at 44–45.

17. *See* Human Rights First, AG Ashcroft Sends Domestic Violence Case Back to Appeals Board, http://www.humanrightsfirst.org/ asylum/torchlight/newsletter/newslet_35.htm (2005); Angela Chazaro & Jennifer Casey, Getting Away with Murder: Guatemala's Failure to Protect Women and Rodi Alvarado's Quest for Safety, 17 Hastings Women's L.J. 141 (2006).

18. These grounds are the applicant's race, religion, nationality, political opinion, or membership in a particular social group.

19. In her chapter in this volume, Audrey Macklin, who served on the Canadian Immigration and Refugee Board for two years, states that "based on experience (mine and others') . . . credibility is the single most important determinant of outcome." *Infra* chapter 7, p. 137.

20. Affirmative asylum applicants who are in immigration court proceedings will at least have told their stories, under oath, to an asylum officer months before testifying in court. The court may take note of any inconsistencies between the versions told to the officer and the version to which the applicant testifies in court.

21. For a discussion of the difficulty of an immigration judge's task, given the inaccuracy demonstrated by social scientists of judgments based on demeanor evidence, and of the importance of consistency and detail, *see* Mitondo v. Mukasey, 523 F.3d 784 (7ᵗʰ Cir. 2008).

22. For a detailed description of an asylum applicant's process of recalling a more accurate version of events, with the help of two law students and of a therapist, while preparing for an immigration court hearing, *see* David Ngaruri Kenney & Philip G. Schrag, Asylum Denied: A Refugee's Struggle for Safety in America 121–33, 142–45 (2008).

23. For a thoughtful discussion of the difficulties that an adjudicator of asylum cases must face when judging the credibility of asylum applicants, *see* Robert Thomas, Assessing the Credibility of Asylum Applicants: EU and UK, 8 Eur. J. of Migration and Law 79 (2006).

24. The applicable law states that a trier of fact

> *may* base a credibility determination on the demeanor, candor, or responsiveness of the applicant or witness, the inherent plausibility of the applicant's or witness's account, the consistency between the applicant's or witness's written and oral statements (whenever made and whether or not under oath, and considering the circumstances under which the statements were made), the internal consistency of each such statement, the consistency of such statements with other evidence of record (including the reports of the Department of State on country conditions), and any inaccuracies or falsehoods in such statements, without regard to whether

an inconsistency, inaccuracy, or falsehood goes to the heart of the applicant's claim (emphasis added).
8 U.S.C. § 1158(b)(1)(B)(iii). The law therefore gives a good deal of latitude to immigration judges.

25. *See also* Judge Richard Posner, *Speech before the Chicago Bar Association*, at 5 (Apr. 21, 2008), *available at* http://38.105.88.161/search/basic.asp?ResultStart=1&ResultCount=10&BasicQueryText=Posner ("[I]f you have an adjudicative setting in which it is extremely difficult to derive a kind of objective judgment of the facts . . . , the greater the uncertainty facing the adjudicator the more the decision is likely to reflect personal factors on the part of the adjudicator. His background, his values, his attitude toward immigration, his impressions of particular foreign cultures.").

26. Thomas, *supra* n.23, at 84–85.

27. *See* David A. Martin, Asylum Case Law Sourcebook (7th ed. 2007) (1,124-page book containing summaries of U.S. court of appeals decisions in asylum cases to June 2007).

28. *Id.*

29. Stephen H. Legomsky, Deportation and the War on Independence, 91 Cornell L. Rev. 369, 376 (2006).

30. *Id.* at 377.

31. Board of Immigration Appeals: Composition of Board and Temporary Board Members, 71 Fed. Reg. 70,855 (Dec. 7, 2006).

32. In 2008, the Bush administration appointed five members to the Board, increasing its size to thirteen members and leaving two vacancies still to be filled.

33. Legomsky, *supra* n.29, at 373, 379. *Id.* at 377. One authority termed Ashcroft's statement a "largely unveiled threat." Linda Kelly Hill, Holding the Due Process Line for Asylum, 36 Hofstra L. Rev. 85, 91 n.23 (2007).

34. Immigration judges are "Schedule A" career appointees, as opposed to "Schedule C" political appointees, so the civil service laws prohibiting discrimination in hiring apply to these appointments. 5 C.F.R. Sec. 213.301. Moreover, Justice Department policy bars discrimination on the basis of politics in selecting career appointees. Department of Justice, Offices of Professional Responsibility and of the Inspector General, *Investigation of Allegations of Politicized Hiring by Monica Goodling and Other Staff in the Office of the Attorney General* (hereafter "Inspector General's Report"), http://www.usdoj.gov/ opr/goodling072408.pdf (July 28, 2008), at 70.

35. Executive Office for Immigration Review, AILA-EOIR Liaison Agenda Questions: For Oct. 17, 2005, http://www.usdoj.gov/eoir/statspub/eoiraila101705.pdf.

36. Emma Schwartz & Jason McLure, *DOJ Made Immigration Judgeships Political*, Legal Times, May 28, 2007, at 12.

37. Inspector General's Report, *supra* n.34, at 83.

38. *Id.*

39. *Id.* at 115.

40. Former Immigration and Naturalization Service General Counsel David A. Martin asks whether this was the case in David A. Martin, *Another Second-Class Citizen: How the Justice Department Has Been Debasing Immigration Courts for Years*, Legal Times, Aug. 11, 2008.

41. By the end of FY 2007, sixteen of the thirty-one judges had decided at least one hundred asylum cases. On average, those judges granted asylum at a rate that was seven percentage points lower than their peers on the immigration courts on which they sat. One judge granted asylum only 20% of the time while hearing cases in Orlando, while during the same period, other judges in Orlando had an average grant rate of 51%. Charlie Savage, *Vetted Judges More Likely to Reject*

Asylum Bids, N.Y. Times, Aug. 24, 2008. A graphic available only online demonstrates these judges' asylum denial rates in comparison to the national average denial rates for FY 2007 as well as the average denial rates of other judges sitting on the same court in FY 2007. *By The Numbers*, N.Y. Times, Aug. 24, 2008, *available at* http://www.nytimes.com/ imagepages/2008/08/24/ washington/24judges-graphic.html.

42. In July 2007, after Monica Goodling had revealed that she had improperly used political criteria to select immigration judges, Attorney General Gonzales testified that he had introduced a new process that would make the hiring of judges and Board members "more routine, consistent, and transparent" by placing the "initial vetting, evaluation, and interviewing functions" within the Executive Office for Immigration Review, rather than in his Department of Justice headquarters staff. However, placing these functions in one part of the department rather than another will not necessarily make appointments more consistent or transparent, and as Linda Kelly Hill has pointed out, the word "initial" in Gonzales's testimony implies that the attorney general would continue to make the ultimate decisions about who would become an immigration judge.

43. Inspector General's Report, *supra* n.34, at 124.

44. *Id.* at 88–89.

45. *Id.* at 108.

46. Department of Justice, *Attorney General Mukasey Appoints Five New Members to the Board of Immigration Appeals*, May 30, 2008 (press release).

47. "When we seek a truly independent adjudicator, institutional separation is nearly as important a tool as a tenure guarantee." Harold H. Bruff, Specialized Courts in Administrative Law, 43 Admin. L. Rev. 329, 345 (1991).

48. An "Article I" court is a court created by an act of Congress that is housed in the executive branch of government and has no function other than to adjudicate cases. *Id.*

49. The idea of citizen participation in judicial selection is not novel; U.S. Senators from thirteen states use nominating commissions to screen candidates for federal court vacancies. http://www.judicialselection.us/federal _judicial_selection/federal_judicial_nominating_commissions. cfm?state=FD.

50. Under the Federal Advisory Committee Act, P.L. 92–463, advisory committee meetings are generally open to public view, but meetings may be closed for deliberations concerning personnel issues. *See* General Accounting Office, *Federal Advisory Committee Act Brochure*, http://www.gsa. gov/Portal/gsa/ep/ contentView.do?contentId=11869&contentType=GSA_BASIC&noc=T (visited Sept. 28, 2008).

51. U.S. Comm'n on Immigration Reform, Becoming an American: Immigration and Immigrant Policy 174 (1997), *available at* http://www.utexas.edu/lbj/uscir/ becoming/full-report.pdf. In the interest of full disclosure, Andrew Schoenholtz was the deputy director of this commission.

52. *Id.* at 178.

53. *See* Dana Leigh Marks, *A System at Its Breaking Point*, L.A. Daily Journal (Aug. 29, 2008).

54. 8 C.F.R. Sec. 1003.1(h)(1)(i).

55. 8 C.F.R. Sec. 1003.1(h).

56. David Martin, *Another Second-Class Citizen: How the Justice Department Has Been Debasing Immigration Courts for Years*, Legal Times, at 2 (Aug. 11, 2008); Justin Chasco, Judge Alberto Gonzales? The Attorney General's Power to Overturn the Board of Immigration Appeals' Decisions, 31 Southern Illinois University L.J. 363, 383 (2007). On January 7, 2009, Attorney General Michael Mukasey used this power to overturn two decades of BIA precedent by ruling that foreign nationals have no constitutional right to assert "ineffective assistance of counsel" as a challenge to a deportation ruling. Matter of Compean, 24 I&N Dec. 710 (A.G. Jan. 7, 2009).

On June 3, 2009, Attorney General Eric Holder vacated that decision and initiated a process of rule-making, after public comment, to determine what procedures and standards should apply to claims of ineffective assistance of counsel. *Matter of Compean,* http://www.ailf.org/lac/chdocs/Compean-Holder.pdf (A.G., June 3, 2009).

57. Chapter 5, note 6, *supra.*

58. *See, e.g.,* Giday v. Gonzales, 434 F.3d 543 (3d Cir. 2006); Recinos de Leon v. Gonzales, 400 F.3d 1185 (9th Cir. 2005). For a more recent and, in our view, particularly shocking case in which a court of appeals exhibited a good deal of restraint when it stated that the immigration judge "mischaracterized" the asylum seeker's testimony, misunderstood her, and made conclusions that were "not supported by logic," *see* Tekle v. Mukasey, 2008 U.S. App. LEXIS 15272 (9th Cir., July 18, 2008).

59. Anna O. Law, *Crossing Legal Borders: Immigrants at the U.S. Courts of Appeals and Supreme Court* (manuscript submitted for publication).

60. In addition to the Seventh Circuit's *Benslimane* decision and the cases summarized therein, *see* the cases described in Hill, *supra* n.33, at 103 n.72 through 105 n.78.

61. Stuart L. Lustig, Niranjan Karnik, Kevin Delucchi, Lakshika Tennakoon, Brent Kaul, Dana Leigh Marks & Denise Slavin, Inside the Judges' Chambers: Narrative Responses from the National Association of Immigration Judges Stress and Burnout Survey, 23 Geo. Immig. L.J. 57 (2008) (hereafter "Lustig Survey").

62. Candidates vetted by the Executive Office for Immigration Review, as opposed to those chosen by political officials in the Department of Justice, are required to have seven years of "relevant" postbar legal experience (but not necessarily immigration knowledge or experience). In addition, the Office of the Chief Immigration Judges desires at least three of the following qualifications: knowledge of immigration law, substantial litigation experience, experience conducting administrative hearings, or knowledge of judicial practices and procedures. Government Accountability Office, U.S. Asylum System, Significant Variation Existed in Asylum Outcomes across Immigration Courts and Judges, GAO-08-940 at 17 n.23 (2008) (hereinafter "GAO Variation Report"). Note that these qualities are only desired and not required, that immigration law experience is not required, and that even knowledge of immigration law is only one of several alternative qualifications for this job. Also, any lawyer who has litigated for a few years is bound to have two of the three qualifications: substantial litigation experience and knowledge of judicial practices and procedures. These standards are completely silent regarding judicial temperament and sensitivity to issues of intercultural communication and the effects of trauma and torture. Furthermore, as noted above, the Department of Justice can dispense with all of these requirements and desired qualifications and did so extensively during the second term of President George W. Bush.

63. The Canadian system of appointing adjudicators may be better on paper than it is in practice. According to one authority,

> the shadow of patronage still hovers over the IRB as the federal cabinet continues to delay or deny the reappointment of superior members while reappointing manifestly mediocre ones. Similarly, strong candidates without political credentials are repeatedly passed over and many potential candidates do not bother to apply. . . . [Nevertheless, a] majority of IRB members have done a very difficult job well, hearing thousands of cases each year with an admirable record of consistency.
> (Peter Showler, Refugee Sandwich: Stories of Exile and Asylum (2006))

Showler is a former IRB chair. *See also* the chapter by Professor Audrey Macklin in this book, concluding that

> the appointment and renewal system introduced in Canada in 2004 offers one model of a merit-based system that functioned reasonably well within a regime

where executive still retained final authority. However, the subsequent undermining of this system, first by the Minister who replaced the initiator of the policy, and then by the Conservative government, demonstrates the crucial importance of political will in making it work.

64. In terms of education, they must have "a university degree OR an acceptable combination of education, training and/or experience" such as "relevant training or experience (5 to 10 years) demonstrative of a breadth of vision and scope, demonstrative of a capacity for enquiry and ability to synthesize information and reach reasonable conclusions, demonstrative of working with various ethnic communities for purposes of integration and settlement, [and] demonstrative of a breadth of vision in the field of human rights." They must also have a "minimum of five years professional experience: experience as a decision maker in a quasi-judicial administrative tribunal; or experience in presenting cases before a quasi-judicial administrative tribunal; or experience in cross-cultural communication; or research and writing in social sciences or law; or experience in the field of human rights; or an acceptable combination of relevant experience in other fields." In addition, they must have "knowledge of the mission, vision and values of the IRB and the role of Members; knowledge of world cultures; contemporary international affairs; human rights concerns and principles of natural justice; knowledge of international migration trends." Immigration and Refugee Board of Canada, Statement of Qualifications for IRB GIC Members, http://www.irb-cisr.gc.ca/en/about/employment/members/soq_e.htm (visited May 23, 2008).

65. Immigration and Refugee Board of Canada, The Selection Process for Governor in Council Appointments to the Immigration and Refugee Board of Canada, http://www.irb-cisr.gc.ca/en/about/employment/members/process_e.htm, and in Immigration and Refugee Board of Canada, Backgrounder: Immigration and Refugee Board of Canada Governor in Council Competency Profile, http://www.irb-cisr.gc.ca/en/media/ background/back_comp_e.htm (visited May 11, 2008).

66. How widely the chief immigration judge advertised for candidates, even before the Department of Justice began to bypass that office in 2004, is not clear. In 2005, EOIR noted that it had listed a position publicly by posting it on www.usajobs.gov, *see* EOIR, AILA-EOIR Liaison Agenda Questions, *supra* n.35, but that is not a site that private practitioners or academics would necessarily know about. One practitioner reports,

> I applied for an IJ position in the 1980s and again in the 1990s. I don't recall how I learned of the openings the first time. The second time, a colleague told me about it at the very end of the application period. Certainly there were many other "casting calls" that I did not hear about because new IJs have appeared willy-nilly since I started doing asylum work in the early 80s. Except possibly for the 1980s application, my impression all along, and it's only an impression, is that the jobs were "wired." You hadda be in the know. . . . Maybe my ignorance of openings is a sign of insularity. I focused on doing actual work, didn't hobnob with movers and shakers, didn't "network" or read gossip rags. I did read Interpreter Releases, was no stranger to the courts; perhaps that wasn't enough. Other people found out about these jobs somehow, but . . . maybe some "casting calls" were made only to insiders. . . . I got the feeling that after the wave of good people who came on in the 1990s, many of whom still top the "asylum grant" lists, [Chief Immigration Judge Michael] Creppy was determined to rebalance (or unbalance) by appointing "prosecutors" like himself. After all, it was he who boasted that the extreme differences in grant rates that you and others have noted, were a sign of judicial independence instead of a sign of dysfunction and a lack of standards. (Email to Philip Schrag from an immigration practitioner, May 15, 2008)

67. American Bar Ass'n., The Standing Comm. on the Federal Judiciary: What It Is and How It Works, http://www.abanet.org/scfedjud/federal_judiciary07.pdf at 4 (2007) (visited May 11, 2008).

68. In FY 2007, only 15% of immigration court hearings were conducted in English. Executive Office for Immigration Review, FY 2007 Statistical Yearbook, http://www.usdoj.gov/eoir/statpub/fy07syb.pdf at F1, Fig. 8 (2008) (visited May 11, 2008). Respondents spoke 265 different languages. *Id.* at F1.

69. Executive Office for Immigration Review, FY 2007 Statistical Yearbook, http://www.usdoj.gov/eoir/statpub/fy07syb.pdf at G1 (2008) (visited May 11, 2008).

70. Our study included 225 judges, but at any given time there are a few vacancies. Regarding the number 215, *see* Linda Kelly Hill, *supra* n.33, at 105 n.75. For the total annual caseload, *see* FY 2007 Statistical Yearbook, *supra* n.69, at A1.

71. *Immigration Litigation Reduction Hearing before the S. Comm. on the Judiciary,* 109th Cong. 5–7 (2006) (statement of Hon. John M. Walker, Jr., C.J., U.S. Court of Appeals for the Second Circuit), *available at* http://www.aila.org/content/ default.aspx?docid=18996.

72. As does Judge Richard Posner, a frequent and thoughtful commentator on the state of the immigration courts. *See* Judge Richard Posner, *Speech before the Chicago Bar Association,* at 2 (Apr. 21, 2008), *available at* http://38.105.88.161/search/ basic.asp?ResultStart=1&ResultCount=10&BasicQueryText=Posner.

73. In 2007, Section 701(b)(3) of Senate Bill 1348 and section 701(b)(3) of House Bill 1645 would have created at least twenty new immigration judges and "not less than 80" new positions to support the immigration judges. S. 1348, 110th Cong. § 701(b)(3) (2007); H.R. 1645, 110th Cong. § 701(b)(3) (2007). But the bills did not pass.

74. Chris Guthrie, Jeffrey J. Rachlinski, & Andrew J. Wistrich, Blinking on the Bench: How Judges Decide Cases, 93 Cornell L. Rev. 1, 31–32. The authors note that intuitive decision making may be the hallmark of expertise, but caution that accurate and reliable feedback on the validity of earlier judgments may be necessary to create expertise. Immigration judges do not currently receive this type of feedback. Judge Posner's *Iao* decision (400 F.3d 530 (7th Cir. 2005)) has a very useful list of problems with unreasoned decisions at 533–35. *See also* Guthrie et al. at 36 (written decisions induce deliberation).

75. *Id.* at 35.

76. Transactional Records Access Clearinghouse, Improving the Immigration Courts: Effort to Hire More Judges Falls Short, http://trac.syr.edu/immigration reports/189/ (2008).

77. *Id.*; Inspector General's Report, *supra* n.34, at 116; *see also* Sandra Hernandez, *Immigration Reforms Result in Fewer Judges, More Prosecutors,* Los Angeles Daily Journal at 1 (Aug. 27, 2008).

78. Sandra Hernandez, n.77 *supra.*

79. Government Accountability Office, *U.S. Asylum System: Agencies Have Taken Actions to Help Ensure Quality in the Asylum Adjudication Process, but Challenges Remain* (hereafter "Asylum Challenges") at 8, GAO-08-935 (2008).

80. Hearing on Oversight of the Department of Justice's Executive office for Immigration Review before the House Subcomm. on Immigration, Citizenship, Refugees, Border Security, and International Law, Sept. 23, 2008 (testimony of Susan B. Long, codirector, Transactional Records Access Clearinghouse). As of the fall of 2008, "there were fewer immigration judges than when Attorney General Gonzales ordered new hires [in 2006]." Jennifer Ludden, "Immigration Crackdown Overwhelms Judges," All Things Considered, Feb. 9, 2009, http://www.npr.org/templates/player/mediaPlayer.html?action=1&t=1&islist=false&id=100420476&m=100469523.

81. Tony Mauro, *Appeals Judges Decry Immigration Case "Tsunami,"* The Blog of Legal Times (Aug. 10, 2008) (quoting Juan Osuna, chair, Board of Immigration Appeals), *available at* http://

legaltimes.typepad.com/blt/2008/08/appeals-judges.html. Fifty-four law clerks served about the same number of immigration courts around the country in fiscal year 2007–2008. Telephone communication from Brigette Frantz, Office of the Chief Immigration Judge, EOIR, to Andrew I. Schoenholtz on May 22, 2008. *See* http://www.usdoj.gov/eoir/sibpages/ICadr.htm for number of immigration courts (fifty-four when visited on May 25, 2008).

82. Transactional Records Access Clearinghouse, Improving the Immigration Courts: Effort to Hire More Judges Falls Short (2008), *available at* http://trac.syr.edu/ immigration/ reports/189/.

83. Attorney General Gonzales announced plans to upgrade the recording equipment in immigration courts, but how long this process will take remains to be seen. *See* Dep't of Justice, Attorney General Alberto R. Gonzalez Outlines Reforms for Immigration Courts and Board of Immigration Appeals, August 9, 2006 (press release), http://www.usdoj/opa/ pr/2006/ August/06_ag_520.html. Section 701(b)(3) of Senate Bill 1348 and section 701(b)(3) of House Bill 1645 would have created at least twenty new immigration judges and "not less than 80" new positions to support the immigration judges. S. 1348, 110th Cong. § 701(b)(3) (2007); H.R. 1645, 110th Cong. § 701(b)(3) (2007).

84. Telephone conversation between Andrew I. Schoenholtz and a senior DOJ official on May 12, 2008.

85. Dana Leigh Marks, *A System at Its Breaking Point*, L.A. Daily Journal (Aug. 29, 2008).

86. Jennifer Ludden, *Complaints Prompt Government Review of Immigration Courts*, Morning Edition (National Public Radio broadcast Feb. 9, 2006), *available at* http://www.npr.org/templates/ story/story.php?storyId=5198044.

87. The statement was made to a federal commission that has been very critical of EOIR's protection of asylum seekers. U.S. Comm'n on Int'l Religious Freedom, Expedited Removal Study Report Card: Two Years Later 10 (2007), *available at* http://www.uscirf.gov/ reports/scorecard_FINAL.pdf. The Department of Justice held a training conference for immigration judges in August 2006, and it held another conference in 2007, at which Andrew Schoenholtz presented the research published in this book. *Id.*

88. Telephone conversation between Andrew I. Schoenholtz and a senior DOJ official on May 12, 2008.

89. GAO Variation Report, *supra* n.62, at 47.

90. Interview of an immigration judge by Philip Schrag, Sept. 25, 2008.

91. Government Accountability Office, *Asylum Challenges, supra* n.79, at 35.

92. In January 2007, the Department of Justice advised the U.S. Commission on International Religious Freedom that it would explore mechanisms (for example, peer review) to reduce "the significant variations in approval and denial rates among immigration judges." U.S. Comm'n on Int'l Religious Freedom, Expedited Removal Study Report Card: Two Years Later 10 (2007), *available at* http://www.uscirf.gov/reports/scorecard_FINAL.pdf. Three months later, the outgoing director of the Executive Office for Immigration Review announced that its objective had been to "[r]eview a study [apparently the TRAC report, TRAC Immigration Report, Immigration Judges, http://trac.syr.edu/immigration/ reports/judgereports] which highlights disparities in asylum grant rates among immigration judges and make recommendations with respect to this issue" and that this objective had been "[i]mplemented." Memorandum from Kevin D. Rooney, Dir., Executive Office for Immigration Review, to EOIR Employees, in 12 Bender's Immigr. Bull. 597, 601 (2007). However, the director's explanation of what he meant by his statement that the objective had been "implemented" suggests that little had yet been done. He reported that "the Office of the Chief Immigration Judge is improving training for judges, is developing a peer observation and mentoring program to encourage immigration judges to share best practices, and is closely supervising those immigration judges who have unusually high or low asylum grant rates." *Id.* However the Department of Justice has not committed itself to serious initial and regular training through conferences, simulations, lectures, consultations, or other educational events. For a later TRAC scorecard on the degree to which EOIR had improved its performance from 2006 to 2008, *see* Transactional Records Access Clearinghouse, Bush Administration Plan to Improve Immigration Court Lags, http://trac.syr.edu/ immigration/reports/194/ (visited Sept. 28, 2008).

93. Posner, *supra* n.72 at 3.

94. *See id.*

95. In 2006, Attorney General Alberto Gonzales took note of "reports of immigration judges who fail to treat aliens appearing before them with appropriate respect and consideration and who fail to produce the quality of work that I expect from employees of the Department of Justice." Memorandum from Alberto Gonzales, Att'y Gen., to Immigration Judges (Jan. 9, 2006), *available at* http://www.humanrightsfirst.info/pdf/06202-asy-ag-memo-ijs.pdf. In view of these reports, he commissioned a study of the work of the immigration judges. After receiving the study, he announced that he would "establish regular procedures [for the Board of Immigration Appeals] . . . to report adjudications that reflect immigration judge temperament problems." Dep't of Justice, Measures to Improve the Immigration Courts and the Board of Immigration Appeals 3 (2006), *available at* http://trac.syr.edu/tracatwork/ detail/P104.pdf. In April 2007, the outgoing director of the Executive Office for Immigration Review announced that "Board members now report instances where an immigration judge failed to display the appropriate level of profession-alism so that the Office of the Chief Immigration Judge can take appropriate action." Memorandum from Kevin D. Rooney, *supra* n.92, at 601.

96. Guthrie et al., *supra* n.74, at 38.

97. *Id.*

98. The data on immigration courts in this book end in August 2004, but more recent grant rates for each judge are periodically posted on www.asylumlaw.org and on the website of the Transactional Records Access Clearinghouse.

99. Canada's Immigration and Refugee Board (IRB) was concerned about substantial disparities in grant rates from one regional office to another and took steps to address the problem in the late 1990s. It set as a standard a thirty-percentage-point spread in the grant rates between two regions for awards of asylum to applicants from any particular country that produced a substantial number of cases. Note that this measure, a spread of thirty percentage points, rather than a 30% rate difference, was in many cases considerably more tolerant of disparity than the 50% rate difference standard used in our study. When the standard was exceeded, the Board would focus its attention on reducing the disparity through such means as reviewing whether the country-of-origin information was current and promoting discussion among the decision makers. Over time the number of countries with a significant variance in decision making was reduced from over ten to only one or two. More recently, the Canadian headquarters office began to code cases by type of claim as well as by country (for example, claims by Iranian monarchists are classified separately from those by Iranian converts to Christianity). It began to focus on disparities within as well as among regional offices. In addition, the Board has at times designated decisions as jurisprudential guides or as persuasive authorities, with a view to promoting consistency in adjudication with respect to particular types of claims. Telephone Interview with Paul D. Aterman, Dir. Gen. of Operations, Immigration and Refugee Bd. of Canada (June 14, 2007); *see also* Immigration and Refugee Board of Canada, Legal and Policy References, http://www.irb-cisr.gc.ca/en/references/

policy/ index_e.htm. Of course, expressing a preferred position on legal issues or on the state of human rights protection in a country of origin cannot resolve differences among adjudicators in their judgments of the credibility of applicants.

100. E-mail from Joanna Ruppel, Deputy Dir., Asylum Div., U.S. Citizenship and Immigration Servs., Dep't of Homeland Sec., to Andrew I. Schoenholtz (Dec. 18, 2006) (on file with authors).

101. Guthrie et al. note that written opinions induce deliberative thinking (rather than intuitive thinking), supporting the idea that written opinions will be better reasoned on the whole than oral opinions. Guthrie et al., *supra* n.74, at 36.

102. Executive Office for Immigration Review, 2007 Statistical Yearbook, http://www.usdoj.gov/ eoir/statspub/fy07syb.pdf (2008) at G1. This figure includes all immigration court proceedings, not only those involving asylum claims. EOIR's annual statistics do not provide any breakdown on asylum representation. Previous studies have noted higher levels of representation in asylum cases than in general based on special data runs by EOIR (see chapter 3, n. 3), but those studies refer largely to representation at merits hearings. Statistics have not been reported regarding the significant number of asylum cases that do not reach merits hearings. In such cases, representation could play a critical role in ensuring that all asylum seekers assert appropriate claims for relief.

103. Tony Mauro, *Appeals Judges Decry Immigration Case "Tsunami,"* The Blog of Legal Times (Aug. 10, 2008) (quoting Judge Robert Katzmann of the Second Circuit and Juan Osuna, acting chair of the Board of Immigration Appeals), *available at* http://legaltimes.typepad.com/ blt/2008/08/appeals-judges.html. See also the discussion by Judge M. Margaret McKeown and Allegra McLeod in chapter 13 of this book.

104. *See* In Re Gault, 387 U.S. 1, 36–37 (1967).

105. Already in 1924, the Supreme Court said in Mabler v. Eby, 264 U.S. 32, 39: "It is well settled that deportation, while it may be burdensome and severe for the alien, is not a punishment."

106. Ambati v. Reno, 233 F.3d 1054 (7th Cir. 2000); Lopez v. Mukasey, 2008 U.S. App. LEXIS 17010 (10th Cir. 2008); Nehad v. Mukasey, 2008 U.S. App. LEXIS 16245 (9th Cir. 2008); Dakane v. United States AG, 399 F.3d 1269, 1273 (11th Cir. 2005); Cubillos v. United States AG, 2008 U.S. App. LEXIS 13224 (11th Cir. 2008); Afanwi v. Mukasey, 526 F.3d 788 (4th Cir. 2008) (citing: Romero v. U.S. INS, 399 F.3d 109, 112 (2d Cir. 2005); Al Khouri v. Ashcroft, 362 F.3d 461, 464 (8th Cir. 2004); Goonsuwan v. Ashcroft, 252 F.3d 383, 385 n.2 (5th Cir. 2001); Hernandez v. Reno, 238 F.3d 50, 55 (1st Cir. 2001); Xu Yong Lu v. Ashcroft, 259 F.3d 127, 131 (3d Cir. 2001); Mejia-Rodriguez v. Reno, 178 F.3d 1139, 1146 (11th Cir. 1999); Mustata v. United States DOJ, 179 F.3d 1017, 1022 n.6 (6th Cir. 1999); Gandarillas-Zambrana v. Board of Immigration Appeals, 44 F.3d 1251, 1256 (4th Cir. 1995); Castaneda-Suarez v. INS, 993 F.2d 142, 144 (7th Cir. 1993); Michelson v. INS, 897 F.2d 465, 467–68 (10th Cir. 1990); Baires v. INS, 856 F.2d 89, 90 (9th Cir. 1988)).

107. Peter L. Markowitz, *Straddling the Civil-Criminal Divide: A Bifurcated Approach to Understanding the Nature of Removal Proceedings*, 43 Harvard Civ. Rights–Civ. Liberties L. Rev. 289, 346 (2008). Despite his analysis showing that the consequences of deportation can be similar to those of criminal incarceration, Markovitz would extend Sixth Amendment protection only to persons who had been lawfully admitted to the United States, not to asylum applicants, a limitation that the authors do not support.

108. Donald Kerwin, *Revisiting the Need for Appointed Counsel*, in Insight, at 1 (Migration Policy Inst., No. 4, 2005), *available at* http://www.migrationpolicy.org/insight/ Insight_Kerwin.pdf.

109. ABA House of Delegates, Resolution 112A (2006), http://www.abanet.org/ media/ docs/112Arevised.pdf (emphasis added); ABA House of Delegates, Resolution 107A (2006), http://www.abanet.org/publicserv/immigration/107a_right_to_counsel.pdf.

110. We reject the suggestion that "the movement of the law schools into the immigration clinic business . . . will alleviate the representation problem sufficiently." Posner, *supra* n.72. Because law school clinics are and should be primarily devoted to educating students, they will always have low caseloads and cannot satisfy more than an infinitesimal fraction of the need for representation in the many thousands of cases per year in which immigrants are unrepresented (in the Asylum Office as well as in immigration court).

111. See the discussion by Judge M. Margaret McKeown and Allegra McLeod in chapter 13 of this book.

112. Some have suggested simply increasing the size of the Board. *See, e.g.,* Posner, *supra* n.72. We recommend a more systemic approach to improving the administrative appellate role than such a "quick fix" can accomplish. Increasing the number of members in and of itself is unlikely to improve the quality of Board decision making. This is so because the Board must resolve tens of thousands of appeals each year. Of necessity, in the vast majority of those cases, the members assign to the Board staff the duty of preparing recommended decisions. Increasing staff resources, including the number and training of the staff lawyers, and requiring the Board to address the contentions of the appealing party in writing, would ensure more careful review and consistency.

113. If, in some instances, one Board member makes the actual adjudication while another signs the paperwork, the statistics should reflect the actual adjudicators, not those who merely processed the decision.

114. In January 2007, EOIR advised a federal commission that it was drafting a new rule to allow the Board to "increase" the number of written decisions and to refer more cases to three-judge panels, but the commission noted "that this does not respond directly to the [commission's previous] recommendation that all asylum appeals receive written decisions." U.S. Comm'n on Int'l Religious Freedom, *supra* n.92, at 11.

115. Social psychology studies have found that the perception that the decision maker has given "due consideration" to the "respondent's views and arguments" is crucial to individuals' acceptance of both the decision and the authority of the institution that imposes the decision. *See* E. Allan Lind & Tom R. Tyler, The Social Psychology of Procedural Justice 80–81, 104–6 (1988).

116. We would not necessarily require the restoration of three-member panels in every asylum case. It might be sufficient to assign two members to review each case and to discuss their views on it. If, after discussion, the two members continued to disagree, they could either remand the case to the immigration judge (thereby giving the benefit of the doubt—but not granting asylum—to the alien) or request the assignment of a third member to break the tie. This system would presumably be more expensive than one-member decision making but less expensive than assigning three members to each appeal.

117. For example, immigration cases took up only 4% of the Second Circuit's docket six years ago, but now comprise 39% of the court's caseload. Tony Mauro, *Appeals Judges Decry Immigration Case "Tsunami,"* The Blog of Legal Times (Aug. 10, 2008) (quoting Judge Robert Katzmann of the Second Circuit), *available at* http://legaltimes.typepad.com/blt/2008/08/appeals-judges.html.

118. Dep't of Justice, *supra* n.95, at 4. Apparently the key word in this pronouncement is "allow," as opposed to "require." The Executive Office for Immigration Review has stated that it will issue a rule that "will provide a Board member with the ability to refer a case to a three-member panel if the case presents complex or unusual issues of law or fact." Rooney, *supra* n.92 at 603. If this is how the final rule reads, the individual member will have discretion to decide a complex or novel case individually rather than referring the case for a more extensive opinion by a panel.

119. DOJ, EOIR, "Board of Immigration Appeals: Affirmances without Opinion, Referral for Panel Review, and Publication of Decisions as Precedents," 73 Fed. Reg. 35654, 35656 (June 18, 2008), http://www.usdoj.gov/eoir/vll/fedreg/ 2008_2009/fr18jun08.pdf.

120. *See, e.g.,* American Immigration Law Foundation, "Comments on Board of Immigration Appeals: Affirmances without Opinion, Referral for Panel Review, and Publication of Decisions as Precedents; EOIR Docket No. 159P," Aug. 18, 2008, http://www.ailf.org/lac/chdocs/BIAAWO-regcmts.pdf.

121. For a powerful statement of why reasoned decisions are important, *see* Hearing on Oversight of the Department of Justice's Executive Office for Immigration Review before the House Subcomm. on Immigration, Citizenship, Refugees, Border Security, and International Law, Sept. 23, 2008 (testimony of Stephen H. Legomsky). Legomsky also points up an oddity in the Justice Department's ongoing "reform" of asylum adjudication practices: the department's Office of Immigration Litigation, which defends BIA decisions in federal court, is being permitted to "report" adjudications that "reflect . . . poor immigration court or BIA quality," which may affect performance evaluations for immigration judges. But immigrants and their representatives are not given the same reporting opportunity. This differential treatment could result in complaints against judges with high grant rates, but not against judges with low grant rates, and if the judges respond by adjusting their decisions to avoid poor evaluations, it could skew future decisions in favor of lower overall grant rates.

At least one additional change in Board procedures seems warranted. With narrow exceptions (e.g., cases involving denials of asylum because of the bar on filing asylum applications more than a year after entering the United States), a Board decision that rejects the claims of an immigrant may be appealed within thirty days to a United States court of appeals. If the immigrant is represented by a lawyer, the attorney is likely to be aware of that right to appeal. But some immigrants are unable to find or afford lawyers, and they take their appeals to the Board without representation. At present, the Board's order rejecting their claims does not include a notice of the right to a further appeal to federal court. Unrepresented immigrants may not realize that they can appeal until after the thirty-day period has passed. In view of the hardships that accompany deportation, the Board should amend its decision form to inform unsuccessful immigrants of the right to appeal and the tight deadline that they must meet.

122. Asylum Challenges, *supra* n.79, at 59.

123. *Id.* at 61.

124. Judge Richard Posner agrees with this recommendation. *See supra* n.72.

125. S. 2454, 109th Cong. § 501 (2006).

126. We are grateful to Jonathan Le, a student at Georgetown University Law Center, for sharing with us his unpublished paper that identifies these defects with the Frist proposal.

127. In the words of a member of the Board of Immigration Appeals,

> In many respects, the "ball game" in examining issues such as we examine today is the standard of review. For example, the Board is compelled by regulation to affirm an immigration judge's finding that an asylum applicant is not credible unless that decision is "clearly erroneous." The circuit courts operate under similar limitations: the administrative findings of fact are "conclusive unless any reasonable adjudicator would be compelled to conclude to the contrary." These are very deferential standards. It is clear that various circuit judges view the terms "reasonable adjudicator" and "compelled" through different lenses. (Edward R. Grant, Laws of Intended Consequences: IIRIRA and Other Unsung Contributors to the Current State of Immigration Litigation, 55 Cath. U.L. Rev. 923, 961–62 (2006))

128. 8 U.S.C. § 1252(b)(4)(B) (2000).

129. *See, e.g.,* FTC v. Indiana Federation of Dentists, 476 U.S. 447 (1986).

130. Congress should also repeal another provision of the Refugee Act that also limits judicial review, a provision that was added in 2005 without hearings. As amended, the act specifies that an immigration judge may deny asylum if the applicant fails to supply corroboration and the judge believes that corroborating evidence should have been available. It goes on to provide that "no court shall reverse a determination made by a trier of fact with respect to the availability of corroborating evidence unless the court finds that a reasonable trier of fact is compelled to conclude that such corroborating evidence is unavailable." 8 U.S.C. § 1158 (b)(1)(b)(iii) (2008).

131. *See* Stephen H. Legomsky, An Asylum Seeker's Bill of Rights in a Non-Utopian World, 14 Geo. Immigr. l.J. 619, 622 (2000).

PART II

International, Judicial, and Scholarly Perspectives

7 Refugee Roulette in the Canadian Casino
Audrey Macklin[1]

Introduction

The authors of the Refugee Roulette study comprising the first part of this book have produced a truly superb piece of scholarship.[2] Even prior to publication, news of the findings reverberated beyond the legal academy and reached civil society, government, and the front page of the *New York Times*.[3] Indeed, anyone concerned about the public administration of justice should read this book with interest and, dare I say, with alarm. Anyone with experience wresting potentially embarrassing data from a public agency will appreciate the tenacity and commitment required by the authors to complete the task. The Refugee Roulette study is rigorous, thorough, and reflective of enormous diligence.

My remit is to provide a comparative perspective on the Refugee Roulette study, and I will preview my remarks by stating that available statistics on Canadian asylum claim acceptance rates over time also reveal lower but still significant disparities among decision makers and regions. The first part of my comments reflects on possible reasons for the variance in outcomes of asylum adjudication. The second part describes the various institutional and jurisprudential mechanisms deployed by Canada's Immigration and Refugee Board to encourage consistency in decision making.

The government of Canada established the Immigration and Refugee Board (IRB) in 1989. The Refugee Protection Division (RPD) of the IRB performs asylum adjudication. The process that the IRB replaced did not mandate an oral hearing before a decision maker. In one of its early decisions under the Canadian Charter of Rights and Freedoms, the Supreme Court of Canada ruled that the absence of an oral hearing in situations where credibility is at stake violated the right of refugee claimants to security of the person in a process that did not accord with the principles of fundamental justice.[4]

The IRB determines the claims of all eligible asylum seekers. It is an independent tribunal and its Members are appointed by the executive (Cabinet) for fixed but renewable terms. Every eligible refugee claimant receives an oral hearing before a Member, except for those whose claims are considered manifestly well founded. These claims may be determined via an expedited process whereby the claimant is interviewed by a refugee claims officer (RCO), who then makes a recommendation to the Member. If this expedited process does not result in a positive decision, the claimant enters the ordinary stream.

The IRB maintains statistics on the acceptance rates of RPD Members, and the data is obtainable (with considerable effort and expense) through Access to Information Requests. Over the years, the media has periodically reported wild variations in acceptance rates among individual Members and among regional offices. Depending on the commentator, these reports were presented as evidence of the alleged failings of a politicized appointment process that favored patronage over competence, or as evidence of decision makers' gullibility, or their insensitivity, or some combination of the foregoing. Of course, whether the problem resided among those with relatively high or low acceptance rates was often a function of the critic's ideological preferences. In any event, the very fact of the variation seemed to indicate a departure from principled, consistent decision making and a move toward random arbitrariness.

The IRB offers various explanations to account for disparities in acceptance rates among Members and regions.[5] For example, Members who are responsible for the expedited process would be expected to have high acceptance rates attributed to them. Members in the larger offices (especially Toronto and Montreal) work in regional or country teams. Members who usually hear cases from countries that are relatively democratic, stable, and respectful of human rights will understandably have lower acceptance rates than Members whose countries include prominent and chronic human rights–abusing regimes. Moreover, the type of claim from a given country may differ across the IRB offices in Canada. For example, in 1999–2000, the majority of Chinese refugee claimants in Vancouver came from Fujian province, whereas the majority in Toronto came from Tibet. An apparent disparity between Vancouver and Toronto in acceptance rates for Chinese asylum seekers might reasonably be explained by this difference in the dominant profile of the Chinese claimants in each city.

No systematic, longitudinal, and comprehensive academic study of acceptance rates been conducted in Canada. However, a recent analysis of 2006 acceptance rates reveals significant disparities in these rates across Canada.[6] Grant rates among adjudicators who decided at least fifty cases ranged from a low of 6.67% to a high of 96%, with an overall mean of 54.08%. However, once expedited claims were removed from the pool and the data was controlled for country of origin and claim type, the variance still ranged from 35% below the mean to 41% above the mean. The sheer magnitude of the disparities in the Refugee Roulette study (where a variance of 50% from the mean was the minimum of statistical significance) makes the Canadian data appear almost benign, but I would suggest that the Canadian data remains troubling. Suffice it to say that the Immigration and Refugee Board regards it as a matter of concern.

One notable difference between the U.S. and Canadian system is that most refugee claimants in Ontario, Quebec, and British Columbia are represented by lawyers or by immigration consultants. About 90% of refugee claims are referred to either the Toronto, the Montreal, or the Vancouver offices.[7] The competence and quality of representation remains variable, not least because legal aid rates for asylum claims are so low that lawyers may devote less time to a file than it warrants, and because immigration consultants operate under minimal regulation.[8]

Before inquiring into the reasons for variance in acceptance rates, it is worth pausing to consider what makes asylum decisions amenable to this type of comparison in the first place. The authors note similar studies of rulings on procedural challenges to the Environmental Protection Act rules, postconviction sentencing patterns, and reversals of disability benefit denials. But outside of attempts to correlate criminal verdicts to race and gender, I doubt that many studies have compared disparities in judicial conviction rates for armed robbery, or in civil liability for medical malpractice, with a view to drawing inferences about the competence or ideological bent of trial judges. Yet, we might reasonably presume that some judges are more "law and order" oriented than others, and some judges accord physicians undue reverence more than others.

One reason for the dearth of empirical research on rates of criminal conviction or civil liability is that the complexity and idiosyncrasies of each civil or criminal case defy the methodological premise that one can isolate a pool of cases that seem sufficiently alike to test the principle of treating like cases alike.

Asylum seekers are surely no less unique than plaintiffs or defendants, and the events that bring them before a tribunal are no less rich, multilayered, or complex than those of civil plaintiffs or criminal defendants. But one reason why it is possible to undertake the kind of study that the authors have produced is that the asylum process, like any form of mass adjudication of individual cases, tends to flatten out difference, demand simplicity over nuance, and compel the distillation of messy, complicated lives down to a manageable set of narrative fragments that can be inserted into the legal pigeonholes of the refugee definition. Typical features of asylum claims, such as the absence of witnesses (except the claimant), the linguistic and cultural barriers to communication, and the near impossibility of independently corroborating specific events, also create incentives to shear away the indeterminate and indeterminable, leaving behind a skeletal narrative containing only a few salient components. After adjudicating scores of claims from the same region over a period of months or years, I can attest to the eventual extrusion of a few predictable case profiles that more or less described a significant proportion of cases.

I can also offer the observation, based on experience (mine and others), that credibility is the single most important determinant of outcomes. Yet the process of credibility determination remains opaque and undertheorized. Indeed, as I have contended elsewhere, adjudication of credibility is an uncultivated field of normativity whose role and impact in any system of justice dwarfs statutory and constitutional adjudication.[9] As the authors rightly point out, the practice of drawing unsupportable inferences from evidence is a systemic problem that reviewing courts seem unable or unwilling to discipline effectively. If anything, the problem has been exacerbated by the shift from two- to single-member panels, discussed in grater detail below.[10] My tenure as a decision maker convinced me that deliberation about credibility (and other issues) between two competent decision makers was an invaluable mechanism for surfacing, challenging, and correcting the assumptions, inferences, prejudices, and intuitions that determine outcomes, yet are rarely subject to scrutiny. The efficiency gains from the reduction in the size of the panel are obvious; the cost imposed on the quality of decisions and ultimately on asylum seekers is more difficult to articulate and to measure.

If asylum adjudication were more thoroughly individualized, meaningful comparison of outcomes might be less feasible for the same reasons that apply in the criminal or civil litigation context. Of course, the entire asylum regime would collapse under the logistical strain of providing full trial-type hearings, just as the criminal or civil litigation regimes would grind to a halt if not for plea bargains and settlements out of court. If asylum adjudication were less individualized—if, for example, we decided that the human rights situation in Burma was so horrendous that Burmese asylum seekers should be presumptively regarded as refugees (unless they fell into some stipulated exception)—consistency would be easier to achieve. The system as it now exists, however, manages to generate what appears to be the worst of both worlds: inefficiency *and* inconsistency.

One need not endorse a mean acceptance rate as empirically correct to conclude that the narratives generated by the asylum process are too thin to provide any plausible explanation for the huge disparities in grant rates. In light of the authors' recommendations for how the U.S. asylum determination regime might begin to address the crisis they have identified, it may be helpful to examine how Canada's Immigration and Refugee Board manages the issue. The range of factors and strategies begins with the selection and renewal of decision makers, moves forward through judicial review and institutional mechanisms for fostering quality and consistency, and ends with management-driven initiatives in relation to statutory interpretation, country conditions, or claim profiles.

Appointment of Members to the Immigration and Refugee Board

The authors suggest, and I concur, that the results of the Refugee Roulette study give cause for deep disquiet about the overall competence of the corps of asylum adjudicators. Of course, too little variation in acceptance rates might generate anxiety about the independence of decision makers: one might suspect that adjudicators were conforming to actual or tacit direction about whom they ought to accept or reject. This conjecture is buttressed by a recent U.S. Justice Department report that documents how aides to U.S. Attorney General Gonzales explicitly and illegally factored Republican political affiliation and conservative ideological commitments into the appointment process of various public officials, including immigration judges.[11] A subsequent study confirmed that these appointees rejected a disproportionately high number of asylum seekers compared to their peers.[12] Presumably, one would take cold comfort in a finding that this pool of immigration judges demonstrated internal consistency in their acceptance rates.

The criteria for the appointment and reappointment of decision makers obviously affect the overall competence demonstrated in the performance of tribunal functions, which in turn has an impact on the quality of decisions and, one anticipates, on the variability and variance in outcomes for roughly similar cases. The influence of the appointment process on the actual and perceived integrity of the asylum system is undeniable, yet difficult to correlate in quantifiable terms. Suffice it to say that the appointment and reappointment process matters a lot, and in the absence of a critical mass of competent decision makers, little else that one does to promote consistency matters very much.

The IRB is Canada's largest federal tribunal. At one point in the early 1990s, the IRB had over two hundred Members in seven cities across the country. At present, the IRB Refugee Protection Division has 127 Members.[13] Virtually from its inception in 1989, media commentators, lawyers, opposition politicians, and refugee advocates criticized the appointment process as little more than an opportunity for the government to award party faithful and repay political debts.[14] They charged that competence was sacrificed at the altar of political patronage, with the result that the overall quality of IRB decision makers was markedly worse than it would be under a system of genuinely merit-based appointment. Successive governments have promised to neutralize the appointment and reappointment process, and move to a more merit-based system.[15] There is no dearth of alternative models of appointment and reappointment, and while some governments have behaved more egregiously than others, no government thus far has demonstrated the political will to fully relinquish partisan control over the process or the outcomes.[16]

Not all appointments are based on patronage, and not all patronage appointees are incompetent, but there can be little doubt that the overall level of competence among a pool of patronage appointees is lower than what might be achieved from a purely merit-based system. Since the Immigration and Refugee Board is an independent tribunal, Members are not employees of the Department of Citizenship and Immigration Canada, but rather are appointed by Cabinet for fixed terms, usually ranging from two to five years. During the term of appointment, Members enjoy virtually unassailable security of tenure (except for extreme cases of personal misconduct).[17] Apart from judicial review, they cannot be instructed to interpret or apply the refugee definition in a certain manner. Neither can IRB management order decision makers to raise or lower acceptance rates, or to grant or deny a particular application. Of course, it would be naïve to suggest that decision makers are impervious to the political currents circulating around them, or oblivious to the possibility that a controversial decision might displease the politicians who ultimately determine future reappointment. To choose a recent example, the IRB Members assigned to determine the refugee claims by U.S. army deserters from the Iraq War were not blind to the political ramifications and signaling effect of their decisions.

Nevertheless, overt political interference in individual cases is rare. After all, the institutional autonomy of the Immigration and Refugee Board gives politicians a valuable means of deflecting direct criticism of specific decisions—from the media, the public, and even foreign governments—by pointing to the tribunals' independence from government.

The appointment process has evolved from the IRB's inception. At the outset, under the Conservative government of Brian Mulroney, it was entirely opaque: positions were not publicly advertised, there was no discernible process, and many appointees seemed to be people who possessed no obvious qualifications other than political connections to the government. A 1993 newspaper article by an investigative journalist curtly dismissed the Immigration and Refugee Board as a "haven for wives, widows and very good friends" of politicians.[18]

The Liberal government subsequently undertook to advertise positions, and in 1994 introduced a ministerial advisory committee to assist in the selection of Members. Suffice it to say that this did not allay concerns. A Montreal newspaper report in 2001 concluded that thirty-two of fifty-eight IRB Members in that city were "defeated Liberal candidates, former party officials, onetime employees or financial backers of the Liberals, members of previous Liberal governments, former aides to Liberal politicians or friends and family members of prominent Liberals or their campaign contributors."[19]

For those involved in refugee determination, whether as decision makers, lawyers, or advocates, the integrity of the reappointment process was at least as critical as (if not more critical than) the initial appointment process.

In a 2006 interview, former IRB chair Peter Showler indicated that the system in place during his tenure from 1999 to 2002 did little to temper the executive's enthusiasm for partisan appointments. He estimated that of the Members appointed during that period, about half possessed known Liberal party connections, about 10–15% had experience in immigration and refugee matters, and about 30–40% of the total had relevant cross-cultural experience in other fields. Among sitting Members, he felt that about 20% were irredeemably incompetent, another 20% were mediocre, and the remaining 60% (which included patronage appointees) "were just really solid fine Members and all you could really ask of somebody in terms of doing their job."[20]

Responding to persistent complaints and proposals for reform, the Liberal government revised the appointment system again in 2004. The changes appeared significant. For the first time, the IRB identified six specific competencies required to perform the tasks of a Member: oral communication, information seeking, organizational skills, results orientation, self-control, and cultural competence. Two new bodies replaced the ministerial advisory committee: an independent and nonpartisan advisory panel, consisting of representatives from the bar, academe, civil society, and the human resource sector, and a selection board, led by the chair of the IRB and composed of senior IRB officials and experts drawn from other tribunals. On paper, the minister retained the capacity to nominate members of the advisory panel in collaboration with the chair of the IRB. In practice, she delegated the nomination power entirely to the chair, thereby advancing the appearance and reality of a nonpartisan advisory panel.[21] The chair alone was authorized to choose the members of the selection board.

The press release by the minister of citizenship and immigration of the day described the revised process as follows:

> The selection process will include five elements—initial screening, a written test, advisory panel prescreening, selection board interview and reference checks—based on redefined competency standards, which will identify target levels of competence and raise the measurement bar to ensure high quality candidates for appointment.[22]

On the basis of the assessment of the advisory panel and the selection board, the chair of the IRB would submit a list of "highly qualified" candidates to the minister, who in turn would exercise her discretion to recommend appointments to Cabinet, "taking IRB operational requirements, gender, diversity and linguistic requirements into consideration".[23] Crucially, the minister (and Cabinet) would be limited to appointing members from the list presented by the chair of the IRB on behalf of the selection board.

The 2004 reforms revised the reappointment process so that it explicitly takes account of merit, albeit in terms that still leave the minister considerably wider discretion: the IRB chair would assess all Members according to merit-based evaluation criteria, and these performance evaluations would in turn form the basis for recommendations to the minister regarding reappointment. Such evaluations were already in place prior to 2004, and so the reform altered little. As before, the minister would merely be required to "take note" of the chair's recommendations in proposing reappointments to Cabinet.[24]

The following illustration[25] summarizes the revised appointment process instituted by the 2004 reform.

FIGURE 7.1
2004 Revised IRB Appointment Process

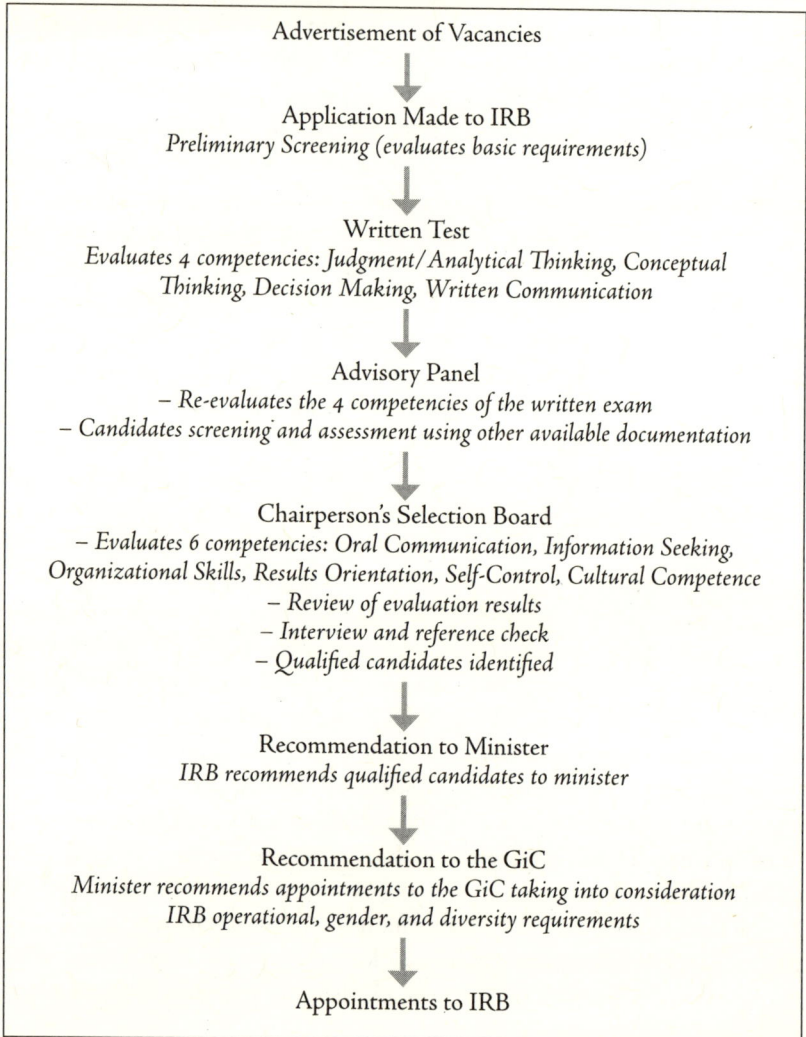

Advertisement of Vacancies

↓

Application Made to IRB
Preliminary Screening (evaluates basic requirements)

↓

Written Test
Evaluates 4 competencies: Judgment/Analytical Thinking, Conceptual Thinking, Decision Making, Written Communication

↓

Advisory Panel
– Re-evaluates the 4 competencies of the written exam
– Candidates screening and assessment using other available documentation

↓

Chairperson's Selection Board
– Evaluates 6 competencies: Oral Communication, Information Seeking, Organizational Skills, Results Orientation, Self-Control, Cultural Competence
– Review of evaluation results
– Interview and reference check
– Qualified candidates identified

↓

Recommendation to Minister
IRB recommends qualified candidates to minister

↓

Recommendation to the GiC
Minister recommends appointments to the GiC taking into consideration IRB operational, gender, and diversity requirements

↓

Appointments to IRB

The new system was rolled out in 2004 and, in the view of the Canadian Bar Association, resulted in "a more transparent and effective IRB."[26] One member of the advisory panel recalled that the quality and self-presentation of applicants improved quickly and dramatically once the message got out that the IRB appointment process would genuinely operate on merit.[27] The competencies captured the relevant skill set, and the written examination was considered fair and appropriately correlated to aptitude. He estimated that about thirty excellent appointments were made to the IRB under the 2004 system, and that the IRB was extremely pleased with the caliber of the new Members. In 2006, a new minister of citizenship and immigration was appointed who did not share his predecessor's commitment to surrendering patronage for merit, and the process stalled at the minister's door.

By January 2007, a newly elected Conservative government retained a consulting firm to redesign the appointment process yet again. The resultant report recommended reviving executive involvement in the evaluation of applicants. It did so by proposing that the advisory panel merge with the selection board, and that the minister appoint half the members of the newly constituted committee, which would in turn generate the list of candidates submitted to the minister and ultimately to Cabinet.[28] The report declined to engage with the reappointment process and blandly remarked that "since these are [executive] appointments, positive performance does not automatically lead to a renewed term."[29] Of course, the executive's lack of commitment to rewarding positive performance with renewal remains one of the most contentious and demoralizing facets of the system, especially for existing Members and IRB management.

Commentators, refugee advocates, and the immigration bar reacted quickly and negatively to the proposed reversion to a more politicized process. A letter from the chair of the National Citizenship and Immigration Section of the Canadian Bar Association conveys the frustration and disappointment provoked by this resumption of overt political involvement in the selection of the pool of nominees for appointment and renewal:

> One of the key concerns leading to the 2004 reforms was that patronage should not govern—or be perceived as governing—the appointment of members to the IRB. . . . Given the IRB's history of rampant patronage in the very recent past, it is imperative that nothing be done to permit it to gain a new toehold. If the Minister appoints any of the external members of the committee screening IRB board members, it will inevitably lead to an increased public perception that patronage, not merit, plays a role in the appointments process, thereby undoing the efforts of the 2004 reforms.

Notably, the chair of the Immigration and Refugee Board and the entire advisory panel resigned shortly after the government announced its intention to introduce the new appointment process. The new process was formally adopted in July 2007.[30]

Despite the articulation of substantive, qualitative criteria for assessing qualifications and performance, as well as the introduction of a written exam designed to test for the relevant skill set, the reinsertion of the executive into the selection of the committee assigned to recommend appointments and reappointments to the minister almost certainly ensures that the current process will fail to live up to the promise of a merit-based system. Political influence and affiliation (with attendant assumptions about ideological commitments) can still matter more than demonstrated (in)competence.

Having said that, it is difficult to gauge the impact of the new appointment process because for the most part, the Conservative government strategy up to the present has been less directed at appointing political supporters than at simply letting the appointments of existing Members lapse without reappointment or replacement. The effect has been both to deprive the IRB of a cadre of experienced personnel and to starve the IRB of decision makers in general. As the outgoing chair of the IRB remarked after his departure, "When I left it had been a very difficult year in terms of appointments and reappointments . . . we lost 300 years of experience in one year."[31] By September 2007, more than a third (37%) of the IRB Member positions remained vacant.[32] The backlog of cases had grown from approximately twenty thousand at the end of 2005 to over thirty thousand by 2007, with a projected increase in processing time from around a year to over two years.[33]

This decline in efficiency and the concomitant escalation in the backlog was manufactured by the Conservative government's inertia well after panels had been reduced from two to one Member (thereby freeing up more decision makers), and during a period when numbers of asylum seekers had actually declined precipitously, largely due to the constrictive impact of the Canada-U.S. Safe Third Country Agreement. Nevertheless, the independent refugee determination system is once again derided as chaotic and inefficient, and Canada is depicted as collapsing under the weight of an unmanageable deluge of asylum seekers. These familiar refrains serve the interests of those on the political right who have always objected that refugee determination should be performed not by an independent tribunal but by civil servants within the Department of Citizenship and Immigration who would answer directly to the minister.

Techniques for Promoting Consistency

1. Judicial Review

The challenge of promoting consistency as a trait of a fair adjudicative regime is that pursuit of this objective collides with and subverts the protection of another equally important virtue, namely, the independence of decision makers. While the discipline of judicial review offers one means of fostering consistency through precedent, several factors render it largely ineffective in Canada. First, access to the Federal Court is constrained by the requirement that judicial review will only be granted by leave of the Federal Court, and the court seldom grants leave and gives no reasons for its leave decisions. Moreover, in order to appeal a decision of the Federal Court to the Federal Court of Appeal, the Federal Court judge must certify a "question of general importance."

These gate-keeping mechanisms are clearly motivated by judicial anxiety over docket control.

A 2000 report by the Inter-American Commission on Human Rights quotes the following statistics, supplied by the Canadian government, on access to judicial review: "[a]pproximately 75% of all persons who receive a negative [refugee] decision seek leave for judicial review of the decision, representing one third of all finalized claims. Of these, about 10% are granted leave; 40% of decisions reviewed are set aside by the Federal Court."[34] This works out to a success rate of 4% for the original pool who applied for judicial review. According to statistics published on the Federal Court website, roughly 14% of leave applications were granted in 2006.[35] In other words, the Federal Court leave requirement constitutes a tightly meshed filter on the access of noncitizens to the courts. Among other things, this practical unavailability of judicial review for the vast majority of rejected asylum claims signals the denigrated status of asylum seekers qua legal subjects. In Canada, as in other common law systems, the entitlement of an individual to seek review of public actors by an independent judiciary is understood as a key component of the rule of law. Yet asylum seekers are routinely denied access to the "ordinary courts" by the ordinary courts themselves.

Despite the low rates of leave, the relatively large numbers of asylum claims (over thirty-five thousand in 2004–2005)[36] and a declining acceptance rate before the IRB meant that around 55% of the Federal Court's workload in 2006 involved disposing of applications for judicial review, or adjudicating judicial reviews in immigration matters (including, but not limited to, refugee cases).[37] About 23% of actual hearings concerned judicial review of rejected asylum claims.[38] In other words, only a tiny proportion of asylum cases end up before the Federal Court, but they make up a disproportionately large component of the Federal Court caseload.

Apart from the procedural obstacles limiting access to judicial review, the available grounds for judicial review are relatively narrow, and preclude a thorough review of the decision on the merits.[39] This limits the utility of judicial review as a means of resolving inconsistencies that do not turn on a narrow question of legal interpretation alone. Relatedly, the Federal Court tends to adopt a deferential stance toward issues of fact or mixed law and fact, with the result that the Court may decline to intervene unless the decision wanders into a zone deemed unreasonable. Moreover, jurisprudence from the Supreme Court of Canada specifically rejects inconsistency within an administrative agency as a reason for applying a more exacting standard of judicial review.[40] Indeed, the reluctance of the Federal Court to resolve divergent interpretations of the refugee definition in relation to the citizenship of Jews from the former Soviet Union figured as a persistent problem for IRB decision makers in the 1990s.[41]

The 2001 Immigration and Refugee Protection Act created a Refugee Appeal Division within the IRB.[42] The mandate of the Refugee Appeal Division was to provide an internal review on the merits, and to thereby reduce the caseload pressure on the Federal Court. Successive governments have refused to proclaim the relevant statutory provisions in force; nor has Parliament repealed the relevant provisions. This systematic refusal to proclaim into force and implement a law duly enacted by Parliament also raises questions about executive compliance with basic principles of the rule of law.

Given the absence of an internal appeal and the limited role of judicial review in fostering consistency, the task falls to the Immigration and Refugee Board itself to devise mechanisms for managing the tension between consistency and independence. Some of these will be recognizable as Canadian analogs to the proposals made by the authors of the Refugee Roulette study.

2. Two-Member Panels

Until the passage of the 2001 Immigration and Refugee Protection Act, asylum decision makers usually sat in panels of two. In the event of disagreement, the decision of the panel was to accept the claimant. Although this practice was not necessarily devised as a tool for promoting consistency, my impression is that two-Member panels did have, or at least could have had, a positive impact on consistency.

As a newly appointed Member, I initially thought the two-Member panel arrangement peculiar, but I quickly came to appreciate the benefits of adjudicating alongside a competent colleague. Sitting with a colleague on a case means that two decision makers read the same documentation, hear and observe the same testimony, weigh the same evidence, and, most importantly, deliberate together. Errors, omissions, or misunderstandings can be caught, assumptions exposed, inferences challenged, and plausibility debated. I recall lengthy and intense discussions about the cogency of the evidence and the credibility of the claimant. In the end, there were probably fewer divergent outcomes than might have occurred had each decision maker made a decision in the case in isolation from the other, a consequence that I attribute in part to the enlargement of perspective and greater reflexivity that deliberation enables. The regular rotation and recombination of

Members into different panels ensured that Members would have the benefit of deliberating with a number of Members, each of whom brought their own distinctive adjudicative capabilities and perspectives to bear. In other words, I believe that two-Member panels offered the potential for fostering greater consistency, at least where Members were competent, qualified, and humble enough to engage meaningfully with the other Member.[43]

As noted earlier, credibility determination is probably the primary function and the most challenging task facing asylum adjudicators. The Anglo-American legal system tends to value deliberation about facts among lay people (juries), but not among judges, who only sit in panels at the appellate level. My experience as a decision maker leads me to wonder whether there is at least as much value in judicial triers of fact sitting in panels as there is for juries or for appellate judges.

Based on my particular experiences, I believe that the overall quality of decisions made by two competent decision makers probably exceeded the quality of decisions made by individual competent decision makers. Two heads are, after all, better than one. Indeed, this helps explain the political dynamics leading to the eventual demise of two-Member panels. In consultations leading up to the Immigration and Refugee Protection Act, refugee advocates urged the adoption of an internal appeal on the merits for failed asylum seekers. The government replied with the Refugee Appeal Division, but simultaneously proposed to move from two-Member to single-Member panels, partly in order to redeploy resources to the new appeal process. The refugee advocacy community largely (if reluctantly) accepted this trade-off. The implicit calculus was that any decline in the quality of decision making attributable to a reduction in panel size would be offset and compensated by the availability of an internal merit-based appeal mechanism for rejected claimants. In the end, however, the advocacy community was sucker-punched: the government reduced the size of the panels but, as recounted above, never implemented the Refugee Appeal Division.

3. Harmonization Strategies

Apart from whatever indirect enhancement of consistency the two-Member panel model could offer, the Immigration and Refugee Board also developed formal channels for communication and consultation among Members in furtherance of encouraging a degree of commonality of approach and, hopefully, consistency in outcomes. At least two institutional features of the IRB warrant special mention, because they furnish the organizational structures that supported and facilitated programmatic initiatives directed at promoting consistency.

The first is the organization of Members in the larger offices into country or regional teams, and the appointment of a team leader within each group. The country/regional team model permits greater specialization and accumulation of expertise among Members because they repeatedly hear claims from the same country or cluster of countries. Members can confer regularly with other Members from the same team, a practice that can only grow in importance with the demise of two-Member panels. In addition, the team leaders in each IRB office can confer with team leaders from other offices around the country in order to compare trends, identify differences, and exchange views. Members from smaller offices, who did not routinely hear a significant number of cases from the same country, profited from participating in discussions with those who had more frequent exposure to a given country. Obviously, this communication among Members could not extend to seeking or offering views about case-specific factual or credibility aspects of a particular case.

The second important structure within the IRB is the Research Documentation Centre. Its contribution to the development of a common evidentiary base deserves special mention. The center is staffed by analysts and researchers with country- or issue-specific expertise. Many are bi- or multilingual. The Research Documentation Centre generates a range of publicly available research products that are intended to address a variety of needs. A brief survey of the documents produced about Somalia is illustrative. The Research Documentation Centre produces a "National Documentation Package: Somalia" containing sixteen standardized topic headings, including "Human Rights"; "Identification Documents and Citizenship"; "Gender, Domestic Violence, and Children"; "Media Freedom"; "Sexual Orientation"; "Religion"; "Nationality, Ethnicity, and Race"; "Political Activities and Organizations"; "Judiciary, Legal, and Penal Systems"; and "Police and Security Forces."[44] Sources of documents contained in the package include nongovernmental organizations (Amnesty International, Reporters Without Borders, WomenWarPeace.org), national and international governmental organizations (United Nations, United States Department of State, United Kingdom Home Office, Norway) and media outlets (*The Australian*). The "National Documentation Package" also contains various documents generated by the Research Documentation Centre itself, such as issue papers, a fact sheet for Somalia, and a selection of responses to information requests submitted by IRB Members on specific topics such as the treatment of children of mixed ethnicity, or the sect of Islam followed by the Bravanese ethnic group.[45] Additional issue papers, an extended response to an information request, and country fact sheets for Somalia are also available on the IRB website,[46] as well as all nineteen responses to information requests produced by the Refugee Documentation Centre since 2003.[47]

In the mid-1990s, IRB management began tracking variations in acceptance rates for specific countries among different IRB offices around the country.[48] After controlling for claim profiles and other potential explanations for divergent outcomes, a disparity of at least 30% over two consecutive quarters was regarded as significant. The IRB then compiled a list of countries with notably discrepant acceptance rates across the country. From the late 1990s onwards, the IRB introduced and refined techniques for mining the statistical data (in order to discern meaningful disparities) and for addressing incongruities among IRB offices.

Thanks to the country team approach, team leaders from the different offices can discuss general issues raised by claims from specific countries, and then take the fruits of that conversation back to the Members in the offices. One response to disparities involves comparing the standard country information file utilized in the different offices. Sometimes, one office relies heavily on a document that another office did not use or to which decision makers attach less weight. The networking facilitated by the team approach enables decision makers to share, discuss, and evaluate documentation with a view to promoting a common evidentiary foundation that decision makers in different cities can utilize and interpret.

The legal services branch of the IRB plays an important role by analyzing a sampling of positive and negative reasons for decisions from the various offices in order to determine sources of discrepancy predicated on divergent legal analyses. Sometimes, different legal analyses can be linked to reliance on different documentation.

The Research Documentation Centre of the IRB, with input provided by country or regional team leaders, produced standardized country documentation packages that are distributed to all the offices. These are disclosed to claimants in advance of the case, and relied upon by Members in assessing claims, in addition to any evidence submitted by the claimant. By 2005, the country files were standardized throughout the country.

Finally, the IRB also orchestrates occasional "Member exchange" programs, where a highly regarded Member from one office sits temporarily in an office where acceptance rates varied significantly. The Member remains in the office at least long enough to participate in a team meeting with all the Members from a given country or regional team. According to former IRB chair Peter Showler, the Member exchange has proven distinctly effective in exposing the reasons for variance:

> This was often the best way to discover the variances in analysis and use of document package. There were occasions where some members of a regional team had to admit that they were using an out-moded analysis or were using credibility in inappropriate ways given the prevailing objective information. . . . At the end of the day, there were regions that stuck to differing views but often it became apparent that there were one or two difficult members within a team who had fixed and biased views. Often the analysis would expose a difference between team members in a particular region. On a few exceptional cases where a member was particularly recalcitrant, the member was transferred to another team.[49]

Showler cautions, however, that Member exchanges only succeeded where they comprised one element of a wider consistency strategy. On the basis of his own experience sitting as a Member in another IRB office before the broader strategy was implemented, he observed, "there wasn't much traction to accomplish anything significant or lasting. Osmosis rarely works on its own."[50]

In addition to these various ongoing activities, the IRB also organizes day-long seminars with in-house experts from the IRB's Resource and Research Documentation Centre and/or academic and external experts who make presentations on country conditions and respond to questions from decision makers and refugee lawyers. For example, conferences were held in the 1990s that addressed the situation of Russian immigrants to Israel (some of whom later came to Canada and claimed refugee status), and Czech Roma.

Measuring the success of the consistency policy is challenging, but the following statistics certainly give reason for optimism: for the years between 1999 and 2003, between eight and twelve major source countries had acceptance rates that varied more than 30% between offices (with some fluctuation over time). By 2004, only four countries remained on the list. It seems reasonable to attribute this shift to the combined and possibly synergistic impact of the package of initiatives adopted by the IRB to promote consistency in decision making.

4. Member Training

The IRB does not officially track individual decision makers' acceptance rates, nor does it undertake to rectify the nonconformity of "outlier" decision makers. At the same time, the IRB does offer customized training for decision makers who demonstrate specific skill deficits. The IRB runs an extensive, lengthy, and ongoing training program for all Members from appointment onwards, and the customized training is designed for those decision makers who fail to develop the requisite skills in case preparation, conduct of a hearing, legal or factual analysis, or explanation of decisions. Insofar as remediable incompetence may lie behind the statistically aberrant acceptance rates of certain Members, customized training can, in principle, promote consistency.

Written reasons for decision are subject to review by IRB's in-house legal counsel prior to release. Legal counsel cannot interfere with the substance or comment on the outcome of the decision; this would run afoul of the public law principle that "she who hears must decide." Nevertheless, legal counsel may draw to the decision maker's attention any aspects of the reasons that misconstrue the law, misapply it to the facts, or fail to effectively explain the legal or factual basis of the decision. This practice has withstood legal challenge that alleged it to be an encroachment on the adjudicative function of decision makers.[51] In principle, the opportunity of legal counsel to detect a Member's pattern of poorly reasoned decisions could be brought to the attention of IRB management with a view to providing the Member with customized training tailored to address the Member's deficiencies.

IRB management evaluates individual Members' performance on an annual basis and prior to reappointment. Members are permitted to read and comment on their performance review. The assessment generally involves, among other things, observation of a Member in the hearing room and review of a sampling of written reasons. This annual evaluation provides another mechanism that feeds into the overall strategy of promoting quality and consistency in decision making.

5. Chairperson's Guidelines

Section 159(1) of the Immigration and Refugee Protection Act (IRPA) authorizes the chairperson to issue guidelines in order to address specific legal or procedural issues, mixed questions of law and fact, or the exercise of discretion. Thus far, guidelines issued for the Refugee Protection Division have concerned gender-related persecution, the application of the refugee definition to civilian noncombatants in civil war situations, and procedural considerations specific to minor and vulnerable refugee claimants.[52] Because guidelines are not enacted by statute or regulation, they do not have the force of law and cannot be regarded as mandatory. However, compliance with the guidelines is strongly encouraged, and recalcitrant decision makers are burdened with the additional task of justifying in writing any decision to deviate from the guidelines.

> Although not binding, members are **expected to follow guidelines,** unless compelling or exceptional reasons exist to depart from them. A member must **explain in his or her reasoning** why he or she is not following a set of guidelines when, based on the facts or circumstances of the case, they would otherwise be expected to follow them.[53] (emphasis in original)

It would be fair to describe the content of most IRB guidelines as embodying a liberal approach to the refugee definition. Indeed, the IRB's path-breaking guidelines on gender-related persecution have been hailed and emulated in many countries, including the United States, as a progressive and gender-sensitive model for interpreting the refugee definition. For reasons that I explore below, Canada's relatively liberal interpretation of the refugee definition does not necessarily correlate with relatively high acceptance rates.

6. Lead Case

In the late 1990s, the IRB grew concerned about an increasing flow of Roma asylum seekers from Central and Eastern Europe. According to reports in the

Canadian media, news of relatively high acceptance rates for Czech Roma had circulated back to the Czech Republic, leading both to consternation from the Czech government and to open promotion of migration to Canada among the Roma community. When it appeared that a similar trend was developing with respect to Hungarian Roma, the IRB developed the "lead case" initiative to cope with the anticipated influx of claims. A "Lead Case Backgrounder" issued by the IRB in March 1999 framed the initiative as a mechanism to "foster consistency and assist decision makers" where shifts in country conditions can result in a surge of claims from a specific country that "often raise issues that recur in many cases":

> To facilitate the efficient, in-depth examination of these recurring issues, the IRB may decide to select a representative sample of similar claims to be dealt with as "lead cases."
>
> A lead case has two objectives. It permits the IRB to establish a baseline of up-to-date and expert information on country conditions in respect of a country from which there is a sudden shift in the volume or type of refugee claim. A lead case also gives focus to the principal legal issues that arise from those facts. This is consistent with the role of the Board's Refugee Division, which acts as an expert tribunal having specialized knowledge of human rights conditions in countries from whose nationals the Board received claims.
>
> The decision to use this concept in dealing with the current influx of Hungarian Roma claimants arose from recent IRB experiences with large influxes of refugee claims from the Czech Republic (also Roma) and Chile.[54]

The methodology of the lead case involved selecting two "typical" cases being handled by the same experienced counsel. With the consent of counsel and the claimants, the IRB would invest resources in bringing as much evidence as possible (including viva voce expert testimony) before a single panel of decision makers. A representative of the minister of the Department of Citizenship and Immigration Canada would participate in an adversarial capacity. (Although, IRPA permits a minister's representative to appear for purposes of opposing any refugee claim, the option is very seldom exercised.) Following the hearing, the panel would render a written, comprehensive, detailed set of reasons that could guide subsequent decision makers hearing substantially similar Hungarian Roma cases.[55] Owing to the horizontal structure of the IRB, decisions by one panel ordinarily cannot bind any other panel. Thus, it appears that the lead case was intended to operate as persuasive, if not formally binding, authority.

The Hungarian Roma lead cases were planned and staged without official publicity, although the event was not a secret within the refugee bar. Neither Canadian nongovernmental organizations involved with Roma and/or refugees (apart from those called as witnesses) nor members of the refugee bar (apart from counsel for the claimants) were consulted or allowed to participate at any stage.

The Toronto hearing spanned over fourteen days in October and November 1998, compared to the half- or single day usually allocated to an ordinary case. In addition to the testimony of the claimants, the panel heard from two expert witnesses for the claimants, and four expert witnesses called by the minister's representative. Apart from claimant-specific evidence, the panel also received extensive documentation regarding country conditions for Hungarian Roma.

In January 1999, the panel dismissed both refugee claims. The panel ruled that the claimants lacked credibility and had exaggerated the severity of the harm they experienced. The panel preferred the evidence of expert witnesses and documentation, and concluded that what the claimants feared was discrimination that did not amount to persecution and/or that Hungary was able and willing to provide adequate state protection.[56] It is important to note that to the extent that the decision turned on doubts about the claimants' credibility, the panel's reasons could not sustain any precedential attribution—unless one (impermissibly) read the reasons as authorization for stereotyping Roma as liars. However, the panel goes on to draw inferences about what these Roma claimants (and presumably other Roma) did experience, namely, discrimination not amounting to persecution. It then supplements this finding of nonpersecution by the alternative conclusion that even if the claimants feared persecution, adequate state protection was available. One can only surmise that these latter two bases for the decision (discrimination short of persecution and adequate state protection) were intended as the precedential elements of the decision, while individual decision makers remained notionally free to make their own findings about the credibility of the claimants before them. Of course, the documentary and expert evidence about the treatment of Roma in Hungary plays an important role in deeming the testimonial evidence of the claimants regarding persecution (versus discrimination) implausible and thus noncredible. Thus, one might contend that the lead case tacitly (if impermissibly) purported to influence decision makers' approach to credibility determination.

In March 1999, only after counsel for the claimants filed an application for leave to seek judicial review did the IRB publicly release the "Lead Case Backgrounder," quoted above. The backgrounder preemptively responded to the allegation that the lead case strategy infringed tribunal independence:

> The use of lead cases does not infringe on the independence of Board decision makers. Neither the evidence presented in lead cases, nor the decisions reached in those cases, are binding on subsequent panels. It is the role of the panel in a subsequent case to assess the evidence presented and examined in a relevant lead case, as well as the reasoning used to arrive at that decision. Given the expertise of the witnesses called by the parties and the quality of the documentary materials introduced in evidence in lead cases, it is expected that the evidence will be given

appropriate weight by subsequent panels. It is also expected that subsequent panels will carefully consider the reasoning applied by the panel in arriving at its decision.

A lead case is not, in itself, determinative of other cases. It is the right of counsel in subsequent cases to call further or better evidence or to bring to light relevant distinctions to be made between the facts of a lead case and those before the subsequent panel. Nothing in the concept of the lead case limits the rights of any party to call evidence or conduct their case in a manner appropriate to the requirements of that case.[57]

The Federal Court dismissed the judicial review application by the claimants, but certified the following question for appeal: "Did the IRB have jurisdiction to conduct a 'lead case' under the Immigration Act?"[58] The Federal Court of Appeal allowed the appeal, but declined to answer the certified question. Instead, the Court of Appeal ruled that the specific steps taken by the IRB to organize the lead case gave rise to a reasonable apprehension of bias and a loss of decisional independence. The Court of Appeal defined the former as circumstances that would lead a reasonable observer to believe that the decision makers had been influenced by an "extraneous or improper consideration," while the latter connoted an "improper" surrender of decision-making autonomy.[59]

The Court of Appeal explicitly sympathized with the IRB's difficult task of "maintaining and enhancing the consistency and quality of its decisions, which is of critical importance to its ability to perform its statutory functions and to retain its legitimacy."[60] At the same time, the Court of Appeal cautioned that the goal of consistency cannot be pursued "at the expense of the duty of each panel to afford to the claimant before it a high degree of impartiality and independence."[61]

Because the Federal Court did not hear the judicial review until 2003, evidence about the acceptance rate of Hungarian Roma before and after the "lead case" was available. The Federal Court of Appeal summarized the data as follows:

[T]he percentage of positive decisions dropped from 71% in December 1998 to 27% in the three months after the decisions in the lead cases were released and to 9% in the next three months. In the first six months of 2002, the percentage of positive decisions in Toronto was 6%, well below the average for this period in Montréal, Calgary and Vancouver.[62]

Notably, several Roma claimants rejected after the lead case was released sought judicial review before the Federal Court on the grounds that decision makers relied too heavily on the documentation supplied in the "Hungarian Lead Case Information Package" and did not conduct their own analysis of the information. Some succeeded, others did not.[63]

The Court of Appeal did not explicitly rely on the decline in the acceptance rate as evidence of bias or interference with independence. Rather, the judges concluded that the cumulative effect of several incidents cast the impartiality of the decision makers into doubt. First, despite the emphasis on consistency as the objective of the lead case, the evidence indicated that only a few Hungarian Roma cases had been decided at the time the IRB decided to launch the lead case. The overwhelming majority of those claims had been accepted, so inconsistency was not actually a problem. However, rumors abounded of a potential influx of several thousand Hungarian Roma claimants. The Court of Appeal remarked that a reasonable person could infer that "the lead case strategy was not only designed to bring consistency to future decisions and to increase their accuracy, but also to reduce the number of positive decisions that otherwise might be rendered in favor of the 15,000 Hungarian Roma claimants expected to arrive in 1998, and to reduce the number of potential claimants."[64]

Secondly, the selection by the IRB of the lead cases and the lawyer with no wider consultation of the refugee bar "would also trouble the reasonable observer."[65] Thirdly, one of the decision makers who heard the case was also part of the management team who devised and organized the "lead case" strategy for Hungarian Roma claims. Thus, "the panel may reasonably be seen to have been insufficiently independent from Board management and thus tainted by the Board's motivation for the leading case strategy."[66] Finally, news of the negative decision in the "lead case" was apparently leaked to the Hungarian media before the decision itself was communicated to the parties, much less the Canadian media. This would lead to a reasonable suspicion that "even before the decisions in the lead cases were signed, officials of the Board or CIC had started to ensure that they were known in Hungary, in order to deter Hungarian Roma from coming to Canada to claim refugee status."[67]

Although the Federal Court of Appeal declined to rule on whether the lead case strategy was unlawful per se, the IRB abandoned it in favor of other instruments that are functionally similar to the lead case but do not engage IRB management in advance of the hearing. In this way, the IRB continues to pursue the general strategy of developing an inventory of precedential decisions while avoiding the legal errors that the Court of Appeal identified as fatal in the Hungarian Roma lead case.

7. Jurisprudential Guides and Persuasive Decisions

Section 159(1) (h) of IRPA authorizes the chairperson of the IRB to "identify decisions of the Board as jurisprudential guides . . . to assist members in carrying out their duties." The reasons for seeking a jurisprudential guide include the need to address an important or emerging issue or to resolve an "ambiguity in the law" or "inconsistency in decision-making."[68] The criteria for designating a given decision as a jurisprudential guide are the cogency of reasoning, the quality of writing, the ventilation of all relevant issues, and the clarity and thoroughness of analysis.[69] The designation of a decision as a jurisprudential guide is publicly communicated in English and French so that counsel and claimants are aware of its status. The chairperson also issues a statement disclosing the scope of applicability of the jurisprudential guide. Decision makers are expected to follow the jurisprudential guide in a manner similar to guidelines:

> Members are **expected to follow the reasoning** in a decision identified as a jurisprudential guide to the extent set out in the accompanying statement, unless there is reason not do so, where the facts underlying the decision are sufficiently close to those in the case being decided to justify the application of the reasoning in the jurisprudential guide. A member must **explain in his or her reasoning** why he or she is not adopting the reasoning that is set out in a jurisprudential guide when based on the facts of the case; they would otherwise be expected to follow the jurisprudential guide.[70] (emphasis in original)

Thus far, the chairperson of the IRB has designated two decisions as "jurisprudential guides." Both concern the availability of state protection in Costa Rica, one for a gay man fearing persecution on grounds of sexual orientation,[71] the other for a young man fearing persecution by gang members.[72] In each case, the claim was rejected on the grounds that the claimant had not discharged his burden of demonstrating that Costa Rica, a functioning, stable, constitutional democracy, was neither able nor willing to furnish adequate state protection.

Because the jurisprudential guides draw conclusions of mixed law and fact about the availability of state protection based on specific documents, the IRB has also developed a "Policy on Document Harmonization in Support of Jurisprudential Guides"[73] in order to ensure that all decision makers use a common set of materials. The IRB has a protocol for amending the documentary packages in support of jurisprudential guides. Claimants, of course, remain free to submit additional documents. Obviously, a significant change to the factual foundation of a jurisprudential guide could justify a departure from the reasoning expressed in that guide, and indeed may lead to a decision by the chairperson to rescind the jurisprudential guide.[74]

Persuasive decisions are functionally identical to jurisprudential guides except that they are not authorized by enabling legislation. The IRB process for identifying a persuasive decision is less formal, and the IRB appears less assertive about promoting it:

> Persuasive Decisions are decisions that have been identified by a Division head as being of persuasive value in developing the jurisprudence of the Division. They are decisions that decision-makers are encouraged to rely upon in the interests of consistency and collegiality.

The application of persuasive decisions by the Division enables the Division to move toward a consistent and transparent application of questions of law or of mixed law and fact. Their designation promotes efficiency in the hearing and reasons writing process by making use of quality work done by colleagues within the tribunal.

Unlike Jurisprudential Guides, decision-makers are not required to explain their decision not to apply a persuasive decision in appropriate circumstances. Their application is voluntary.[75]

To date, the chairperson has identified seven cases as persuasive decisions.[76] One persuasive decision dealt with a pure question of statutory interpretation and was revoked when the Federal Court of Appeal came to the opposite conclusion in a case addressing the same issue.[77] Another persuasive decision concerned the prerequisites for internal flight alternative, which the decision maker interpreted narrowly, leading to rejection of the claim.[78] Three persuasive decisions from October 2006 dealt with unsuccessful Mexican claims. Two were rejected on the basis of adequate state protection and the third on the availability of an internal flight alternative in Mexico City.[79] All three persuasive decisions on Mexico were revoked by the chair in May 2008 because "over time, the evidence on which the above-noted decisions was based may have become dated and the reasoning in the decisions, based on the evidence, may no longer have persuasive value relevant to more recent claims."[80] However, another persuasive decision on state protection in Mexico was added the same day in which the result was also negative.[81] The sole positive persuasive decision in circulation concerns the availability of state protection for a Colombian claimant fearing persecution by armed insurgents or paramilitaries on account of actual or imputed political opinion.[82]

Conclusion

The authors' study of U.S. asylum adjudication is also a study in excellence in advocacy scholarship: empirically grounded in method, measured and constructive in tone, and yet so scandalous in its findings that it demands attention and action. It is difficult to imagine another adjudicatory regime where such apparent disarray and arbitrariness would be tolerated. I am of the view that it is not coincidental that the subjects of this regime happen to be noncitizens, whose claims for protection are typically misread as appeals to charity rather than appeals to justice. It is as if their noncitizen status somehow exempts the state from the ordinary demands imposed by the rule of law on exercises of state power over individuals. Asylum adjudication is only one domain in which one might find evidence in support of this hypothesis.

Canada's Immigration and Refugee Board has been experimenting for at least the past dozen years with various strategies for encouraging consistency without sacrificing independence. A few conclusions about the nature and efficacy of these initiatives warrant emphasis. First, disparities in acceptance rates persist; they can be managed, and diminished, but elimination is neither possible nor reconcilable with the principle of independence. Secondly, without a cadre of qualified, competent decision makers with some degree of adjudicative independence from the executive, virtually all other reforms will be futile. The appointment and renewal system introduced in Canada in 2004 offers one model of a merit-based system that functioned reasonably well within a regime where executive still retained final authority. However, the subsequent undermining of this system, first by the minister who replaced the initiator of the policy, and then by the Conservative government, demonstrates the crucial importance of political will in making it work. Given a system that reserves to the executive the ultimate decision about appointment and renewal, the best-designed system will falter and fail if the executive is not politically committed to the primacy of merit over patronage.

Thirdly, the positive record of the IRB in implementing a consistency strategy that deploys the institutional structure and resources of the IRB, and mobilizes the participation and collaboration of the Members and staff, provides a template that merits the attention of other jurisdictions. The record of success for top-down initiatives from management appears rather mixed, in terms of both fostering consistency and maintaining the balance between consistency and independence. The guidelines dealing with the interpretation of the refugee definition tend toward a broad and generous approach, while initiatives directed at the application of law to a specific factual context almost invariably tend toward the negative. Bluntly stated, guidelines mainly instruct decision makers about "getting to yes" on the law, while the lead case, persuasive decisions, and jurisprudential guides mainly counsel decision makers about "getting to no" on the evidence. The practical consequences of this incongruity become salient once one appreciates that in practice, the overwhelming majority of asylum applications are determined not on the legal question of whether the claim fits within the refugee definition, but on factual assessments of claimant credibility and documentary evidence about country conditions, especially the availability of state protection.[83]

This apparent vacillation at the level of policy maps onto an endemic conflict within the culture of the IRB: palpable tension exists between those decision makers who understand themselves as gatekeepers, tasked with protecting Canada's borders from unscrupulous and undeserving migrants who abuse the asylum system to gain entry, and those who conceive of their mandate in terms of fulfilling Canada's human rights obligations under the Refugee Convention and Canadian law.[84] That is not to suggest that the gatekeepers are without compassion, or that the human rights protectors are incorrigibly naïve. It is to suggest that the ideological orientation of decision makers profoundly shapes the manner in which they engage in their assigned tasks, including legal analysis, evaluation of documentary evidence, and credibility determination. At least some struggles over consistency are, in some sense, proxy wars that erupt because of an inability or unwillingness to directly engage this ideological conflict.

Finally, even if one remains agnostic on the disposition of the Canadian Immigration and Refugee Board, or its U.S. counterparts, toward asylum seekers, there can be little doubt about one matter: these institutions of asylum adjudication operate in an environment of pervasive suspicion regarding asylum seekers. The popular narrative in most Western industrialized states casts asylum seekers as presumptively fraudulent, potential security threats, and probable drains on the public fisc. In consequence, governments remain uncommitted to resourcing inland adjudication agencies with adequate numbers of qualified and competent decision makers. Moreover, these same governments simultaneously invest considerable resources into perfecting techniques for more rapidly and effectively deflecting, deterring, immiserating, and otherwise preventing asylum seekers from accessing protection without the prior approval of the state.[85] On this, there is remarkable consistency.

NOTES

1. The author is an Associate Professor at the Faculty of Law of the University of Toronto and was a Member of the Immigration and Refugee Board from 1994 to 1996. I am grateful to the authors of Refugee Roulette for inviting me to comment on their study, for offering incisive and constructive editorial comments, and for their patience. I also thank Marie-Josée Hadaya and Brigitte Desmeules of Canada's Immigration and Refugee Board for their assistance in providing information. Peter Showler and Nick Summers also provided invaluable information and insights.

2. Introduction, chapters 1 through 6, and the Methodological Appendix of this book (hereinafter "Refugee Roulette study").

3. Julia Preston, *Big Disparities in Judging of Asylum Cases*, New York Times, 31 May 2007, A1, http://www.nytimes.com/2007/ 05/31/washington/31asylum.html?_r=2&hp=&adxnnl=1&oref=slogin&adxnnlx=1180616794-IQUZZZnMofeQlTfPyw/XHw&oref=slogin.

4. Singh v. Canada [1985] 1 SCR 177.

5. Immigration and Refugee Board, "Members' Acceptance Rates: Explanatory Note," June 2007, http://www.ccrweb.ca/ documents/rehaag/LetterIRB2008.pdf.

6. All data regarding acceptance rates in this paragraph from Sean Rehaag, Troubling Patterns in Canadian Refugee Adjudication (2008) 39(2) Ottawa Law Review 335, tables 4, 5, 6, 8, appendix 1.

7. See John Frecker, "Immigration and Refugee Legal Aid Cost Drivers" (Department of Justice Canada, 2002), at 49–50, http://www.justice.gc.ca/en/ps/rs/rep/2003/rro3lars-17/rro3lars-17. pdf (accessed 8 August 2007).

8. John Frecker, Pierre Duquette, Donald Galloway, Fernand Gauthier, William Jackson, Gregory James, "Representation for Immigrants and Refugee Claimants: Final Study Report," Legal Aid Research Series, Department of Justice Canada, October 2002, http://www.justice-canada. ca/en/ps/rs/rep/2003/rro3lars-16/rro3lars-16.pdf. In 2003, the Canadian Society of Immigra-

tion Consultants (CSIC) was established as a voluntary, self-regulating professional body with a mandate to protect the public from unscrupulous consultants and to ensure the competence and professionalism of their members. In 2008, the Standing Committee on Citizenship and Immigration released a report on immigration consultants, which concluded that the CSIC's performance was deficient in a number of ways. Among its recommendations were several directed at statutory reforms to empower the CSIC to investigate, adjudicate, and enforce matters relating to consultant misconduct. See House of Commons Standing Committee on Citizenship and Immigration, "Regulating Immigration Consultants" (Report No. 10), June 2008, http://www2.parl. gc.ca/content /hoc/Committee/ 392/CIMM/Reports/RP3560686/cimmrp10/cimmrp10-e.pdf.

9. I explore the ethical implications of this observation in *Truth and Consequences: Credibility in Refugee Determination*, International Association of Refugee Law Judges, Realities of Refugee Determination on the Eve of a New Millennium (Haarlem: IARLJ 1999).

10. This change was effected by s. 163 of the Immigration and Refugee Protection Act, SC 2001, c. 27.

11. See discussion in chapter 6, pp. 101–103.

12. *Vetted Judges More Likely to Reject Asylum Bids*, New York Times, http://www.nytimes. com/2008/08/24/washington/24judges.html (last accessed 25 August 2008).

13. *Refugee Backlog Headed for Record High as Tories Slow to Appoint Adjudicators*, Canadian Press, 8 April 2008,www.immigrationwatchcanada.org/index.php?module=pagemaster&page_user_ op=view_page&PAGEID=30978NMN_position=92:90.

14. See, e.g., Peter Showler, Refugee Sandwich (Montreal: McGill-Queen's Press, 2006), at 225–26.

15. See, e.g., Immigration and Refugee Board of Canada, "Minister Sgro Announces Reform of the Appointment Process for Immigration and Refugee Board Members" (Press Release), Ottawa, March 16, 2004.

16. Macleans.ca, "Refugee Board in Flux: With Its Chairman Departing, Critics Suggest the IRB Is Moving Backward," 28 February 2007, http://www.macleans.ca/ article.jsp?content=20070228 _101241_7772 (accessed 3 March 2008).

17. Incidents that have led to suspension include attempting to extract sex or money in exchange for a favorable decision. For an example, see Ctv.ca, "Refugee Judge Charged with Breach of Trust," 12 October 2006, http://www.ctv.ca/servlet/ ArticleNews/print/CTVNews/20061012/ Refugee_judge_061012/20061012/?hub=TorontoHome&subhub=PrintStory (accessed 3 March 2008).

18. Stevie Cameron, *A Haven for Wives, Widows, and Very Good Friends: The Immigration and Refugee Board Shows What Can Go Wrong in a Patronage System*, Globe and Mail, 5 June 1993, at D4.

19. Quoted in "Refugee Board in Flux," *supra* note 16.

20. Christin Schmitz, *Bar Condemns Conservatives' Treatment of Refugee Board*, lawyers weekly, 11 May 2007, http://www.lawyers weekly.ca/index.php?section=article&articleid=472.

21. Nick Summers (former member of Advisory Panel), Personal Interview, 3 October 2008.

22. Citizenship and Immigration Canada, "Backgrounder: Reform of the Immigration and Refugee Board's Governor-in-Council Appointment Process," http://www.cic.gc.ca/english/ department/media/backgrounders/2004/2004-03-16.asp (last accessed 25 August 2008).

23. Id.

24. Id.

25. Public Appointments Commission Secretariat, "Governor in Council Appointments Process: Immigration and Refugee Board of Canada (Annexes)," January 2007, http://www.cic.gc.ca/ ENGLISH/ pdf/pub/irb-annexes.pdf, at ii (last accessed 25 August 2008).

26. Jean-Philippe Brunet, chair, Canadian Bar Association, National Citizenship and Immigration Section, "Change to IRB Selection Committee Appointment Process," Letter to Norman Doyle, MP, chair, Standing Committee on Citizenship and Immigration, 16 April 2007, http://www.cba.org/cba/submissions/pdf/07-22-eng.pdf.

27. Nick Summers, *supra* note 21. Whereas past applications would often emphasize political activities related to the government in power, the applications began to highlight applicants' skill set in relation to the job of adjudicating refugee claims.

28. Public Appointments Commission Secretariat, *supra* note 25.

29. Id.

30. Citizenship and Immigration Canada, "Minister Finley Announces Revised Selection Process for Appointments to the IRB" (News Release), 7 July 2007, http://www.cic.gc.ca/english/department/media/releases/2007/2007-07-09.asp.

31. Christin Schmitz, *Bar Condemns Conservatives' Treatment of Refugee Board*, lawyers weekly, 11 May 2007, http://www.lawyers weekly.ca/index.php?section=article&articleid=472.

32. Canadian Council for Refugees, "Canada Refugee System Made Vulnerable by Government Inaction" (Media Release), 25 September 2007, http://www.ccrweb.ca/eng/media/pressreleases/25sept07.htm.

33. Id.

34. Inter-American Commission on Human Rights, *Report on the Situation of Human Rights of Asylum Seekers within the Canadian Refugee Determination System*, 2000, para. 83, http://www.cidh.org/countryrep/canada2000en/table-of-contents.htm (accessed 3 March 2008). Leave rates also vary dramatically between Federal Court judges, suggesting that consistency might be an issue for them as well.

35. Federal Court of Canada, *Activity Summary: January 1 to December 31, 2006*, http://cas-ncr-nter03.cas-satj.gc.ca/portal/page/ portal/fc_cf_en/Statistics_dec06 (accessed 3 March 2008).

36. Immigration and Refugee Board, *Performance Report 2004-5*, p. 22, http://www.tbs-sct.gc.ca/rma/dpr1/04-05/IRB-CISR/IRB-CISRd45_e.pdf (accessed 3 March 2008).

37. Federal Court of Canada, *Activity Summary: January 1 to December 31, 2006*, supra n.35 .

38. Id. In addition to immigration and citizenship matters, the jurisdiction of the Federal Court includes admiralty, aboriginal law, tax, intellectual property, and judicial review of federal boards, agencies, and tribunals.

39. Judicial review is available for a breach of due process, an error of law, a decision or remedy that is ultra vires, or an "erroneous finding of fact that [the board] made in a perverse or capricious manner or without regard for the material before it." Federal Courts Act, RSC 1985, c. F-7, s. 18.1(4).

40. Domtar Inc. v. Quebec (Commission d'appel en matière de lésions professionnelles), [1993] 2 S.C.R. 756 (inconsistency in statutory interpretation by two different tribunals not a basis for judicial intervention in the absence of operational conflict).

41. See, e.g., Grygorian v. Canada (1995), 33 Imm. L.R. (2d) 52 (Israeli Law of Return confers automatic citizenship on Russian Jews, so asylum seeker must establish fear of persecution against Russia and Israel); Katkova v. Canada (1997), 40 Imm. L.R. (2d) 216 (Russian Jews are not virtual citizens of Israel).

42. IRPA, s. 110–111.

43. I reflect further on the significance of two-Member panels in Macklin, *Truth and Consequences*, supra note 9.

44. Immigration and Refugee Board, "National Documentation Package, Somalia," 2 April 2008, http://www.irb-cisr.gc.ca/en/research/ndp/index_e.htm?id=635 http://www.irb-cisr.gc.ca/en/research/ndp/index_e.htm?id=635.

45. Id.

46. Immigration and Refugee Board, Country of Origin Research, Issue Papers, Extended Responses, and Country Fact Sheets (Somalia), http://www.irb-cisr.gc.ca/en/ research/publications/index_e.htm?cID=202.

47. Immigration and Refugee Board, Country of Origin Research, Response to Information Requests, Somalia (2003–2008), http://www.irb-cisr.gc.ca/en/research /rir/index_e. htm?action=search.results&ft_criteria=&subject_criteria=&Country=202&lng=1&y1=2003&y 2=2008&sortby=date.

48. The description accompanying notes 48–50 is based on the account of Peter Showler, former chair of the Immigration and Refugee Board (1999–2002), e-mail correspondence with author, 3, 4 October 2008 (on file with author).

49. Id.

50. Id.

51. Bovbel v. Canada, [1994] 2 FC 563.

52. For a description of the Chairperson's Guidelines and links to the individual guidelines, see Immigration and Refugee Board, "Chairperson's Guidelines," http://www.irb-cisr.gc.ca/en/references/policy/guidelines/index_e.htm (accessed 9 September 2007).

53. Immigration and Refugee Board of Canada, "Policy on the Use of Chairperson's Guidelines," Policy no. 2003–7, 23 October 2003, at 5, http://www.irb-cisr.gc.ca/en/references/ policy/policies/guides_e.htm (accessed 9 September 2007).

54. Quoted in Geza v. Canada (Minister of Citizenship and Immigration) (F.C.), [2005] 3 F.C.R. 3 at para. 5.

55. At the relevant time, refugee claims were normally heard in panels of two; since the implementation of IRPA in 2002, the panel is usually a single decision maker.

56. Cited in Geza v. Canada, *supra* note 54 at para. 9 (FC).

57. IRB, "Lead Case Backgrounder," quoted in Geza v. Canada, *supra* note 54 at para. 5 (FC).

58. Kozak v. Canada (Minister of Citizenship and Immigration), [2006] 4 FCR 377 (CA), at para. 6.

59. Id. at para. 57.

60. Id. at para. 56.

61. Id.

62. Id. at para. 39.

63. See cases cited by the Federal Court of Appeal in Kozak, *supra* note 58 at para. 41.

64. Id. at para. 61.

65. Id. at para. 63.

66. Id. at para. 65.

67. Id.

68. Immigration and Refugee Board, "Policy on the Use of Jurisprudential Guides," Policy no. 2003-01, 21 March 2003, at 3, http://www.irb-cisr.gc.ca/en/references/policy/ policies/jurisguides_e.htm (accessed 9 September 2007).

69. Id.

70. Id. at 4.

71. Refugee Protection Division, TA0-15870, 31 March 2003, EA Schlanger, http://www.irb-cisr.gc.ca/en/references/ policy/juriguides/tao-15870_e.htm (accessed 9 September 2007).

72. Refugee Protection Division, TA2-14980, 27 May 2003, EA Schlanger, http://www.irb-cisr.gc.ca/en/references/ policy/juriguides/ta2-14980_e.htm (accessed 9 September 2007).

73. Policy no. 2003-3, 15 May 2003, http://www.irb-cisr.gc.ca/en/references/policy/policies/harmon_e.htm (accessed 12 September 2007).

74. Id. at 3.

75. Immigration and Refugee Board, "Persuasive Decisions," http://www.irb-cisr.gc.ca/en/references/policy/ persuasive/index_e.htm (accessed 10 October 2007).

76. For the list of persuasive decisions, see Immigration and Refugee Board, Persuasive Decisions, http://www.irb-cisr.gc.ca/en/references/policy/persuasive/index_e.htm.

77. Immigration and Refugee Board, "Policy Note: Notice of Revocation of Persuasive Decision," 13 December 2005, http://www.irb-cisr.gc.ca/en/references/ policy/polnotes/rev_ma200869_e. htm (accessed 10 October 2007) (standard of proof for internal flight alternative under s. 97 of IRPA).

78. MA1-10302, 27 August 2002, G. Ethier, http://www.irb-cisr.gc.ca/en/references/policy/persuasive/ma1-10302_e.htm (accessed 10 October 2007).

79. TA4-17681, 17 January 2006, D. Morrish (adequate state protection in Mexico for claimant fearing persecution from drug dealers), http://www.irb-cisr.gc.ca/en/references/ policy/persuasive/ta417681_e.htm (accessed 10 October 2007); TA4-10802 & T4A-10803, 28 November 2006, V. Rangan (internal flight alternative in Mexico City for gay couple), http://www.irb-cisr.gc.ca/en/references/policy/persuasive/ta41080203_e.htm (accessed 10 October 2007); TA4-18833, December 2006, G. Griffith (adequate state protection in Mexico for claimant fearing persecution by drug dealers), http://www.irb-cisr.gc.ca/en/references/policy/persuasive/ta418833_e.htm (accessed 10 October 2007).

80. IRB, "Policy Note: Notice of Revocation of Persuasive Decisions," http://www.irb-cisr.gc.ca/ en/references/ policy/polnotes/rev_ta417681_10800203_18833_e.htm, 8 May 2008 (accessed 28 August 2008).

81. The persuasive decision added is TA6-07453, 26 November 2007, S. Alidina (Mexican claim rejected because of availability of adequate state protection).

82. MA4-04467, February 2005, Me. Martial Guay, http://www.irb-cisr.gc.ca/en/references/policy/persuasive/ma4-04467_e.htm (accessed 10 October 2007).

83. Macklin, *Truth and Consequences, supra* note 9.

84. For a very recent, nuanced, extensive, and compelling empirical exploration of the IRB institutional culture, see François Crépeau and Delphine Nakache, Critical Spaces in the Canadian Refugee Determination System: 1989–2002 20 International Journal of Refugee Law 50–122 (2008).

85. A legal challenge to the Canada-U.S. Safe Third-Country Agreement succeeded before the Federal Court and was overturned by the Federal Court of Appeal. In February 2009, the Supreme Court of Canada denied leave for a further appeal. For an account of the Canada-U.S. Safe-Third Country Agreement, see Disappearing Refugees 36 Columbia Human Rights Law Review 101–61 (2005); Andrew Moore, Unsafe in America: A Review of the U.S.-Canada Safe Third-Country Agreement 47 Santa Clara L. Rev. 201–84 (2007).

8 Refugee Roulette
A UK Perspective
Robert Thomas[1]

THE DISPARITIES IN asylum adjudication, as evidenced by part I of this book,[2] are without doubt a cause for concern. At the same time, it is important to caution against any temptation to castigate the asylum process as operating as nothing but a random or arbitrary lottery. When the decision task is viewed from the perspective of decision makers, with the same information available to them, it often reveals a patterned and rational process at work, albeit one undertaken under various pressures that can militate against the pursuit of quality decisions. While consistency is certainly desirable, it can be difficult to attain because of the inherently problematic nature of the asylum decision task itself, that of prognosticating the risk of persecution or ill treatment often only on the basis of limited and uncertain evidence. In this chapter, I explore how the problem of inconsistency in asylum adjudication is handled in the United Kingdom and consider whether there are any useful comparisons for the U.S. system. In doing so, I suggest that there is certainly scope for the quality of the asylum process, in both the United States and the United Kingdom, to be improved and that such improvements may exert some influence on reducing the scope for disparate outcomes among different decision makers. At the same time, despite our best efforts, a degree of inconsistency may well remain because of the especially difficult challenges posed by asylum decision making.

Asylum Adjudication in the UK and Consistency

The UK's asylum process is perhaps not too dissimilar from that which operates in the United States. Like the U.S. system, it comprises a complex process of administrative and judicial decision making.[3] Initial decisions are taken by the responsible governmental department, the Home Office.[4] Rejected claimants may appeal to the Asylum and Immigration Tribunal (AIT), the specialist independent judicial tribunal staffed by some seven hundred immigration judges, who undertake a fact-based merits appeal and give detailed written reasons for their decisions.[5] There is then a further right of challenge to the higher courts for any error of law.[6] Like the U.S. system, the UK asylum process has, over the last decade, experienced a high volume of cases. Furthermore, the UK asylum process has, alongside its U.S. counterpart, often been criticised for operating as an asylum lottery, and concerns as regards the overall quality of the process have been persistently raised.[7]

However, in the UK, there is a dearth of empirical data to substantiate the degree of (in)consistency among different decision makers and at the different stages of the process. Occasionally, particular instances arise that illustrate the scope for disparate decision making. Consider, for example, the case of *Otshudi*, in which the appeal of a Congolese asylum applicant had been dismissed by one immigration judge while that of his brother, on almost identical evidence, had been allowed by another judge. This was, the Court of Appeal noted, "an illustration, if an alarming one, of the fact that two conscientious decision-makers can come to opposite or divergent conclusions on the same evidence."[8] The court held that while the discrepant outcomes were a matter for concern, they did not give rise to any legal ground of challenge.

There is also much anecdotal evidence that decision making is often inconsistent. One comment frequently made by those representing both asylum seekers and the Home Office before the Tribunal is that they can often predict the outcome of an appeal simply by knowing which particular judge is to hear the appeal.[9] Those who represent and campaign on behalf of asylum applicants have often discussed whether they should expend the necessary resources to collect the evidence with which to test these assumptions. One argument against this has stemmed from the concern that such an effort could be counterproductive: given the highly charged political context of asylum adjudication, the risk is that the media and a section of political opinion might use such data in order to highlight how generous some decision makers are and therefore suggest that they ought to be reined in.

From the perspective of asylum decision makers themselves, there would appear to be every incentive not to produce such data because of the political risks associated with it. Consider recent experience in the Republic of Ireland. Here, a legal challenge was made to the Irish Supreme Court by three asylum applicants against having their appeals heard by an individual member of the Refugee Appeals Tribunal on the ground of that member's perceived bias. The member concerned was reported to have rejected the vast majority of the one thousand appeals he had heard.[10] While the case was settled out of court, the individual tribunal member resigned amidst political controversy over the Tribunal's independence and calls for greater transparency in the appointment of its members and in the allocation of cases to its members.[11] Given the acute political sensitivities attached to asylum decision making, it is unsurprising, though also regrettable, that both the Home Office and the AIT have been reluctant to publish, or even collect, relevant data.

In this context, the Refugee Roulette study is, from a UK perspective, of particular significance. It presents valuable and robust empirical evidence that the outcomes of asylum decisions in the United States often vary—not as a result of individual cases but because of the identity of the decision maker. While it is impossible to know whether or not this is also the case in the UK, it would indeed be surprising if the UK system had somehow managed to attain a greater degree of consistency.

The Asylum Decision Problem and Consistency

How then can we approach the problems raised by inconsistency in asylum adjudication? One way to do this is to begin by considering the nature of the asylum decision problem itself. The task of determining whether someone is a refugee, or otherwise in need of protection, is a peculiar type of decision making.[12] It normally requires an assessment of two different, though related, aspects of that person's claim: first, whether the asylum applicant's story is credible; and, secondly, whether conditions in the relevant country would place her at risk of persecution or serious ill treatment if she were returned. The decision maker must then assess the particular circumstances of an individual's case, but that assessment must be made within the general context of what is known about the conditions in the country from which refuge is being sought.

The distinctiveness of the decision task is matched by its notoriously problematic nature and the high error costs of incorrect decisions. In many cases, there are acute difficulties in deciding whether or not someone is genuinely in need of protection. The difficulties posed by fact finding in asylum cases are often acute because of the language and cultural differences between claimants and decision makers, the paucity, changeability, and unreliability of evidence that corroborates or contradicts the claimant's case, the emotional and other pressures on claimants, and the administrative and time pressures on decision makers. In some cases, the law governing eligibility for asylum may be unclear. Even when the facts are established and the law is clear, "there can be room for legitimate differences of opinion as to whether a claimant to refugee status has made good his claim."[13] Few other decision system are regularly required to produce decisions that might, if wrong, directly result in an individual suffering persecution, torture, or even death—or, alternatively, the admission of people into a country who would otherwise not be entitled to enter it. Few other decision systems operate within such a highly charged political environment, one that often assumes that many, if not most, asylum claimants are in reality economic migrants and are abusing the system.

Clearly, consistency is a desirable feature of any large-scale adjudication process; the principle of ensuring that like cases are treated alike is often held up as an inherent aspect of justice.[14] Apparent inconsistency can also be an indicator of inaccuracy. Indeed, as the task of objectively assessing the accuracy of decisions that normally depend not on issues of law but on issues of fact is impossible, consistency can be a useful proxy for testing accuracy. If a decision-making process produces inconsistent outcomes in essentially similar cases, then surely some of its decisions must also be substantively incorrect—either because genuine cases have been rejected or because nongenuine cases have been accepted.

Consistency can, though, be a difficult value to pin down because few cases are ever exactly alike. Asylum cases, in particular, are often recognised as being highly fact-specific. The culture of asylum decision making, certainly in the UK, tends to exhibit a strong sense that every case is different and that each case turns on its own individual facts. While justice requires the like determination of like cases, it does not require the like determination of cases that merely share some similarity.

Alternatively, there is the risk that consistency may be achievable in particular classes of asylum cases but only because the relevant tests have been raised to such a height that few, if any, claimants will succeed in mounting them. Something like this has been occurring in the UK in relation to HIV/AIDS cases, those cases in which claimants with either condition claim that their removal to a country that cannot provide adequate medical care will drastically reduce their life expectancy and therefore amount to serious ill treatment, contrary to article 3 of the European Convention on Human Rights. Conscious of the sheer volume of potential applicants from, amongst other places, sub-Saharan Africa, both the UK courts and the European Court of Human Rights have held that removal in such cases will be unlawful only in those rare instances where very exceptional circumstances mean that the humanitarian grounds against removal are compelling.[15] Decision making in such cases is therefore likely to be more consistent simply because the majority of claims will be rejected; decision makers have little room for maneuver because the test has been placed so high.

While of considerable importance, consistency—and with it, accuracy—are only two goals underpinning the asylum adjudication process. They must be mediated with other important values such as efficiency, speed, and cost. Asylum decision processes, in particular, are often under intense pressure to process cases quickly so that those individuals who do not qualify for asylum can be removed in order to maintain immigration control. For these reasons, attempts to ensure absolute consistency are likely to be unattainable. The more realistic objective may then be one of seeking to limit undue inconsistency.

In any event, even this modest goal presents a challenge because the fact- and judgment-based nature of the asylum-decision task requires an essentially evaluative or interpretive appraisal of various kinds of evidential material against the eligibility criteria for asylum.[16] The evidential material will often include the claimant's own (oral and written) evidence; documentary evidence particular to the claim; perhaps a medical report to the effect that the scarring on the claimant's body is consistent with past persecution or torture; and country information reports (from various governmental and nongovernmental agencies) detailing the social and political conditions in the country from which refuge is being sought. The range of evidence will, though, often be of variable quality and frequently contain little that is either firm or objectively verifiable. To decide whether a claimant has established the relevant facts to the appropriate standard of proof—which in the UK is the reasonable-degree-of-likelihood test—the decision maker will have to assess the relative weight of the evidence, a task inextricably bound up with subjective questions of value. What decision makers make of the evidential material presented to them is a matter for their own conscientious judgment. If we assume that different decision makers bring different values to bear on the highly individualistic task of making asylum decisions, then inconsistency is inevitable.

Other sources of inconsistency may emanate from procedural aspects of the decision system. As chapter 3 of this book indicates, the presence of representation for asylum claimants at hearings is a key factor in explaining differential success rates.[17] In the UK, for an asylum applicant to benefit from publicly funded representation before the Tribunal, she must fulfill the "merits test" (that is, be assessed as having a 50% or above chance of success).[18] While most appellants benefit from publicly funded representation at the appeal stage, the number of unrepresented appellants has increased due to restrictions on publicly funded representation introduced in 2005; although there are no statistics on this matter, anecdotal evidence suggests that unrepresented appellants tend to experience a lower rate of success than represented appellants. There has also been the problem of the frequent absence of a Home Office representative before the Tribunal, presenting difficulties for the immigration judge, who will want to avoid undermining the perception of judicial impartiality by cross-examining the claimant and thereby "descending into the arena," while at the same time wanting to have the evidence properly tested in order to make findings of fact.[19]

A related issue is that of the appropriate judicial posture at appeal hearings: should the process be an adversarial contest between the parties or should the judge take an active or interventionist role in collecting relevant information? In the UK, the asylum appeals jurisdiction has traditionally adopted an adversarial approach: the appellant bears the burden of proof; it is for the parties to decide which evidence they wish to rely upon; and, to maintain their independence, judges should refrain from asking too many questions.[20] However, some judges do take a more proactive approach, for instance, through direct questioning of appellants or by conducting internet searches for relevant country information, which may be decisive to the outcome of a case either way.[21] By contrast, others take the view that responsibility for producing evidence rests solely with claimants, as they bear the burden of proof. This difference of approach can only compound the risk of inconsistency.

While decision makers may themselves appreciate the scope for inconsistency, they are often not in a position to remedy it. Promoting consistency across a large number of decision makers will often require the establishment of systems or processes of oversight. But this can create difficulties if those decision makers are to remain independent. Moreover, proposals to control against inconsistency by *ex post* oversight often encounter objections that they will impose additional cost and delay. The better way might then be to devise *ex ante* methods of promoting consistency that themselves form part of the inputs into the decision-making task rather than controlling outputs. However, for this to be successful, such methods need to be attuned to the particular character of the decision problem. It is a central aspect of asylum decision making, that of assessing credibility, to which we now turn.

Credibility

The task of assessing the credibility of an asylum claimant, whether she is telling the truth, is often the most decisive aspect of asylum decision making. The vast majority of cases either succeed or fail depending on the decision maker's view of the claimant's credibility. Along with the principal authors of this book, I suspect that most of the disparities in asylum adjudication relate to decision makers' judgments of claimants' personal credibility.[22] The risk is always that credibility assessments by different decision makers will be inconsistent. Indeed, it may be no exaggeration to state that there is scope for inconsistent credibility assessments by the same decision makers.

In the UK, it is widely recognised that decision makers may well reach inconsistent credibility assessments. As the Court of Appeal has explained, judging credibility "is inevitably a difficult and imperfect exercise. Different tribunals hearing the same witnesses may reach quite different views. A search for theoretical perfection is doomed to failure."[23] The view within the Tribunal is no different. As an immigration judge has noted, "it is a lot like a lottery when it comes to credibility because we all have such different views and different approaches."[24]

The reason why there is such scope for inconsistency when assessing credibility is, I would suggest, the same reason why it is so difficult to reduce it: the intrinsically problematic nature of the task. There is no rule book by which credibility can be assessed, only a number of pointers or indicators, each of which has to be applied with care. One approach is to assess the internal cogency of an applicant's story: surely, a genuine claimant would present a coherent and internally consistent story? However, the problem is that someone genuinely in fear of his life might well advance a story that contains various discrepancies while a competent liar may present a perfectly coherent account. The decision maker's task is then to determine whether the discrepancies are sufficiently significant to cast doubt on the story. Of course, assessing the weight to be attributed to such discrepancies clearly requires the decision maker's own subjective preferences; questions of fact and value are inseparable.

Another approach is to consider whether or not the claimant's story corresponds with what is known about his country of origin: if it does, then this may lend weight to it. At the same time, it does not necessarily follow that an individual's story is true merely because it is consistent with the background country information: those facts may be well known by nationals of that country who will not be at risk on return. Similarly, the decision maker might consider whether the claimant's story is plausible given what is known about his country, but this provides only limited assistance: a story may be implausible but nevertheless be accepted as true; or it may be plausible but yet not properly believed.[25] Then there are the difficulties posed by assessing credibility in the cross-cultural context in which asylum adjudication operates. By definition, much of the evidence will refer to societies with customs and circumstances that are very different from those familiar to the decision maker. Indeed, it is likely that the country an asylum seeker has left will be suffering from the sort of problems and dislocations with which the overwhelming majority of residents of the decision maker's country will be wholly unfamiliar. The decision maker must then be cautious before finding an account to be inherently incredible, because there is a considerable risk that he will be overly influenced by his own views on what is or is not plausible, and those views will have inevitably been influenced by his own background. At the same time, the decision maker need not take at face value factual assertions that are completely contrary to common-sense human experience.[26]

Alternatively, a claimant might produce medical evidence of physical scarring in support of her claim that they have suffered past persecution—itself a serious indicator of a future risk of persecution.[27] However, if the claimant has scarring and even if this scarring is consistent with having been caused by torture, it may equally be consistent with other causes also.[28] Such medical evidence will then often not corroborate a claimant's story but only have the more limited role of not negating it; whether or not the decision maker accepts that the scarring was caused in the manner described (for instance, through torture) will depend on the view taken of the claimant's overall credibility. Likewise, someone suffering from Post-Traumatic Stress Disorder (PTSD) might experience difficulties in presenting her story. There is then a great need to take account of any psychological difficulties when it comes to assessing credibility, but this cannot mean that *all* individuals diagnosed with PTSD have a memory loss that prevents them from giving a proper account of themselves in the context of an asylum claim.[29] In any event, it can be difficult for a decision maker to decide what weight ought to be placed on a psychiatric report diagnosing PTSD because of the different possible causes for that condition. A claimant may have PTSD as a result of past persecution, which, if accepted, would lend weight toward reaching a positive credibility finding. At the same time, there may be other obvious potential causes for the signs of the claimant's anxiety, stress, and depression; for instance, the claimant may be depressed because he is facing return to the country that he has left, at some expense, and that may well not be a pleasant place to which to return.[30]

As none of the indicators of credibility is conclusive one way or the other, in practice, the task of assessing credibility is highly dependent on that nebulous aspect of decision making: human judgment and visceral reaction to the evidence presented. Measuring the influence of decision makers' presuppositions and tacit assumptions on their substantive decision making is always a tricky endeavour. I would, though, concur with the authors that much of the disparity in asylum adjudication can be attributed to the differing degrees of scepticism or credulity that decision makers bring to bear when assessing credibility.[31] Some decision makers may approach the stories of many asylum claimants, arriving from war-torn countries with poor human rights records, with both an accommodating mindset and a propensity to believe what they are told. By contrast, other decision makers may adopt the view that many foreign nationals falsely claim asylum because of a desire to improve their conditions of life and consequently adopt a more suspicious approach. Given the frequent absence of firm, objective evidence as to whether a claimant would be at risk on return, this then is the problematic nature of asylum adjudication: the great difficulty, if not impossibility, of knowing whether or not claims are being decided accurately; the elusive nature of fact finding; and the inherent difficulty of not really being able to determine what the truth is. The risk is that some decision makers may become too cynical and case-hardened whereas others may become too credulous and willing to believe. It is because of such features that it has been argued that asylum adjudication requires a very particular conception of impartiality: that of abstention from preordained or conditioned reactions to what one is being told; this means not so much knowing others as knowing oneself—perhaps the hardest form of knowledge for anyone to acquire.[32] At the same time, given the complex array of factors involved, it seems virtually impossible to ensure consistency across decision makers.

There have, though, been a number of responses to this view. One is to suggest that initial asylum claims and appeals should not, as they normally are, be decided by a single Home Office case worker or immigration judge but by a panel of such people. This could, of course, enable greater understanding among different decision makers, as reaching joint decisions requires panel members to come to a closer understanding of each other's perspective. At the same time, it would also add to the length and cost of the process and to the time needed to write up decisions. In any event, making decisions by a panel provides no guarantee that its members will necessarily reach the same views on credibility. As one AIT member has explained, it is not unknown for immigration judges, when sitting as a panel, to be unable to reach a common view on credibility so that the case has to be reheard by a different panel.[33] Nevertheless, decision making by a panel may reduce the prospects of disparate decision making.

Another response has been to attempt to formulate rules as to how decision makers are to assess credibility as a means of promoting consistency. The difficulty here is that this may produce only rules laden with discretion. To illustrate, the European Community Qualification Directive states that where an applicant's statements are not supported by documentary or other evidence, then those aspects shall not need confirmation when the applicant has made a *genuine* effort to substantiate his claim; has given a *satisfactory* explanation as to the absence of such supporting evidence; has given *coherent* and *plausible* statements; has lodged his claim at the earliest opportunity unless there was *good reason* for not doing so; and has established his *general credibility*.[34] Of course, decision makers' assessments of all of these aspects may well differ.

Alternatively, the legislature might introduce rules intended to steer decision makers toward consistently negative credibility assessments, but this can result in an adverse reaction if decision makers view such rules as an attempt to interfere with their independent fact-finding role. In 2004, the UK Parliament introduced legislation to guide the assessment of credibility by requiring, for instance, that decision makers take into account a failure by an individual to claim asylum in a safe country before he reached the UK (of course, a failure to claim asylum en route cannot mean that an individual is not at future risk on return).[35] This provision, viewed by both the AIT and the courts as an unwarranted interference with independent judicial fact finding, exerts little, if any, influence on substantive decision making.[36]

Beyond this, the general approach adopted in the UK might appear to be a somewhat fatalistic one, as it acknowledges the risk of inconsistency while simultaneously drawing succour from its existence elsewhere. When presented with concerns over inconsistent decision making, many immigration judges simply accept it and emphasize that it is not unique to asylum adjudication but also a feature of, for instance, the criminal justice process. Of course, the reassurance that immigration judges draw from disparities in other litigation contexts may be illusory if, as the Refugee Roulette study found with regard to U.S. circuit courts, the disparities in asylum cases are much greater than, for instance, in civil cases.[37] A second view held by some judges is that they neither record nor wish to know the consistency or otherwise of their decision making, as this may itself exert an influence on their future decision making at the expense of considering the merits of each individual case. A third view, articulated by one judge, is that it is necessary for judges to exercise their own individual judgment rather than attempt to reduce asylum law to the application of rigid formulae. On this view, decision making is, of course, messy, imperfect, and based on the decision maker's own life experiences, preconceptions, and prejudices and hence variable and unpredictable. While this seems to detract from the predictability we would ordinarily desire from an adjudication process, what else can realistically be expected when making the right decision on asylum cases is inherently difficult and no one really knows what is meant by the "right" decision anyway?[38]

The causes of inconsistency in credibility assessments are difficult to suppress; whether or not a claimant is believed might depend largely on the luck of the draw. At the same time, some decision has to be reached. This, it might be thought, is a counsel of despair—one shared, as it happens, by some decision makers. But it is not to say that there is no way forward. As this book suggests, training decision makers better and equipping them with greater resources so that they may acquire both a better appreciation of their task and the capacity with which to undertake it can do much to improve the quality of their decisions. However, it is extremely difficult to suggest how greater consistency can be secured as regards credibility when there are no firm standards for decision makers to go by. The upshot is that the risk of inconsistency becomes an accepted feature of the process.

Country Information and Consistency

What then of the second aspect of the asylum decision problem—the assessment of conditions in the country from which asylum applicants fear to be returned? In order to determine whether or not a claimant's fear of persecution is objectively well founded, it is necessary for the decision maker to consider country-of-origin information detailing the conditions in the relevant country. The prospects for inconsistency here arise because of the different range and quality of country information presented by the parties: some claimants may present more complete and up-to-date country information than others. Then there are also the difficulties in evaluating the significance of such information. While guidelines exist on the criteria by which country information is to be evaluated, different decision makers may nevertheless draw different conclusions from such evidence as to whether or not asylum claimants would be at risk on return.[39] The AIT has on occasion been criticised by the courts for reaching differential assessments of the relevance of country information. For instance, in a line of cases concerning religious apostasy in Iran, some tribunal panels decided that Christian converts would be at risk on return to Iran whereas other panels, drawing upon much the same country information, arrived at exactly the opposite conclusion.[40] Such inconsistency was, the courts recognised, understandable because it is perfectly possible for different decision makers to arrive at different conclusions, even from the same country information, as to whether or not asylum claimants would be at risk on return. However, it was not satisfactory. As the Court of Appeal noted in 1997, "consistency in the treatment of asylum-seekers is important in so far as objective considerations, not directly affected by the circumstances of the individual asylum-seeker, are involved."[41] Moreover, it would also be inefficient for the Tribunal to undertake multiple assessments of the same situation in the same country. The courts were then defining a role for the Tribunal in order to secure consistency in the assessment of country conditions, a role subsequently defined by the Tribunal as its "country guidance" system.

The Tribunal has then produced various country guidance decisions containing generic and authoritative guidance on recurring country issues as to how decision makers should handle asylum cases raising those issues. The basic purpose of the country guidance system is for the Tribunal to consider a particular country issue in depth and then produce guidance that is then to be applied by immigration judges deciding subsequent appeals that raise the particular issue. These determinations are produced by the Tribunal's twenty-five senior judges, typically after a thorough review of all relevant country information and often also country-expert evidence.[42] These decisions should normally be followed by immigration judges in subsequent appeals.[43] The senior judges seek to produce country guidance on those country issues that are frequently raised in appeals before immigration judges. In this way the Tribunal seeks to promote consistency of decision making in relation to the general circumstances obtaining in individual countries and to ensure that generally recurring factors relating to country conditions are periodically the subject of careful and authoritative assessment.[44] Country guidance determinations therefore give no guidance on individual personal facts: the guidance is limited to the general circumstances, or the circumstances for a group of people with a particular characteristic, in the country in question.

To illustrate this technique, consider the issue of whether or not Somali nationals who are members of minority clans would be at risk on return. Given the number of Somali nationals who have sought asylum in the UK over recent years, this has been an important and recurrent country issue. If it were left to each immigration judge hearing appeals in which this issue was raised to examine the wealth of country information concerning the treatment of Somali minority clans and draw her own conclusions, then there would be substantial risks of inconsistency. Some judges might conclude that minority clan members would be at risk while others might not. Even though differing views could reasonably be reached through the same material, the resulting inconsistency would be undesirable. However, the senior judges have issued guidance to the effect that minority clan members will generally be at risk.[45] The role of the judge hearing a Somali appeal is therefore one of applying this guidance and determining questions of credibility specific to the particular claimant (Is this individual claimant a member of a minority clan? If so, might she still be able to access an area of safety?). As the general country issue has been resolved, at least until country conditions change or new country information comes to light, this promotes both consistency and efficiency in the decision-making process.

Given the range of different nationalities of asylum applicants and the country issues that commonly arise in asylum cases, country guidance decisions have assumed a central role throughout the asylum process. There are currently some 276 country guidance determinations covering some fifty-eight countries generating asylum applicants.[46] Many important country issues have received detailed and repeated examination by the senior Tribunal judiciary.[47] Furthermore, country guidance decisions have been used to identify positive risk categories in addition to those categories of person who will not be at risk. So, for instance, the Tribunal has issued guidance to the effect that Congolese nationals with an ethnic, political, or military profile in opposition to the Congolese government comprise recognised risk categories whereas failed asylum seekers are not for that reason generally at risk on return to the Democratic Republic of Congo.[48]

In essence, the Tribunal's country guidance system is a form of judicial policy-making through adjudication. These cases establish either the generic categories of asylum applicants who may or may not be at risk on return or the risk factors that should be taken into account when assessing any particular case. It still remains for the decision maker to assess credibility in the specific case, but once this has been done, country guidance should normally be applied unless country conditions have changed. In other words, country guidance concerns "risk-group existence" while the individual decision maker must still determine the question of an individual claimant's "risk-group affiliation."[49] While the higher courts have encouraged the Tribunal to establish and develop its country guidance system, highlighting its "beneficent and valuable role . . . in achieving consistency," they also set down certain safeguards as to how it is to operate.[50] When issuing country guidance, the Tribunal needs to set out its reasons with particular rigour. It should also take special care to ensure that its decision is effectively comprehensive by considering all relevant country information and by explaining what is made of it.[51]

However, even in relation to country conditions, consistency has its limits. Country guidance concerns assessments of country conditions, which, by definition, are liable to change. The ever-present risk is that of promoting consistency in the assessment of country conditions when those conditions have changed. If country guidance decisions are to promote consistency, they need to possess an element of binding authority, but if they possess too much, then this risks pursuing artificial consistency. Therefore, the general status of country guidance decisions is that they are not to be regarded as legally binding but as authoritative in subsequent appeals so far as that appeal relates to the country guidance issue in question and depends upon the same or similar evidence.[52] In light of the importance of consistency, any failure by an immigration judge to follow a clear, apparently applicable country guidance case or to show why it does not apply to the case in question is likely to be regarded as grounds for review.[53] At the same time, it is always possible for an asylum claimant to advance fresh country evidence to show that an applicable country guidance decision is either wrong or has been overtaken by changes in country conditions.[54] The fact that the Tribunal has produced country guidance does not mean that the situation in the relevant country cannot change, nor that an individual's relationship to it does not have to be distinctly gauged in each case. A flexible rather than a rigid approach is required in relation to both the status of country guidance and its application.

While the purpose of the country guidance system is to attempt to promote consistency, it is not, though, without its own difficulties. Country guidance determinations are always susceptible to becoming out of date and are not subject to any sunset-date provision—it would be more satisfactory if they were, as this would require the Tribunal regularly to consider whether fresh country information necessitated modification of its guidance. While it is always possible for claimants in a subsequent appeal to adduce evidence to show that a country guidance decision was wrong or that country conditions have changed in the meantime, there is no guarantee that a claimant, especially if unrepresented, will be in a position to do this. There is also the risk that the decision maker may apply country guidance by rote rather than by attuning it to the particular circumstances of an individual claimant. As country guidance cases can affect literally thousands of asylum applicants, they have sometimes been challenged before the courts, which have on occasion remitted cases back to the Tribunal, thereby prolonging the process.[55] There has also been debate as to whether the senior judges themselves possess the necessary expertise with which to evaluate country conditions and set wide-ranging guidance.[56] At the same time, there have been improvements in the quality of the country guidance issued. While initial country guidance decisions were criticised because they did not live up to the promise of an effectively comprehensive examination of available country information, there has been a marked change of approach as, more recently, the Tribunal has undertaken far more thorough analyses.[57]

Of course, other asylum systems may not have developed a formalized country guidance system like that which exists in the UK simply because there is relative agreement or informal guidance on those classes of claims who may or may not be at risk on return. Alternatively, some asylum decision systems, like the Canadian Immigration and Refugee Board, may have their own country-of-origin information units that respond to focused queries or requests for information from decision makers.[58] On balance, the AIT's country guidance system, while not perfect, provides an input into the decision-making process designed both to assist decision makers and to secure a degree of consistency. Its other advantages are that it promotes legal certainty, as both parties to the process and the immigration judiciary are able easily to find what guidance exists. If the parties wish to dispute a particular aspect of established guidance, then they know what needs to be the focus of their evidence or argument. The system also enables the Tribunal to refine its own understanding of country conditions as successive decisions lead to the production of up-to-date country information and the identification of consequential country issues to be grappled with had previously been unrecognised. Moreover, there are no real concerns as regards judicial independence because it is the senior tribunal judges who issue country guidance, which immigration judges, as their subordinates, are expected, in the absence of good reason to do otherwise, to follow.

Does the AIT's country guidance system provide a model that could be adopted by the U.S. asylum process? To some extent, this would depend on the extent to which the degree of disparity in the U.S. asylum process could properly be attributed to differential assessments of country conditions by decision makers. On this point, this book is inconclusive; the principal authors suspect that many of the disparities arise from the different ways decision makers approach the task of assessing credibility, but they cannot be sure that this is actually the case. If it is the case that the disparities that the study has uncovered are not caused by differential assessments of country conditions, then there is no real case for developing a country guidance system. If, on the other hand, such differentials do exist, then this might at least justify some consideration as to whether some move toward a country guidance system may be a suitable means of seeking to reduce the levels of disparate decision making. If so, then we might also note that this would also provide a strong case for a change of approach in respect of the provision of publicly funded representation for asylum applicants in the United States. After all, if an individual asylum claimant's case is selected for the purpose of issuing generic country guidance that might influence many other similar cases, then there is an overwhelming case for that claimant to receive, at no expense to herself, high-quality representation to ensure that the relevant country information materials are well researched and that the resultant guidance is also of high quality. In any event, this would seem to be precisely the type of issue that ought, following the ground-breaking study that forms the core of this book, to be the focus of subsequent research.

Enhancing Consistency?

The posture of the UK system toward inconsistency in asylum decision making could be summarised as follows. With regard to assessing credibility, it is probably impossible, because of the nature of the task, to eliminate inconsistency because so much depends on subjective factors. However, insofar as decision making concerns more objective considerations, such as the assessment of country information, consistency can be promoted by establishing country guidance decisions that lay down the approach to be taken toward a particular country issue until overtaken by changes in country conditions. Despite the development of the country guidance system, there still remains considerable scope for inconsistency outcomes.

So, what then is to be done? Like the principal authors of this book, I would reject the idea of quotas for decision makers.[59] Codification is often a matter of degree, but the dynamic nature of asylum adjudication may preclude detailed codification; alternatively, codification may, like the European Community Qualification Directive considered above, still leave scope for discretion.

Certainly, most of the proposals suggested by the authors would exert a beneficial effect in terms of improving the general quality and reliability of asylum adjudication and thereby possibly reduce the scope for inconsistent decisions. Depoliticization of asylum decision making at both the initial and appeal stages is a *sine qua non* for an independent asylum process that can command public confidence—as are both adopting rigorous hiring standards for judges and providing them with the necessary resources and training. Peer-review performance appraisals of decision makers, combined with better training and support, are certainly important. Continuous training for judges on general "judgecraft" skills—how to conduct hearings, undertake fact-finding in relation to both credibility and country information, and write well-reasoned decisions—needs to be complemented with training in the particular skills required by asylum adjudication. This training could cover the following matters: developing a greater awareness and knowledge of other cultures; learning how to handle medical and country-expert evidence; and developing a greater appreciation of the difficulties that traumatised victims of torture and persecution may experience when giving evidence. Better feedback from higher-level to subordinate decision makers on the quality of their decisions, in addition to discussion forums, could also be beneficial in terms of encouraging decision makers at different levels of the process both to reflect upon their role and to learn each other's perspectives with the view to enhancing the quality of decision making.[60] At the same time, while these suggestions are necessary, they are not sufficient. They must also be matched by decision makers themselves recognizing the importance and special demands of impartiality in asylum adjudication, that is, by their seeking to approach each case with a mental attitude of open-mindedness and a willingness to consider any story presented by an asylum claimant irrespective of how improbable or implausible it may at first appear. There are also aspects of the decision process that can be improved. Ensuring that all claimants are represented would be a major enhancement of the process, but, given constraints on public spending, this may not be realistic.

Proposals such as these would without doubt improve the overall quality of asylum decision making, and for that reason alone they are desirable. Will they, though, be effective in reducing the disparities identified in this book, especially when, as the book indicates, such disparities are so deeply ingrained? It is far more difficult to answer this question, but I would express some caution in this regard. Improving the quality of the process may, to some extent, reduce the disparities in asylum adjudication, but it is difficult to know for certain whether this would actually be the case. The basic challenges and difficulties posed by asylum adjudication will, of course, remain. Decision makers may still differ in the ways in which they approach cases and in the outcomes they reach. The problematic aspects of asylum adjudication will also remain; they are permanent and not merely transient features.

As an illustration of this point, consider the suggestion that immigration judges in the U.S. system should issue written decisions after merits hearings.[61] Such a change would certainly raise the quality of decision making and also professionalize decision makers by requiring them to act in the same way that most other judicial office holders are required to—provided, of course, that they are given adequate time to produce well-reasoned written decisions. I am confident that this would be a valuable improvement to the U.S. asylum process. However, the following question arises: would the provision of written reasons reduce the level of disparities in decision making? Drawing upon experience in the UK, I am not sure that it can be assumed that this would necessarily be the case. The reason for this is that while a requirement to produce written reasons may lead to those decisions being of better quality, it does not absolve the decision maker from grappling with the problematic aspects of the asylum decision itself. The decision maker will still have to make findings of fact as to the credibility of the claimant's story by assessing the weight that should be attributed to the evidence presented, and it is perhaps in this respect that the prospects for inconsistent decisions are greatest.

Consider the practice of issuing written decisions in the UK. In each asylum appeal determined by the AIT, an immigration judge must produce a written determination containing both the decision and the reasons for it.[62] These written determinations are usually divided into the following subheadings: the applicable rules and principles of refugee, asylum, and human rights law; the basis of the claimant's case; the evidence advanced by the parties and an analysis of that evidence; the parties' submissions; any points of law that may have arisen; and, crucially, the judge's findings of fact and conclusions as to whether or not the claimant is a refugee or otherwise in need of protection.[63] Within the AIT, it is considered *essential* for immigration judges to produce written determinations in each appeal if the judge is to make clear findings of fact on the material issues, and to give proper, intelligible, and adequate reasons for arriving at those findings.[64] In general administrative law terms, reason giving serves both non-instrumental and instrumental purposes: it can enhance the claimant's sense of fairness and human dignity; and it can also perform an important role either by persuading those affected by the decision that it is a just and reasonable one or by enabling them to identify grounds for challenge. Reason giving can enhance the decision makers' own understanding of the nature of their decision task; it can also promote accurate decision making.[65] In the specific context of asylum adjudication, giving reasons serves a number of important functions. Adequately reasoned decisions are particularly important when the credibility of an appellant is in issue; a lack of reasoning may demonstrate a failure adequately to address the fundamental question, is the applicant telling the truth?[66] Giving reasons in support of an adverse credibility finding is important not only for the discipline that it imposes upon the fact finder but also in order to distinguish between those aspects of the claimant's story that are central to its veracity or otherwise and those aspects that are only peripheral.[67] Furthermore, reason giving is important to ensure that the decision maker has properly analysed the relevant country-of-origin information and, in the UK, applicable country guidance.

The production of written, as opposed to oral, reasons may then impose an important discipline requiring the judge to consider carefully the grounds for the decision rather than merely arriving quickly at an instinctive decision. However, while the production of written reasons may lead to better decisions, it does not necessarily follow that the inconsistencies would be reduced to an acceptable level. That the AIT produces written decisions has not in any way moderated the concerns over the inconsistency of decision making; if anything, it has fuelled them because observers can compare the different reasons provided by different judges and see the variations of approach among them. While judges give written reasons, it is still possible that there are wide variations in the outcomes of those decisions. This is the case because so much is dependent on the assessment of credibility and, as we have seen, it is often possible for a decision maker to arrive at either possible outcome—case allowed or dismissed—because there is no fixed or ascertainable way to assess a claimant's credibility. Underlying all this, of course, is the intractable nature of the asylum decision problem and the different presuppositions that decision makers bring to it. Furthermore, the vast majority of AIT decisions are simply ordinary determinations by immigration judges. Unlike country-guidance determinations, they possess no precedential value whatsoever; they merely are adjudication decisions based on the evidence presented before the immigration judge in the appeal of one individual appellant and dealing with the situation in a particular country at a particular moment in time. In short, giving written reasons may promote better decisions and instill greater confidence in decision making, on behalf of both the general public and the appellate courts, but it may not follow that it will necessarily reduce the range of disparities among decision makers.

Conclusion

I do not wish to be taken as implying that it is not worthwhile implementing the reforms proposed by the principal authors of this book; on the contrary, any effort that can be secured to improve the asylum process is self-evidently worthwhile. Most asylum-decision systems operate under pressure to process a high volume of cases quickly, and the quality of both their processes and substantive decisions have often been criticised; for instance, the Canadian Immigration and Refugee Board, sometimes held up as an exemplar of a high-quality asylum-decision-making system, has been subjected to withering criticism.[68] In this respect, the UK system is no different and has often been criticised in terms of the quality of decision making and the governmental emphasis on speed and efficiency at the expense of fairness and quality. Pursuing a quality agenda is therefore the most productive way ahead. At the same time, it is likely, I suspect, that a degree of inconsistency in asylum adjudication will always remain because of the inherent uncertainties and ambiguities that attend asylum decision making. Moreover, this is probably inevitable in the context of an adjudication process that must make notoriously difficult decisions often only on the basis of limited and uncertain evidence and with respect to which there is usually much scope for differences of view.

1. The author is a Senior Lecturer in Administrative Law at the School of Law of the University of Manchester. This paper draws upon data drawn from empirical research into the asylum appeal process in the United Kingdom funded by the Nuffield Foundation (AJU/00124/G). The views expressed herein are mine alone.

2. Introduction, chapters 1 through 6, and the Methodological and Ninth Circuit Appendices of this book.

3. On the UK asylum process, see generally Iain MacDonald & Ronan Toal, Macdonald's Immigration Law and Practice (London: Butterworths, 7th edn., 2008).

4. In 2007, the Home Office received 23,430 asylum applications. However, in addition to these new applications, there were some 450,000 older, undecided "legacy" cases that had accumulated over the previous decade. See Home Office, Asylum Statistics 1st Quarter 2008 (London: Home Office, 2008).

5. The AIT determines ordinary immigration appeals in addition to asylum appeals. In 2007–2008, immigration judges determined a total of 161,517 appeals, of which 13,700 were asylum appeals (Asylum and Immigration Tribunal, Provisional Statistics for 2007–2008 [2008], obtained from www.ait.gov.uk [visited July 25, 2008]). As the AIT is overseen by the Tribunals Service of the Ministry of Justice (MoJ), it is structurally independent of the Home Office. At the same time, because the MoJ and the Home Office share a Public Service Agreement concerning the processing of asylum claims, the Tribunal is placed under managerial targets concerning its performance; for instance, it aims to determine 75% of asylum appeals within a period of six weeks. See Tribunals Service, Annual Report 2007–08 (2007–08 HC 802), page 98.

6. Asylum and Immigration (Treatment of Claimants, etc.) Act 2004, s.26. The UK's immigration and asylum appeals processes have both been regularly reformed. See Geoffrey Care, The Judiciary, the State, and the Refugee: The Evolution of Judicial Protection in Asylum—A UK Perspective, 28 Fordham Int'l L.J. 1421 (2004); Robert Thomas, Evaluating Tribunal Adjudication: Administrative Justice and Asylum Appeals, 25 Legal Studies 462 (2005). In August 2008, the Home Office consulted on a further set of reforms, see Home Office, Consultation: Immigration Appeals—Fair Decisions, Faster Justice (London: Home Office, 2008).

7. See Raekha Prasad, The Asylum Lottery, The Guardian, January 25, 2002. For a recent critique of the UK asylum process, see the Independent Asylum Commission, Fit for Purpose Yet? The Independent Asylum Commission's Interim Findings (London: Independent Asylum Commission, 2008). For specific concerns over the quality of initial Home Office decisions, see House of Commons Home Affairs Committee, Asylum Applications (2003–04 HC 218); Amnesty International, Get It Right: How Home Office Decision-Making Fails Refugees (London: Amnesty International, 2004). Partly in response to such concerns, the Home Office has allowed the United Nations High Commissioner for Refugees to establish a "quality initiative project" to monitor both the procedures and the application of the refugee criteria by initial decision makers. See http://www.bia.homeoffice.gov.uk/sitecontent/documents/aboutus/reports/unhcrreports/ (visited July 25, 2008).

8. Otshudi v Secretary of State for the Home Department [2004] EWCA Civ 893, para.11. See also Ocampo v Secretary of State for the Home Department [2007] Imm AR 225.

9. This in turn can lead to "forum-shopping"; for instance, an appellant before the Tribunal might apply for her appeal hearing case to be adjourned so that it will be set back to be heard at a later date by a different judge, who may be more favourably disposed towards her. In the United States, it is not possible for claimants to deploy this tactic because the case will remain with

the same immigration judge even if a lengthy adjournment is granted (except in those very rare instances when the judge is retiring).

10. See Nyembo v Refugee Appeals Tribunal [2007] IESC 25 (Supreme Court of Ireland); Carol Coulter, *Call for Review of up to 1,000 Rejected Asylum Applications*, Irish Times, March 20, 2008.

11. The claim of the Tribunal's chairman that the decision record of the member concerned was not at variance with other members was itself contested by three other members. In response, the responsible government minister defended the Tribunal's record. See *Refugee Appeals Body*, Irish Times, March 10, 2008; *Minister Defends Refugee Tribunal*, Irish Times, March 12, 2008.

12. In the UK, the legal obligation under the Refugee Convention, 1951, is supplemented by that of article 3 of the European Convention on Human Rights ("No-one shall be subjected to torture or to inhuman or degrading treatment"). Furthermore, under the Immigration Rules (1994 HC 395), rule 339C, someone who is not a refugee may nevertheless qualify for humanitarian protection if on return he would face a real risk of suffering serious harm, which consists of the death penalty or execution; unlawful killing; torture or inhuman or degrading treatment or punishment; or a serious and individual threat to his life or person by reason of indiscriminate violence in situations of international or internal armed conflict.

13. Saad, Diriye, and Osorio v Secretary of State for the Home Department [2002] Imm A.R. 471, 479.

14. See Introduction, page 1.

15. N v Secretary of State for the Home Department [2005] UKHL 31; N v United Kingdom (Application no. 26565/05, May 27, 2008, European Court of Human Rights). A similar trend is evident in "suicide" cases, those cases in which the applicant claims that he will, if returned to his country of origin, commit suicide. While it is theoretically possible for a claimant to succeed in such a claim under article 3 (see J v Secretary of State for the Home Department [2005] Imm A.R. 409), there have been few, if any, successful claims.

16. See especially Karanakaran v Secretary of State for the Home Department [2000] 3 All E.R. 449 at 477–480 (Sedley LJ).

17. Chapter 3, pages 45–46. In the UK, see also Hazel Genn & Yvette Genn, The Effectiveness of Representation at Tribunals (London: Lord Chancellor's Department, 1989).

18. This test is administered by the Legal Services Commission (LSC), the public agency that runs the legal aid system in England and Wales. LSC caseworkers and representatives work together to process funding applications for asylum applicants. Legal aid is also available for expenses such as external reports and translations. If an asylum appellant passes the merits test, LSC funding will only cover five hours' work per case by a representative. These restrictions, introduced in 2005, have led to many experienced immigration law firms withdrawing from offering advice to asylum applicants. See Independent Asylum Commission, *supra* note 7, at pages 36–37.

19. The Home Office is entitled to be represented before the Tribunal; usually this role is undertaken by an agency official known as a presenting officer. However, with the increase in asylum appeals over the period 2000–2005, the number of appeal hearings that proceeded in the absence of presenting officers increased. In this situation, the judge may ask questions of the claimant but for clarification purposes only. See MNM v Secretary of State for the Home Department (Surendran Guidelines for Adjudicators) Kenya [2000] INLR 576.

20. See Oyono v Secretary of State for the Home Department [2002] UKIAT02034; K v Secretary of State for the Home Department (Côte d'Ivoire) [2004] UKIAT00061; SA v Secretary of State for the Home Department (Clarificatory Questions from IJs—Best Practice) Iran [2006] UKIAT00017.

21. This latter practice has not been encouraged by the Tribunal's senior judges because, to be procedurally fair, the judge should then reconvene the hearing to allow the parties an opportunity to comment on the material, which would in turn prolong the length of the appeal process. See EG v Entry Clearance Officer, Lagos (Post-hearing Internet Research) Nigeria [2008] UKAIT00015, para.5.

22. See chapter 6, page 99.

23. HF (Algeria) v Secretary of State for the Home Department [2007] EWCA Civ 445, para.25.

24. Interview with an immigration judge.

25. MM v Secretary of State for the Home Department (DRC—Plausibility) Democratic Republic of Congo [2005] UKIAT00019.

26. See HK v Secretary of State for the Home Department [2006] EWCA Civ 1037, paras.29–30; Y v Secretary of State for the Home Department [2006] EWCA Civ 1223, paras.25–27.

27. Immigration Rules (1994 HC 395), rule 339K.

28. RT v Secretary of State for the Home Department (Medical Reports—Causation of Scarring) Sri Lanka [2008] UKAIT00009.

29. Jane Herlihy, Peter Scragg, and Stuart Turner, Discrepancies in Autobiographical Memories—Implications for the Assessment of Asylum Seekers: Repeated Interviews Study, 324 British Medical Journal 324 (2002); A (Turkey) v Secretary of State for the Home Department [2003] UKIAT00061.

30. HE v Secretary of State for the Home Department (DRC—Credibility and Psychiatric Reports) Democratic Republic of Congo [2005] Imm AR 119.

31. Chapter 6, page 99.

32. Stephen Sedley, *Asylum: Can the Judiciary Maintain Its Independence?* Paper presented at the International Association of Refugee Law Judges World Conference, Wellington, New Zealand, April 2002.

33. Interview with an immigration judge.

34. EC Council Directive 2004/83/EC on minimum standards for the qualification and status of third-country nationals or stateless persons as refugees or as persons who otherwise need international protection and the content of the protection granted, OJ L304/12 of September 30, 2004 (the "Qualification" Directive), art.4(4) as transposed into UK law under the Immigration Rules (1994 HC 395), rule 339L.

35. Asylum and Immigration (Treatment of Claimants, etc.) Act 2004, s.8.

36. Concerned about the effect of section 8 on judicial impartiality, the courts have interpreted it so as to reduce much of its impact, see JT (Cameroon) v Secretary of State for the Home Department [2008] EWCA Civ 878. Meanwhile, the Home Office intends to repeal this provision, see Home Office, Draft (Partial) Immigration and Citizenship Bill, Cm 7373 (2008), schedule 3, part 1.

37. See chapter 5, pages 79–80.

38. Tony Talbot, Credibility and Risk: One Adjudicator's View, 10 Immigration Law Digest 29 (2004).

39. International Association of Refugee Law Judges (IARLJ): Country of Origin Information–Country Guidance Working Party, *Judicial Criteria for Assessing Country of Origin Information (COI): A Checklist.* Paper for the 7th Biennial IARLJ World Conference, Nov. 2006.

40. See Shirazi v Secretary of State for the Home Department [2004] 2 All E.R. 602.

41. Manzeke v Secretary of State for the Home Department [1997] Imm A.R. 524, 529 (Lord Woolf MR).

42. On the use of country-expert evidence in asylum appeals, see Anthony Good, "Undoubtedly an Expert"? Country Experts in the UK Asylum Courts, 10 Journal of the Royal Anthropological Institute 113 (2004).

43. Country-guidance decisions also exert an influence on primary decision making. The Home Office refers extensively to the country-guidance determinations in its "Operational Guidance Notes," which instruct its caseworkers assessing initial claims on the main types of claim that are likely to justify the grant of asylum.

44. KA v Secretary of State for the Home Department (Draft—Related Risk Categories Updated) Eritrea CG [2005] UKAIT00165, para.10; AS and AA v Secretary of State for the Home Department (Effect of Previous Linked Determination) Somalia [2006] UKAIT00052, para.63.

45. NM v Secretary of State for the Home Department (Lone Women—Ashraf) Somalia CG [2005] UKIAT00076; HH & Others v Secretary of State for the Home Department (Mogadishu: Armed Conflict: Risk) Somalia CG [2008] UKAIT 00022.

46. The AIT maintains a list of country-guidance decisions on its website: www.ait.org.uk (visited July 24, 2008).

47. Furthermore, the Home Office will occasionally halt removals to a particular country pending a country-guidance decision from the Tribunal. In July 2008, the Home Office announced that it would defer enforcing the return of non-Arab Darfuri asylum seekers to Sudan until the Tribunal had issued country guidance on the safety of return to Khartoum (Hansard HL Deb., vol.703 col.WA263, July 22, 2008).

48. AB and DM v Secretary of State for the Home Department (Risk Categories Reviewed, Tutsis Added) Democratic Republic of Congo CG [2005] UKAIT00118; BK v Secretary of State for the Home Department (Failed Asylum Seekers) Democratic Republic of Congo CG [2007] UKAIT00098.

49. Henrik Zahle, *Competing Patterns for Evidentiary Assessments* in Gregor Noll (ed.), Proof, Evidentiary Assessment, and Credibility in Asylum Procedures (Leiden/Boston: Martinus Nijhoff Publishers, 2005), page 21.

50. R. (Iran) v Secretary of State for the Home Department [2005] Imm AR 535, 564 (Brooke LJ).

51. S & Others v Secretary of State for the Home Department [2002] INLR 416, 436 (Laws LJ). More recently, the Court of Appeal has encouraged the Home Office to provide information about the risks facing asylum applicants from officials stationed at UK diplomatic and consular posts in the country concerned in order to enable the Tribunal to produce high-quality country guidance. See AH (Sudan) v Secretary of State for the Home Department [2007] Imm AR 584, 601 (Buxton LJ).

52. Asylum and Immigration Tribunal, *Practice Directions* (2007), para.18.2. The AIT also produces "starred" determinations that clarify a point of law and that are, unlike country-guidance decisions, legally binding unless they have been overturned by the higher courts.

53. Ibid., para.18.4.

54. See *NM*, *supra* note 45, paras. 140–41. As the Court of Appeal, in KH (Sudan) v Secretary of State for the Home Department [2008] EWCA Civ 887, para.4 recently noted, ". . . no country guidance case is for ever; it is a factual precedent . . . and as such is open to revision in the light of new facts—new either in the sense of being newly ascertained or in the sense that they have arisen only since the decision was promulgated—provided in each case that they are facts of sufficient weight."

55. For instance, from 2005 to 2008, the Tribunal issued three country-guidance cases on the risks facing Zimbabwean asylum applicants (of whom there are several thousand in the UK) on their return, after the Court of Appeal twice remitted the case back to the Tribunal for

reconsideration. The most recent decision is HS v Secretary of State for the Home Department (Returning Asylum Seekers) Zimbabwe CG [2007] UKAIT00094.

56. Country experts, such as Anthony Good, have disputed the Tribunal's claim to possess expertise in country conditions while the House of Lords, in AH (Sudan) v Secretary of State for the Home Department [2007] UKHL 49, para.30 (Baroness Hale), has noted that it is "an expert tribunal charged with administering a complex area of law in challenging circumstances." See further John Barnes, Expert Evidence: The Judicial Perspective in Asylum and Human Rights Appeals, 16 International Journal of Refugee Law 349 (2004); Anthony Good, Expert Evidence in Asylum and Human Rights Appeals: An Expert's View, 16 International Journal of Refugee Law 358 (2004); Anthony Good, Anthropology and Expertise in the Asylum Courts (London: Routledge-Cavendish, 2007).

57. Colin Yeo (ed.), Country Guideline Cases: Benign and Practical? (London: Immigration Advisory Service, 2005). For instance, in country-guidance decisions promulgated in 2007–2008, the Tribunal usually considered a wide range of country information and evidence from country experts; this resulted in some lengthy decisions. See, for instance, the Tribunal's 144-page determination in BK, supra note 48, to the effect that failed Congolese asylum seekers would not be at risk on return.

58. See Canadian Immigration and Refugee Board, http://www.irb-cisr.gc.ca/en/research/origin_e.htm (visited September 2, 2008).

59. Chapter 6, pages 96–97.

60. Having discussion forums among immigration judges may seem a rather elementary suggestion. However, from my own research into asylum appeals in the UK, immigration judges noted that their initial training contained very little coverage on assessing credibility and, furthermore, once they had been hearing appeals, there was little opportunity to enter into discussions with each other as to how they approached the decision-making task despite the desire of many judges to have such an opportunity. The reason for this is simple: the pressure of the Tribunal's caseload.

61. Chapter 6, pages 112–113.

62. The Asylum and Immigration Tribunal (Procedure) Rules SI 2005/230, rule 22.

63. Although the length of determinations varies, their average length, according to my own experience, is around thirteen pages.

64. AK v Secretary of State for the Home Department (Failure to Assess Witnesses' Evidence) Turkey [2004] UKIAT 00230, para.10.

65. See generally Frederick Schauer, Giving Reasons, 47 Stanford L.R. 633 (1995); Jerry L. Mashaw, Reasoned Administration: The European Union, the United States, and the Project of Democratic Governance, 76 George Washington L.R. 99 (2007).

66. Malaba v Secretary of State for the Home Department [2006] EWCA Civ 820, para.29 (Pill LJ).

67. Detamu v Secretary of State for the Home Department [2006] EWCA Civ 604, para.19 (Moses LJ).

68. Peter Showler, Refugee Sandwich: Stories of Exile and Asylum (Montreal & Kingston: McGill-Queen's University Press, 2006), pages 222–29; François Crépeau and Delphine Nakache, Critical Spaces in the Canadian Refugee Determination System: 1989–2002, 20 International Journal of Refugee Law 50 (2008).

9   Consistency, Credibility, and Culture
Bruce J. Einhorn[1]

I.

Now the whole earth had one language and few words. And as men migrated from the east, they found a plain in the land of Shinar and settled there. And they said to one another, "Come, let us make bricks, and burn them thoroughly." And they had brick for stone, and bitumen for mortar. Then they said, "Come, let us build ourselves a city, and a tower with its top in the heavens, and let us make a name for ourselves, lest we be scattered abroad upon the face of the whole earth." And the LORD came down to see the city and the tower, which the sons of men had built. And the LORD said, "Behold, they are one people, and they have all one language; and this is only the beginning of what they will do; and nothing that they propose to do will now be impossible for them. Come, let us go down, and there confuse their language, that they may not understand one another's speech." So the LORD scattered them abroad from there over the face of all the earth, and they left off building the city. Therefore its name was called Babel, because there the LORD confused the language of all the earth; and from there the LORD scattered them abroad over the face of all the earth.

Genesis 11:1–9

DURING MY ALMOST seventeen years as a United States immigration judge in Los Angeles, I often felt as if my colleagues and I were still smarting from the curse incurred by the hubris of our common ancestors (who apparently became among the first reported refugees). We were fellow judges and friends; we shared our lunches and reveled in our bull sessions caffeinated by twice-cooked coffee only a litigation addict could love. Indeed, among the more than two hundred immigration judges in courts across the United States, I counted many men and women whom I had known, respected, and liked from our days as lawyers to our time on the bench. Notwithstanding my close relations with my fellow judges—or perhaps precisely because of them—I was constantly confounded and confused by our conversations on the subject of asylum law. I was even more at a loss for words (no small matter, given my nature) by the manner in which many of my colleagues approached asylum applicants and adjudicated their cases.

In fairness, I note that my colleagues were just as unable to understand much of what I did in my courtroom in my own proceedings.

Trial judges experience the aloneness and autonomy of adjudication in a way appellate judges do not. The camaraderie that we immigration judges experienced at rest and in each other's chambers was replaced by a constant scattering of our sensibilities about asylum law when we donned our robes and voluntarily departed to our separate corners of the world, our own tiny principalities, our own courtrooms. We may have shared a taste for good food, bad coffee, and even worse jokes, but we seemed to speak very different legal languages when we heard and decided asylum claims. The curse of Babel was ever present in the way we judged others and their alleged fears of persecution abroad.

Our shared war stories, the tall tales we told of our judicial talents, made us seem very similar in our approaches to asylum, but then, people's golf games always improve with the telling of them, far from the fairways and greens and the balls lost in between. The truth was that far more often than not, we judges just did not reason or speak in the same language in the exercise of our role as asylum adjudicators. The results of this dramatic diversity in the decision-making process were and continue to be made clear in the research and conclusions of Professors Ramji-Nogales, Schoenholtz, and Schrag. I share their concerns about the serendipity of asylum adjudication, and admit to being an especially large stakeholder in the future of asylum availability. As a young lawyer with the U.S. Department of Justice engaged in the prosecution of human rights violators,[2] I was assigned to help draft what became the Refugee Relief Act of 1980—the modern law of asylum.[3] I retain a strong parental interest in the continuing viability of asylum as a form of relief subject to relatively and reasonably consistent (and, I admit, compassionate) parameters of application by the immigration courts. I fear that without the changes and reforms proposed by the authors of the Refugee Roulette study, the curse of Babel will continue the crazy-quilt method of asylum adjudication that neither the best-prepared lawyers nor the most credible relief applicants could contemplate: a method wherein, in each case in each separate courtroom, the "law is what the judge ate for breakfast."[4] Like any dutiful parent, I trust that my contribution to those changes and reforms will help engender health and hardiness in asylum as a rightful remedy for those who seek protection from a broken world confounded not just by the language but by the practice of persecution.

II.

In my experience, and in the frank and frequent conversations I've held with my colleagues from the court, the single most significant factor in an immigration judge's assessment of an asylum claim is *credibility*. It has also been my experience that credibility is the single most inconsistently assessed variable in asylum adjudication. In the complex chemistry of credibility determinations, there are a number of free radicals that bedevil and divide judges.

Credibility determinations in asylum hearings have always been difficult to make. Reasons for this difficulty include, but are not limited to, "*differences in cultural norms*, the effect of an asylum seeker's *past traumatic experiences* and flight on her ability to recall events, *language* barriers, the adversarial nature of the hearing, the asylum seeker's *limited access to counsel*, and the adjudicator's sometimes *inaccurate perceptions of foreign culture*."[5]

An additional and constant aggravating element in determining credibility is the often crushing caseloads of Immigration Judges, particularly in large and multi-cultural cities like Los Angeles or New York, which cause even the best-intentioned adjudicators to lose patience and perspective.[6] It was not unusual for me, and remains standard operating procedure for many of my colleagues, to have to conduct "master calendar" hearings in more than twenty-five or thirty removal cases in a single morning. In these hearings, preliminary but critical matters are resolved (including language determinations, the sufficiency of time for the aliens[7] to seek counsel, the admissions or denials made by aliens to the allegations and charges made against them by the government in the court proceedings, and the submission of relief applications, like those for asylum) and "individual calendar" sessions of three or more hours on the merits are scheduled for the majority of litigants whose issues of removal and especially relief require more than a few minutes of discussion. To continue the metaphor, then, all of the free radicals described above make for a most combustible chemistry of credibility determinations that are grossly unpredictable to asylum seekers and their lawyers (should they have any) and injurious to asylum seekers and to the reputation of immigration judges.

Take, for example, the recently decided case of *Mousa v. Mukasey*.[8] Mousa, an Iraqi Chaldean Christian, was denied asylum by both an immigration judge and the Board of Immigration Appeals (BIA) despite her testimony that she and other family members had been pressured to join Saddam Hussein's Ba'ath Party, and that she and her brother had been interned for forty-seven days at the party's compound, during which time she was raped by the party's representatives. Both the immigration judge and the BIA found as a fatal flaw in Mousa's credibility her failure to mention her rape on her pretestimonial written asylum application. The Ninth Circuit Court of Appeals rejected that finding, however, noting that "the assumption that the timing of a victim's disclosure of sexual assault is a bellwether of truth is belied by the reality that there is often delayed reporting of sexual abuse." In remanding her case and finding Mousa's claim of rape to be a credible one, the court of appeals added that "[m]any victims of sexual assault feel so upset, embarrassed, humiliated, and ashamed about the assault that they do not tell anyone that it occurred." The *Mousa* court emphasized that the psychology behind the reluctance to report rape becomes more pronounced when the country of the sexual assault—in this case, Iraq—is one "where reported rapes often go uninvestigated, and where rape victims are sometimes murdered by members of their own families because they have 'dishonored' their families by being raped."[9] In sum, the court of appeals concluded that, in addition to her demonstrated psychological stress, "Mousa provided a compelling explanation for her failure to mention her rape at an earlier time in the proceedings: her cultural reluctance to admit the fact it had occurred."

Another example of convoluted credibility determinations in asylum proceedings may be found in the case of *Zhou v. Gonzales*.[10] Zhou had applied for asylum because of his opposition to the Chinese government's policies of coercive population control. The immigration judge and the BIA found against Zhou's claim, citing his lack of credibility. The immigration judge (IJ) concluded that Zhou had testified inconsistently about whether he and his wife suffered forced sterilization in China. The Second Circuit Court of Appeals disagreed, however, and in remanding the proceedings found that "this purported inconsistency appeared to be the result of a translation error rather than an attempt to mislead the IJ." More specifically, the court of appeals cited to what it regarded as a "nonsensical translation of Zhou's testimony on this exact point: 'I said they forced me to be sterilized and had not been sterilized.'" The Second Circuit went on to criticize the IJ for relying on the translation to reject Zhou's credibility instead of rejecting the interpreter:

> The IJ recognized that the translator was having difficulty, [but] dismissed the problem because Zhou had elected to speak in Mandarin instead of Foo Chow, and subsequently characterized the confusing translation as an example of Zhou's deceitfulness. Under these circumstances, the IJ's finding is based on an "inaccurate perception of the record" and thus is insufficient.... Further, the IJ placed considerable weight on her misapprehension: what she perceived as a lie, as she set forth in her decision, "flavored the entire hearing."[11]

The circuit court also concluded that the IJ's adverse credibility determinations "seemed to reflect a lack of cultural sensitivity by treating what were obvious translation difficulties as evasiveness that 'flavored the entire hearing.'"

As a last example, consider the case of *Agbor v. Gonzales*,[12] in which the female copetitioner sought asylum on the basis of her fear of female genital mutilation following her marriage in her native Cameroon. In denying her and her copetitioning spouse asylum relief, the IJ found Agbor not to be credible, in part because of the "alleged implausibility that the petitioners only know Mr. Daniel—the man who provided them shelter and passports—by his first name." By contrast, the court of appeals cited to the testimony of another witness who told the IJ that Mr. Daniel was a "mere" business acquaintance and not a friend of the petitioners. Furthermore, the circuit court noted the testimony of Ms. Agbor, "that in Cameroon it is customary only to know and refer to an acquaintance by his first rather than his full name." The Seventh Circuit reversed the decisions of the IJ and BIA to deny asylum and related forms of relief, and remanded the Agbors' proceedings. Once again, an immigration judge's failure to incorporate cultural factors into his or her credibility assessment proved to be a fatal flaw that occasioned an independent appeals court to question the credibility of the IJ rather than the asylum seeker.

These examples reveal that from coast to coast and in between, the inability or unwillingness of at least some IJs to let issues of individual psychology, language, lawyerly skills, and, above all, culture inform the content of credibility determinations has created an atmosphere in asylum proceedings that often resembles the crap shoot of a casino more than the judicious proceedings of a court of law.

In defense of my former workplace, I should add that some immigration judges have attempted to recognize both the reality of cultural diversity and the need to pay heed to it in resolving asylum claims. Frankly, the reality of culture clashes between the Byzantine labyrinth of immigration laws and regulations that govern asylum proceedings and the mindset of the asylum applicants was for me hard to miss. During the first term of the Clinton administration in the 1990s, as the brave but failed efforts of the U.S. military to bring peace to Somalia became front-page news, I had in my courtroom an asylum seeker from that poor and war-torn country. She was single, barely out of her teens, with no knowledge of English and understandably no expertise in the workings of the immigration court. Despite my urgings to the contrary, the female respondent elected to represent herself and did so with the assistance of a court-contracted Somali language interpreter. In the course of the asylum phase of her deportation proceedings, she produced a document given to her in Kenya after she fled Somalia and before she arrived in the United States. The document appeared to identify the respondent as a refugee from potential persecution in Somalia on account of her tribal (i.e., national and ethnic) origin, and thus also appeared to corroborate her reasons for seeking asylum. Government counsel suggested, and I agreed, that respondent should provide a copy of the document to the court for possible introduction into the evidentiary record of the case. I thereupon asked the respondent whether she would be willing to "make a Xerox of the document" during a brief recess. In the most polite and straightforward way, respondent replied in the affirmative, but then added these revealing words: "Excuse me, Your Honor, but what is a Xerox?" This young woman, intelligent but indigent and barely familiar with the gadget-goofy and technology-dependent ways of the West, illustrated better than

I ever could the cultural disconnect between her background of desperation—of drought, famine, and internecine tribal warfare unrestrained by the anarchy of the state—and mine. I promptly withdrew my request of her, and made the photocopies myself, a practice that I and indeed almost all of my Los Angeles court colleagues continued in all *pro se* cases.

In another asylum case brought before my court, I was confronted by a Russian-speaking respondent from the then newly independent state of Estonia. Like the young woman from Somalia, this respondent declined my invitation for her to take some time in order to seek counsel. She too represented herself, and claimed that she had been harassed and mistreated by agents of the new government on account of her activities as an organizer and spokesperson for the ethnic Russian minority in Estonia who in turn complained that they had become second-class citizens in their own country following the end of Soviet rule. In her written asylum application, prepared through an interpreter before the initiation of her removal proceedings, the respondent contended that Estonian government agents had "raped" her. However, in her courtroom testimony, respondent swore only that she had been "violated" by the government agents as they fondled her through her clothes. Government counsel argued that the inconsistency evidenced a lack of credibility on a matter central to her asylum claim. I was not persuaded that this was necessarily so, however: never before had I witnessed a case in which an asylum applicant had actually downgraded the degree of abuse she suffered because of her political activities. I therefore gently pressured government counsel to try to find the interpreter who had assisted respondent in the preparation of her asylum application. Fortunately, the interpreter was located and testified in my court that the Russian-language word for rape—phonetically spelled in Latin letters as "na-seal-a-veats"—may also be used to denote a lesser violation of a woman's body. The interpreter's testimony resolved any reasonable doubts about the respondent's representations, and my grant of asylum to her was not appealed.

Another challenge to which some of my fellow judges and I have been sensitive is gauging the credibility of an asylum applicant through the latter's perception of time. Psychiatric and psychological studies have taught us that traumatic recollections are maintained by the mind in a different way than less jarring memories: the former are saved as fragments, contain a more sensory quality, "do not seem to carry a 'time-stamp,'" and cannot be evoked at will as easily as more routine recollections.[13] The individual stressors that complicate temporally accurate recollections are often aggravated by cultural factors like the application of non-Western (e.g., Persian and Ethiopian) calendars and systems that measure time according to specific events without reference to any standardized durational units.[14] Some immigration judges, particularly those without the benefit of psychological and cultural experts, but burdened by large and looming caseloads, pounce on the difficulty victims of past persecution have in clearly dating their episodes of abuse and in doing so conclude that the asylum seeker's credibility is lacking. Some of us have resisted going in that direction, perhaps because some of us as lawyers propounded the testimony of immigrant witnesses (in my case, Holocaust survivors)[15] with similar problems in temporal discussions, however accurate they were in describing people, places, and events critical to their credibility. Federal courts of appeals have often held that discrediting the testimony of a foreign-born asylum seeker because of the difficulty he or she evidences in dating important activities is often based as much on the psychological impatience and cultural ignorance of the immigration judge as on the weaknesses of the respondent's testimony.[16] Time, therefore, like language, must be considered with psychological and cultural care in assessing asylum seekers' credibility assessments.

Finally, all of the problems that attach themselves to the difficulty in determining credibility in asylum proceedings are made worse by the *newness* of asylum seekers to the United States and its processes for resolving immigration disputes. While many applicants for relief from removal must establish a considerable number of years of uninterrupted presence in the United States,[17] asylum seekers tend to be more recent arrivals to this country. In fact, since 1998 Congress has barred asylum for those who apply for it more than one year after arriving in the United States.[18] Consequently, because they are newer to the country, asylum applicants tend to be even more "alien" to the psychology, culture, language, and legal profession they encounter than are other foreign-born respondents in immigration court. It is therefore not surprising that a significant disparity exists in the way asylum applicants respond to immigration judges and, more importantly, vice versa. Nevertheless, while the disparity is explicable, it is not acceptable: the nature and quality of an asylum decision is often literally a matter of life and death. It therefore behooves all of us involved in asylum law and adjudication to discern how best to correct the problems identified by the Refugee Roulette study and in doing so implement the reforms proposed by the authors regarding better appointments, training regimens, and resources for immigration judges, and more and better counsel for asylum seekers.

III.

Old but persistent problems with the body of our legal institutions and those who operate them require new prescriptions. My new bromide is for a new and autonomous United States Asylum Court (USAC), which, while it would not contemplate or guarantee (since, indeed, no mortal solution could contemplate or guarantee) a complete uniformity of results from one trial judge to the next, could put in place a set of procedures and methods designed to prevent problems of psychology, culture, and language from making it a Herculean task (rather than just a human one) for judges to better understand the newcomers in their courtrooms and thus decide their cases more on the facts presented and less on the frustrations caused in immigration litigation. A new cure for the problems of Refugee Roulette can come only from a new court invested with new priorities and new resources. Justice, as well as the sanity of judges, calls for a court tailor-made to adjudicate credibility in cases unlike those that involve events in *this* country and respondents who have lived here longer.[19]

Essentially, I am calling for two courts to handle removal proceedings brought by the U.S. Department of Homeland Security. An immigration court would have more general jurisdiction and would hear cases that involve non-asylum-based relief claims such as cancellation of removal, adjustment of status, and waivers of inadmissibility.[20] The Asylum Court would be assigned all removal proceedings in which protection from persecution or torture is requested.[21] Cases would be assigned to either the general immigration court or the USAC by judges at master calendars. Both the general immigration court and the USAC could still function within their current agency, the Justice Department's Executive Office of Immigration Review (EOIR), or, as this book's authors suggest and as is my preference, within an immigration court that is independent of the executive branch, created by an act of Congress pursuant to Article I of the U.S. Constitution.[22] Regardless of the conditions for the divorce, a separate USAC would no longer overcook the judicial temperament of its judges by pouring on them all kinds of cases with all kinds of deadlines. The USAC, and for that matter the new immigration court, would enjoy a lighter (though still not light) caseload to which it could give greater attention in a less hectic and exhausting atmosphere. My proposal would require additional IJ appointments so that each of the two courts would possess approximately the same number of judges as the present, malfunctioning immigration court has.[23] Thus, the USAC and the new general immigration court would possess the personnel to efficiently adjudicate its cases without prejudice to the workload of the other. Such a proposal would require a not insignificant amount of money, but the problems and embarrassments caused by the current adjudication system necessitate a commitment of additional funds and human resources.

Reassignments of current IJs to the USAC and new appointments to the new court would be made or at least cleared by a merits panel composed of current judges, leaders, and specialists in the area of international human rights (both governmental and nongovernmental), and prominent academics and practitioners (both government and private) in the field of immigration law. The result of such a selection system would be the appointment of USAC judges who are truly qualified for and dedicated to the challenges of asylum adjudication. Additionally, all USAC members would be required to submit to initial and subsequent periodic training in asylum and refugee law, and the psychological, cultural, and other anthropological aspects of examining and assessing asylum claims. Such training would be conducted by incumbent asylum judges, legal scholars, and experts in the already mentioned and related disciplines. Such training would also include review of recent precedent-setting case law on asylum, and at least some review of the legal developments at the international level (e.g., the reports and guidelines provided by the United Nations High Commissioner for Refugees and his *UNHCR Handbook on Procedures and Criteria for Determining Refugee Status*) and even of the decisions of foreign courts in democratic adjudication systems, like Canada.[24] Indeed, our adjudication system has much to learn from our neighbors to the north, particularly in the emphasis they accord psychology and culture in credibility determinations. For example, the Federal Court of Canada ruled that an expert medical doctor's psychological report on an asylum applicant cannot be rejected solely because the doctor's conclusion is based on information that the claimant related to the doctor, when it is clear from the report that the doctor's own professional observation of the claimant was material to the conclusion reached.[25] Canadian courts also emphasize that care be taken to understand the asylum applicant's "ability to observe and recall events in the course of a hearing; nervousness caused by testifying before a tribunal; the claimant's psychological condition (such as post-traumatic stress disorder) associated with traumas such as detention or torture; the claimant's young age; cognitive difficulties and the passage of time; gender considerations; the claimant's educational background and social position; and cultural factors."[26] These admonishments comport with very recent studies conducted both in North America and Europe that conclude as follows:

> Cultural factors may strongly influence the types of information asylum seekers are comfortable sharing, as well as the pace of disclosure. In many cultures, victims of sexual abuse, rape, or sexual torture experience an overwhelming amount of shame. Because in many cultures it is important to not lose face, these painful experiences would be difficult to share with loved ones, let alone strangers in a public setting, especially government officials who might evoke memories of the perpetrators in cases where applicants have been terrorized by the agents of the state.... Eye contact is another culturally variable pattern of behavior.... Lewdness or aggression is associated with prolonged eye contact in many cultures, though not in the U.S..... Thus, in U.S. culture, ironically, some asylum seekers may arouse suspicion by the aversion of gaze that to them is innately ingrained as a sign of respect or deference.[27]

Thus it is critical that the USAC have regular access to expert witnesses in the disciplines of psychology and culture to mediate between the court and the often difficult-to-understand asylum applicants.

To that end, the USAC should have access to its own court-appointed experts with "no dog in the fight," no vested interests, financial or otherwise, in the outcome of asylum litigation. "In much of the rest of the world, expert witnesses are selected by judges and are meant to be neutral and independent. Many foreign lawyers have long questioned the American practice of allowing the parties to present testimony from experts they have chosen and paid."[28] Moreover, by having the experts selected by and responsible to the court, the judges will find it easier and less threatening to inform the content of their decisions, and of the asylum law itself, with the various medical and social disciplines necessary to the proper adjudication of cases based on foreign events and often on complex psychological factors affecting witness credibility. Again, the proposal to have court-appointed experts will cost the government money, money indigent and poor asylum applicants often do not have to pay the same witnesses under the current system. Again, however, if the quality and consistency of asylum decisions are to be increased, a capital investment of public funds is appropriate.

On the subject of funds, a new USAC (and, for that matter, a separate general immigration court) should be allocated more resources, human resources, in the form of additional law clerks to allow for more research and more written decisions regarding those cases that prove more complicated and demanding. Currently, the overwhelming majority of rulings made by immigration judges are conveyed by means of oral decisions, delivered from the bench immediately after respondents' hearings are concluded. Although the immigration laws and regulations do not require oral as opposed to written decisions, the former are actively encouraged by EOIR as a way of accelerating the completion of the hundreds of thousands of pending removal and deportation proceedings. With additional law clerks, written decisions needed to "flesh out" difficult questions of asylum law, and credibility resolution will become more likely.[29] Moreover, judges should be given authority they do not now have to publish some of their written decisions, even in cases that go unappealed. Then, at periodic retraining sessions, asylum judges could share and discuss their written rulings and what led to them. Additionally, in larger court jurisdictions like Los Angeles, Miami, and New York, immigration judges might adopt the suggestion of the principal authors of this book, that more complex asylum cases be heard and decided by panels of three IJs, who could collaborate in decisions while comparing their approaches to adjudication and perhaps contribute to a more cohesive pattern and practice of decision making. A true and deep dialogue could begin that would lead to a continuing legal education on asylum in general, and credibility resolution in particular, for judges and lawyers alike. A consistent methodology of credibility resolution would surely emerge, and with it a lessening of extremes in asylum rulings.

Lastly, it is time to join the authors of the Refugee Roulette study in calling for a "civil *Gideon*" rule that would release public funds for the representation of asylum applicants (and indeed, all indigent respondents) in federal removal proceedings.[30] The better the preparation and representation on both sides in asylum cases, the better informed the asylum judge will be and the better quality asylum decisions will have. I cannot count the many times my fellow immigration judges and I have lamented the inadequacy or even absence of counsel in cases where a better preparation of asylum claims could prevent cultural misunderstandings and enhance the possibility that documentary evidence and corroborating witnesses be discovered and introduced at trial. Given the time pressures under which most immigration judges operate, IJs are neither inclined nor encouraged to grant multiple continuances for respondents to seek counsel, or to slow down to a trickle the pace of merits hearings on the possibility that with the unlikely emergence of representation in the midst of proceedings, issues might emerge that could make a relief claim clearer or more credible. Given that the burden of proving asylum eligibility lies with the asylum applicant,[31] the absence of sufficient attorney resources is perceived by immigration judges as just another problem through which they must muddle and over which they lack control. A civil *Gideon* standard would solve this problem, empower asylum applicants in their presentations, and allow IJs to adjudicate more thoroughly vetted relief claims in an efficient fashion. Frankly, an adequate supply of adequate counsel would make it just as easy for even busy immigration judges to grant asylum as to deny it.[32]

IV.

As I write this in August 2008, the United Nations estimates that about one hundred thousand civilians have been displaced by warfare between Russian and Georgian armed forces on the territory of the former Soviet republic of Georgia. The cold, hard reality faced by large numbers of refugees, and the humanitarian basis upon which the asylum law was predicated, are very much needed in our difficult world. The key to a more just application of that law, of greater consistency in assessing the credibility of asylum seekers, lies in an interdisciplinary approach to adjudication that gives recognition to the complexities inherent in modern human rights casework:

> Let us look the facts of human conduct in the face. Let us look to economics and sociology and philosophy, and cease to assume that jurisprudence is self-sufficient. . . . Let us not become legal monks.[33]

1. Bruce J. Einhorn served as a United States Immigration Judge in Los Angeles from July 1990 through January 2007. He is currently a Professor of Asylum and Refugee Law, and Director of the Asylum Litigation Clinic, at the Pepperdine University School of Law in Malibu, California. He also serves as a radio and newspaper commentator on issues of law and public policy, international human rights law, and the laws of war.

2. From October 1979 through June 1990, I served as a special prosecutor and then as chief of litigation in the Justice Department's Office of Special Investigations (OSI), the unit responsible for seeking the identification, denaturalization, and deportation of Nazi war criminals who resided illegally in the United States. OSI continues its good work to this day.

3. These provisions are codified at Title 8, Sections 1101(a)(42) and 1158(a)–(d) of the Immigration and Nationality Act, as amended. I make no claim to any revisions in the asylum law that occurred after its initial passage. I especially disavow any role in the drafting of the REAL ID Act, Pub. L. No. 109–13, 119 Stat. 302 (2005), which I believe has made it more difficult to grant asylum to credible applicants without in any meaningful way enhancing the nation's post-9/11 security.

4. This less than cherished scenario is generally but falsely attributed to the late Judge Jerome Frank of the United States Court of Appeals for the Second Circuit, a philosopher in the school of legal realism. In fact, Frank urged a less flippant and more serious study of the often extrajudicial elements that affect judicial decisions. In his work Courts on Trial (1949) at 161, Frank commented, "Many legal scholars, instead of giving serious consideration to that subject ['the numerous non-rational factors in the decisional process'], resort to derision. Absurdly lumping together all the non-rational, non-logical elements, and describing them as the 'state of the judge's digestion,' these scholars often jeeringly speak of 'gastronomical jurisprudence.' Under the heading of gastronomical ailments, one cannot subsume all the irrationalities of judges." My chapter of this book is a small attempt to go beyond the glib analysis of such a theory of jurisprudence to a more realistic analysis of why and how immigration judges rule as they do in asylum cases.

5. Daniel Forman, Improving Asylum-Seeker Credibility Determinations: Introducing Appropriate Dispute Resolution Techniques into the Process, 16 CARDOZO J. INT'L & COMP. L. 207, 209 (2008) (footnote omitted) (emphases added).

6. See Tun v. Gonzales, 485 F.3d 1014, 1027–29 (8th Cir. 2007), cited in Michele Benedetto, Crisis on the Immigration Bench, 73 BROOK. L. REV. 467–68 (2008) (footnote omitted).

7. The term "alien" is not one I would choose to use in immigration law. It implies beings of an extraterrestrial origin, instead of fellow flesh-and-blood humans. Unfortunately, the general term applied to the foreign-born who are in the United States but not citizens or nationals of the United States is "alien," pursuant to 8 U.S.C. 1101(a)(3). The immigration law's selection of the term "alien" is, in my view, a powerful example of a long-running theme, that "[a] citizen democracy can only work if most of its members are convinced that their political society is a common venture of considerable moment that requires a special sense of bonding amongst the people working together." Charles Taylor, *Why Democracy Needs Patriotism*, in FOR LOVE OF COUNTRY: DEBATING THE LIMITS OF PATRIOTISM (Martha Nussbaum ed., 1996). The theme was put more bluntly by Thomas Jefferson, who noted that newcomers to the United States bring "their principles, with their language, which they will transmit to their children," and that as to America, "[t]hey will infuse into it their spirit, warp and bias its direction, and render it a heterogeneous, incoherent, distracted mass." Frederick Whelan, *Citizenship and Free Movement: An Open Admission Policy*, in OPEN BORDERS? CLOSED SOCIETIES? THE ETHICAL

AND POLITICAL ISSUES (Mark Gibney ed., 1988). It is no great wonder that the chemistry of credibility determination in asylum cases is poisoned by a culture of paranoia, aggravated by a culture of misunderstanding and caseload crunching.

8. 530 F.3d 1025 (9th Cir. 2008).

9. The court cited European Council on Refugees & Exiles, Guidelines on the Treatment of Iraqi Asylum Seekers and Refugees in Europe, 18 INT'L J. REFUGEE L. 452, 458 (2006). There is no evidence in the record of proceedings in *Mousa* that her attorneys ever submitted the above-cited journal piece, which the court of appeals understandably found so persuasive and which it apparently found for itself. The failure of Mousa's counsel, particularly at her removal hearing, to address and advance the issue of culture as a basis for understanding her reluctance to admit to her rape clearly did not help her case for relief and delayed her procurement of the same.

10. 193 Fed. Appx. 98 (2d Cir. 2006).

11. Id., citing Tambadou v. Gonzales, 446 F.3d 298, 302 (2d Cir. 2006).

12. 487 F.3d 499 (7th Cir. 2007).

13. Jane Herlihy, *Evidentiary Assessment and Psychological Difficulties in Proof*, in EVIDENTIARY ASSESSMENT AND CREDIBILITY IN ASYLUM PROCEDURES 126 n.84 (Gregor Noll ed., 2005).

14. Walter Kaelin, Troubled Communication: Cross-Cultural Misunderstanding in the Asylum Hearing, 20 INT'L MIGRATION REV. 230, 236–37 (1986).

15. As a prosecutor and as chief of litigation for OSI, I interviewed, deposed, and took the testimony of thousands of refugees from Nazi persecution and of Nazi collaborators who agreed to serve as witnesses against the subjects of my office's investigations and court proceedings. Many of the most credible witnesses, especially among Holocaust survivors, described the murderous and/or violent actions of OSI defendants as if those actions had been "frozen in time." Oftentimes, the more convincing the recollections of the survivors, the more convoluted seemed their ability to "date-stamp" those memories. With the patience of the witnesses and the courts who heard them, and the aid of experts on psychology and on foreign cultures, the credibility of these brave and good survivors survived and even flourished in the course of the trials. OSI taught me much about building bridges of communication between individuals from other times and places and those lawyers and judges who dwell in the very different, more neat and tidy world of the Anglo-American courtroom. But for my work at OSI, I may well have become one of those overworked, insufficiently assisted immigration judges who have suffered excoriation at the hands of U.S. courts of appeals.

16. See Fiadjoe v. Attorney General, 411 F.3d 135, 137 (3d Cir. 2005).

17. For example, Title 8, Section 1229b(1) of the United States Code allows for the possible cancellation of an alien's removal (and his resulting procurement of lawful permanent residence) if, *inter alia*, he proves that he has maintained continuous physical presence in the United States for at least ten years from the date of his relief application.

18. 8 U.S. Code Section 1158(a)(2)(B). There are some exceptions, but they do not cover all of the situations that might explain a late application. See Michele R. Pistone and Philip G. Schrag, The New Asylum Rule: Improved but Still Unfair, 16 GEORGETOWN IMMIGRATION LAW JOURNAL 1 (2001) and Philip G. Schrag, A Well-Founded Fear (Routledge, 2000).

19. For example, under 8 U.S.C. 1220b(a), a lawful permanent resident of the United States may obtain a grant of cancellation of his removal if, despite his criminal convictions (almost always ones recorded in the United States), he demonstrates the following: (1) that he is an alien lawfully admitted to the United States for not less than five years; (2) that he has resided in the United States continuously for five years after having been admitted in any status; and (3) that he has not been convicted of an "aggravated felony," a term of art defined at 8 U.S.C. 1101(a)(43) that generally excludes all but the most serious offenses, like "rape" and "murder." Section 1229b(a) is a form of relief within the sound discretion of an immigration judge to grant or deny, by weighing the criminal record of the alien in the United States against his time here, his family contacts here, his rehabilitation here, his personal and filial hardships here, and the positive achievements he has accomplished here. Thus the critical issues to be weighed are domestic ones usually well within the common understanding of the respondent, the attorneys for both sides, and the judge. The stress on asylum proceedings brought on by culture shock is therefore far less severe in a cancellation of removal case, and other litigation that involves aliens who have lived in the United States for more significant periods of time.

20. 8 U.S.C. 1229(a) and (b), 1255, and 1182(h).

21. These include, along with applications for asylum, claims for withholding of removal and protection under the Convention Against Torture. See 8 U.S.C. 1231(b)(3) and the United Nations Convention Against Torture ("CAT") and 8 C.F.R. 208.16–.18. Section 1231(b)(3) prohibits the removal of an alien to a country where "the alien's life or freedom would be threatened in that country because of the alien's race, religion, nationality, membership in a particular social group, or political opinion." Eligibility for a withholding of removal must be proven by "clear and convincing evidence." See INS v. Stevic, 467 U.S. 407 (1984). By contrast, asylum eligibility may be proven by a lower standard of "a well-founded fear of persecution on account of race, religion, nationality, membership in a particular social group, or political opinion." INS v. Cardoza-Fonseca, 480 U.S. 421 (1987). Under 8 C.F.R. Section 208.16(a) "an immigration judge may adjudicate both an asylum claim and a request for withholding of removal whether or not asylum is granted." Relief from removal under CAT is available if the alien establishes "that it is more likely than not that he or she would be tortured if removed to the proposed country of removal." 8 C.F.R. 208.16(c)(2) and 208.17(b)(1).

22. It is unseemly for a supposedly impartial court of such consequence to hundreds of thousands of litigants to be subject to control by a litigation and law enforcement agency like the Department of Justice, particularly one that has been found to have illegally employed partisan politics in the appointment of immigration judges. Bruce J. Einhorn, Op-Ed, *Tainted Justice*, L.A. TIMES, June 29, 2008. I would also elevate the Board of Immigration Appeals, which reviews the decisions of immigration judges, to a Court of Immigration Appeals that includes experienced and well-reviewed IJs from various regions of the country. Finally, I would eliminate the Board's policy of "streamlining" review of "routine cases by a single-member adjudication process." *See* DEPARTMENT OF JUSTICE, BOARD OF IMMIGRATION APPEALS: FINAL RULE (August 23, 2002). Cursory review of removal decisions, especially life-and-death decisions regarding asylum eligibility, should not trump a thorough appellate examination in the purported interests of efficiency. In a democracy, safety must always take precedence over efficiency.

23. Of course, adjustments in the number of new IJs assigned and appointed to each court should comport with rising and falling caseloads.

24. Canada's Immigration and Refugee Board (IRB) functions as that country's USAC. The IRB has published an Assessment of Credibility in Claims for Refugee Protection available to both its judges and its practitioners and the public at large (2004). The Assessment calls for judges in asylum cases to consider "all of the evidence, both oral and documentary" and "not just selected portions of the evidence." Id. at 1 (footnote omitted). Adjudicators are admonished that they "should not selectively refer to evidence that supports its conclusions without also referring to evidence to the contrary." Id. (footnote omitted). The Assessment also warns that in cases where "the claimant provides personal documentary evidence or medical reports, specific to and corroborative of his claim, it is not sufficient to simply make a blanket statement, without explanation, that no probative value was assigned to this evidence because of a general lack of credibility on the part of the claimant." Id. at 13 (footnote omitted). Finally, the Assessment cites a major Canadian appeals case, Maldonado v. Canada (Minister of Employment and Education), [1980] 2 F.C. 302 (C.A.) at 305, which held that "[w]here [a claimant] swears to the truth of certain allegations [of persecution], this creates a presumption that those allegations are true unless there be reason to doubt their truthfulness." The Assessment is national in scope, and thus supports less deviation and eccentricity in judicial findings on credibility.

25. Zapata, Carlos Alberto Ruiz v. M.E.I., (F.C.T.D., no. IMM-4876-93), Gibson, June 29, 1994.

26. Immigration and Refugee Board, Assessment of Credibility in Claims for Refugee Protection (2004) at 83–84. It is high time that we in the United States abandon our parochialism and look for guidance if not precedent to the actions of asylum courts in other parts of the democratic world, particularly those within the Anglo-American legal tradition. As former U.S. Supreme Court Justice Sandra Day O'Connor thoughtfully observed in a similar context, "I think that we . . . will find ourselves looking more frequently to the decisions of other constitutional courts, especially other common-law courts that have struggled with the same basic constitutional questions we have. . . . All of these courts have something to teach us about the civilizing function of constitutional law." Sandra Day O'Connor, The Majesty of the Law: Reflections of a Supreme Court Justice 234 (2003). What applies to constitutional questions should equally apply to asylum issues, all of which arise out of the 1951 United Nations Convention, 189 U.N.T.S 150, and the 1967 Protocol Relating to the Status of Refugees.

27. Stuart L. Lustig, M.D., Symptoms of Trauma among Political Asylum Applicants: Don't Be Fooled, 31 HASTINGS INT'L & COMP. L. REV. 725, 730–31 (2008).

28. Adam Liptak, In U.S., Partisan Expert Witnesses Frustrate Many, NEW YORK TIMES, August 11, 2008, at A1.

29. Given that the REAL ID now allows for adverse credibility determinations based on "demeanor" and on an array of misrepresentations that may arise in asylum hearings, the need for extra care in crafting asylum decisions, and the need for expert witness testimony, have become even more critical to a balanced appraisal of a respondent.

30. See Gideon v. Wainwright, 372 U.S. 335 (1963).

31. See 8 C.F.R. 208.13(a). In busy jurisdictions where asylum cases are sometimes complicated, poorly elaborated, and even more poorly represented (if at all), the burden of proof becomes a convenient and justifiable excuse for expeditious denials of relief. Like Pontius Pilate, an over-worked and overwrought IJ may wash his or her hands of an alleged target of persecution where no spirited defense has been advanced on the respondent's behalf.

32. Since 2000, according to its current website, EOIR has had the Legal Orientation Program and the Pro Bono Program, which include a BIA Pro Bono Project and an unaccompanied Alien Children Initiative. While EOIR's efforts in this regard are commendable, they are no substitute for a paid public defenders program that would guarantee counsel to every indigent respondent in immigration court proceedings, and thus ensure a more equal playing field for all asylum applicants.

33. Roscoe Pound, Law in Books and Law in Action, 44 AMERICAN L. REV. 36 (1910).

10 Asylum in a Different Voice?

Judging Immigration Claims and Gender

Carrie Menkel-Meadow[1]

Perhaps the most interesting result of our cross-tabulation study was that the gender of the judge had a significant impact on the likelihood that asylum would be granted. Female immigration judges granted asylum at a rate of 53%, while male judges granted asylum at a rate of 37.3%. An asylum applicant assigned by chance to a female judge therefore had a 44% better chance of prevailing than an applicant assigned to a male judge.[2]

A. Introduction: Gender Difference in Theory and Practice

The extraordinary (and quite robust) findings of Professors Ramji-Nogales, Schoenholtz, and Schrag that gender matters in the outcomes of claims for asylum is not as surprising as it might seem (at least to some of us!). The idea that women judges and lawyers might behave differently from men has been debated in legal scholarship for several decades. The current study provides some of the most powerful and interesting evidence that such a claim about gender in judging in some contexts is valid. What we ought to do about this result as a policy matter remains a quite complicated and debatable issue.

As I will suggest in this essay, women may not only arrive at different outcomes in some kinds of cases, but they are likely to "reason" differently, or consider different facts, circumstances, and conditions as they consider what to decide in granting asylum or not (and perhaps in judging other matters, as well, including those beyond the scope of the present study). I will argue that women should not be the only repositors of those values, attitudes, or considerations that lead them to grant asylum more readily. What women do "differently" should perhaps be more the norm, so that denials, not grants, of asylum status would be more the outliers and departures from justice, or that, at least, a deeper contextual, relational, empathic credibility assessment and factual analysis of asylum cases might be appropriate, rather than the current set of assumptions, presumptions, and evidentiary considerations that seem to lead to arbitrary, or at least inconsistent, asylum denials.[3] To the extent that women judges may be more likely to preside over "conversational" or empathetic hearing processes, they may encourage fuller narratives from troubled asylum claimants. That women judges actually do behave differently in more formal court settings still needs empirical verification. Differences in judicial behavior may vary depending on the setting (formal or informal) and the nature of the claim (and legal rules and evidence rules that govern the proceedings).

Twenty-five years ago, in a book that ruptured the arguments of "equality" feminist theorists and activists in law[4] and elsewhere, Carol Gilligan suggested that girls (and women) might engage in "different" patterns of moral reasoning and decision making. Her path-altering book, *In A Different Voice: Psychological Theory and Women's Development* (1982), argued that girls were more concerned about "connection and relationships" than they were about solving algebraic questions of justice that forced them to solve problems by choosing one legal right (or one person) over another.

In her empirical studies of how adolescents made decisions about such matters as whether to have an abortion or resist the military, she noticed a pattern of difference, not always in actual decisions but frequently in modes of decision making and rationales used for particular choices. Gilligan used a hypothetical of moral reasoning (originally developed by her graduate-school colleague, friend, and noted psychologist Lawrence Kohlberg)[5] to ask young people how they would reason to achieve justice. The hypothetical or moral fable was known as Heinz's Dilemma. It asked whether Heinz, whose wife was suffering from a terminal and painful disease, would be morally wrong in stealing a drug to ease suffering, and, perhaps, prolong the life of his wife, from a pharmacist who was charging a price for the drug that was beyond Heinz's means to pay. Carol Gilligan queried young boys and girls about what they thought about Heinz's choices.

In her book Gilligan reported on two "typical" responses she received that marked different narratives of moral reasoning. Jake, consistent with many of the subjects of Kohlberg's (mostly, if not exclusively male) subjects, used universalistic, legalistic, and "algebraic" reasoning. The drug belonged to the pharmacist—it was his property. Stealing property is both morally wrong and against the law, unless there is a more important right that trumps the right of property. Jake reasoned, by "balancing rights," that since life was "worth" more than property, it was morally permissible for Heinz to steal the drug. Thus, Jake solved the "equation" of justice by declaring that Heinz was entitled to steal the drug because his was the "superior" and therefore morally "trumping" right.[6]

Amy, on the other hand, engaged in a different sort of reasoning, what I then described as "like a bad law student, fighting the hypo."[7] Amy tried to see the needs, rights, and interests of all the parties. Perhaps, she suggested, Heinz and the druggist could sit down and talk about the problem. They might arrange an installment payment plan for the drug, thus holding constant the needs of Heinz's wife for the drug and the pharmacist's need to make a living. Maybe they should ask Heinz's wife (who is most affected by the decisions made) what she thinks should be done. For Amy the dilemma involved more people and had a wider and deeper context than a simple "yes or no."

On Kohlberg's scale of "universal" moral development, Amy scores lower than Jake because she equivocates, she focuses on the facts and personalistic aspects of the problem, and she does not adequately address the larger "universal" issues of justice, precedent, and the need to rank "clear" hierarchical moral choices.

Soon after Gilligan's book was published and a torrent of controversy was unleashed among feminists, lawyers, sociologists, biologists, and anthropologists about whether men and women were more alike or more different in their attitudes, beliefs, and actions, I wrote an article provocatively titled, "Portia in a Different Voice: Speculations on a Woman's Lawyering Process,"[8] in which I argued that Gilligan's work, joined by the work of other scholars of human behavior at that time,[9] supported a notion that women might engage in "different" forms of legal reasoning, valuing highly human connection, relationships, not just rules, and especially the contexts in which legal and moral problems were situated.

Portia was chosen (both by me and by Carol Gilligan) as an evocative figure because she pleaded for mercy (not just cool justice) in Shakespeare's *Merchant of Venice*.[10] Portia's plea for mercy facilitated the expansion of Carol Gilligan's original notion of "an ethic of care" to a wide variety of political and legal contexts.[11] While Jake displayed an "ethic of justice" of rights balancing and clear choices, Amy tried to keep the connections of parties in conflict in relationship to each other and to herself and worried a lot about everyone's (not just the legal winner's) well-being. Amy became a symbol of legal actors and scholars who saw care, human flourishing, and so-called positive rights as an equally, if not more, important part of the justice system than "negative" rights of freedom from (governmental restraint).[12] The kind of "care for the other" that Amy and Portia came to represent in this highly contested literature may hold some of the explanatory clues to the Ramji-Nogales, Schoenholtz, and Schrag findings of gender differences in asylum decisions (what I will from here on call "the gender judging findings").

Twenty-five years ago, I also argued that women were (more) likely to use different sorts of processes and modes in their legal and moral reasoning than relatively "simple," blunt-cut determinations made according to formal, bright-line legal rules. This argument included not only more contextual and relational reasoning (suggesting more mediational and negotiated, rather than decisional, processes) but also different outcomes (more "shared," contingent, or jointly managed solutions to problems, both moral and legal). In the asylum context these claims would suggest that women judges might be more likely to facilitate less formal conversations in the hearing process, be less rigid with respect to evidentiary admissibility rulings, cabin or control extraordinarily harsh cross-examinations, and empathize with claimants. On the other hand, since the asylum decision is a binary one—yes or no—there is little room in this environment for "compromise" or intermediate rulings.

I went on to speculate (as the article's title honestly announced) on a variety of other gender differences that might play a role in the legal system, including more inclusive forms of evidence rules (what is "admissible" or "relevant" might vary more in different legal contexts), less draconian decision making, both in rules and outcomes, a generally less adversarial approach to both process (more open, inclusive, and conversational or "dialogic") and outcomes (avoidance of binary outcomes), participation by more parties affected by legal decision making, and, most relevant to the present inquiry, different modes and outcomes of "judging."[13]

Immediately following these claims, several things happened. First, some other legal analysts joined or expanded the argument, suggesting that women would reason in a different voice, change the legal rules and legal processes, practice law differently, treat their clients and opponents differently, use different qualities of "judgment" in deciding cases, or otherwise transform the legal system.[14] Second, a few legal scholars applied these theories specifically to the acts of judging.[15] Third, at both theoretical levels, and ultimately in a wide variety of empirical studies, scholars from many different fields argued about the validity of these claims and the alleged "sources" of gender difference (whether in biology, socialization, or political oppression and subordination).[16]

I will review some of those claims and empirical findings here, but it is also true that the issue of "gender difference" in legal work has more recently receded to a more quiescent period of simply documenting numbers of participants in the legal and judicial professions, without much speculation about or evidence to confirm gender differences in the structure or performance of legal and judicial work.[17] The findings of the Refugee Roulette study[18] change all that, and we are back to speculating on what it all means.

In this essay I will first provide some review of what we already know about gender differences in legal and judicial behavior, and then I will recap what Ramji-Nogales, Schoenholtz, and Schrag have uncovered about gender differences in decisions about whether to grant asylum in the immigration context. Finally, I will take up once again some speculations about what it all means, including why those differences in asylum grant rates exist, and offer some further thoughts about the policy implications of the present findings. I say "speculation" because although the data are clear and robust here, the present study does not include qualitative data or interviews with the decision makers to test any of the hypotheses or speculations I (or Ramji-Nogales, Schoenholtz, or Schrag) offer here. Clearly, more empirical work is required. For example, to the extent that future researchers could get access to study hearings, they could code for differences in process behaviors and rulings. Simple interview studies could also at least let the judges speak for themselves about what they think they do in judging claims so that at least at the self-reporting level we could see if there are gender differences in beliefs about or conceptions of what judges are doing.

B. Empirical Findings on Gender Differences in Legal Decision Making

For decades political scientists have been studying the correlations of a variety of demographic and political factors with particular judicial outcomes. In short (more detail provided below), the results are quite mixed and, I would say, inconclusive, with many researchers proclaiming that there is little to no support for the claim that women judges behave differently than men judges.[19] In addition to the empirical data, there is the claim, often made, that judging, by role definition, demands neutrality and so women don their judicial robes and roles to literally "disembody" themselves and assimilate to a "neutral" or male model of judging so as to draw the least amount of attention to their biological or "embodied" gender.[20] Judging is, after all, about being "neutral," "impartial," and unbiased, not letting personal characteristics or relationships interfere in any way with decision making. Consider the image of "Lady Justice" (yes, a woman representing justice) who is blindfolded so she weighs her scales of justice without "seeing" who the parties before her really are.[21] Both the judge and the parties are "disembodied," representing only their legal claims and not their personhood.

On the other hand, there is a growing body of empirical work that does find some gender differences in judicial behavior,[22] noting that among other things, women judges may be more likely to find discrimination in employment (by both race and gender),[23] that women are both more and less harsh in criminal sentencing,[24] including in cases where criminal offenders have done great harm to women, as in rape or sexual assault cases,[25] but are also sometimes "harsher" on women in family law cases.[26] An early study found that women were more sympathetic to those seeking to avoid the draft,[27] supporting theoretical arguments that because women are mothers they are more inclined to disfavor war and military solutions and more likely to seek "peace" in a variety of different contexts.[28] Other studies have found that women were more likely to vote with claimants and mothers (in criminal-justice and family-law settings), while male judges were more likely to protect individual interests of accused persons.[29] In another study, women judges on state courts were more likely to vote "liberally" on obscenity and death penalty issues. In such cases just the presence of one woman on a state supreme court could increase the probability that the rest of the court would follow a more "liberal" position.[30]

Clearly, there is "conflict in the circuits" (and trial courts and appellate courts) and in the data on the issues of whether there are gender differences in judging and, if there are, in what direction they operate ("protectionist" of same-gender interests as in family and discrimination matters, or harsher for differential expectations of different genders, especially in criminal and family law matters).

As I will discuss more fully below, these complex, and sometimes contradictory, empirical findings on gender differences in judging track the contradictory and inconclusive literature on whether there are gender differences in legal practice generally.[31] There is empirical work that supports claims that women perform certain lawyering tasks differently,[32] or are more "ethical,"[33] or have different goals with respect to the purposes of their legal work, such as being more oriented to public interest work,[34] and other studies that claim that no significant differences in practice protocols can be observed.[35] For many years (indeed, one could say for centuries), it was widely assumed that women would practice and interpret law differently or at least disrupt the study of law, as is evidenced in the many successful efforts to exclude women from law schools for most of human (and American) history.[36]

There is fairly consistent research on the continuing occupational segregation of women in the profession, women being disproportionately represented in the public sector and still not present in the upper reaches of the large corporate law firm partnership.[37] As studies of gender difference in the practice of law and judging continue, I suspect we may be in the middle of a generational shift. The way women are recruited and socialized to the profession in times of scarcity as opposed to times of "critical mass"[38] may determine the relative "freedom" that women (or other "minorities" in the workplace) have to express particular views, attitudes, or behaviors. Early gender-difference literature confirmed that early recruits to a male- (or white-) dominated profession were quite likely to "conform" or assimilate to traditional patterns of behavior. As the more recent studies of gender differences in judging are demonstrating, the numbers of findings of difference seem to be increasing, perhaps signaling larger samples from which to observe and study differences, as critical mass and representation of women increases in both the judiciary and the practice of law generally.[39] Since there are a relatively large number of women judges in the immigration system (32%), perhaps women judges in this system are within the "critical mass" range and feel "freer" to rule and decide on their own terms and interpretations of the law and facts. Or, it is also possible that since the immigration judiciary suffers from being less "public" and is less "prestigious" than other court settings, women may feel "liberated" (without much scrutiny or because no one really "cares" about what they do) to decide cases in ways they think are appropriate and just, without needing to "conform" to a male "norm" of higher denial rates.

It is also quite important to observe that more recent studies of women as judges are focusing on differences where there are "mixed panels" of judges, as in various appellate courts, as opposed to the single trial judge making decisions on her/his own. The present study looks at judges at the trial and some appellate levels (Board of Immigration Appeals, circuit courts of appeals) but, due to lack of adequate data, has not looked closely at differences in the gender composition of multiple-judge panels.[40] A growing body of work on the paths of influence and collegiality in multiperson judging situations suggests that mere representation of women (or other nonmajority male judges) may alter the decisional processes and outcomes.[41]

C. The "Gender Gap" in Asylum Judging

In addition to the primary finding of a wide gap in asylum grant rates for women and male judges (53% rate of granting asylum for women, versus 37.3% for men, making it 44% more likely for a claim to result in a grant of asylum when brought before a woman immigration judge), other empirical findings of the present study illuminate the power of "gender plus." When gender is combined with other variables, the "gender gap" in judging rates may be even more profound. Prior employment settings and reactions to the presence of claimants' dependents and family members are among the factors that interact with "simple" gender differences.

Paths to the traditional bench are quite different for women,[42] as the findings of difference in pre-judicial employment of immigration judges in this study confirms. More women than men who ascend to the immigration bench work in nongovernmental organizations (29% for women to 9% for men), but, in contrast, many more men than women come from governmental enforcement agencies like the Department of Homeland Security or the previously named Immigration and Naturalization Service (56% of men compared to 51% for women). Men were more likely to come from governmental enforcement agencies potentially more sympathetic to enforcement and exclusionary practices and policies than women, who worked in settings more "sympathetic" to asylum seekers, including both government and private practice. On the trial bench generally women are more likely to come from government, legal education, and other public services than are male judges, who disproportionately come from large law firms and prosecutorial roles. Thus, differences in judicial behavior may simply be a further reflection of earlier gender differentiation in opportunities for socialization in different work environments. Whether women "choose" or are "pulled" toward public service or are "pushed" toward it through exclusion from other work environments remains a much-studied question in occupational segregation and socialization studies.[43]

Prior work experience clearly affects grant of asylum rates (according to the gender judging data here). Those with prior government service granted asylum in 39.6% of cases compared to 47.1% of those from NGOs or private practice, with prior DHS and INS experience explaining much of the variance (those without DHS and INS experience granted asylum 48.2% of the time, compared to 38.9% of those with DHS/INS experience). Judges with experience in academia, private law practice, and NGOs were all more likely to grant asylum than those with DHS/INS experience. A few female judges, who are beginning to write about their experiences as judges, have reported that their experiences as women jurists *qua* women, including both work and family roles (as mothers, academics, reformists, particular kinds of lawyers, such as family lawyers), and their needs to be sympathetic to differences, do and will affect how they perform as judges.[44] Thus, Baroness Hale, the highest judge in the United Kingdom, for example, has been studied as one who has used her experience in family law and as an academic to understand and write differently about some women's issues, such as family (dis)connections and appropriate clothing for Muslims in public schools. Female immigration judges may understand from inside experience (through personal or professional and representational experience) some of the particularities of women's asylum claims (such as those that are explicitly gendered, such as domestic violence or cultural practices like female circumcision).

Nevertheless, the gender judging findings here found a strong gender difference in asylum grant rates, independent of prior work experience, demonstrating just how profound and robust the "gender gap" findings in asylum grant rates are here. As the data demonstrate, female judges still have higher asylum grant rates regardless of work location. Gender differences in asylum grant rates persist and indeed get stronger when gender is combined with other variables such as whether applicants were represented by counsel (female judges granted asylum in 55.6% of cases with representation while male judges granted asylum in only 14.3% of cases where the applicants were unrepresented).

One additional finding of this study is relevant to the issue of gender differences in judging. Professors Ramji-Nogales, Schoenholtz, and Schrag found that the presence of dependents (usually children, but sometimes also spouses) also dramatically increased the likelihood of a grant of asylum. Those with no dependents had a 42.3% grant rate, whereas having one dependent increased that rate to 48.2%, a statistically significant difference. The existence of these family members may mark both increased credibility and increased sympathy for the claimant. Knowing that by denying the claim a judge may be sending a whole family to their deaths or serious injury or to a parentless living situation may cause those who "care" about family and child well-being to increase their likelihood of granting asylum. As I discuss more fully below, this "family" effect is consistent with some of the theoretical claims made about what female judges may consider as relevant and appropriate in deciding such cases.

Thus, despite somewhat equivocal findings about gender differences in previous studies of judicial behavior in courts, gender differences in judging asylum cases noted in this study are quite pronounced.

D. What It Means: Why Are Women Judges More Likely to Grant Asylum?

The dramatic findings of this study demonstrating that women immigration judges are 44% more likely to grant asylum than male judges revitalizes the debates of gender differences in judging and legal behavior of the last few decades. The current study has probably a bigger database of cases and judges than most, if not all, of the prior studies of this phenomenon and so may provide a more rigorous test of gender-difference claims. On the other hand, immigration cases, and the asylum claim in particular, are located in a unique context, conjuring up terrible harms and suffering if asylum is not granted, relying on relatively vague legal standards, being very fact intensive in proof requirements, requiring a great deal of discretion, and, at the same time, are overshadowed by highly contentious immigration-policy concerns about how "open" to make our borders. Whether the strength and robustness of the gender-gap findings here would be replicated in other judicial settings is less clear. Consider, as one possible comparison, Social Security disability claims. These are also claims that rely on testimony about levels of pain and suffering; there may also be a "critical mass" of female judges in this system, but the legal regulations and definitions of disability are more delineated and more rigid. Studies of other judicial settings would provide an interesting test of the true extent of this "gender gap" in judging behavior.

In trying to understand why there are gender differences in judging asylum cases, it might be useful to revisit one of Carol Gilligan's other moral fables, a more recent one that is remarkably close to the issues presented by asylum cases. In her work on "the two moralities," Gilligan posed the following problem to young girls and boys:

> Two industrious moles have worked all summer to build themselves a shelter for the winter. When winter arrives, a less forward-looking porcupine pleads with the moles to share their comfortable hole. In their concern, they take the porcupine into their close and small space and then are hurt by the sharpness of the porcupine's quills. What should the moles do?[45]

In Gilligan's studies, adolescents with a "rights" or "justice" orientation (more often, but not exclusively, boys) suggest that the porcupine should be thrown out (or excluded from the comfortable hole) because the moles built the hole with their hard labor and earned moral desert. Indeed, if the porcupine refuses to leave "voluntarily," many young boys in the study said it would be morally permissible for the moles to shoot the porcupine. Sound familiar? Is this the brutal boundary defense with a theory of border-based moral desert that our immigration policy enacts? Why should those who have not participated in creating the American polity be allowed to enter, just because, like the porcupine, they have a "need" to get out of the cold (or more dangerous situations of persecution)?

Young girls in the study were much more likely to be sympathetic to the porcupine and looked for other ways to account for and satisfy the needs of both the moles and the porcupine. They were more likely to develop solutions like using a blanket to cover the porcupine, asking the porcupine to work with the moles to enlarge the living space, or creating a separate space for the porcupine to use. Those who responded by trying to find a solution for getting the porcupine out of the cold are labeled those who reason with an "ethic of care."

As studies using this fable have accumulated, data indicate that most men and about one-third of all women use the first, "rights"-based approach to the moral dilemma and about two-thirds of women and a smaller group of men use the latter approach.[46] In the first approach, like Jake's reasoning in the Heinz Dilemma, reasoning is from abstract, rational, and universal principles—land, holes, housing, and property belong to those who work for them—moral desert based on effort and boundaries. For those who seek to include the porcupine (even if he didn't contribute, initially, to making the hole) values of human need, care, connection, social responsibility, and sharing dominate concerns about efforts, boundaries, and rights. If you don't like to see suffering of any other sentient being, then it is hard to "exclude" the needy.

The Porcupine's Dilemma of moral desert or human need aptly represents some of the challenges faced by immigration judges, who, after all, have a statute to interpret. What is a "well-founded fear of persecution on the basis of race, religion, nationality, membership of a particular social group or political opinion" on account of which a person outside of his country is "unable or owing to such fear, unwilling to avail himself of the protection of that country" and therefore should be granted asylum as a refugee?[47] Is the porcupine's fear of the cold within a qualifying category? How much suffering must he endure? Is he excluded because his species/race/nationality of porcupine is disfavored by his native habitat and "country" or by those who rule in his native land, or because he is different from the moles? Judgments about how to characterize groups, categories, facts, and the relationship of individual harm(s) within collective entities (e.g., social groups, religions, nationalities, political groups) require much discretion, as well as evidence, and interpretation. Like the porcupine who pleads for "mercy" and empathy, asylum applicants tell stories of suffering, fear, and serious physical harm. Whether they are allowed to crawl into the safe "hole" may depend on whether the deciding moles are male or female, whether they are considering rational and abstract principles, and precedent, or simply human need.

Since there are no settled quotas on successful asylum applicants, individual judges must determine in each individual case, with the aid of whatever precedent exists from past decisions, BIA decisions, and the appellate cases from the relevant circuit court of appeals, whether to let a particular candidate "in" or not. The fact-dependent nature of these cases and their individuality makes it relatively easy to treat each case almost *sui generis*. Thus, unlike many other settings in which the effects of gender in judging have been studied, immigration cases may provide an arena of greater discretion, greater fact specificity, and broader relevance, and a site where particular stories of human need and suffering may, at least for some decision makers, "trump" the more broad, vague, and abstract legal standards. It would be useful to study more rigorously whether gender differences in judging vary with respect to the confines or specifics of the law being applied. For example, Rand and Dana Jack found in their studies of lawyers' ethical behavior that men and women acted or opined about ethical matters quite similarly when the ethical rules were clear (e.g., applying confidentiality rules) but were quite different when there was little specific direction or more discretion in a particular rule interpretation (such as when to disclose information to the other side in a contested matter).[48]

If Amy, Portia, and female moles reason with an "ethic of care" rather than an "ethic of rules and justice," then female immigration judges may be more likely to listen to stories of human need and suffering with a more empathic, or sympathetic, ear. If, as the data above show, women judges are more likely to be sympathetic to (or rule in favor of) claimants in discrimination and family law cases, perhaps the combination of persecution for ethnic, national, religious, or even political affiliations, coupled with concerns about the harms visited upon possibly abandoned dependents, makes asylum claims more likely to be validated by women judges.

To the extent that immigration cases combine intensive fact determinations with a relatively vague and broad statutory standard, they are precisely the kind of case in which appeals to need, emotional elements, and nonlegal factors may be particularly salient. Thus, like the studies that demonstrate that men and women do not differ much in their judging behavior unless gender itself is salient (as in discrimination, family law, and a variety of other case types), immigration may fall on the side of personal or human need (rather than commercial or other civil claims) that may be, in some cases, gendered.[49] Where determinations of cases are more dependent on human considerations, both in terms of evidence (credibility, storytelling, degree of personal fear, suffering, and harm) and in terms of directly observable outcomes (if asylum is not granted, the losing claimant is automatically "removed" and may be detained, if not already in detention), the tearing or breaking of human connections and lives may be salient by gender (in a disproportionate number of, if not in all, cases). As Robin West has eloquently argued, the law needs to take account of women's hedonic needs, including claims (like relationship and familial [dis]connection) that have previously been underprotected in the law.[50]

In another context, I have reported on my own experience as a judge (arbitrator) in a gender-salient set of cases.[51] For some years I was an arbitrator in some of the thousands of hearings attended by victims of a mass tort, involving a defective product, the birth control device Dalkon Shield, which caused injuries ranging from death to infertility, unwanted pregnancies, excessive bleeding, infections, and pain to exclusively female claimants.[52] The Dalkon Shield Claimants Trust (which managed the arbitration hearings from inside the bankruptcy proceedings of the manufacturer, the A.H. Robins Company, and was administered by Duke University's Private Adjudication Center) initially sought to use as decision makers labor arbitrators, who turned out to be more or less exclusively male. I was recruited as the first woman, followed by many others, to begin to hear these cases, as the program's managers realized that all the claimants were women who were to testify about very intimate details of their lives. While both I and other researchers had hoped to formally study this claims process as an excellent study of gender differences in judging, among other things, formal data analysis was never completed (the outcomes of the arbitration awards were confidential). Nevertheless, in many informal meetings of the arbitrators and the management of the program, gender differences in judging were revealed (not always in a predictable direction). In some cases male judges were more likely to grant higher amounts of damages (there was a monetary cap on all cases) because they were moved by the pain and suffering they heard about; in other cases male judges admitted an inability to assess the "female" pain of bleeding and reproductive organ pain and malfunction. In many cases women arbitrators had first-hand knowledge and experience of the symptoms and injuries and thus could both empathize with, but also discount, the claims made by injured claimants. Though we have no formal data on outcome differentials, it was clear to us that there were some (in both directions of harshness and generosity of awards, even within a relatively small range of awards within the cap). Nevertheless, during the hearings and afterward, I, and many of the other women arbitrators, received tearful acknowledgments and letters of gratitude for the processes we had presided over with care (providing tissues, among other things), and for providing some relief to the claimants who had to testify about intimate "female" problems and their sexual history to a female, rather than male, judge.

This is not to say that some male arbitrators did not also provide fair and caring processes (as some of the males responding to Gilligan's Porcupine Dilemma did), but my own experience in the Dalkon Shield hearings confirms what much of the empirical data on judging is now suggesting: the gender of judges may matter if the issue being decided is *gender salient*. What is gender salient (biological concerns, family issues, discrimination claims) of course remains highly contested. Here it is important to note several different issues—where a contested issue in a case does involve gender, there may be gender differentials (and those gender differentials can operate in contradictory directions, such as more harsh or lenient treatment of female criminal offenders, less credibility attached to particular kinds of claims and injuries) in outcomes. This is consistent with some of the findings of studies of individual judges and justices such as Sandra Day O'Connor and Baroness Brenda Hale, on the highest courts of the United States and United Kingdom.[53] Second, gender behavior in the court or hearing room (judicial temperament, process, rulings on what is relevant, salient, admissible) may be "different," irrespective of final outcome. To the extent that we know from the literature of procedural justice that process matters for participants' valuation of legal processes,[54] the way judges behave during the hearing may be extremely important to claimants and participants in legal processes, irrespective (or unrelated to separate assessment) of outcomes. Thus, the role of gender in judicial processes is complex.

While many have argued that because judging requires "neutrality" there will be little evidence of difference in either process or outcome, several legal scholars have suggested a variety of characteristics that women judges might bring to the bench, including compassion, a broader sense of relevance and admissibility, patience, a greater sense of "connection" to the litigants, a broader sense of context, more generous conclusions about credibility (especially in cases of pain and suffering), more attention to storytelling and narrative than crisper, leaner, more legalistic testimonial evidence, and more sympathy for particular kinds of claimants (the helpless, children, other oppressed or subordinated people).[55] Imagine how the descriptions of the "rational" judge of Ronald Dworkin's Hercules[56] would have to be broadened to include some of these characteristics. While many descriptions of appropriate judicial characteristics include such abstractions as detachment, impartiality, disengagement, neutrality, independence, discernment, analytic ability, strength, clarity, decisiveness, freedom from bias, open-mindedness, and commitment to equal justice,[57] those arguing that women judges will bring more of their "gendered" experiences, in both personal and professional roles, to the bench suggest that other and appropriate characteristics should be added to any description of judging, including the values of compassion, Portia's empathy and mercy, connection to (not disengagement from) litigants, courtesy, sensitivity, and a deeper sense of context. Such authors (and I am among them) have argued that to add these qualities of judging is not to challenge or change the values of neutrality and lack of bias—indeed, they add to the justice and fairness of decision making by adding human and appropriately affective (emotional)[58] considerations to what are not always totally rational or rule-/law-based decisions. Thus, while often protesting that women will not "do justice" differently, many commentators still argue for representativeness of judicial bodies, suggesting that in order to represent all the values that make up "just" decisions, women (as well as other underrepresented groups) should be on the bench to reflect the full range of values that exist in a society that defines justice democratically.

Several literary and cultural sources provide stark representations of these empirical findings and arguments (if not through rigorous social science). In Susan Glaspell's famous play and short story, *A Jury of Her Peers*,[59] the wives of the legal investigators and prosecutors of a murder of a local farmer in a remote region of the Midwest consider "evidence" of the crime that is outside the "view" or literal understanding of the male professionals. While the men look at conventional sources of proof for determining who committed the murder, the wives discover that the wife of the farmer (the main suspect) has had her pet bird's neck broken, cruelly. They infer from this "evidence" that she has been the subject of her husband's brutality and probably killed in "self-defense." They, without words, "judge" her nonguilty by virtue of excuse or justification and quietly remove the evidence their legalistic and conventional husbands could neither "see" nor interpret properly. This story illustrates what has been called by feminist analysts a "women's way of knowing"—deeply contextual thinking, looking at facts or "evidence" that would not necessarily or conventionally be considered legal, and understanding motivations and facts that might not be formally considered relevant. The women in this story act as judge and jury and "acquit" their "fellow" wife from a place of empathetic understanding of what and how hard her life was. This story evokes complex reactions. To those who think the wives have "violated" formal law by collaborating in the destruction of evidence, they are "lawless." To a large number of commentators, they are performing a higher justice (especially in an era when women could not serve as actual judges or jurors) in considering the facts outside the murder scene and seeing the wife's action in the context of her life of terrible suffering. Glaspell based her play and story on a real case, which she covered as a journalist, and she has been read as criticizing the formality and limitedness of conventional (male) legal systems, which, with their formal and narrow rules, do not do justice.

More recently, the film *Frozen River*[60] demonstrated a similar "women's justice" on the U.S.–Canadian border as two women, one Native and the other Anglo-White, become reluctant partners in an unlawful human smuggling operation across the border. They know that what they are doing is unlawful, but both of them are working to make money to provide for their children—a home for the white children and an attempt to regain custody of her lost child for the Native woman. In the course of their work they discover they have almost killed an innocent baby belonging to one of their smugglees and they return at great danger to themselves to rescue and resuscitate the baby. (Many viewers of the film in the commercial theater at which I viewed it openly discussed whether male human traffickers would have done the same!) Eventually, despite their initial distrust of each other, these women care for each other and each other's children. The white woman (Ray Eddy) helps the Native Woman (Lila) recapture her own child and then Lila becomes the caretaker for all their children as Ray Eddy takes the "rap" for their activities and is incarcerated. The film is a searing look at one of the least-known sites of border crossings (the Mohawk region on the New York-Quebec border) and its brutal honesty and frigid landscape all the more dramatically reveal the little bit of human warmth provided by the female characters as they attempt to raise their families alone and facilitate the desire of illegal border crossers to find a better life.

True, another recent film about immigration, *The Visitor*,[61] depicts the growing human connections between a male widower college professor, Walter Vale, and the Syrian and Senegalese immigrants who are squatting in his New York apartment. But this film also demonstrates the futility of individual stories and narratives to achieve immigration justice in the period of post-9/11 immigration rules and practices. In this film the connections are ultimately severed as Tarek (the young Syrian musician) is deported back to Syria, separating him from his girlfriend, his mother (Mouna, who lives in the Midwest,) and Professor Vale. All are helpless at changing the legal turns of events and Tarek's mother (yet another female heroine marked by her connection to family) returns (at great risk to herself) to Syria to be with her son, sacrificing many things, including a budding romance with the now rehumanized professor, who, perhaps because he is so law-abiding and timid, is less efficacious than the "lawless" women of *Frozen River*. In juxtaposition these films demonstrate how a man (Professor Vale), slavishly following the law and passively obeying it, may do greater injustice (at a deeper moral, not legal, level) than women (Lila and Ray Eddy), challenging the law and living as "outlaws" on the "edge" of countries and lives.

Certainly, these are only fictional, if powerful depictions of the modern world of immigration, from both sides of legality and lawless borders,[62] but the filmmaker storytellers, like asylum applicants, are trying to demonstrate the individual pain and suffering that occurs with vague and harsh rules and arbitrary and often brutal enforcement, and in their different ways, they also appeal to our emotional and human, as well as legal, sense of (in)justice.

Thus, in a system of judging asylum claims that requires claimants to tell their stories of persecution, harm, and suffering and not only to satisfy the statutory standards but also to persuade a judge that a particular case has merit, both for the individual and for the political issues implicated in refugee law, it should not be surprising that emotional appeals, good storytelling, affidavits, and narratives from family members and others who have been persecuted might draw greater responsiveness from (at least some) women judges, especially those who have worked within the immigration legal system.

The findings of this study are consistent with my claims of twenty-five years ago that women judges might encourage more participatory, less adversarial-like, more "conversation-like" proceedings within formal evidence rules and, therefore, might be more likely to elicit a stronger, longer, and more detailed narrative from a traumatized asylum claimant.[63]

Finally, as both quantitative and more qualitative studies of gender judicial behavior demonstrate, women judges themselves have suffered disproportionately from discrimination[64] (at work and in other aspects of their lives) and thus may be more inclined to believe (credibility assessments) and empathize with asylum claimants. Perhaps, at least for some, this experience of discrimination permits them, literally, to "hear" better the "different" voices in their courtrooms, including the literally hundreds of different languages represented in asylum hearings.

The particular findings of gender differentials in asylum grant rates here do continue to raise some interesting, and as yet unstudied, questions, calling for more research. First, and most importantly here, how do these judges describe their own judicial behavior? How would both male and female immigration judges react or respond to the findings here? Would they be surprised? Would they offer illustrations of their own motivations or explanations about why they might differ in their rulings from each other by gender? Second, are asylum cases *gender salient* as I have described that concept here—does freedom from persecution, connection to family members, or other aspects of this claim make it more like a discrimination, subordination, or family claim than other kinds of cases in which there appear to be little or no gender disparities in outcomes?

The gendered nature of asylum claims has been most pronounced in a variety of contested cases involving genital mutilation[65] and domestic violence[66] as "persecutions" on the basis of membership in a "social or political" group, that of persecuted women, not yet recognized by most courts as a qualifying category. And, to measure another possible influence of gender, it would be interesting to compare grant and denial rates by gender of the asylum applicant (and to look at interactions of the gender of the applicant and the judge).[67] Unfortunately, such data were not provided in the current study.

Third, can we test empirically some of the claims I have made here about more inclusive evidence, more conversational, less adversarial hearings—both the existence of these possibly differential processes and their effects? (Not likely, given the lack of transcripts in most cases, especially those that are not appealed.)

Fourth, how should we account for the fact that asylum cases call for binary (yes or no) decisions? This is not an environment in which, like Amy, we can search to meet the needs of all the parties. Either asylum is granted or it is not—no negotiation, mediated process, or intermediate outcome is permitted under the rules. Are women more likely to resolve a doubt or use a different standard of proof if the evidence is not totally clear on one side in favor of granting asylum while male judges exercise their blunt cuts more often in the other direction? Does the gender disparity in outcomes hold true for other kinds of immigration claims (removal, etc.)?

Finally, what might the consequences be for the asylum judicial system of knowledge of these findings? How will represented claimants try to "game" the system to be assigned to female judges, despite the clerk's random assignments? How will unrepresented claimants fare in an environment where experienced or well-educated lawyers know of these results but unrepresented parties will not? (Badly, we can assume, since their grant rates are already much lower than those who have counsel [45.6% of those who are represented are successful in seeking asylum, compared to 16.3 % who do not have counsel].) All of these unanswered questions call for more research and make the policy implications of the present study difficult to assess.

E. Policy Implications of the "Gender Gap" in Asylum Judging

Though the findings are clear, strong, and relatively robust (even when tested against and combined with other important variables) that women immigration judges are much more likely to grant asylum than their male colleagues, what we should do about these findings is much less clear. The danger, of course, is that such findings will be used to proclaim women judges too "soft" or "lenient" in an era of immigration phobia, especially after September 11, 2001, has hardened our immigration policies and, in principle, if not in actuality, hardened our borders. This could cause a serious backlash against women judges, both in appointing them and in monitoring their behavior. Even worse, those already serving as immigration judges might see these results and decide to "overcompensate" by increasing denial rates to prove their even-handedness and neutrality. Worse yet, these findings could "infect" judicial appointments generally, not just to the immigration courts, by providing fodder for those who want to argue about women judges being too "soft."

On the other hand, we could look at what makes women judges more likely to grant asylum as a sign that our system needs redirection. Perhaps the "ethic of justice" (and rules and formality) should, in Portia's words, "be tempered with mercy." Perhaps women judges encourage more respectful courtrooms with active listening that allows traumatized victims of persecution to tell a more complete and accurate story. Perhaps a little compassion is appropriate in a potentially life-ending judicial proceeding. We know we cannot admit everyone who wants to come to the United States, but do we know what an "optimal" or "appropriate" number of refugees is, given both world conditions and our capacity to offer safety and shelter to those who need it from outside of our well-constructed "hole" of warmth in winter? Perhaps two sorts of heads and hearts (both male and female) can give us better answers when they work additively and together.

Like the principal authors of this book, I do not think we should deal with gender disparities by issuing quotas or numbers for immigration judges to measure themselves against. I do think we should pay some attention to who our immigration judges are and how they are selected, trained, and evaluated.[68] Most state and federal judges are accountable, in some cases by election, in others by appellate review or publication of decisions, opinions, and reversal rates. Just learning what we have from this study should demonstrate the importance of seeing and understanding those "social facts" that we learn from statistical analysis— the patterns in the aggregate that are often not readily apparent to the "naked" human eye. Clearly we need to study more the *why* and the *how* of the differences in gender judging in immigration.

In the meantime, however, I would suggest that we reorder what we think the "norm" ought to be. Perhaps in a world that is brutish and getting ever "smaller" and at the same time continues to have its share of cruelty, we might consider how appropriate it might be in a system of refugee protection to consider other factors and different processes—including more inclusive, less formal hearings, consideration of family connections and emotions, and a generous benefit of the doubt in credibility determinations, rather than overly harsh cross-examinations—for those who have usually undergone enormous hardship just to get here and make an asylum claim in the first place.[69] Perhaps the processes that produced a higher grant rate for women judges should be the processes and decision rules for all. Perhaps asylum in a "different" voice might be asylum in a "better" voice as well.

1. Carrie Menkel-Meadow is A. B. Chettle Jr. Professor of Law, Dispute Resolution and Civil Procedure, Georgetown University Law Center, and Professor of Law, University of California, Irvine. I thank my colleague and friend Philip Schrag for the invitation to reflect on these important issues and for the opportunities he has provided over the years for me to participate in the supervision of clinical students undertaking representation of asylum seekers. I come from a family of those who were persecuted for their "ethnicity and religion" (though they were, in fact, not practitioners of any religion) and who would have faced sure death in the Holocaust's concentration camps, but for their perseverance, bravery, hard work, luck, and social connections. I have learned from personal and professional experience how random justice in this arena (or any other) can be and dedicate this essay to the hope that if we understand better the human roulette we are playing we can increase the chances for true justice to be done. Thanks to Bert Kritzer, Tranh Nyugen, and Timothy Moore for substantive and bibliographic assistance and support.

2. See chapter 3, page 47.

3. As the data here show, grant rates vary enormously by region, ranging from a low of 26% (Region H) to a high of 62% for Region D, see chapter 2, page 22, table 2.1. In addition, grant and denial rates vary by nation of origin of the asylum applicant. In some regions, there is relative uniformity about the level of "persecution" in a particular nation, such as China or Colombia; in other regions there may be wide disparity among decision makers within a region about how to treat the conditions of particular countries, see chapter 2, pages 22–28.

4. Wendy Williams, The Equality Crisis: Some Reflections on Culture, Courts, and Feminism, 7 Women's Rts. L. Rep. 175 (1982).

5. Lawrence Kohlberg, THE PSYCHOLOGY OF MORAL DEVELOPMENT: THE NATURE AND VALIDITY OF MORAL STAGES (1984); id., THE PHILOSOPHY OF MORAL DEVELOPMENT: MORAL STAGES AND THE IDEA OF JUSTICE (1981).

6. Carol Gilligan, IN A DIFFERENT VOICE: PSYCHOLOGICAL THEORY AND WOMEN'S DEVELOPMENT (1982) at 25–31.

7. E. Dubois, Mary Dunlap, C. Gilligan, C. MacKinnon, C. Menkel-Meadow et al., The 1984 James McCormick Mitchell Lecture: Feminist Discourse, Moral Values, and the Law—A Conversation, 34 Buffalo L. Rev. 11, 36 (1985).

8. 1 Berkeley Women's Law Journal 39–63.

9. Such as N. Chodorow, THE REPRODUCTION OF MOTHERING (1978); J. Miller, TOWARD A NEW PSYCHOLOGY OF WOMEN (1976); N. Noddings, CARING: A FEMININE APPROACH TO ETHICS AND MORAL EDUCATION (1974); A. Schaef, WOMEN'S REALITY (1981). Cf. E. Maccoby & C. Jacklin, THE PSYCHOLOGY OF SEX DIFFERENCES (1974).

10. Shakespeare, MERCHANT OF VENICE. Of course, it is also true, as I argued later, see infra note 31, that Portia was quite an effective traditional lawyer in arguing her case, disguised as she was, as a male jurist.

11. Leslie Bender, From Gender Difference to Feminist Solidarity: Using Carol Gilligan and an Ethic of Care in Law, 15 Vt. L. Rev. 1 (1990); Joan Tronto, MORAL BOUNDARIES: A POLITICAL ARGUMENT FOR AN ETHIC OF CARE (1993); Eva Feder Kittay, WOMEN AND MORAL THEORY (1987); C. Menkel-Meadow, What's Gender Got to Do with It? Morality and the Ethic of Care, 22 N.Y.U. Rev. of Law and Social Change (1995); Stephen Ellmann, The Ethic of Care as an Ethic for Lawyers, 81 Geo. L. J. 2665 (1993); Eric L. Muller, The Virtue of Mercy in Criminal Sentencing, 24 Seton Hall L. Rev. 288 (1993).

12. See e.g. Robin West, CARING FOR JUSTICE (1997); Robin West, Unenumerated Duties, 9 Univ. of Penn. J. Constitutional Law 221 (2006).

13. Portia in a Different Voice, *supra* note 8 at 49–55.

14. 38 Journal of Legal Education 1, Symposium on Women in Legal Education (1988); 25 Law and Society Review 221, Symposium on Gender and Sociolegal Studies (1991); C. Menkel-Meadow, Mainstreaming Feminist Legal Theory, 23 Pacific L. Rev. 1493 (1992); C. Menkel-Meadow, *Women's Ways of Knowing Law: Feminist Legal Epistemology, Pedagogy, and Jurisprudence*, in KNOWLEDGE, DIFFERENCE, AND POWER (Bilenky, Clinchy, Goldberger, Tarule, eds. 1996).

15. J. Resnik, On the Bias: Feminist Reconsideration of the Aspirations for Our Judges, 61 S. Cal. L. Rev. 1877 (1988); id., Feminism and the Language of Judging, 22 Arizona St. L. J. 31 (1990); S. Sherry, Civic Virtue and the Feminine Voice in Constitutional Adjudication, 72 Virginia Law Review 543 (1986) (focusing on the gendered jurisprudence of Supreme Court Justice Sandra Day O'Connor); C. Menkel-Meadow, Taking the Mass Out of Mass Torts: Reflections of a Dalkon Shield Arbitrator on Alternative Dispute Resolution, Judging, Neutrality, Gender, and Process, 31 Loyola-Los Angeles L. Rev. 513 (1997–98).

16. See e.g. Linda Kerber, Catherine G. Greeno, Eleanor Maccoby, Zella Luria, Carol B. Stack, and Carol Gilligan, On *In a Different Voice*: An Interdisciplinary Forum, 11 SIGNS 304 (1986); Women and Morality, 50 Social Res. 487 (1983) (methodological, sociological, and epistemological critiques of Gilligan's claims); Lawrence Blum, *Gilligan and Kohlberg: Implications for Moral Theory*, in AN ETHIC OF CARE: FEMINIST AND INTERDISCIPLINARY PERSPECTIVES 49 (Mary J. Larrabee, ed. 1993).

17. Edward Laumann, John Heinz, & Robert Nelson, URBAN LAWYERS: THE SOCIAL STRUCTURE OF THE BAR (2005); J. Hagan & F. Kay, GENDER IN PRACTICE: A STUDY OF LAWYERS' LIVES (1996); Clare MS McGlynn, *The Status of Women Lawyers in the United Kingdom*, in WOMEN IN THE WORLD'S LEGAL PROFESSIONS (U. Schultz and G. Shaw, eds. 2003); C. Menkel-Meadow, *Feminization of the Legal Profession: The Comparative Sociology of Women Lawyers*, in LAWYERS IN SOCIETY: COMPARATIVE THEORIES (R. Abel and P. Lewis, eds. 1989); C. Menkel-Meadow, Exploring a Research Agenda of the Feminization of the Legal Profession: Theories of Gender and Social Change, 14 Law & Social Inquiry 289 (1989). Cf. WOMEN IN THE WORLD'S LEGAL PROFESSIONS (U. Schultz and G. Shaw, 2003).

18. Introduction, chapters 1 through 6, and the Methodological Appendix of this book (hereinafter Refugee Roulette study).

19. See e.g., David W. Allen and Diane Wall, Role Orientation and Women State Supreme Court Justices, 77 Judicature 156 (1993) and Orley Ashenfelter, Theodore Eisenberg, and Stewart Schwab, Politics and the Judiciary: The Influences of Judicial Background on Case Outcome, 24 J. Legal Studies 257 (1995) (finding gender played no role [with a small sample] in explaining outcome differences among federal judges); Jon Gottwchall, Carter's Judicial Appointments: The Influence of Affirmative Action and Merit Selection on Voting on the U.S. Courts of Appeals, 67 Judicature 165 (1984). This research is now extending into other countries, see e.g. Erika Rackley, Difference in the House of Lords, 15 Social Legal Studies 163 (2006) (U.K.); Guy Seidman, Women as the *Court*: The Israeli Experience (2005), *available at* SSRN, http://ssrn.com/abstract=743944; Ulrike Schultz, Empathy and Emotions: Do Women Judge Better? (2006) (Germany), *available at* SSRN, http://ssrn.com/paper=910043; Elaine Botelho Junqueira, *Women in the Judiciary: A Perspective from Brazil*, in WOMEN IN THE WORLD'S LEGAL PROFESSIONS (U. Schultz and G. Shaw, eds. 2003); Bertha Wilson, Will Women Judges

Really Make a Difference? 28 Osgoode Hall L. J. 507–22 (1990) (Canada); and to international bodies, see e.g. Kimi Lynn King and Megan Greening, Gender Justice or Just Gender? The Role of Gender in Sexual Assault Decisions at the International Criminal Tribunal for the Former Yugoslavia, 88 Soc. Sci. Q. 1049–71 (2007) (finding that women judges sentence male offenders of sexual assaults against women more harshly than do male judges); S. Kutnajak Ivkovic, Does Gender Matter: The Role of Gender in Legal Decision Making by Croatian Mixed Tribunals, 22 Int'l. J. of Soc. of Law 131–56 (1995).

20. Anne Boigeol, *Male Strategies in the Face of the Feminization of a Profession: The Case of the French Judiciary*, in WOMEN IN THE WORLD'S LEGAL PROFESSIONS, supra note 17 at 416.

21. Dennis Curtis and Judith Resnik, Images of Justice, 96 Yale L. J. 1727 (1987).

22. J. Gruhl, C. Spohn, and S. Welch, Women as Policy Makers: The Case of Trial Judges, 25 Am. J. of Political Science 308 (1981); Elaine Martin, Men and Women on the Bench: Vive la difference? 73 Judicature 204 (1990).

23. S. Davis, S. Haire, and D. Songer, Voting Behavior and Gender on the U.S. Courts of Appeals, 77 Judicature 129 (1993) (finding women judges were much more likely to find in favor of discrimination claimants and also to support the claims of criminal defendants, especially in search and seizure motions); Jennifer A. Segal, The Decision Making of Clinton's Nontraditional Judicial Appointees, 80 Judicature 279 (1997); Elaine Martin and Barry Pyle, Gender, Race, and Partisanship on the Michigan Supreme Court, 63 Alb. L. Rev. 1205 (2000).

24. Madhavi McCall, Structuring Gender's Impact: Judicial Voting across Criminal Justice Cases, 36 American Politics Res. 264 (2008) (finding that women judges were more likely to find on behalf of criminal justice defendants); Todd Collins and Laura Moyer, Gender, Race, and Inter-sectionality on the Federal Appellate Bench, 61 (2) Political Res. Q. 219–27 (2008) (finding that minority women judges were more likely to support criminal defendants' claims); Darrell Stef-fensmeier and Chris Hebert, Women and Men Policymakers: Does the Judge's Gender Affect the Sentencing of Criminal Defendants? 77 (3) Social Forces 1163–96 (1999) (finding women judges generally harsher on sentencing but more contextual in weighing effects of defendant character-istics).

25. Interestingly, while more recent studies show women's sometimes leniency in sentencing, an early study (perhaps one of the first) on gender differences in judging found that women trial judges were more likely to convict for certain criminal offenses and were harsher sentencers. The explanation offered is that these early women judges who had "made it in a man's world" had to demonstrate their toughness, see Herbert Kritzer and Thomas Uhlman, Sisterhood in the Courtroom: Sex of the Judge and Defendant in Criminal Case Disposition, 14 Soc. Sci. J. 77–88 (1977). More salient for differences in sentencing rates was the gender of the defendant; male judges were more likely to sentence more lightly female defendants. See also K. King and M. Greening, Gender Justice or Just Gender: The Role of Gender in Sexual Assault Decisions at the International Criminal Tribunal for the Former Yugoslavia, 88 Soc. Sci Q. 1049–71 (2007) (find-ing that female jurists more severely sanctioned defendants who assault women, while all-male panels of judges do the same for male victims).

26. Demanding that women go to work and receive less spousal support, see e.g. Junqueira, supra note 19.

27. Beverly Cook, Sentencing Behavior of Federal Judges: Draft Cases, 42 University of Cincin-nati L. Rev. 597 (1979).

28. Sara Ruddick, Maternal Thinking: Toward a Politics of Peace (1989) (arguing that maternal "caring" behavior translates into greater concerns for caring, connection, and the desire for peace-ful relations in the political as well as personal spheres).

29. Moin Yahya and James Stribopoulos, Does a Judge's Party of Appointment or Gender Matter to Case Outcomes? An Empirical Study of the Court of Appeal for Ontario, *available at* SSRN, http://ssrn.com/abstract=981300.

30. Donald Songer and Kelley Crews-Meyer, Does Judge Gender Matter? Decision Making in State Supreme Courts, 81 Soc. Sci. Q. 750–62 (2000).

31. See studies collected in Menkel-Meadow, Portia Redux: Another Look at Gender, Feminism, and Legal Ethics, 2 Va. J. Soc. Pol'y & L. 75 (1994–95); Rand Jack & Dana Jack, MORAL VISION AND PROFESIONAL DECISIONS: THE CHANGING VALUES OF WOMEN AND MEN LAWYERS (1989); Kathryn Abrams, Feminist Lawyering and Legal Method, 16 Law & Soc. Inquiry 373 (1991); see also Charles Craver, The Impact of Gender on Clinical Negotiating Achievement, 6 Ohio St. J. Disp. Res. 1 (1990); Naomi Cahn, Styles of Lawyering, 43 Hastings L. J. 1039 (1992); Bryna Bogoch, Gendered Lawyering: Difference and Dominance in Lawyer-Client Interaction, 31 Law & Soc'y Rev. 677 (1997).

32. See e.g. Eve Hill, Alternative Dispute Resolution in a Feminist Voice, 5 Ohio St. J. on Disp. Resol. 337 (1990); Ann Shalleck, The Feminist Transformation of Lawyering, 43 Hastings L. J. 1071 (1992); Eve Spangler, Marsha Gordon, and Ronald Pipkin, Token Women: An Empirical Test of Kanter's Hypothesis, 84 Am J. of Soc. 160 (1978).

33. Rand Jack & Dana Jack, MORAL VISION AND PROFESSIONAL DECISIONS: THE CHANGING VALUES OF WOMEN AND MEN LAWYERS (1989).

34. Women are disproportionately represented among those seeking public interest fellowships of various kinds, including those of my own institution—Georgetown's Public Interest Law Scholars (http://law.georgetown.edu/clinics/pils)—and the Skadden Fellowships in the public interest (source: Judith Areen, former dean of Georgetown and selection committee, Skadden Fellows, see http://www.skaddenfellowships.org/sitecontent.cfm?page=recentFellows).

35. Cynthia Fuchs Epstein, DECEPTIVE DISTINCTIONS (1988) (suggesting that "differences" are in the eyes of the perceiver); W. L. F. Felstiner, B. Pettit, E. A. Lind, and N. Olsen, *The Effect of Lawyer Gender on Client Perceptions of Lawyer Behavior*, in WOMEN IN THE WORLD'S LEGAL PROFESSIONS (U. Schultz and G. Shaw, eds. 2003)(finding clients did not find gender differences in how lawyers related to them, finding so-called women's behaviors in both men and women and valuing those qualities of listening, being informed of case progress, willingness to deal with the emotional aspects of the representation, returning calls or other communications, treating a case as important, and willingness to consider client's desires, needs, and suggestions for representation choices).

36. As Harvard Law School Professor J. B. Thayer said in 1876, "Imagine women on the bench. Would not their peculiarities of sentiment, and difference in degree and measure and intensity with which they hold them, show itself in determining what is law" (as an argument that women should not be admitted to Harvard Law School for fear they would change the meaning of law). James B. Thayer Papers, Special Collections 1 and 3, Criminal Law Teaching Notebook (Oct. 30, 1876), Harvard Law School Library, quoted in Bruce Kimball and Brian S. Shull, The Ironical Exclusion of Women from Harvard Law School, 1870–1900, 58 (1) Journal of Legal Educ. (2008). Dean Erwin Griswold several decades later (early 1950s) very reluctantly admitted women and queried them about what they would do with their degrees, see Karen Morello, THE INVISIBLE BAR: THE WOMAN LAWYER IN AMERICA, 1638 TO THE PRESENT (1986).

37. See Laumann et al.; and Hagan and Kay, supra note 17.

38. See Rosabeth Kanter, MEN AND WOMEN OF THE CORPORATION (1977), demonstrating that it takes a "critical mass" of women or minorities in any occupational setting to be "free" to act, either in conformity or contrary to gender expectations. When women are below the critical mass (which can differ in different contexts), the pressures to conform or assimilate to the "male" patterns of work are quite strong and it is virtually impossible to see any "gendered" effects on the workplace.

39. Other studies continue to document lower pay for women, fewer promotional opportunities, and differential satisfaction rates with the profession, see e.g. F. Kay and J. Hagan, Raising the Bar: The Gender Stratification of Law Firm Capitalization, 63 (5) Am. Soc. Rev. 728 (1998); F. Kay and J. Brockman, *Barriers to Gender Equality in the Canadian Legal Establishment*, in WOMEN IN THE WORLD'S LEGAL PROFESSIONS (U. Schultz and G. Shaw, eds. 2003).

40. In 2002, policy changes made by Attorney General John Ashcroft made single-member BIA panels and decisions more or less the norm, thereby reducing the possibilities of more collegial processes and decision making in appeals from immigration court cases, see p. 000. In any event, the data provided by the BIA for this study did not permit analysis of how individual judges (or multiperson panels) ruled on cases by individual. Similarly, data were insufficient for analysis of individual judges on the federal circuit courts of appeals.

41. See e.g. Jennifer Peresie, Female Judges Matter: Gender and Collegial Decision-Making in the Federal Appellate Courts, 114 Yale L. J. 1759 (2005); Songer and Crews-Meyer, infra note 30; Seidman, supra note 19; Ivkovic, supra note 19.

42. E. Slotnick, The Paths to the Federal Bench: Gender, Race, and Judicial Recruitment Variation, 67 Judicature 370 (1984).

43. See e.g. Martha Blaxall & Barbara Reagan, eds., WOMEN AND THE WORKPLACE: THE IMPLICATIONS OF OCCUPATIONAL SEGREGATION (1976); Barbara Reskin & Heidi Hartmann, eds., WOMEN'S WORK, MEN'S WORK: SEX SEGREGATION ON THE JOB (1986); see also C. Menkel-Meadow, The Comparative Sociology of Women Lawyers: The Feminization of the Legal Profession, 24 Osgoode Hall L. J. 897 (1986).

44. See e.g. The Hon. Lady Brenda Hale, Why Should We Want More Women Judges?, Public Law, 489–504 (Autumn 2001).

45. This is my paraphrase of the moral fable, see Menkel-Meadow, Portia Redux, supra note 31 at 79; see discussion of Gilligan's use of this fable (derived from an Aesop's fable) in Diana T. Meyers, *The Socialized Individual and Individual Autonomy*, in WOMEN AND MORAL THEORY (Eva Kittay and Diana Meyers, eds. 1987).

46. Menkel-Meadow, Portia Redux, supra note 31 at 80; Meyers, supra note 45 at 141–42.

47. This language, adapted from the UN Charter creating the Office of the UN High Commissioner for Refugees (UNHCR), moved into the 1951 Convention Relating to the Status of Refugees (not ratified by the United States but imported through the United States's ratification of the related Protocol Relating to the Status of Refugees almost two decades after the Convention was written), and ultimately into American law in the Refugee Act of 1980, see Philip G. Schrag, A WELL-FOUNDED FEAR: THE CONGRESSIONAL BATTLE TO SAVE POLITICAL ASYLUM IN AMERICA (2000).

48. Jack and Jack, supra note 33.

49. Several scholars have noted after studying the decisions of the highest-ranking woman in the British judiciary, the Honorable Baroness Brenda Hale, that her decisions in particular cases (involving familial [dis]connection, unwanted parenthood, indecent assault, and the contentious issue of Muslim dress for girls in public education) may differ not just in outcome but in mode of reasoning—what is considered relevant and salient to decisions and how litigants are connected to other family members or those who harm or control them. This does not compromise "neutrality" or justice, argue these scholars, but instead broadens what is legally salient and relevant from the perspective of one (a woman) who understands something about women's roles

in society. See e.g. Erika Rackley, Difference in the House of Lords, 15 (2) Social & Legal Studies 163 (2006); John Mikhail, Cultural Legality and Orientalism: A Comment on Roger Cotterrell's *Struggle for Law* and a Criticism of the House of Lords' Opinion in *Begum*, 5 International J. of Law in Context (2009) (commenting favorably on the concurrence of Baroness Hale in her discussion of brotherly domination of a young female Muslim student in appropriate dress litigation in the British courts, in which she suggests that a young Muslim "woman might indeed choose a veil or garment as an act of her defiant political identity," see *R on the application of Begum, by her litigation friend, Rahman v. Headteacher and Governors of Denbigh High School* (2006) UKHL 15.

50. Robin West, The Difference in Women's Hedonic Lives: A Phenomenological Critique of Feminist Legal Theory, 15 Wisconsin Women's L. J. 149 (2000).

51. C. Menkel-Meadow, supra note 15, Taking the Mass Out of Mass Torts: Reflections of a Dalkon Shield Arbitrator.

52. See Richard Sobol, BENDING THE LAW; THE STORY OF THE DALKON SHIELD BANKRUPCY (1991).

53. See Sherry, supra note 15, and Rackley and Mikhail, supra note 49.

54. E. Allan Lind & Tom Tyler, THE SOCIAL PSYCHOLOGY OF PROCEDURAL JUSTICE (1988).

55. See e.g. Resnik, supra note 15; West, supra note 12.

56. Ronald Dworkin, LAW'S EMPIRE (2003).

57. See e.g. Resnik, supra note 15; ABA Code of Judicial Conduct, 2006; John Leubsdorf, Theories of Judging and Judge Disqualification, 62 NYU L. Rev. 237 (1987).

58. Susan Bandes, THE PASSIONS OF LAW (2001).

59. Susan Glaspell, A JURY OF HER PEERS (2005), play version, Trifles, published in THE PLAYS OF SUSAN GLASPELL (2008); see also C. Menkel-Meadow, Feminist Legal Theory, Critical Legal Studies, and Legal Education; or, The Fem-Crits Go to Law School, 38 J. Legal Educ. 61 (1988); Marina Angel, Teaching Susan Glaspell's Jury of Her Peers and Trifles, 53 J. Legal Educ. 548 (2003).

60. FROZEN RIVER, Courtney Hunt (writer and director) (2008).

61. THE VISITOR (2008), Thomas McCarthy (writer and director).

62. There is also the recent *Babel* (Alejandro Gonzalez Inarittu, dir. 2006) for the depiction of a cruel deportation as a long-time nanny returns, with her American charges, to visit her hometown for the wedding of her son and is captured recrossing in the desert, putting herself and her charges at risk. She is depicted in the film as a more concerned caretaker than the children's biological mother.

63. See Menkel-Meadow, supra note 17 and this volume, p. 000.

64. Elaine Martin, Men and Women on the Bench: Vive la difference? 73 Judicature 204 (1990).

65. Fauziya Kassindja, DO THEY HEAR YOU WHEN YOU CRY? (1999).

66. Haley Schaffer, Domestic Violence and Asylum in the United States: In Re R- A-, 95 Northwestern L. Rev. 775 (2000–01) (discussing denial of asylum of domestic violence victim, Rodi Alvarado Pena, a case involving a Guatemalan woman who claimed that her husband's domestic violence was essentially government [in]action; her case remains caught up in political reversals at the Board of Immigration Appeals, see http://www.nilc.org/ immlawpolicy/asylrefs/ar106.htm); Karen Musalo and Stephen Knight, *Unequal Protection: When Women Are Persecuted They Call It a Cultural Norm Rather Than a Reason to Grant Asylum*, in THE UPROOTED, BULLETIN OF THE ATOMIC SCIENTISTS (2005).

67. For example, one excellent and rigorous study of race and ethnicity differences in judges and mediators by claims was able to analyze the outcome variations by race, ethnicity, and gender

"matching" of disputants in court and mediation settings to test differences in outcomes (and perceptions of differential satisfaction rates of the participants), see Gary LaFree and Christine Rack, The Effects of Participants' Ethnicity and Gender on Monetary Outcomes in Mediated and Adjudicated Civil Cases, 30 Law & Soc'y Rev. 767 (1996).

68. They have long protested their inadequate working conditions and resources, see Dana Leigh Marks, *A System at Its Breaking Point*, Los Angeles Daily Journal, August 29, 2008 at 6 (appointment of immigration lawyers in the Department of Justice has increased exponentially while the number of judges has been stagnant or decreasing; caseloads are staggeringly high, few law clerks, no court reporters or bailiffs). Thus, the author of this piece, the president of the National Association of Immigration Judges, has argued for independence from the Justice Department and the creation of an independent and better-funded agency.

69. See e.g. David Ngaruri Kenney & Philip G. Schrag, ASYLUM DENIED: A REFUGEE'S STRUGGLE FOR SAFETY IN AMERICA (2008); Kassindja, supra note 65.

11 Refugee Roulette in an Administrative Law Context

The *Déjà Vu* of Decisional Disparities in Agency Adjudication

Margaret H. Taylor[1]

Introduction

In *Refugee Roulette: Disparities in Asylum Adjudication and Proposals for Reform* (the Refugee Roulette study),[2] Professors Ramji-Nogales, Schoenholtz, and Schrag provide a comprehensive analysis of new data to document decisional disparities that undermine the fairness of asylum adjudication. The Refugee Roulette study is an empirical project of remarkable scope. It examines patterns of asylum decisions at four different adjudication levels: at the asylum office interview, in immigration court, on administrative appeal to the Board of Immigration Appeals (BIA), and on petition for review to the federal courts of appeals. At each level, the Refugee Roulette study generates empirical findings to support what we knew mostly by anecdote—that there are eye-popping disparities in the grant rates of asylum adjudicators that cannot be explained by the underlying merits of the cases.

What are we to make of these findings? One could derive an answer from a variety of perspectives. My response places the Refugee Roulette study in its broader administrative law context, considering what we can learn from a long history of attempts to redress decisional disparities in a parallel adjudication system: disability determinations made by the Social Security Administration. As someone whose teaching and research covers immigration law and administrative law, I believe that the Refugee Roulette study should be required reading for scholars, practitioners, and policymakers in both fields. Those who study agency adjudication often limit their focus to a single administrative context; they are overlooking some of the most important and challenging administrative law questions if they do not expand their field of vision to consider immigration adjudication. On the flip side, immigration law specialists may be surprised to discover a *déjà vu* component to the Refugee Roulette study. In fact, the problem of decisional disparities in agency adjudication is a landmine of administrative law, which has already exploded on those who suggest that increased managerial control over agency adjudicators is a possible route to reform.

A. A Primer on the Structure of Agency Adjudication

The authors of the Refugee Roulette study recommend that Congress create an independent Article I immigration court, moving immigration judges and the Board of Immigration Appeals out of the Department of Justice and into an executive branch agency that is not part of any department.[3] This recommendation falls at one end of the spectrum of models of decisional independence for agency adjudicators. To understand its implications, we must identify the full range of choices and consider the conflicting goals inherent in structuring administrative adjudication.

Adjudication of cases within an executive branch agency rests on a premise that is inconsistent with the norm of judicial independence embodied in our Article III courts. In most administrative contexts, the adjudicators—those individuals who decide whether to grant or deny a benefit, or to impose a civil penalty under a particular statute—are employees of the very agency whose caseload they adjudicate. They are, in other words, potentially subject to the supervision and control of one of the interested parties.[4] This is the case because administrative adjudication, traditionally conceived, is not simply about deciding individual cases; it is a means to effectuate the statutes enacted by Congress in accordance with the priorities of the executive branch. Agencies develop and implement policy when they adjudicate.[5] In order to promote policy consistency and ensure accurate outcomes, agency heads may exercise supervisory oversight over agency adjudicators, and usually have some degree of control over their decisions as well.[6]

A second divergence from Article III norms also comes into play when agencies, not courts, adjudicate. One rationale for lodging policymaking authority in an administrative agency is the expertise that can develop within the agency staff. While our legislators and our Article III judges are generalists, our bureaucrats are often specialists, with technical knowledge and experience that can usefully be employed to further the agency's mission. We expect scientists to have a hand in developing food-safety standards, and physicians and pharmacologists to determine whether a new drug application should be approved. In some administrative contexts, agency adjudicators are specialists as well, selected because their background and expertise suits them to hear a particular type of case.[7] Moreover, in the federal system all agency adjudicators specialize to some degree after they are hired, because they by and large decide the cases of one particular agency.

There is an obvious tension between the oversight that promotes consistency and accuracy and the decisional independence of agency adjudicators. This tension has bedeviled administrative law from its inception.[8] The founding document of the modern administrative state—the federal Administrative Procedure Act (APA)—offers one model for resolving this tension, which centers on the particulars of employing and supervising administrative law judges. Since the APA was enacted in 1946, a number of additional models have sprung up, reflecting a sliding scale of decisional independence for agency adjudicators.[9] These models reflect different choices that can be made on two critical issues: the degree of managerial control over adjudicators, and the degree of control over their decisions.

One option is reflected in the solution proposed in the Refugee Roulette study: to jettison the idea of policy control by executive branch officials through *complete separation* of adjudicators from the administrative agency whose cases they decide. Complete separation could be accomplished by creating a statutory Article I court for immigration adjudication, as recommended in the Refugee Roulette study.[10] It also could be achieved by what is known in administrative law as the "split-enforcement" model, where adjudicators remain lodged in an executive branch agency but that agency is formally separate from the entity that administers or enforces the law.[11]

The hallmark of complete separation is that adjudicators are emancipated from the policy control that comes from vesting a presidential appointee who also oversees enforcement with the authority to review their decisions. According to proponents, this leaves adjudicators "free to focus on adjudicative fairness and efficiency, unfettered by the competing concerns of prosecutorial imperatives."[12] The complete separation model is a perennial favorite reform proposal among those who value expert adjudicators with decisional independence; it has been proposed time and again as an appropriate model for immigration judges and the BIA.[13]

At the opposite end of the spectrum are agency decision makers who decide cases under a strong system of *managerial control* of individual adjudicators and their decisions. Asylum officers who decide affirmative claims provide an example of how this system can be coupled with the idea of an adjudicator with substantive expertise. The asylum officer corps was created in 1990 to replace Immigration and Naturalization Service (INS) examiners, who decided affirmative asylum applications along with a variety of other benefits petitions. The central premise of reform was that asylum cases should first be adjudicated in a nonadversarial environment by a cadre of professionals whose background, experience, and ongoing training especially suited them to hear these sensitive claims.[14]

Asylum officers are not exempt from the supervision experienced by other government employees; they must meet strict timetables for deciding cases and undergo regular performance evaluations.[15] They also are subject to a high degree of decisional control. Asylum officers must secure their supervisor's assent in every case before a decision issues. There also are procedures in place for advance clearance from headquarters for especially controversial or difficult decisions.[16] These features illustrate the tradeoff inherent in adjudication systems that stress managerial control: decisional independence is greatly reduced, but the system is thought to promote policy consistency and greater uniformity of decisions.

Between the poles of complete separation and strong managerial control are a wide variety of administrative adjudication systems that balance these competing factors in different ways. Those not governed by the formal adjudication provisions of the APA may provide *de facto independence* that to some degree insulates agency adjudicators from managerial control, but authorizes postadjudication review of their decisions by the agency.

Immigration judges and members of the BIA operate in such an environment. They are employed by the Executive Office for Immigration Review (EOIR), lodged within the Department of Justice, rather than by the Department of Homeland Security (DHS), whose enforcement cases they adjudicate.[17] This structure looks something like the split-enforcement model, except that the attorney general and the secretary of DHS (along with the chairman or a majority of the BIA) can refer Board decisions to the attorney general for review.[18] IJ decisions, in contrast, are not subject to any oversight within the agency, either before or after they are issued. The only review of an IJ's work product happens via party-initiated appeals to the BIA. EOIR issues case completion guidelines for immigration judges and Board members, and is in the process of establishing a formal system of performance evaluation as well.[19]

The features of de facto independence vary from agency to agency and—unless incorporated in an agency's governing statute—can be revised by executive branch officials. In contrast, administrative law judges (ALJs)[20] employed in a number of federal agencies experience a particular form of independence established by the APA. *ALJ independence* includes a number of features that insulate ALJs from the managerial control of their employing agencies. An agency that employs ALJs cannot seek out candidates with relevant expertise and hire them directly; instead, ALJ candidates must be screened through procedures established by the Office of Personnel Management and selected according to rigid statutory criteria.[21] Once hired, ALJs cannot be supervised by anyone who performs investigative or prosecuting functions within the agency.[22] They also are exempt by statute from the annual performance appraisals conducted for virtually all other federal employees.[23] Finally, ALJs can be removed only for "good cause" after a hearing before the Merit Systems Protection Board.[24] While ALJs are personally insulated from agency control by these provisions, their decisions are subject to reconsideration within the agency.[25] Thus, ALJ independence all but extinguishes an agency's authority over hiring, firing, and supervision of its ALJs, but gives an agency control—according to whatever administrative-appeal or quality-assurance procedures the agency might establish—over ALJ decisions.

A system of administrative adjudication can incorporate different models of decisional independence at different levels. This is true, as I have noted, for the asylum process. In addition, multitiered systems use different procedures for moving cases up to the next adjudication level, and can adopt different decisional standards—such as de novo consideration or a particular standard of review—at each level.

B. Comparing Asylum and Disability Adjudication

Armed with this understanding of the structure of agency adjudication, we now turn to consider the *déjà vu* aspect of the Refugee Roulette study. For administrative law scholars, the Refugee Roulette study's findings immediately call to mind the long history of attempts to redress decisional disparities in disability determinations made by the Social Security Administration (SSA).

Social Security disability adjudication has spawned the classic book on agency adjudication—Jerry Mashaw's *Bureaucratic Justice*,[26] written in 1983—along with a dizzying array of scholarly studies[27] and reports issued by government agencies[28] and outside consultants.[29] The process of resolving disability claims is "the largest system of administrative adjudication in the Western world."[30] SSA receives some five million disability applications each year,[31] and its ALJs annually resolve almost five hundred thousand contested cases.[32] A just and efficient resolution of these claims is vitally important to deserving beneficiaries, for whom "disability benefits often provide the barest cushion against destitution,"[33] and to the integrity of America's promise to provide a means of support for those who are unable to work because of serious disabling conditions.[34] Building an adjudication system to deliver on this promise has been extraordinarily difficult, however. Among the most visible and intractable problems—indeed, a central theme of multiple studies and several attempted reforms of disability adjudication—is a concern that "the outcome of cases depends more on who decides the case" than on the underlying facts or applicable legal standards.[35]

Disability adjudication therefore provides a portal to the administrative law context of the Refugee Roulette study because the SSA system is plagued with decisional disparities quite similar to those documented in the Refugee Roulette study.[36] Asylum and disability cases also share two features that contribute to the problem of inconsistent decisions: a multitiered adjudication system, which provides multiple opportunities to present a claim under different procedures, and an underlying claim that is both legally complex and fact-specific.

While the particulars vary in several respects, applicants for asylum and SSA disability claimants move through adjudication systems with some structural features in common. Both systems start with an application filed in a nonadversarial setting, which is adjudicated by an officer who decides applications within a system of managerial control. Disability applications are decided in the first instance by examiners in state Disability Determination Service agencies, who review the paper record.[37] Asylum applicants are interviewed in person by an asylum officer.[38] In both systems, disappointed claimants get another "bite at the apple" when their claim is heard de novo at the next level. In the asylum context, this happens automatically because applicants who do not convince the asylum officer are referred to removal proceedings before an immigration judge.[39] Disability applicants who lose at the state level may choose to present their case anew to an administrative law judge employed by the Social Security Administration.[40]

Both systems currently provide for administrative appeals from the ALJ or IJ decision, but here procedures in the two agencies diverge significantly. In the asylum context, the party that loses before an IJ—either a disappointed applicant or the government—can appeal to the BIA. The Board uses a "clearly erroneous" standard to review IJs' findings of facts, and a de novo standard for questions of law, discretion, and judgment.[41] Asylum applicants who lose before the BIA can petition for review in the circuit courts of appeals.[42]

In the Social Security context, a disappointed claimant (but not the government) can request a review of an ALJ decision before the administrative appeals unit, currently known as the Appeals Council. There is no right to administrative appeal, however, and the Appeals Council may decline review.[43] The Appeals Council also decides a number of cases on its own motion, as part of quality assurance review. Under this procedure (which has varied over time, as discussed below), ALJ decisions can be selected for review before they take effect, and will be modified or reversed if the Appeals Council finds error.[44]

The administrative appeals body has recently become a flashpoint in the SSA and asylum adjudication systems. In both contexts, a crushing caseload has prompted procedural reforms and a concomitant shift in the role of the appeals unit.[45] As described in the Refugee Roulette study, the BIA now decides administrative appeals under streamlined procedures that promote single-member decisions.[46] This has greatly reduced its role of promoting uniformity and policy consistency through precedent decisions. The Social Security Administration has recently promulgated regulations to create a new body, the Decision Review Board, to perform the quality assurance function of Appeals Council own-motion review.[47] Under the new regulation, the Appeals Council is being phased out; once it is eliminated disappointed claimants will no longer be able to seek administrative review of an ALJ decision.[48] Their only recourse after an ALJ denial will be a petition for judicial review in federal district court.[49]

In addition to moving through multitiered adjudication systems with some structural similarities, disability and asylum cases are specialized, highly complex, and require adjudicators to make a binary yes-or-no decision on a claim that could fall anywhere along a continuum.[50] In both contexts, decision makers must navigate a "dense thicket" of statutes, regulations, and case law, but at the same time the ultimate decision turns on "fine-grained attention to the intimate facts on the record"[51] and an assessment of whether the applicant is telling the truth. Because credibility looms so large in asylum claims,[52] and in many contested disability cases,[53] the accuracy of any given decision may be unknowable.[54] As Stephen Legomsky notes in his contribution to this book, these factors all promote a high degree of variance among agency adjudicators.[55]

C. The Unhappy History of Attempted Reform in the Disability Adjudication Context

The earliest studies of the adjudication system for disability claims found "that a claimant's success . . . is substantially affected by the identity of the presiding ALJ."[56] Since then, the oft-repeated wisdom is that decisional disparities in disability adjudication are "patent"[57]—or even "manifest and alarming."[58] Some studies assess "horizontal inconsistency,"[59] documenting differences in allowance rates among different hearing offices or different decision makers at the same adjudication level.[60] (This is similar to the analysis in the Refugee Roulette study, which analyzes horizontal consistency at four levels of asylum adjudication.) But the key concern in the Social Security context has been "vertical inconsistency"[61] between state disability examiners and federal ALJs.[62]

State disability examiners allow roughly 40 percent of initial claims.[63] Allowance rates for federal ALJs, whose caseload consists of claimants who were denied benefits at the state level, have fluctuated between 58 percent and 72 percent since 1985.[64] Although there are a number of factors that might feed into this apparent generosity,[65] policymakers have long been concerned with the seeming anomaly of a relatively high allowance rate in a pool of cases that initially were rejected.

Reflecting this concern, efforts to reform disability adjudication have sometimes been coupled with a desire to reduce the overall allowance rates of ALJs.[66] And that helps to explain why reform efforts created such controversy, resulting in "an agency at war with itself."[67] I will relate the story of two skirmishes in this war: programs that targeted individual ALJs or their decisions for special review, and a proposal to subject all ALJs to greater oversight through performance evaluations.

Social Security ALJs with high grant rates or low productivity have, at various times, had their decisions subject to special scrutiny or (for a handful of low-producing judges) been subject to "for cause" removal actions. This targeting began in the 1970s, when the director of SSA's hearing office, Robert Trachtenberg, established a Quality Assurance Review program with several components. Director Trachtenberg issued productivity memos to ALJs stating quotas for decisions per month; he then revised personnel policies to create incentives to reach the productivity goals.[68] Trachtenberg also instituted a program of postadjudicatory review of ALJ decisions. The most controversial part of this program would have singled out the decisions of low-producing ALJs for Regional Chief Review.[69] Several ALJs sued, contending that the Trachtenberg policies unlawfully intruded on various aspects of ALJ independence. The lawsuit was settled when SSA agreed to modify these programs significantly to meet ALJ objections.[70]

Congress then entered the fray. A 1980 amendment to the Social Security Act, known as the "Bellmon Amendment," directed the SSA Appeals Council to create a significant program of own-motion review of ALJ decisions.[71] The legislative history indicated that Congress was concerned with the high allowance rate of ALJs after state disability denials, and with the considerable disparity in the allowance rates among individual ALJs.[72] The resulting Bellmon Review Program had several phases; most controversial was the initial decision to target those ALJs with high allowance rates for more extensive review. ALJs who allowed more than 70 percent of claims, for example, would have *all* of their decisions screened for review under the Appeals Council own-motion procedures.[73]

A number of lawsuits were filed to challenge the Bellmon Review Program, including one by the Association of Administrative Law Judges, which contended that targeting the decisions of ALJs with high allowance rates created considerable pressure for them to deny benefits in violation of ALJ independence guarantees.[74] While that case was pending, the Bellmon Review Program was modified considerably, so that the individual targeting components of own-motion review were removed before the district court ruled in 1984.[75] Finding that these changes were "significantly for the better," the court declined to enjoin operation of the program.[76] Nevertheless, the court concluded that the SSA's "unremitting focus on allowance rates in the individual ALJ portion of the Bellmon Review Program created an untenable atmosphere of tension and unfairness which violated the spirit of the APA, if no specific provision thereof."[77]

Both the Trachtenberg initiatives and the Bellmon Review Program targeted the *decisions* of ALJs with high grant rates or low productivity for special review. While SSA ALJs perceived that they could be subject to adverse personnel actions if their productivity or the outcome of their decisions did not eventually fall in line with agency expectations, no such actions were taken under the Bellmon program.[78] In the mid-1980s, however, the SSA brought "for cause" removal actions before the Merit Systems Protections Board (MSPB) against three low-producing ALJs.[79] The board held that low productivity could in principle form the basis for removing an ALJ. It also concluded, however, that the SSA's evidence that an ALJ's case disposition rate was one-half the national average was not sufficient to establish "good cause" "[i]n the absence of evidence demonstrating the validity of using its statistics to measure comparative productivity."[80]

As Jeffrey Lubbers, former research director of the Administrative Conference of the United States (ACUS), describes it, the Social Security Administration's attempts throughout the 1970s and 1980s to assert managerial control over its ALJs resulted in a set of "mixed signals" about the legal contours of ALJ independence and the limits of agency management prerogatives.[81] Courts affirmed the agency's authority to set "reasonable production goals, as opposed to fixed quotas."[82] Meanwhile, the MSPB recognized that an ALJ's failure to meet production goals could be grounds for removal, but set a "virtually insurmountable burden of proof" in such cases.[83] Finally, quality assurance through own-motion review by the Appeals Council was upheld, but only after the SSA abandoned a system that targeted ALJs with high allowance rates for this procedure. Perhaps the most significant legacy of this era, however, is not found in the annals of reported cases. The APA's uneasy compromise establishing ALJ independence was severely tested during this period, resulting in a "legacy of tension" between Social Security ALJs and their employing agency.[84]

It was against this backdrop that ACUS, at the request of the Office of Personnel Management (OPM), undertook a study of the federal administrative judiciary in the early 1990s.[85] ACUS was an advisory agency whose mission was to study and improve the functioning of federal bureaucracy. It had funded a number of significant research studies on Social Security disability adjudication.[86] The authors of this broader study on the administrative judiciary—all preeminent scholars of administrative law—were well attuned to the details of SSA's efforts to assert greater managerial control over its ALJs. Thus, they waded carefully into the debate, seeking to find some middle ground to balance adequate protection of ALJ decisional independence against an employing agency's need to ensure a reasonable degree of uniformity, productivity, and adherence to law and agency policy in administrative adjudication.

The study authors concluded that the "good cause" standard for removal of ALJs was an important component of decisional independence, and that removal actions should be considered a "last resort" for extreme instances of misconduct, insubordination, or low productivity.[87] At the same time, they stressed that agencies needed "other approaches for assessing and dealing with apparent or alleged instances of misbehavior, bias, or unacceptably low productivity on the part of their ALJs."[88] Among the recommendations to emerge from the ACUS study was that Congress should authorize a system whereby the chief ALJ in an agency that employed more than one ALJ would, in consultation with other agency ALJs and with oversight from OPM, "[c]onduct regular ALJ performance reviews, based on relevant factors, including case processing guidelines, judicial comportment and demeanor, and the existence, if any, of a clear disregard of or pattern of non-adherence to properly articulated and disseminated rules, procedures, precedent, and other agency policy."[89]

The political fallout was swift and fierce. The ACUS proposal met "indignant opposition" from a well-organized ALJ lobby,[90] which decried the notion that agency managers—who "look too much at computer printouts, read too little history, and fail to provide for the individual nature of each case"[91]—should exercise greater oversight over their productivity and their adherence to precedent and agency policy. The fact that the ACUS proposal would lodge this function in the chief ALJ (which the study authors described as a form of peer review)[92] and would impose various safeguards on the exercise of this authority did little to blunt the opposition. Ultimately, the issue became linked to larger political agendas, including a promise by Republicans who had just gained control of the House of Representatives to shrink the federal government.[93] ACUS was a "low-profile" agency without a natural constituency, virtually unknown outside circles of administrative law.[94] Despite the fact that its budget was "minuscule" and its mission was to foster government reform,[95] it became a tempting target for a Congress looking to "show the taxpayers that once an agency is created, it does not have eternal life."[96] And so in 1995 the Administrative Conference of the United States lost its congressional funding. A thorough study of the legislative history of its demise concludes that vocal opposition from some ALJs who were outraged at the ACUS proposal to subject them to greater oversight played a significant role.[97]

D. Policy Choices in Context

Our case study of attempted reform of disability adjudication shows that efforts to promote uniformity and policy consistency through increased managerial control over agency adjudicators and their decisions have generated significant controversy with limited results. One might therefore conclude that it is a good idea to steer well clear of this approach. This is the route taken by the authors of the Refugee Roulette study. In addition to proposing enhanced resources, better training, and more rigorous hiring standards for immigration judges and the BIA (all important and necessary reforms), the study authors call for complete separation of EOIR adjudicators from the Department of Justice.

In the meantime, the DOJ and EOIR, through a number of management directives, seem to be moving in the opposite direction. Responding to harsh criticism of the BIA and immigration judges, former Attorney General Gonzales announced in January of 2006 that DOJ would conduct an internal review of EOIR. In August of that year, he released a memorandum outlining initiatives that DOJ and EOIR would undertake to improve the operation of immigration courts and the BIA. First on the list was establishing a system of "performance evaluations to enable EOIR leadership to review periodically the work and performance of each immigration judge and member of the Board of Immigration Appeals."[98] In September of 2007, DOJ published a final rule to make explicit the legal authority to establish a system of performance appraisals for immigration judges and Board members.[99] Implementation is "targeted for the July 2007–June 2008 rating period."[100] This program has been developed internally, without input from stakeholders outside EOIR and without public disclosure of the procedures or criteria for evaluating IJs and Board members.

With this recent action, we see two policy options on the table. As scholars call for greater independence for EOIR adjudicators, the executive branch moves toward exercising greater managerial control. In my mind, neither option can be fully embraced until we know important details: how an independent agency for immigration adjudication would be structured, for example, or what criteria will be used and what possible sanctions lurk in IJ performance review. We can, however, identify some potential problems that might be overlooked by those who consider EOIR reform in isolation, apart from its administrative law context, and we can consider how these options ought to be implemented if pursued.[101]

Turning first to EOIR's performance evaluation proposal, the agency is moving toward the landmine that exploded on SSA and ACUS. That is not to say that a similar blowback is inevitable. The legal context is different for ALJs and EOIR adjudicators, because ALJ protection from managerial control is enshrined in the APA. The political context is different as well. Efforts to reign in agency adjudicators might be greeted with opposition, support, or indifference, depending on the extent of publicity, the degree of sympathy for beneficiaries of the program, the particulars of how control is exercised, and the political clout of the judges' union. Recent assaults on the decisional independence of immigration adjudicators, however, have created a climate of mistrust within EOIR and among its stakeholders that may fuel opposition to EOIR's performance evaluation system.

The agency's new regulation promises to "[p]rovide for performance appraisals for immigration judges and Board members while fully respecting their roles as adjudicators."[102] But this promise to protect decisional independence is accompanied by statements that EOIR adjudicators "do not serve in a purely judicial capacity" and "are subject to the Attorney General's direction and control"[103]—assertions echoed in other regulations that have undermined decisional independence within EOIR over the past few years.[104] Against the backdrop of a recent "war on independence" against EOIR adjudicators, which Professor Legomsky has detailed elsewhere,[105] these qualifiers come across as saber rattling and create suspicion that "subject to the Attorney General's . . . control" will be the operative principle in any system of performance evaluation.[106]

A lack of transparency may also generate opposition to EOIR's new performance evaluation system. In liaison meetings with the American Immigration Lawyers Association (AILA), the agency has deflected questions about what criteria will be used to evaluate judges and how evaluations will be conducted. EOIR has also rebuffed requests to provide AILA and other stakeholders with an opportunity to review and comment on the program.[107] Although an agency's management directives and procedural rules are exempt from notice and comment procedures, EOIR has waived this exemption in the past.[108] And EOIR could solicit public input on the design and implementation of performance reviews outside of the rulemaking process. In light of the significant negative publicity that has surrounded EOIR adjudication over the past year, it is a poor tactical choice for the agency to be so close-lipped about its plans (although it is possible that—despite public statements to the contrary—this silence might simply reflect a lack of progress on this initiative).

The opportunity for public input is particularly important given that EOIR's new regulation promises an evaluation system that will include a "process for reporting adjudications that reflect temperament problems or poor decisional quality."[109] There is a reservoir of potential support for a system that deals appropriately with misconduct by a minority of immigration judges, conduct that includes (in the words of the Third Circuit Court of Appeals) "bullying . . . browbeating . . . hostility . . . abusive treatment," "bias-laden remarks," and "crude (and cruel)" behavior.[110] Immigration attorneys have long perceived unfairness in the fact that EOIR routinely sanctions private attorneys for misconduct, but does nothing to address serious misbehavior by its own immigration judges or government attorneys. They might welcome managerial intervention to deal with the few bad actors but—given the accompanying risk to decisional independence—must be assured that the system is operating fairly. Although EOIR cannot discuss disciplinary action taken against an individual judge, it should be more forthcoming about the substantive criteria and the procedures it will use in the new system of performance evaluation.

In sum, I do not believe that *any* system of performance evaluation is a bad idea.[111] It is true, however, that "in the wrong hands, with the wrong attitude, and without constant vigilance," increased managerial control of EOIR adjudicators "could cause a serious setback to the system of administrative justice."[112] The ACUS study identified several criteria for a system of performance evaluation that appropriately protects decisional independence. They include peer review and oversight of the program from the Office of Personnel Management.[113] EOIR would do well to implement these recommendations and—by opening up its proposal for public input—to allow others to assess whether the program is in fact being designed to "fully respect[]"[114] the role of the adjudicator.

Administrative law also provides a perspective to evaluate the more conceptual reform proposals of the Refugee Roulette study. Our primer on the structure of agency adjudication discloses a fundamental disconnect between the problem of decisional disparities documented in the Refugee Roulette study and the solution proposed by the study authors. Creating an independent agency to insulate immigration judges, members of the BIA, and their decisions from oversight would jettison the tools traditionally available to achieve policy control and greater uniformity of decisions. Simply put, there is no reason to think that asylum decisions will become more consistent if EOIR adjudicators become more independent, and some reason to suspect the opposite would be true.

The authors of the Refugee Roulette study nevertheless recommend emancipating EOIR from DOJ control to promote other important values, notably "depoliticizing the immigration court and the Board of Immigration Appeals and increasing the professionalism of the adjudicators."[115] A culture of professionalism springs from a number of sources, however, and it is perhaps more closely related to the training, expertise, and sense of mission shared by adjudicators than it is to their place in the administrative bureaucracy. The successful creation of the asylum officer corps within the former Immigration and Naturalization Service aptly illustrates this point.[116] EOIR adjudicators may gain a measure of prestige, and will be insulated from the recent and unfortunate politicization of DOJ, if they are moved to an independent agency. But structural reform by itself will not necessarily improve the judicial demeanor of the intemperate, or make the slipshod judge more careful. It will do nothing to change the fact that there are "too many people who should not be in a position of judging others, especially those with no power," serving as immigration judges.[117]

This problem of intemperate and abusive IJs should not be overlooked as we evaluate reform proposals. The concern could perhaps be addressed with a somewhat counterintuitive idea: the attorney general's directive to establish more managerial control over EOIR adjudicators by instituting performance reviews could be combined with the Refugee Roulette study's proposal to liberate them from policy control. Stated differently, EOIR adjudicators could be separated *from DOJ*, as the Refugee Roulette study authors recommend, and at the same time could be subject to greater supervisory oversight from the head of a newly independent agency.[118] The Department of Justice has so thoroughly undermined the integrity of EOIR adjudication in recent years that a "divorce" between the two agencies is perhaps the only route to a healthy bureaucratic culture of professional adjudication. It is this concern, rather than the problem of decisional disparities so thoroughly documented in the Refugee Roulette study, that seems to animate the authors' policy proposals. Moreover, it is only within such a culture, in the absence of mistrust and lingering tension between agency managers and adjudicators, that management initiatives to promote consistency and evaluate judicial temperament and performance can be implemented successfully.

In a perfect world, we might work our way through these vexing choices in a careful study of the sort that, ironically, used to be funded by ACUS. (An excellent example is an ACUS-funded study conducted by David Martin in the late 1980s, which successfully launched the asylum officer corps.)[119] It seems more likely that Congress or the executive branch will instead lob in a quick "fix" of the asylum system with potentially disastrous consequences.[120] Effective reform is not possible, however, unless we understand the broader administrative law context and talk frankly about the tradeoffs inherent in structuring agency adjudication.

NOTES

1. Margaret Taylor is Professor of Law at Wake Forest School of Law in Winston-Salem, North Carolina. This chapter was originally published, in an expanded version, at 60 Stan. L. Rev. 475 (2007) and is reprinted by permission of the Board of Trustees of the Leland Stanford Junior University. I am grateful to Christina Boyd, Chris Coughlin, Jeff Lubbers, David Martin, Hiroshi Motomura, Sid Shapiro, and Ron Wright for their very helpful comments. While I have learned from the insights of these colleagues, any mistakes are my own.

2. Introduction, chapters 1 through 6, and the Methodological Appendix of this book [hereinafter Refugee Roulette study].

3. See chapter 6, pages 103–104.

4. See generally 2 Richard J. Pierce, Jr., Administrative Law Treatise § 9.9 (4th ed. 2002); Michael Asimow, When the Curtain Falls: Separation of Functions in Federal Administrative Agencies, 81 Colum. L. Rev. 759, 759–65 (1981); James E. Moliterno, The Administrative Judiciary's Independence Myth, 41 Wake Forest L. Rev. 1191, 1219–36 (2006).

5. Daniel J. Gifford, Adjudication in Independent Tribunals: The Role of an Alternative Agency Structure, 66 Notre Dame L. Rev. 965, 978–80 (1991); Moliterno, supra note 4, at 1126. The Supreme Court has affirmed broad agency discretion to choose rulemaking or adjudication as the vehicle for policymaking. NLRB v. Wyman-Gordon Co., 394 U.S. 759 (1969); SEC v. Chenery Corp., 332 U.S. 194 (1947). See generally Charles H. Koch, Jr., Policymaking by the Administrative Judiciary, 56 Ala. L. Rev. 693 (2005); M. Elizabeth Magill, Agency Choice of Policymaking Forum, 71 U. Chi. L. Rev. 1383 (2004).

6. Ronald A. Cass, Allocation of Authority within Bureaucracies: Empirical Evidence and Normative Analysis, 66 B.U. L. Rev. 1, 10–14 (1986).

7. Asylum officers are one example. See infra note 14.

8. See Daniel J. Gifford, Federal Administrative Law Judges: The Relevance of Past Choices to Future Directions, 49 Admin. L. Rev. 1 (1997); Antonin Scalia, The ALJ Fiasco—A Reprise, 47 U. Chi. L. Rev. 57 (1979); Jeffrey A. Wertkin, A Return to First Principles: Rethinking ALJ Compromises, 22 J. Nat'l Ass'n. Admin. L. Judges 365, 389–91 (2002) ("The APA's conception of the ALJ's role . . . involves a curious mixture of autonomy and subservience.").

9. Gifford, *supra* note 8; Jeffrey S. Lubbers, APA-Adjudication: Is the Quest for Uniformity Faltering?, 10 Admin. L.J. Am. U. 65 (1996).

10. *See generally* Harold H. Bruff, Specialized Courts in Administrative Law, 43 Admin. L. Rev. 329 (1991); Rochelle Cooper Dreyfuss, Specialized Adjudication, 1990 BYU L. Rev. 377.

11. *See generally* Gifford, *supra* note 8; Paul R. Verkuil & Jeffery S. Lubbers, Alternative Approaches to Judicial Review of Social Security Cases, 55 Admin. L. Rev. 731, 773–77 (2003) (discussing the split-enforcement model and various proposals for an Article I court within the context of Social Security disability cases).

12. Nat'l Ass'n of Immigration Judges, An Independent Immigration Court: An Idea Whose Time Has Come 13 (2002).

13. *See id.*; U.S. Comm'n on Immigration Reform, Becoming an American: Immigration and Immigrant Policy 175–83 (1997); Maurice A. Roberts, Proposed: A Specialized Statutory Immigration Court, 18 San Diego L. Rev. 1 (1980).

14. *See generally* Gregg A. Beyer, Affirmative Asylum Adjudication in the United States, 6 Geo. Immigr. L.J. 253 (1992); Gregg A. Beyer, Establishing the United States Asylum Officer Corps: A First Report, 4 Int'l J. Refugee L. 455 (1992); Gregg A. Beyer, Reforming Affirmative Asylum Processing in the United States: Challenges and Opportunities, 9 Am. U. J. Int'l L. & Pol'y 43 (1994); David A. Martin, Making Asylum Policy: The 1994 Reforms, 70 Wash. L. Rev. 725, 728–31 (1995).

15. *See* Walter A. Ewing & Benjamin Johnson, Am. Immigration Law Found., Asylum Essentials: The U.S. Asylum Program Needs More Resources, Not Restrictions (2005), *available at* http://www.ailf.org/ipc/ policy_reports_2005_asylumessentials.asp (stating that case completion guidelines require asylum officers to conduct eighteen asylum interviews each two-week pay period); Memorandum from Joseph E. Langlois, Chief, Asylum Div., U.S. Citizenship and Immigration Servs., to All Asylum Office Personnel (Oct. 10, 2006) (on file with author) (detailing asylum office's success in meeting case processing goals).

16. The American Immigration Lawyers Association's quality assurance referral sheet details those categories of cases that must be referred to headquarters for review prior to issuance of a decision. U.S. Citizenship and Immigration Servs., Quality Assurance Referral Sheet (Nov. 6, 2001) (on file with author).

17. When Congress created DHS, responsibility for immigration enforcement was moved from the former INS to DHS. The INS was, like EOIR, lodged within the Department of Justice, giving the attorney general authority over both the enforcers and the adjudicators of immigration law. *See* Margaret H. Taylor, Behind the Scenes of St. Cyr and Zadvydas: Making Policy in the Midst of Litigation, 16 Geo. Immigr. L.J. 271, 288–95 (2002). When Congress abolished the INS and created DHS, but left EOIR within the Department of Justice, it created an unusual agency structure: one presidential appointee (the attorney general) exercises policy control over EOIR adjudicators, but a second (the secretary of DHS) presides over a separate agency with authority over immigration enforcement. *See* David A. Martin, Immigration Policy and the Homeland Security Act Reorganization: An Early Agenda for Practical Improvements, Insight (Migration Policy Inst., Washington, D.C.), Apr. 2003, at 1, 18–19.

18. 8 C.F.R. § 1003.1(h) (2007). The regulation does not specify any substantive criteria for referral. Rather, it delineates those who have authority to invoke this mechanism of policy control.

Referrals of BIA decisions to the attorney general are rare, but this option does give the Department of Justice final say in adjudicated matters of immigration policy. For an explanation of how referral operated before the creation of DHS, *see* Taylor, *supra* note 17.

19. Authorities Delegated to the Director of the Executive Office for Immigration Review, and the Chief Immigration Judge, 72 Fed. Reg. 53,673 (Sept. 20, 2007) (to be codified at 8 C.F.R. pts. 1003, 1240).

20. The phrase "administrative law judge" is a term of art; it is not (as many law students mistakenly assume) a generic phrase that can be used to describe any agency adjudicator. Instead, administrative law judges decide claims under the APA's provisions for formal adjudication. See 5 U.S.C. § 556(b)(3) (2000) ("There shall preside at the taking of evidence [in a formal adjudication] . . . one or more administrative law judges as appointed under section 3105 of this title."). The vast majority of agency adjudications are not formal adjudications under the APA; procedures for these so-called informal adjudications are established by the agency's governing statute and regulations. The term "informal" is not meant to describe the actual formality of a hearing. Removal proceedings conducted by an immigration judge are a good example of administrative adjudications that look quite formal but are not governed by the APA. *See generally* Lubbers, *supra* note 9.

21. *See generally* Jeffrey S. Lubbers, Federal Administrative Law Judges: A Focus on Our Invisible Judiciary, 33 Admin. L. Rev. 109, 112–20 (1981). An oft-criticized feature of the statutory selection criteria for ALJs is the veteran's preference, which adds points to the eligibility score of veterans and restricts an agency's ability to pass over a qualified veteran to choose an applicant without veteran status. 5 U.S.C. §§ 2108, 3309 (2000). Women are significantly underrepresented in the ALJ corps by operation of the veteran's preference. *See* Elaine Golin, Note, Solving the Problem of Gender and Racial Bias in Administrative Adjudication, 95 Colum. L. Rev. 1532, 1549–50 (1995). The statutory selection criteria for ALJs also reflect an overemphasis on litigation experience, and an underemphasis on judicial temperament and substantive expertise. *See* Charles H. Koch, Jr., Administrative Presiding Officials Today, 46 Admin. L. Rev. 271, 292–95 (1994). The Administrative Conference of the United States (ACUS) has criticized the criteria and procedures used to select ALJs and recommended various changes. *See* Paul R. Verkuil et al., Report for Recommendation 92–7: The Federal Administrative Judiciary, *in* 2 Administrative Conference of the United States, Recommendations and Reports 777, 954–67 (1992).

22. 5 U.S.C. § 554(d) (2000).

23. 5 U.S.C. § 4301(2)(D) (2000). *See generally* Jeffrey S. Lubbers, The Federal Administrative Judiciary: Establishing an Appropriate System of Performance Evaluation for ALJs, 7 Admin. L.J. Am. U. 589 (1993); L. Hope O'Keeffe, Note, Administrative Law Judges, Performance Evaluation, and Production Standards: Judicial Independence versus Employee Accountability, 54 Geo. Wash. L. Rev. 591 (1986).

24. 5 U.S.C. § 7521(a) (2000).

25. 5 U.S.C. § 557(b) (2000). The APA specifies that "[o]n appeal from or review of the initial decision [of an ALJ], the agency has all the powers which it would have in making the initial decision." *Id.* Reviewing courts have limited an agency's ability to overturn ALJ decisions that are based on witness credibility or demeanor. *See* Loomis Courier Serv., Inc. v. NLRB, 595 F.2d 491 (9th Cir. 1979); Penasquitos Vill., Inc. v. NLRB, 565 F.2d 1074 (9th Cir. 1977).

26. Jerry L. Mashaw, Bureaucratic Justice: Managing Social Security Disability Claims (1983) [hereinafter Mashaw, Bureaucratic Justice]. Professor Mashaw was also the project director for an earlier study sponsored by the National Center for Administrative Justice, then an entity of the American Bar Association. Jerry Mashaw et al., Social Security Hearings and Appeals (1978) [hereinafter Mashaw et al., Social Security Hearings and Appeals]. A third oft-cited book is a study by a political scientist: Donna Price Cofer, Judges, Bureaucrats, and the Question of Independence: A Study of the Social Security Administration Hearing Process (1985).

27. See, e.g., Frank S. Bloch et al., Developing a Full and Fair Evidentiary Record in a Nonadversary Setting: Two Proposals for Improving Social Security Disability Adjudications, 25 Cardozo L. Rev. 1 (2003); Charles H. Koch, Jr. & David A. Koplow, The Fourth Bite at the Apple: A Study of the Operation and Utility of the Social Security Administration's Appeals Council, 17 Fla. St. U. L. Rev. 199, 229 (1990); Richard E. Levy, Social Security Disability Determinations: Recommendations for Reform, 1990 BYU L. Rev. 461; Verkuil & Lubbers, supra note 11; Jeffrey Scott Wolfe, Are You Willing to Make the Commitment in Writing? The APA, ALJs, and SSA, 55 Okla. L. Rev. 203 (2002).

28. Congress's "watchdog agency," the U.S. General Accounting Office (now known as the U.S. Government Accountability Office), has issued numerous reports on disability adjudication. The general tenor of these reports is captured in the following titles: Jane L. Ross, U.S. Gen. Accounting Office, SSA Actions to Reduce Backlogs and Achieve More Consistent Decisions Deserve High Priority (1997), available at http://www.gao.gov/archive/1997/he97118t.pdf [hereinafter U.S. Gen. Accounting Office, SSA Actions to Reduce Backlogs]; U.S. Gen. Accounting Office, Disappointing Results from SSA's Efforts to Improve the Disability Claims Process Warrant Immediate Attention (2002), available at http://www.gao.gov/new.items/d02322.pdf; U.S. Gen. Accounting Office, More Effort Needed to Assess Consistency of Disability Decisions (2002), available at http://www.gao.gov/new.items/d04656.pdf [hereinafter U.S. Gen. Accounting Office, Consistency of Disability Decisions]. For a succinct summary of the claims adjudication process and the most recent proposed reforms, see Scott Szymendera, Cong. Research Serv., Social Security Disability Insurance (SSDI) and Supplemental Security Income (SSI): Proposed Changes to the Disability Determination and Appeals Process (Apr. 24, 2006), available at http://www.opencrs.com/rpts/RL33179_20060424.pdf. The independent, bipartisan Social Security Advisory Board has also issued reports on SSA adjudication. See Soc. Sec. Advisory Bd., Disability Decision Making: Data and Materials (May 2006), available at http://www.ssab.gov/documents/chartbook.pdf [hereinafter Soc. Sec. Advisory Bd., Disability Decision making]; Soc. Sec. Advisory Bd., Improving the Social Security Administration's Hearing Process (Sept. 2006), available at http://www.ssab.gov/ documents/HearingProcess.pdf [hereinafter Soc. Sec. Advisory Bd., Hearing Process Report].

29. The Lewin Group et al., Evaluation of SSA's Disability Quality Assurance (QA) Processes and Development of QA Options that Will Support the Long-Term Management of the Disability Program (2001), available at http://www.disabilitydoc.com/ssa-disability-quality-assuran.

30. Mashaw, Bureaucratic Justice, supra note 26, at 18.

31. Soc. Sec. Admin., SSA Publ'n No. 13-11700, Annual Statistical Supplement to the Social Security Bulletin tbls.2.F5 & 2.F6 (2007), available at http://www.socialsecurity.gov/policy/ docs/statcomps/supplement/2006/2f4-2f6.pdf (displaying combined totals of Disability Insurance and Social Security Insurance claims received in fiscal year 2005).

32. Szymendera, supra note 28, at 1 (noting that in fiscal year 2004, ALJs issued rulings in 495,029 appeals of initial disability denials).

33. Koch & Koplow, supra note 27, at 229.

34. The disability adjudications discussed in this essay encompass two programs administered by the Social Security Administration. The first, Social Security Disability Insurance, provides cash benefits and medical coverage to persons under sixty-five who meet the statutory definition of disability and have worked a requisite number of qualifying quarters. The second, Supplemen-

tal Security Income, is a means-tested welfare program for persons of limited income who are disabled. Under both programs, "disability" is defined as an "inability to engage in any substantial gainful activity by reason of any medically determinable physical or mental impairment which can be expected to result in death or which has lasted or can be expected to last for a continuous period of not less than 12 months." 42 U.S.C. §§ 423(d)(1)(A), 1382(c)(a)(3)(A) (2000). *See generally* Szymendera, *supra* note 28, at 1–3; Koch & Koplow, *supra* note 27, at 204–25.

35. Mashaw et al., Social Security Hearings and Appeals, *supra* note 26, at xxi.

36. Some courts have noted similarities between the asylum and disability adjudication systems. See Banks v. Gonzales, 453 F.3d 449, 453–54 (7th Cir. 2006) (suggesting that the SSA model of using vocational experts in disability cases should be adapted to the asylum context, to provide immigration judges with "concrete, case-specific" evidence on country conditions); Jacinto v. INS, 208 F.3d 725, 733 (9th Cir. 2000) ("Both administrative settings have the common feature of determining the applicant's eligibility for certain benefits. . . . [B]oth social security and deportation hearings are likely to be unfamiliar settings for the applicant."); Fisher v. INS, 79 F.3d 955, 972 (9th Cir. 1996) (Noonan, J., dissenting) (arguing that an immigration judge has a duty to develop the record similar to that of an ALJ in Social Security disability cases).

37. Levy, *supra* note 27, at 467–71; *see also* Bloch et al., *supra* note 27, at 22–26. Disappointed claimants must file a petition for reconsideration with the state agency before they move to the ALJ hearing stage. *Id.* New regulations will change this, and instead impose review by a federal reviewing official. See Administrative Review Process for Adjudicating Initial Disability Claims, 71 Fed. Reg. 16,424, 16,432–34 (Mar. 31, 2006).

38. See chapter 1 of this book, page 12.

39. *Id.*

40. This constitutes their first chance to appear in person at a hearing; claimants may be represented but no government attorney opposes the application. See Bloch et al., *supra* note 27, at 26; Levy, *supra* note 27, at 471–72.

41. 8 C.F.R. § 1003.1(d)(3) (2007).

42. The Immigration and Nationality Act (INA), Pub. L. No. 82-414, § 242(a)(1)–(b)(2), 66 Stat. 163 (1952) (exempting asylum from the bar on judicial review of discretionary decisions). The INA is codified as amended at 8 U.S.C.A. §§ 1–1178 (West 2007).

43. Koch & Koplow, *supra* note 27, at 243; Soc. Sec. Admin., Social Security's Appeals Council Review Process, http://www.ssa.gov/appeals/appeals_process.html; *see also* 20 C.F.R. § 404.970(a) (2007) (specifying four grounds on which the council will grant review).

44. Koch & Koplow, *supra* note 27, at 245–49.

45. Professors Koch and Koplow describe the Appeals Council circa 1990 in language that also seems apt for the BIA today: "[M]embers of the Appeals Council are snowed under with files . . . ," Koch & Koplow, *supra* note 27, at 258 n.312, "[and] now function almost exclusively as case handlers, not as policymakers, . . . [in an] operation that resembles a factory assembly line," *id.* at 266–67.

46. *See* chapter 4, pages 62–63.

47. Administrative Review Process for Adjudicating Initial Disability Claims, 71 Fed. Reg. 16,424, 16,437 (Mar. 31, 2006).

48. *Id.* at 16,437–38, 16,441.

49. *Id.* at 16,438.

50. Stephen Legomsky identifies this last factor as the "spectrum of choice" of a decision. He explains that "[s]ome subjects provide more than the usual leeway to adjudicators," and posits that for asylum adjudication the spectrum of choice is "exceptionally broad." See chapter 12, page

266–267. David Martin has also developed this point in a discussion of why the factual issues in asylum cases are so difficult to resolve, which is highly relevant to the Refugee Roulette study. David A. Martin, Reforming Asylum Adjudication: On Navigating the Coast of Bohemia, 138 U. Pa. L. Rev. 1247, 1270–87 (1990). Professor Martin observes that "[a]sylum seekers present a spectrum of situations, with only subtle shadings distinguishing the risk levels they face. Adjudication must draw a line at some point on that spectrum." *Id.* at 1278 (footnote omitted). Richard Pierce notes the same phenomenon in disability determinations. He explains that cases disputed up to the ALJ level often involve claims of pain or mental illness, which require ALJs to make subjective "yes-or-no decisions on disability when the applicant's ability to work and the severity of the underlying illness could fall anywhere along a vast spectrum." Richard J. Pierce, Jr., Political Control versus Impermissible Bias in Agency Decisionmaking: Lessons from Chevron and Mistretta, 57 U. Chi. L. Rev. 481, 511 (1990); *see also* Levy, *supra* note 27, at 467 (disability determinations are "highly technical and complex" and require evaluation of evidence that is "inherently subjective") (footnotes omitted).

51. Koch & Koplow, *supra* note 27, at 228.

52. *See* chapter 6, page 99; chapter 12, page 267; Martin, *supra* note 50, at 1281–82.

53. Koch & Koplow, *supra* note 27 at 229; Levy, *supra* note 27, at 467; Pierce, *supra* note 50, at 502 & n.85.

54. Koch & Koplow, *supra* note 27, at 270 ("Accuracy in a disability case is extremely difficult to define, let alone measure or achieve. No one we spoke with was able to articulate a workable definition of 'accuracy.'").

55. *See* chapter 12, part II.E.

56. Mashaw et al., Social Security Hearings and Appeals, *supra* note 26, at 21.

57. *Id.* at xxi.

58. Koch & Koplow, *supra* note 27, at 283.

59. The term is borrowed from Professors Koch and Koplow, who define "horizontal consistency" as "the similarity of decisions in different venues" at the same adjudication level. *Id.*

60. *See* Soc. Sec. Advisory Bd., Disability Decision Making, *supra* note 28, at 29 chart 13 (comparing average allowance rate in each state, at the state Disability Determination Services level and at the federal ALJ level); Szymendera, *supra* note 28, at 13 tbl.4 (showing high, low, and average grant rates for state Disability Determination Services offices).

61. Koch & Koplow, *supra* note 27, at 283 ("'Vertical consistency' is achieved when decisionmakers evaluate a case according to the same procedures and legal standards at each tier of the appellate review ladder. It requires harmony among all the adjudicatory levels regarding standards for case handling, definitions of eligibility, and interpretations of policy.").

62. *See* Soc. Sec. Advisory Bd., Disability Decision Making, *supra* note 28, at 29 chart 13 (comparing initial decision and ALJ allowance rate in each state); U.S. Gen. Accounting Office, Consistency of Disability Decisions, *supra* note 28, at 1, 7, 10–12 (giving figures and assessing causes of vertical inconsistency); U.S. Gen. Accounting Office, SSA Actions to Reduce Backlogs, *supra* note 28; *see also* Daniel J. Gifford, Need Like Cases Be Decided Alike? Mashaw's Bureaucratic Justice, 1983 Am. B. Found. Res. J. 985, 987 (asserting that SSA efforts to achieve more consistent determinations are undermined by the "excessive independence of ALJs").

63. Szymendera, *supra* note 28, at 7.

64. U.S. Gen. Accounting Office, Consistency of Disability Decisions, *supra* note 28, at 1.

65. ALJs may grant applications at a higher level than state offices because they are the only adjudicators who meet the applicant face-to-face, have more opportunity to develop a record, and historically were governed by different rules and guidelines than the state offices. *See* Bloch et al., *supra* note 27, at 26, 33–34; Levy, *supra* note 27, at 498.

66. Ass'n of Admin. Law Judges v. Heckler, 594 F. Supp. 1132, 1137 ("Evidence ... strongly suggested that [the Office of Hearing Administration] had an ulterior goal to reduce ALJ allowance rates."); Mashaw, Bureaucratic Justice, supra note 26, at 174–78. But see Nash v. Bowen, 869 F.2d 675, 681 (2d. Cir. 1989) ("The agency maintained then, and maintains now, that reducing [allowance] rates was not the intent of the policy.").

67. Koch & Koplow, supra note 27, at 231.

68. Levy, supra note 27, at 478; see also Cofer, supra note 26, at 93–96.

69. Cofer, supra note 26, at 87.

70. Id. at 111–12 (describing the June 7, 1979, settlement in Bono v. Social Security Administration). The Trachtenberg initiatives are also described in two reported cases arising from a decade-long lawsuit brought by an ALJ challenging various aspects of the program. See Bowen, 869 F.2d at 675 (holding that individual ALJ did not have standing to challenge SSA's nonacquiescence policy and that other challenged practices did not unlawfully intrude onto ALJ independence); Nash v. Califano, 613 F.2d 10 (2d Cir. 1980) (holding that individual ALJ had standing to challenge allegedly unlawful intrusions onto ALJ independence).

71. Own-motion review by the Appeals Council had been dormant for several years prior to the Bellmon Amendment. Ass'n of Admin. Law Judges v. Heckler, 594 F. Supp. 1132, 1135 n.6 (1984). The Association of Administrative Law Judges decision contains a detailed description of the various phases of the Bellmon Review Program created under this statute. Id. at 1135 & nn.7–8, 1136; see also Cofer, supra note 26, at 117–22; U.S. Gen. Accounting Office, Social Security: Results of Required Reviews of Administrative Law Judge Decisions (1989), available at http://archive.gao.gov/d25t7/139091.pdf; Levy, supra note 27, at 497–500.

72. Ass'n of Admin. Law Judges, 594 F. Supp. at 1134.

73. Id. at 1134–36; U.S. Gen. Accounting Office, supra note 71, at 8. Only ALJ grants, not denials, were originally included in Appeals Council own-motion review. This disparity was justified, according to SSA, by studies that suggested that a high rate of allowance indicated a high rate of ALJ error, and also by the fact that the Appeals Council already reviewed a significant number of ALJ denials via claimant petitions for review. Ass'n of Admin. Law Judges, 594 F. Supp. at 1134.

74. Ass'n of Admin. Law Judges, 594 F. Supp. at 1136.

75. In 1982, SSA discontinued its use of ALJ allowance rates as the selection criteria, and instead targeted individual ALJs according to their "own-motion rates"—the frequency with which the Appeals Council took corrective actions on their decisions. Id. at 1134–35. In 1984, the SSA eliminated the individual ALJ portion of Bellmon Review, and increased the number of cases reviewed from a random national sample. Id. at 1135–36.

76. Id. at 1141, 1143.

77. Id. at 1143; see also Nash v. Bowen, 869 F.2d 675, 680 (2d Cir. 1989) (holding that, while coercion of ALJs to lower allowance rates would infringe decisional independence, "[t]he efforts complained of in this case for promoting quality and efficiency do not"). In a separate lawsuit challenging the procedures used to promulgate the Bellmon Review program, the Ninth Circuit ruled that the Bellmon Review program was a substantive rule that was improperly established without notice-and-comment procedures, and ordered that ALJ decisions that had been set aside by Appeals Council own-motion review should be reinstated. W.C. v. Bowen, 807 F.2d 1502, 1505–06 (9th Cir. 1987).

78. Ass'n of Admin. Law Judges, 594 F. Supp. at 1135, 1142.

79. Soc. Sec. Admin. v. Balaban, 20 M.S.P.R. 675 (1984); Soc. Sec. Admin. v. Goodman, 19 M.S.P.R. 321 (1984); Soc. Sec. Admin. v. Brennan, 19 M.S.P.R. 335 (1984), opinion clarified, 20 M.S.P.R. 35 (1984). These cases, and the broader issue of establishing production standards for ALJs, are discussed in Lubbers, supra note 23, at 599–600; Pierce, supra note 50, at 504–7; James

P. Timony, Performance Evaluation of Federal Administrative Law Judges, 7 Admin. L.J. Am. U. 629, 642–44 (1993); and O'Keeffe, *supra* note 23, at 614–24.

80. Goodman, 19 M.S.P.R. at 331.

81. Lubbers, *supra* note 23, at 595–96.

82. Bowen, 869 F.2d at 680.

83. Lubbers, *supra* note 23, at 599–600.

84. Levy, *supra* note 27, at 502.

85. *See* Verkuil et al., *supra* note 21.

86. Verkuil & Lubbers, *supra* note 11, at 737 n.16 (listing ACUS recommendations emerging from numerous ACUS-funded studies of disability adjudication).

87. Lubbers, *supra* note 23, at 600.

88. *Id.*

89. Recommendations and Statements of the Administrative Conference Regarding Administrative Practice and Procedure, 57 Fed. Reg. 61,759, 61,764 (Dec. 29, 1992) (codified at 1 C.F.R. pts. 305, 310).

90. Lloyd Musolf, Performance Evaluation of Federal Administrative Law Judges: Challenge for Public Administration?, 28 Am. Rev. Pub. Admin. 390, 394 (1998).

91. Timony, *supra* note 79, at 653.

92. Lubbers, *supra* note 23, at 604.

93. Toni M. Fine, A Legislative Analysis of the Demise of the Administrative Conference of the United States, 30 Ariz. St. L.J. 19, 91–92 (1998).

94. *Id.* at 93.

95. *Id.* at 66.

96. *Id.* at 78.

97. *Id.* at 59–61, 95–97. Professor Fine concludes that the Republican Party's desire to eliminate an agency was the "greatest contributing factor" to the demise of ACUS, but that the process "was set in motion by a small but outspoken group of disaffected administrative law judges" unhappy with ACUS's recommendations. *Id.* at 113–14. Congress has recently shown interest in reviving ACUS. *See* Regulatory Improvement Act of 2007, H.R. 3564, 110th Cong. (2007) (authorizing appropriations for ACUS through fiscal year 2011).

98. Press Release, U.S. Dep't. of Justice, Attorney General Alberto R. Gonzales Outlines Reforms for Immigration Courts and Board of Immigration Appeals (Aug. 9, 2006), *available at* http://www.usdoj.gov/opa/pr/2006/August/06_ag_520.html.

99. Authorities Delegated to the Director of the Executive Office for Immigration Review, and the Chief Immigration Judge, 72 Fed. Reg. 53,673, 53,675 (Sept. 20, 2007) (to be codified at 8 C.F.R. pts. 1003, 1240).

100. Memorandum from Kevin D. Rooney, Dir., Executive Office for Immigration Review, U.S. Dep't of Justice, to All Executive Office for Immigration Review Employees (undated) (on file with author) [hereinafter Rooney Memo].

101. Professor Legomsky suggests, for example, that immigration judges could be made into ALJs. *See* chapter 12, page 273. This proposal cuts against the quite sensible idea that immigration judges should be selected with an eye toward the challenges of their specific docket, and that it would be desirable for the judges to have some degree of knowledge or experience with immigration law. (*See* chapter 6, pages 106–107.) Even if one embraces the structural features of ALJ independence as appropriate in this context, the rigid statutory criteria and the procedures for selecting ALJs are fraught with problems that I would not impose on the immigration courts. *See supra* note 21.

102. Authorities Delegated to the Director of the Executive Office for Immigration Review, and the Chief Immigration Judge, 72 Fed. Reg. at 53,676–77.

103. *Id.* at 53,673. The preamble to the new regulation authorizing the director of EOIR to create a system of performance evaluation also quotes the Second Circuit decision upholding SSA efforts to improve the quality and timeliness of ALJ disability decisions. *Id.* at 53,674 (quoting Nash v. Bowen, 869 F.2d 675, 681 (2d Cir. 1989)).

104. Stephen H. Legomsky, Deportation and the War on Independence, 91 Cornell L. Rev. 369, 374, 379 (2006).

105. *Id.* at 371–85.

106. Authorities Delegated to the Director of the Executive Office for Immigration Review, and the Chief Immigration Judge, 72 Fed. Reg. at 53,673.

107. Executive Office for Immigration Review, AILA-EOIR Agenda Questions and Answers (2006), *available at* http://www.usdoj.gov/eoir/statspub/eoiraila101806.pdf. Only the slimmest of details have emerged about the performance evaluation initiative. Former EOIR Director Rooney has stated that EOIR adjudicator performance will be rated as "Satisfactory, Improvement Needed, and Unsatisfactory," and that implementation of the program is subject to statutory bargaining obligations with the IJ union. Rooney Memo, *supra* note 100. EOIR's General Counsel has been detailed to a newly created position of Assistant Chief Immigration Judge for Conduct and Professionalism, serving in an "acting" capacity. Executive Office for Immigration Review, AILA-EOIR Liaison Meeting Agenda Questions 2–3 (2007), *available at* http://www.usdoj.gov/eoir/ statspub/eoiraila041107.pdf. The BIA now reports to the Office of Chief Immigration Judge instances in which IJs have failed to display the appropriate level of professionalism. DOJ's Office of Immigration Litigation makes a similar report to EOIR's Office of General Counsel when a case pending in federal court reflects temperament, conduct, or quality problems on the part of an IJ or BIA member. Rooney Memo, *supra* note 100.

108. *See* Board of Immigration Appeals: Procedural Reforms to Improve Case Management, 67 Fed. Reg. 7309, 7309–10 (Feb. 19, 2002) (codified at 8 C.F.R. pts. 3, 280) (soliciting public comment on a proposed rule to "revise the structure and procedures of the Board of Immigration Appeals, provide for an enhanced case management procedure, and expand the number of cases referred to a single Board member for disposition").

109. Authorities Delegated to the Director of the Executive Office for Immigration Review, and the Chief Immigration Judge, 72 Fed. Reg., 53,673, 53,677 (Sept. 20, 2007) (to be codified at 8 C.F.R. pts. 1003, 1240).

110. Cham v. Attorney Gen., 445 F.3d 683, 686 (3d Cir. 2006). These concerns about the temperament of immigration judges and the quality of their decisions were widely reported in the press. *See, e.g.,* Adam Liptak, *Courts Criticize Judges' Handling of Asylum Cases*, N.Y. Times, Dec. 26, 2005, at A1; Pamela A. MacLean, Immigration Bench Plagued by Flaws: Due Process Abuse, Bad Records Alleged, Nat'l L.J., Feb. 6, 2006, at 1.

111. In his contribution to this book, Professor Legomsky criticizes "[p]erformance reviews that take approval rates into account and serve as a criterion for retention or promotion," chapter 12, page 278. He does not discuss in this section whether "punishing wayward adjudicators," which receives his strong disapproval, includes actions against intemperate and abusive IJs, or how such misconduct can be identified and redressed in the absence of performance reviews.

112. Nash v. Califano, 613 F.2d 10, 15–16 (2d Cir. 1980) (quoting memorandum from Robert Trachtenberg, the SSA official who promoted the controversial targeting of ALJs for quality assurance review, to the Regional Chief ALJs, setting forth a Regional Office Peer Review Program).

113. Lubbers, *supra* note 23, at 605.

114. Authorities Delegated to the Director of the Executive Office for Immigration Review, and the Chief Immigration Judge, 72 Fed. Reg. at 53,676–77.

115. Chapter 6, page 100.

116. *See supra* note 4 and accompanying text.

117. This statement was made with reference to ALJs in Koch, *supra* note 21, at 275.

118. Although the Refugee Roulette study authors do not address the issue of performance evaluations and strongly favor reforms that move in the direction of decisional independence, they make passing reference to this idea. Chapter 3, note 20 (suggesting that data about discrepant grant rates "may be a jumping off point for a more thorough examination of performance and professionalism in the courtroom").

119. *See* Martin, *supra* note 50. Professor Martin later served as a consultant to the INS; his work as a consultant forged the compromise that created our current asylum procedures. *See* Martin, *supra* note 14. ACUS also funded earlier studies in the immigration law arena. *See* Stephen H. Legomsky, A Research Agenda for Immigration Law: A Report to the Administrative Conference of the United States, 25 San Diego L. Rev. 227 (1988); Stephen H. Legomsky, Forum Choices for the Review of Agency Adjudication: A Study of Immigration Process, 71 Iowa L. Rev. 1297 (1986).

120. Attorney General Ashcroft's "streamlining" of BIA adjudication provides one example. These procedures had a number of negative spillover effects, including a dramatic rise in the caseload of the courts of appeals. *See* Legomsky, *supra* note 104, at 375–77; John R. B. Palmer, Stephen W. Yale-Loehr & Elizabeth Cronin, Why Are So Many People Challenging Board of Immigration Appeals Decisions in Federal Court? An Empirical Analysis of the Recent Surge in Petitions for Review, 20 Geo. Immigr. L.J. 1, 56 (2005). A recent near miss was a proposal from a former ombudsman of the U.S. Citizenship and Immigration Services to eliminate asylum officer jurisdiction over any individual who is not in valid immigration status. This proposal, which would have gutted the current system of affirmative asylum adjudication, paid absolutely no heed to the years of study that went into crafting the current procedures. Memorandum from Prakash Khatri, Ombudsman, Citizenship and Immigration Servs., to Emilio Gonzalez, Dir., U.S. Citizenship and Immigration Servs. (March 20, 2006), *available at* http://www.dhs. gov/ xlibrary/assets/CISOmbudsman_RR_24_Asylum_Status_03-20-06.pdf. It was promptly rejected by the USCIS director, who noted that the recommendation was based on a novel legal interpretation and would, if implemented, "eliminate a valuable, time-tested process for the vast majority of asylum applicants." Memorandum from Emilio Gonzalez, Dir., U.S. Citizenship and Immigration Servs., to Prakash Khatri, Ombudsman, Citizenship and Immigration Servs. (June 20, 2006), *available at* http://www.dhs.gov/xlibrary/assets/ CISOmbudsman_RR_24_Asylum_Status_USCIS_Response-06-20-06.pdf.

12 Learning to Live with Unequal Justice
Asylum and the Limits to Consistency

Stephen H. Legomsky[1]

THIS ESSAY IS about consistency in adjudication. It explores why consistency matters, what its determinants are, and whether it can be substantially achieved at a price that is worth paying.

But this essay is also about the U.S. asylum adjudication system. Asylum challenges the national conscience in distinctive ways. It generates hard questions about our moral responsibilities to fellow humans in distress; the recognition of human rights and our willingness to give them practical effect; the extent of our obligations to those who are not U.S. citizens; U.S. legal and moral obligations to the international community; the roles of state sovereignty and borders; foreign relations; allocation of finite national resources; and racial, religious, linguistic, and ideological pluralism.

Into this emotional and political fray, one often better known for polemic than for hard data, Professors Jaya Ramji-Nogales, Andrew Schoenholtz, and Philip Schrag have bravely ventured. Through painstaking and thoughtful empirical research, they collected massive data from several different federal bureaucracies and shed important light on the results asylum adjudicators reach. Their impressive study, *Refugee Roulette: Disparities in Asylum Adjudication and Proposals for Reform* (the Refugee Roulette study),[2] highlights the striking disparities in asylum approval rates from one adjudicator to another at various stages of the process. As the authors convincingly demonstrate, asylum outcomes often depend as much on the luck of the draw as on the merits of the case.

The present essay has two aims. The first, which is asylum-specific, addresses the "so what" question. What are the normative implications of the findings reached in the Refugee Roulette study? What problems have the sharp disparities in asylum approval rates caused, and what, if anything, should we do about them? To answer those questions, the essay sets a second objective—to examine, more generically, the role that consistency should play in any justice system. What, exactly, is the relationship between consistency and justice? What forces influence consistency? What instruments might enhance it? And what trade-offs do those instruments present?

Many readers will find the patterns revealed by the Refugee Roulette study shocking. One's visceral reaction might be that we need to "rein in" the adjudicators. Perhaps, one might think, the answers lie in terminating or demoting the outliers, or subjecting all adjudicators to performance evaluations, or making vastly increased use of agency-head review of adjudicators' decisions, or even imposing mandatory minimum and maximum approval rates.

I argue here that these impulses should be resisted. There are times when we simply have to learn to live with some measure of unequal justice because the alternatives are worse. Disparities in asylum approval rates just might be one of those instances. As long as adjudicators are flesh-and-blood human beings, as long as the subject matter is ideologically and emotionally volatile, and as long as limits to the human imagination constrain the capacity of legislatures to prescribe specific results for every conceivable fact situation, there will be large disparities in adjudicative outcomes and justice will depend, in substantial part, on the luck of the draw.

This is not to suggest that inconsistent outcomes are harmless; to the contrary, they impede justice in several ways that will be explored below. Nor is this a call to throw in the towel; there are several ways to mitigate the problem at the margins. The authors of the Refugee Roulette study outline several possibilities, as do I in the final section of this essay. But more dramatic inroads into adjudicative inconsistency would bear costs that, in my view, are socially unacceptable. The major cost is the erosion of decisional independence, but there are others as well.

Part 1 examines why consistency matters. It considers the costs of unequal justice. Part 2 identifies the determinants of consistency. These are the forces that influence the degree of consistency one might expect from a given adjudicative process. Part 3 then surveys the policy options—both those that would enhance consistency at the margins and those that might well bring more dramatic uniformity gains but that would be bad ideas nonetheless.

I. Why Consistency Matters

> Now, what goes into the definition of justice? . . . We try to be fair.
> And fair to me is consistency.[3]
> A foolish consistency is the hobgoblin of little minds . . .[4]

Which is it? On the scale from innocuous to intolerable, where does inconsistency rank? The answer, of course, depends on the context, and the present context encompasses case-by-case adjudication generally and the asylum process specifically. The concern here is with inconsistent outcomes, not with inconsistent procedures or inconsistent adjudicator credentials (except to the extent that they in turn generate inconsistent outcomes).[5] Nor is this essay confined to the specific problem of systematic discrimination against particular groups, such as those defined by race, religion, gender, country of nationality, or the like. My concern here is more mundane—disparate outcomes, whether conscious or unconscious, for individuals who are similarly situated in all legally relevant respects.

These inconsistencies are of several types. As the Refugee Roulette study dramatically illustrates, outcomes might vary systematically from one court or tribunal to another, or from one adjudicator or panel to another within the same court or tribunal. Even the body of decisions by a single adjudicator might be internally inconsistent.

Inconsistencies also vary by type of issue. The issue might be one of law, one of fact, one of discretion, or one with a mix of ingredients. An interpretation of law might be one of "pure" law—either a broad question like the meaning of the statutory term "particular social group" or a narrower question such as whether female genital mutilation is "persecution" or whether the husbands of women who have been forcibly sterilized qualify under the "refugee" definition.[6] Or the decision might require the application of a broad term to specific facts, such as whether a given instance of physical abuse was severe enough to be "persecution."[7] Similarly, a finding of fact might be one of historic fact, requiring the adjudicator to determine what actually happened. It might be one of predictive fact, such as how likely it is that the feared persecution will occur in the future. Or it might be an assessment of the asylum seeker's credibility, including whether the person is truthful, reliable, and perceptive. Even discretionary judgments can vary from open-ended determinations of whether an individual who is statutorily eligible for asylum should receive it[8] to a more structured discretionary decision, such as whether the hardship a person will experience can be described as "exceptional and extremely unusual."[9]

Two last preliminary observations: balance is not the same as, and does not promote, consistency. At best, balance prevents asymmetric inconsistency. An immigration judge corps that comprises one hundred anti-immigrant zealots and one hundred pro-immigrant zealots would be "balanced" in some sense, but in such a corps the outcomes would be more likely to diverge, not less. Second, inconsistency is a two-edged sword. It can result in an outcome favorable to the asylum seeker when another adjudicator would have reached a different result, or vice-versa. Consequently, neither one's general ideology nor one's specific preferences on immigration or asylum should drive one's degree of tolerance for inconsistent outcomes.

With those introductory caveats, it is possible to examine the reasons why we value consistency in adjudication. At first blush, consistency might seem like a good proxy for accuracy. If, for example, 60 percent of a group of decisions go one way and the remaining 40 percent the opposite way, and the facts are similar enough that the two sets of outcomes cannot be reconciled, it might initially appear that at least 40 percent of the decisions—and perhaps 60 percent—were wrong. For at least two reasons, that assumption should be resisted.

First, some issues do indeed lend themselves to what our legal system regards as uniquely correct results. A particular question of fact might present a dichotomy, and the appellate authority might rule that the evidence did not permit the initial decision maker's finding. In such a case the finding is "wrong" as a matter of law. Similarly, even if the dichotomous issue was discretionary, an appellate authority might conclude that the initial decision maker's determination was an abuse of discretion. But even if we assume the existence of issues that each lend themselves to only one legally correct answer, the assumption that consistency is congruent with accuracy breaks down with respect to the many other issues on which the law recognizes that reasonable minds might disagree. In those cases, the outcomes simply cannot be classified as "right" or "wrong."

Moreover, even in cases where there is truly only one legally correct answer, consistency does not necessarily indicate a low error rate. One hundred percent consistency might mean that all the decisions were right, but it could also mean that all the decisions were wrong.

I concede, however, that rational human choice is still more likely than random selection to produce correct outcomes. On that assumption, a high degree of consensus makes the hypothesis of everyone being right more likely than the hypothesis of everyone being wrong. There is some reason, therefore, to assume that consistency correlates positively with accuracy. Still, correlation is not causation. Even if consistency provides some evidence of accuracy, it does not follow that consistency promotes accuracy. Unless there is some other basis for assuming that consistency generates accuracy, then reasons to promote consistency—or, more realistically, reasons to sacrifice other interests for the sake of attaining consistency—remain to be identified.

As it turns out, reasons to strive for consistency are plentiful. Probably the most intuitive is the principle of equal treatment—the notion that inconsistent outcomes are substantively unfair. When two people are situated identically in all legally relevant respects, the law should treat them the same. To the extent reasonably avoidable, the outcomes should not hinge on the biases of whichever adjudicator the individual had the good or bad luck to draw.[10]

Certainty, and the predictability that it brings, are commonly cited as a second set of reasons to strive for consistent adjudication.[11] Conflicting results breed uncertainty in two ways. They do so directly, by preventing the parties from predicting how their dispute is likely to be resolved. These conflicts seem especially significant when the issues are legal, since by definition legal rules are norms of general applicability. Yet, uncertainty can also result from conflicting conclusions on questions of fact or discretion if the issues are recurring. Even when the facts differ in important respects, as when different asylum applicants allege different harms, one adjudicator's finding that a given harm is not severe enough to be classified as "persecution" might have an a fortiori effect, signaling the same result for cases in which the harm is even less severe. The impact of consistency on certainty and predictability might also vary as between intertribunal and intratribunal conflicts. Intertribunal conflicts might be less serious, at least in cases where the rules of jurisdiction and venue constrain the parties' choices, since consistency within the applicable tribunal at least helps the parties predict how their particular cases will be decided. Inconsistent outcomes within a tribunal, in contrast, do not permit even that.

As I have suggested elsewhere, consistency might also contribute to certainty and predictability in a more indirect way:

> One benefit of consistency is enhanced stability. Conflicts among equally authoritative bodies have ways of being reconciled eventually, either by gradual evolution or by pronouncements from above. The mere presence of a momentary conflict, therefore, can create at least the perception of imminent change, leaving affected sectors of the population uncertain how to plan for the future. Consistency reduces this uncertainty.[12]

Inconsistency can also impair efficiency. The very fact that two decisions are inconsistent means that the second adjudicator had to duplicate the analytical efforts of the first one rather than simply adopt the first adjudicator's reasoning and result. It also means that, at some point, some government actor will have to step in to resolve the issue definitively. Moreover, the resulting uncertainty leaves the parties less incentive to accept the first ruling in their case and more incentive to appeal it. The fact that they cannot predict the result might also discourage future parties from settling.

A final benefit of consistency is acceptability to both the parties and the general public, a central concern of every adjudication process.[13] The public has a direct interest in consistency, since uncertainty can be problematic for the reasons already given. In addition, there is ample evidence that the public simply perceives inconsistent outcomes to be unfair. As the authors of the Refugee Roulette study observe, we inscribe the equal justice admonition at the entrance to the Supreme Court building, follow stare decisis, promulgate uniform federal sentencing guidelines, employ pattern jury instructions, and allow judges to modify civil verdicts that veer too far from the norm.[14]

All else being equal, therefore, it is hard to be against consistency. Indeed, fidelity to the rule of law demands attention to consistency. But all else is seldom equal. Since strategies that enhance consistency can have costs, the real question is how much cost should be accepted in return for whatever amount of increased consistency it will purchase. Conflicts can have positive effects of their own. As others have observed, a judicial conversation that includes differing views expressed over a reasonable time period can be part of a healthy maturation process that ultimately aids the thoughtful resolution of a difficult issue.[15] In addition, even when the net impact of conflicts is negative (as I assume to be the norm), some solutions might be too costly. Strategies like reductions in adjudicators' decisional independence, broader or more frequent agency-head review of adjudicators' decisions, heightened judicial deference to administrative tribunals, or even elimination of judicial review of the decisions by centralized tribunals, for example, might well enhance consistency, but at a price that I argue would be excessive.

II. The Determinants of Consistency

What factors drive consistency? I suggest in this part that there are at least fifteen. Some relate to numbers—the number of people who decide each case, the total number of adjudicators or panels in the entire system, and the number of cases. Some of the other determinants relate to the attributes of the adjudicators, including the criteria and procedures for appointing them and their postappointment training and guidance. Still others relate to the adjudicators' roles—their degree of independence, the level of deference they are expected to give to other decision makers, and their obligations with respect to the preparation of reasoned opinions and the use of stare decisis. Finally, I suggest that the level of consistency reflects the nature of the subject matter—in particular, how specialized, complex, dynamic, ideologically charged, and determinate the concepts are. While these categories can overlap, they serve a useful organizing function.

A. Numbers

1. THE NUMBER OF DECISIONAL UNITS

All else being equal, one can assume that the fewer "decisional units" there are at a given adjudication level, the more consistent the outcomes should be. By "decisional unit," I mean the person or group of people who decide a single case. Thus, the decisional unit might be one adjudicator (in the case of asylum, for example, a USCIS asylum officer, an immigration judge, a single member of the BIA, or the attorney general), a panel that consists of more than one adjudicator but less than the entire tribunal (a three-member BIA panel, a three-judge court of appeals panel, or a limited en banc court of appeals panel), or the full tribunal sitting en banc (the BIA or a court of appeals). It is easier to monitor and conform to the decisions of one's colleagues when they are few in number than it is when they are many.

In the asylum context, I submit, it is the number of decisional units—more so than the number of tribunals—that should be expected to correlate more closely with consistency. There is only one BIA, for example, but even a single-member decision becomes the official decision of the BIA unless a panel later takes up the case. Thus, the degree of consistency within the BIA has to reflect the fact that almost all its decisions are rendered by either single members or three-member panels. Functionally, therefore, we can think of the BIA as a collection of single-member and three-member decisional units rather than as one large decisional unit. Analogous statements could be made about court of appeals decisions; the degree of consistency they can be expected to display must similarly take into account that decisions are normally made by three-judge panels.

I do not want to overstate this point. The fact that BIA members and panels, as well as court of appeals panels, are each part of a single tribunal does have significance. Some cases—a small minority—will be decided en banc. More important, designating selected decisions as precedent can serve as a unifying force by constraining future individual adjudicators or panels. When cases are decided either en banc or by reference to the tribunal's own precedents, the entire tribunal can be thought of as the decisional unit. That subject is taken up separately below.[16] But since not all cases are precedents, and since even precedents can lend themselves to differing interpretations, the degree of consistency one can expect from even a collegial body like the BIA or a court of appeals is reduced when the bulk of that body's decisions are made by less than its full membership.

These considerations are important, because it is often assumed or asserted that centralizing a review function in a single tribunal should improve the consistency of the resulting decisions.[17] One who accepts that assertion might, for example, applaud the BIA as an instrument for bringing consistency to the decisions of the immigration judges, or even advocate substituting a single specialized immigration court or asylum court for the current regime of judicial review of BIA decisions by the twelve courts of appeals of general jurisdiction (not advocated here).[18] But the assertion that centralization itself enhances consistency would require at least one of two assumptions. One assumption is that a fixed number of decisional units will be more consistent if they are in the same tribunal than they will be if they are in different tribunals. An alternate assumption might be that centralization itself will permit a reduction in the total number of decisional units.

The first assumption might be true, but only if there are institutional constraints that cause decisional units to converge, and that would not occur if the decisional units were in different tribunals. That will be the case if all the decisional units within the centralized tribunal are bound to follow that tribunal's precedents but not those of parallel tribunals. Panels of the U.S. courts of appeals, for example, must follow the precedents of their respective courts, but need not follow the precedents of other courts of appeals.[19] Again, however, stare decisis constraints govern only questions of law, not those of fact and discretion, and then only in cases where the prior decisions have been designated as precedents and are indistinguishable. Only in cases where all these conditions are met—question of law, designated as precedent, and indistinguishable on the facts—does centralization alone yield improved consistency.

The alternate assumption would be that centralization permits a reduction in the total number of decisional units for a particular class of cases. Again, an example might be transferring the judicial review function in asylum cases from the general courts of appeals to a single specialized court. Under those circumstances, if the judges of the new specialized court were to decide asylum cases and no others (and assuming they continue to decide cases in three-judge panels), then each of those judges could decide more asylum cases, and fewer judges would thus be needed to decide the entire class of asylum cases. To the extent that the smaller pool of judges improves consistency, however, that is the case because the specialization enables them to be fewer in number, not because they are centralized within a single tribunal.[20] To confirm that this is so, imagine a transfer of the judicial review function to a single centralized court whose judges continued to decide not only asylum cases but also the same general mix of cases—for example, reassigning all judicial review of immigration cases to the U.S. Court of Appeals for the D.C. Circuit. Such a system would be centralized but not specialized, and there would be no reason to think fewer judges could handle the same asylum caseload.

The assertion that reducing the total number of decisional units should generally enhance consistency is subject to one crucial caveat. If the caseload remains constant, and the number of decisional units is reduced, possibly as a fiscal measure, it might initially appear that consistency will improve simply because there are now fewer decisional units whose outcomes have to be reconciled. All else being equal, however, the reduction in the number of decisional units will mean less time and less attention per case. The reduced resources for each case, in turn, might well impair the ability of the decisional units to assure consistent results. Consequently, with a given caseload, a change in the number of total decisional units should have a mixed impact on consistency.

2. THE SIZE OF THE DECISIONAL UNITS

As noted earlier, different tribunals employ decisional units of different sizes, ranging from single-member decisions to panels of less than full membership, to en banc decisions. Generally, increasing the size of the decisional unit should increase the consistency of the decisions both within the tribunal and among tribunals. The larger group diffuses the effects of personal values and subjective biases, thus diminishing the impact of the extremists and pushing the results closer to the middle of the spectrum. To use a simplistic illustration, suppose a tribunal had six members, of whom two always approved the applicants' claims, two always denied them, and the other two approached all cases with complete objectivity. Assume further that the applicant's case is a strong one that an objective adjudicator is almost certain to approve. Thus, four of the six members would be inclined to approve this person's claim and two would be inclined to deny it. If the tribunal decides all its cases by single members, then the chance of the applicant succeeding would be four out of six, or two-thirds. If the tribunal decides all its cases by majority votes of randomly selected three-member panels, the same applicant's chance of success rises to four-fifths.[21] If it decides all its cases en banc, the chance of success becomes one hundred percent. If instead the applicant has a weak case that an objective adjudicator is almost certain to deny, then the same reasoning applies in reverse.

But it is not just a question of mathematics. A panel decision, unlike that of a single member, can be deliberative. There is an opportunity for the various members to persuade one another, thus adding a further check on ill-considered decisions that might otherwise have led to inconsistent rulings.

Moreover, even if an extreme panelist is not actually persuaded, he or she might go along with the decision of more moderate colleagues, either to avoid embarrassment or to present a united front. That check is absent when decisions are made by single members.

Of course, even the use of multimember panels does not guarantee a high degree of consistency. The courts of appeals, for example, decide cases in three-member panels; yet, as the Refugee Roulette study demonstrates, there is a high rate of inconsistency from one circuit to another.[22] Generally, however, utilizing larger decisional units at least helps to bring the results closer to a comfortable center. The added members might outvote or persuade an extremist or produce compromise.

One caveat is that this analysis assumes a constant ratio of cases to decisional units. Suppose instead that the total number of adjudicators stays the same while the size of the decisional unit increases—for example, a tribunal shifts from single-member decisions to panel decisions without adding any adjudicators. Each adjudicator will then have to participate in more cases. The effect could be less attention per case and thus a higher incidence of inconsistent results.

3. THE NUMBER OF CASES

The total caseload of all decisional units combined can also affect consistency. It is easier to reconcile two cases than to reconcile two thousand. Moreover, for any given subject matter, increasing the number of cases increases the number of variations on particular issues, and those variations might require judgment calls as to whether particular cases are similar enough to dictate similar results. Judgment, in turn, invites inconsistency. Finally, when an increase in the total number of cases is not accompanied by a corresponding increase in the number of decisional units, the change in the average caseload of a decisional unit can have additional effects on consistency.[23]

B. Attributes of Adjudicators

I. APPOINTMENT PATTERNS

There is ample evidence that the demographics and prior work experiences of adjudicators can have significant effects on their decisions. The adjudicator's gender, for example, has been found to correlate with particular outcomes in a variety of settings.[24] The Refugee Roulette study reveals that female immigration judges had far higher asylum approval rates than their male counterparts (54 percent versus 37 percent), although no significant gender difference existed among asylum officers' decisions.[25] The authors also found that those immigration judges who had previously worked in the private sector—especially those who had worked in academia, for other nonprofit organizations, or for private law firms—had significantly higher asylum approval rates than those immigration judges who had previously worked for the federal government, particularly those who had worked in a law enforcement capacity for DHS or its predecessor agency, or in the military.[26] In fact, the longer an adjudicator's prior government service, the lower his or her asylum approval rates have been.[27]

At the court of appeals level, the Refugee Roulette study found that Sixth Circuit judges appointed by Democrats appear to vote in favor of asylum applicants at much higher rates than do judges appointed by Republicans.[28] Given these patterns, the diversity of appointees might well contribute to the differing outcomes.

2. TRAINING AND POLICY GUIDANCE

The quality of both the initial and the ongoing training and policy guidance received by adjudicators can similarly affect consistency in at least two ways. To the extent that training enhances the quality of the decision making, it reduces that component of inconsistency attributable to sloppiness or simple inadvertence. If the training and any other substantive guidance provided along the way also impart the agency's views on particular policy issues that are likely to come before the adjudicators, then it can be assumed that those communications will tend to drive the decisions toward some common ground. The magnitude of that effect might well hinge on the adjudicators' degree of independence and, in particular, their job security.[29]

C. The Roles of the Adjudicators

Decisional independence means many things to many people. I am using the term here to describe an adjudicator's freedom to reach the decision that he or she honestly believes the evidence and the law require, without fear of adverse personal consequences. Under that definition, an adjudicator whose job or compensation is at risk when the outcome of a case displeases his or her superiors is not independent.[30] So defined, the same term does not address other forms of intervention, such as attempts by politically accountable superiors to influence decisions by issuing general statements of agency policy through regulations, policy guidelines, and the like. Nor is decisional independence compromised by agency-head or other review of adjudicators' decisions. Both of the latter subjects are considered separately below.[31]

A series of developments in 2002 and 2003 have profoundly drained the decisional independence of immigration judges and BIA members. The selective "reassignments" of the generally liberal BIA members, combined with other regulatory actions that used language broadly applicable to both immigration judges and BIA members, have sent the clear signal that the Justice Department regards these adjudicators as simply department attorneys whose tenure is subject to the unfettered discretion of the attorney general. These developments are summarized above and detailed elsewhere.[32]

At first blush, independence would seem to be at war with consistency. Allowing adjudicators the freedom to sort out the evidence, interpret the law, and even exercise a statutory discretion as they see fit might strike one as a recipe for divergence. The distinguished authors of a major study for the Administrative Conference of the United States on the federal administrative judiciary, for example, saw it that way. They noted the large disparities in the decisions by administrative law judges (ALJs) in Social Security disability cases, ascribed the disparities to the differing personal philosophies of the ALJs, and lamented the fact that ALJ independence hindered efforts by the Social Security Administration to generate greater uniformity.[33] The unspoken assumption was that agency intervention would have caused more of the adjudicators' decisions to converge around a common agency position.

But the net impact of independence on consistency is not quite so obvious. If adjudicators perceive their politically accountable superiors as threats to their job security, they might indeed be influenced to reach the agency's preferred outcome, but to varying degrees. Adjudicators will surely differ in the extent of their willingness to risk the displeasure of their superiors. They might have different family or other personal circumstances; different career aspirations; different levels of integrity, courage, or pride; and differing perceptions of how much their superiors care about a particular issue or even what their superiors' preferred outcome would be. Whether these sources of divergence are strong enough to offset the convergence produced by gravitation toward a common agency position is an empirical question.

2. DEFERENCE AND SCOPE OF REVIEW

Appellate review can either enhance or diminish consistency. It can reduce the consistency of the outcomes when several horizontal tribunals, such as the U.S. courts of appeals, review the decisions of a centralized decision maker like the BIA. In that scenario, absent Supreme Court review, consistency is diminished simply because the final say is lodged in twelve different tribunals and more decisional units at the court of appeals level, rather than in one BIA and fewer decisional units. Conversely, review can enhance the consistency of the outcomes when a single centralized authority like the BIA or the attorney general reviews the decisions of decentralized decision makers, such as the immigration judges.

Appellate review can have these effects for a second reason. Review serves not only a retrospective "error-correcting" function concerned with the outcome of the particular dispute but also a prospective "guidance" function concerned with the future development of the law.[34] If the appellate tribunal has the power to designate selected decisions as binding precedent, then those precedents further increase or decrease consistency, depending again on whether it is a single centralized review body binding numerous decentralized adjudicators or vice-versa. The effects of stare decisis on consistency are taken up separately below.[35]

If those are the effects of appellate review on consistency, then anything that tempers the impact of appellate review should have precisely the reverse effect on consistency. One instrument that tempers the impact of appellate review is a narrow scope of review. In the removal context, which includes asylum, the BIA reviews immigration judges' decisions de novo with respect to conclusions of law and the exercise of discretion. Since 2002, however, it may reverse findings of fact—specifically including the credibility determinations that play particularly crucial roles in asylum cases—only under the "clearly erroneous" standard.[36] Thus, while BIA review of immigration judge decisions should generally enhance consistency for the reasons given above, the degree of enhancement is constrained on fact questions by the narrow scope of review.

As for judicial review of agency decisions, the Administrative Procedure Act generally limits the court to "substantial evidence" review of findings of fact and the "arbitrary, capricious, an abuse of discretion, or otherwise not in accordance with law" standard for the review of agency discretion.[37] Courts reviewing removal decisions (again, including asylum denials) employ roughly similar standards.

And on questions of law, judicial review is constrained by *Chevron* deference to the agency's interpretations of the laws they administer.[38] Thus, while review of BIA decisions by the twelve courts of appeals should generally reduce consistency for the reasons given above, the degree of reduction is itself constrained by the combination of *Chevron* deference on questions of law and a narrow scope of review on questions of fact or discretion.

3. REASONED OPINIONS AND STARE DECISIS

The practice of explaining one's decision in a reasoned, written opinion has to have a positive impact on both the internal consistency of one adjudicator's decisions and the external consistency of the collection of decisions by multiple adjudicators. For one thing, having to offer reasons for the decision forces the adjudicator to put more thought into the issue before reaching a conclusion. Most relevant here, if one possible outcome would potentially conflict with another decision, the adjudicator has to decide consciously whether the two outcomes would be reconcilable. Without a reasoned written opinion, there is more room for gut instinct and visceral reactions based on personal or political outlook. Since those outlooks, in turn, will vary from one adjudicator to another, reasoned written opinions should, all else being equal, enhance consistency.

Regulations issued in 2002 dramatically expanded the categories of BIA cases that require affirmances without opinion.[39] In those cases, as the name implies, BIA members are prohibited from writing reasoned opinions to explain their decisions; instead, they must dispose of the cases with a single boilerplate paragraph contained in the regulations. Under those circumstances, producing accurate and consistent outcomes becomes problematic. Happily, the attorney general has recently announced that the BIA will be "drastically decreasing its reliance on summary one-line decisions."[40]

Reasoned opinions are a prerequisite to another practice that promotes consistency—stare decisis. On questions of law, the institution of stare decisis encourages adjudicative bodies to strive for consistent outcomes. While commonly associated with the judicial setting, stare decisis also applies to the BIA. Those decisions that the BIA chooses to designate as precedent are binding on immigration judges and on all employees of the Department of Homeland Security.[41] The attorney general has recently pledged that the BIA will make greater use of its power to designate decisions as binding precedent.[42]

D. Resources

1. FISCAL RESOURCES

Generally, one can assume that the fiscal resources invested in an adjudicative process, relative to the nature and the size of the caseload, will influence the consistency of the outcomes. The number of adjudicators can cut both ways, for the reasons already discussed.[43] On the one hand, more adjudicators means more sets of potentially conflicting viewpoints to reconcile. On the other hand, for a given caseload, more adjudicators also means more time per case per adjudicator. The latter, in turn, can mean more careful hearings, more thorough review of the evidence and the law, more opportunity to find and consider potential precedents, more thoughtful consideration of the evidence and the arguments on appeal, and more careful drafting of the final opinion.

Resources are about more than the number of adjudicators. The support staff can help to attain both accuracy and consistency through research, analysis, and drafting of memoranda and opinions. Thus, the size, quality, training, and use of the support staff can all affect the degree of consistency. For the same reasons, the pay scales for both the adjudicators and the support staff become determinants of consistency as well. The availability and quality of a documentation center— particularly in asylum cases, where current and comprehensive information on country conditions is critical—is another key fiscal resource. So too is access to all the other information needed to assure accurate and consistent outcomes, such as a good system for cataloguing and retrieving both prior and currently pending cases that present roughly similar issues.

2. PROCEDURAL RESOURCES

The various procedural safeguards built into the adjudicative process have equally obvious effects on the adjudicators' ability to achieve consistency. Practical access to competent counsel—attorneys or other qualified representatives— has repeatedly been shown to be one of the highest correlates of asylum approval rates.[44] As the authors of the Refugee Roulette study acknowledge, some component of that positive correlation undoubtedly reflects sampling bias, since pro bono and other attorneys are less likely to spend their time on cases that have little chance of succeeding.[45] But the complexity of the cases and the amount of corroborating evidence and other preparation required to win an asylum case make it highly likely that representation clarifies the issues and presents the adjudicator with critical information. On that assumption, practical access to counsel at least improves the probability that the adjudicators will reach more informed decisions, thus reducing whatever portion of the inconsistency is otherwise traceable to lack of information or analysis.

Investing in a right of appeal should have similar positive effects on consistency, subject to the caveat that multiple horizontal reviewers of a single tribunal with fewer decisional units (for example, court of appeals review of the BIA) can have countervailing effects. As the Refugee Roulette study demonstrates, that caveat is important in the asylum context, as the various courts of appeals have indeed reached disparate results.[46] Subject to that qualification, however, a right of appeal should generally enhance consistency, depending on both the accessibility and the efficacy of the appeal. The appellate authority is able to take a second look at a case, with a special eye on those aspects of the decision that the opposing counsel have identified as problematic.

E. The Nature of the Subject Matter

I. DEGREE OF SPECIALIZATION

Specialized adjudication has a whole range of benefits and costs that I have discussed more comprehensively elsewhere.[47] The final part of this essay will revisit that discussion in the specific context of asylum. One of the benefits has long been assumed to be consistency. Indeed, the desire for uniform outcomes was one of the driving forces behind the establishment of the multiple-specialty United States Court of Appeals for the Federal Circuit.[48] Over the years, others have put forward similar rationales in support of a specialized immigration court[49] or a specialized administrative law court.[50]

I would suggest that the road from specialization to consistency takes two different routes. One route leads from specialization to expertise to consistency. The other route leads from specialization to fewer adjudicators to consistency.

The link between specialization and expertise has several components. Members of specialized tribunals can be chosen because of their preexisting experience and expertise. Once on board, their expertise grows. As others have observed, the growth results both from their frequent contacts with the governing legislation and from their exposure to the practical results of their decisions through immersion in the overall statutory scheme.[51] If they are equipped with a specialized support staff and other specialized resources, and if their specialization allows them the time to participate in specialized professional associations and other forms of continuing professional development, then their specialized knowledge will expand further. That expertise, in turn, should aid them in achieving consistent outcomes. Familiarity with the issues should alone reduce the incidence of inadvertent deviations from established law and practice. Familiarity with one's own prior decisions and the prior decisions of colleagues is an additional avenue for uniformity.

Specialization also permits a reduction in the number of adjudicators who decide the particular class of cases. Suppose, for example, a given court has jurisdiction over ten unrelated subjects. Assume that in a typical month the court receives twenty new case filings for each of these subjects, for a total of two hundred cases per month, and that each case is equally labor-intensive. Assume further that all the court's decisions are by single members, that one adjudicator can reasonably average ten dispositions per month, that the cases are randomly assigned, and that in a typical month, therefore, each adjudicator decides an average of one case from each of the ten subjects. On those assumptions, it will take twenty adjudicators to staff the court. Now suppose that one of the ten subjects the court handles is transferred to a specialized court that hears only those cases. Since that new court will receive only twenty cases per year, two adjudicators can staff it.[52] Without minimizing the possibility that the two adjudicators might have vastly different ideologies and judicial philosophies, one can still assume that it will be easier for two adjudicators to keep track of each other's decisions than it was when there were twenty.

2. COMPLEXITY

Statutory schemes can be complex for many reasons. Size alone can make a statutory regime complex; the Immigration and Nationality Act now spans more than five hundred pages[53] and is supplemented by hundreds of pages of administrative regulations issued by the Departments of Homeland Security, Justice, Labor, and State,[54] among others, as well as thousands of administrative and judicial decisions. Perhaps more important, it is organizationally intricate. Passed in 1952 and amended countless times, the act is "a hideous creature" whose "excruciating technical provisions . . . are often hopelessly intertwined."[55] It is not unusual for one provision to be qualified by other provisions located in distant reaches of the same statute.

The complexities that result from both size and organizational intricacy can give rise to inconsistent outcomes. With increased complexity comes a greater risk that the adjudicator will simply miss an important provision. There is a heightened potential for logic errors. There is greater potential for reading particular provisions in ways that create conflicts with others. Reconciling those conflicts might require consideration of broader goals and contexts, and those sorts of judgments might vary from one adjudicator to the next. Technical complexity can generate textual ambiguity, with the attendant need to resort more frequently to legislative history. The latter, in turn, can breed further inconsistencies, as adjudicators differ not only in the ways in which they interpret various expressions of legislative intent but also in the weight they place on different sources.

3. DYNAMISM

All else being equal, one would expect a rapidly changing subject matter like immigration—particularly asylum—to produce a good deal of inconsistency along the way. It is hard for one adjudicator to stay even internally consistent, much less maintain consistency with his or her colleagues, when the goal line keeps moving. The changes might stem from new statutes, new regulations, new case law, or new developments elsewhere in the law. Whatever the source of the changes, dynamism makes it more likely that even experienced adjudicators will simply miss new developments entirely. The changes might render precedents—one of the key instruments for consistency—outdated. They might raise doubts—and therefore judgments that differ from one adjudicator to another—about whether existing precedents have been superseded. And the changes can raise whole sets of new issues that have to be decided without the aid of precedent, an additional recipe for inconsistent outcomes.

4. EMOTIONAL OR IDEOLOGICAL CONTENT

Some subjects generate more heat than others. Those subjects that inspire ideological or emotional fervor would seem to have the greatest potential for disparate outcomes, since the flesh-and-blood adjudicators who decide the cases will have extra reason to resolve the more indeterminate questions by resort to visceral beliefs and emotional impulses.

Asylum is such a subject. Both genuine refugees and those asylum seekers who are seen as abusing the system trigger strong emotions. Refugees present compelling cases for protection. They might be fleeing unspeakable atrocities and might be traumatized by their experiences. They are unusually vulnerable and, through no fault of their own, must depend on a foreign state for their most basic needs. For some adjudicators, those factors are paramount. For others, different priorities dominate. Some adjudicators might see their main mission as weeding out fraudulent or other legally insufficient asylum claims in order to prevent illegal immigration generally or asylum abuse in particular. Since asylum adjudication tends to be high-volume and administrative resources are finite, adjudicators will also differ in the trade-offs they make between productivity and accuracy. They will have differing attitudes toward human rights, the role of international law, and perhaps even race, ethnicity, gender, and class.

5. SPECTRUM OF CHOICE

Some subjects provide more than the usual leeway to adjudicators. Statutory language might contain differing degrees of specificity, and regulations and case law might or might not fill in the gaps. The more latitude there is for basic fact finding, the more open-textured the statutory and other relevant law, and the broader the area of delegated discretion, the more judgment the adjudicator will have to exercise, and, therefore, the more room there will be for the ideological and emotional factors discussed above to operate.

The choices, of course, will never be boundless. They will always be constrained by the classic "steadying factors" that Karl Llewellyn assembled as a response to what he perceived as the excesses of legal realism.[56] The professional office occupied by the adjudicator, and the pride and responsibilities that go with it, will surely be among the most important of these constraints. But the points here are that these steadying factors still leave ample margin for variation from one adjudicator to another and, more important, that the size of that variance will itself vary from one area of law to another.

That brings us to asylum. In this field, the spectrum of choice is exceptionally broad. First, asylum claims require determinations of whether individual claimants meet the definition of "refugee."[57] That definition in turn necessitates applications of such broad statutory terms as "persecution," "well-founded" fear, and "social group."[58] Moreover, since asylum claimants can rarely escape their countries of origin with official documentation of the persecution that awaits them if they return, their own testimony assumes special importance. For that reason, claims frequently, if not usually, turn on whether the adjudicator finds their stories credible. Although Congress has provided some specific guidance on how to assess credibility and on when to insist on corroborating evidence of even credible stories, myriad factors and the absence of guidance as to the weight those individual factors should command leave credibility highly indeterminate.[59] Finally, the requirement that the fear of persecution be "well-founded" requires the adjudicator not only to find historic facts but also to make predictions about the treatment an applicant will receive if returned to the country of origin. The latter requires an uncommon degree of judgment and therefore spawns an unavoidably high degree of variance among adjudicators.

III. The Policy Options

> God, grant me the serenity to accept the things I cannot change, the courage to change the things I can, and the wisdom to know the difference.[60]

The authors of the Refugee Roulette study have demonstrated a high rate of variance in asylum outcomes. They have exposed disparities at all levels of the system—from asylum officers and immigration judges to the U.S. courts of appeals. Differences in the asylum seekers' countries of origin do not explain these results, because the authors were careful to control for that variable. Moreover, the Refugee Roulette study revealed specific patterns to the variances, not just random distributions that might otherwise have been the simple result of high numbers of adjudicators or cases. As the study demonstrated, some adjudicators are generally much more inclined to grant asylum than others are. Moreover, the approval rates vary by the genders of the adjudicators, their prior work experience, and, at least on some courts of appeals, the administration that appointed them.

Of the variables identified in the preceding part, which ones might account for the disparate outcomes observed in the asylum setting? Under the circumstances just noted—the persistence of large variances at all levels, the elimination of country of origin as an explanatory factor, and the adjudicator-specific patterns—it seems easy to identify the principal contributors. They include the adjudicators' differing ideologies and attitudes, which affect their preexisting inclinations to grant or deny asylum,[61] and the subject matter, which is indeterminate enough, complex enough, and dynamic enough to give adjudicators relatively broad freedom to reach the outcomes they desire. The attitudes that asylum adjudicators inevitably bring to their work include not only their general philosophies about asylum or immigration but also their normative conceptions of the adjudicative role, their levels of suspicion about the credibility of the applicants, and the weights they attach to erring on the side of either the individual or the government.

That is unequal justice, to be sure, but my basic thesis is that for the most part we shall have to live with it. Unless the adjudicators can be made ideologically homogeneous—a goal I find neither desirable nor achievable—there will always be substantial asylum-approval-rate disparities' and many outcomes will reflect the luck of the draw. That is just the way it is.

This is not, however, a call for complacency. Consistency is a positive virtue for all the reasons offered in part 1 of this essay, and this part will consider steps that can be taken to enhance it at the margins. The key is to aim low and to settle for treating the symptoms.

More substantial fixes are possible to theorize. Some might respond to the Refugee Roulette study by calling for dramatic measures that would infuse the asylum process with greater uniformity. Most of those solutions would probably require more centralized control over the adjudicators. These might include terminating the appointments of the true outliers or otherwise penalizing them for extreme decisional patterns, imposing minimum or maximum asylum approval rates, or more muscular review of adjudicative decisions by an agency head or other politically accountable officials. In the discussion that follows, I argue against all of those options.

A. Worthwhile but Marginal Improvements

I. MORE DETAILED STATUTES, REGULATIONS, AND INFORMAL INSTRUMENTS

As many have noted over the years, the law contains no comprehensive definition of "persecution" that would be concrete enough to offer adjudicators any meaningful guidance.[62] That gap is understandable. It would be hard to anticipate every conceivable means of persecution that "an imaginative despot might conjure up."[63] It would be possible, however, for Congress to express its judgment on a few commonly recurring issues. Similarly, either the Department of Justice or the Department of Homeland Security could issue interpretative regulations or provide other informal policy guidance that adjudicators could consult in relevant cases.[64] Congress, for example, has specifically made subjection to forced abortions or forced sterilizations a basis for refugee status.[65] The former INS issued informal gender guidelines to aid asylum officers in their evaluation of gender-related asylum claims.[66]

The authors of the Refugee Roulette study expressed little enthusiasm for more substantive guidance, not because they identified any affirmative harms but because of the lack of evidence that disagreements about substantive law account for the disparities in grant rates.[67] I agree with the authors that the bulk of the explanation lies elsewhere, but policy guidance on a few specific key issues might help at the margins.

2. MORE ADJUDICATORS

Increasing the total number of adjudicators at each level—asylum officers, immigration judges, BIA members, and court of appeals judges—would have mixed effects on consistency. As discussed earlier, it might seem counterinstinctive to expect greater consistency when there are more human beings whose decisions have to be reconciled.[68] Again, however, increasing the number of adjudicators at a particular level permits either the use of larger decisional units (explored next) or more decisional units. The latter, in turn, allows a decrease in the caseload of the average decisional unit and, therefore, an increase in the amount of time and attention that each decisional unit can devote to the average case. The extraordinary caseload pressures on the immigration judges[69] make reinforcements essential. The extra time and attention should ultimately enhance consistency for all the reasons given earlier.

3. LARGER DECISIONAL UNITS

All else being equal, expanding the size of the decisional unit—changing from mainly single-member BIA decisions to panel decisions, for example—should improve the consistency of the outcomes for numerous reasons considered earlier.[70] Among other things, enlarging the decisional unit diminishes the impact of the extremists by diffusing their subjective biases, permits deliberation, and encourages consensus through moderation.

Until 1988, the BIA—then composed of five members—decided every case en banc.[71] The Justice Department, in fact, initially opposed a 1985 recommendation by the Administrative Conference of the United States that it move to a system of three-member panels.[72] Only three years later did the Justice Department, faced with a rapidly growing backlog, acquiesce in that recommendation.[73] Ironically, the same department that had once staunchly resisted shifting from en banc to three-member panels has now gone to the other extreme, with dramatically increased resort to single-member decisions.[74]

Because the BIA does not keep the statistics that would have made comparison possible, the authors of the Refugee Roulette study were not able to confirm empirically that BIA members have been prone to the same sorts of inconsistency as the asylum officers, immigration judges, and court of appeals judges. But the main sources of the inconsistencies among the latter three groups—differing ideologies and attitudes combined with complex, dynamic, and open-textured subject matter—are equally present for BIA members. Thus there is no reason to expect their decisional patterns to vary any less. Moreover, although based on a much smaller data sample, the Levinson study that was noted earlier certainly suggests similar patterns among BIA members.[75]

On those assumptions, the authors of the Refugee Roulette study urge the BIA to assign all asylum cases to multimember (possibly two-member) panels.[76] More routine use of multimember panels would involve at least two policy trade-offs. The most obvious is the additional fiscal cost. If the number of decisional units is held constant, then it would take more adjudicators and more support staff to handle the same caseload. Two-member panels would not cost twice as much as single-member panels, because part of the work is the writing of the opinion, which would presumably be assigned to a single member at any rate. But they would certainly cost more. The extra expenditures would have to be balanced against the enhanced accuracy and consistency that those resources permit. The less obvious trade-off is the opportunity cost. The extra resources, instead of being allocated to increasing the size of the decisional unit, could instead have been used to increase the total number of decisional units. The latter strategy would cut each BIA member's caseload and thus permit each member to devote more time and attention to each case. Which approach would ultimately yield the greater improvement in accuracy and efficiency is another unanswered empirical question.

Finally, the BIA could make more liberal use of en banc decisions when the issues are commonly recurring, otherwise important, or simply difficult. The regulations currently permit en banc BIA hearings in selected cases.[77] Also possible, however, would be a system of limited en banc decisions in which a majority of the BIA members, but not all, are randomly assigned to a case that warrants more than a two-member panel. Those U.S. courts of appeals that have more than fifteen active judges are authorized to do precisely that.[78] If a substantial increase in BIA en banc decision making were felt to be worthwhile but otherwise too costly, the BIA could adopt a similar practice.

4. STRENGTHENING THE SUPPORT STAFF

The Refugee Roulette study identifies some basic gaps in the support resources for asylum adjudicators—very few law clerks even for immigration judges, no stenographers, and interpreters of uneven quality.[79] Improving the quality of the interpreters would have obvious implications for both the time that hearings take and the reliability, and therefore consistency, of the outcomes. Investing in more law clerks for immigration judges might be more important still. Law clerks can do much of the research, aid with the analysis through carefully written bench memoranda, and draft opinions for the immigration judge to consider. Their work would improve the quality of the decision making not only directly but also indirectly, as it would free up more hearing time for the immigration judges.

5. PROVIDING COUNSEL

The immigration laws give every person in removal proceedings the right to counsel, but not at government expense.[80] The preclusion of government-funded counsel has been problematic, because many of the individuals in removal proceedings are unable to afford counsel and because counsel materially increases the likelihood of success, especially in asylum cases.[81] The authors of the Refugee Roulette study found representation by counsel to be "the single most important factor affecting the outcome of [an asylum] case." There are ways for indigent noncitizens in removal proceedings—including asylum applicants—to obtain counsel, but they are very limited.[82]

For these reasons, the authors of the Refugee Roulette study recommend the appointment of counsel for every indigent asylum seeker in removal proceedings. Without counsel, they point out, it is difficult to produce the affidavits and other documents asylum seekers need in order to establish their claims and nearly impossible to make the technical legal arguments often required. Combining the incalculable harm of erroneous denials with the substantial probability that counsel can help avoid such errors, they argue, the government should provide counsel to indigent asylum seekers when they find themselves in the quasi-legal setting of a removal hearing.[83]

The authors make a strong case. And if representation by counsel increases the asylum approval rate, then assuring that all asylum applicants have access to counsel has the additional effect of evening the playing field, thereby enhancing the consistency of the outcomes. Accuracy and consistency aside, counsel benefits not only the clients but also the immigration court. Counsel can help speed the hearings by focusing the issues,[84] preparing the testimony, assembling the documents, and doing the necessary legal research.

In the present political climate, furnishing counsel for all indigent asylum seekers in removal proceedings seems unrealistic. Some will particularly object to devoting public resources to those applicants whose claims are frivolous or in bad faith. There might even be a fear that the availability of appointed counsel for asylum applicants would create a perverse incentive for individuals in removal proceedings to file frivolous asylum claims merely to get free legal advice. A compromise, therefore, would be to borrow one feature from the otherwise much maligned expedited removal program. Congress could require the appointment of government counsel once an asylum applicant makes threshold showings of indigence and a "credible fear of persecution,"[85] to be determined by the immigration judge. While perhaps still politically unrealistic, the compromise version would at least address the objection to rewarding frivolous claims.

6. QUALITY CONTROL IN HIRING

Whatever the hiring system, of course, adjudicators will arrive with biases. Anyone with specialized experience is likely to have thought about the issues and formed opinions and in that sense, at least, will have a preexisting bias. Therefore, as long as immigration experience is valued as one of the hiring criteria, there will be biases. Further, even if prior specialized experience is discounted as a hiring factor, the adjudicator who arrives with no such experience will still have been exposed to the immigration debate and be likely to have some predisposition on the more controversial issues. Indeed, the chance of appointing a qualified asylum adjudicator who truly has no opinion on the subject is about the same as that of finding a qualified O.J. Simpson juror who had never before heard of the case. And if such a person could be found, one would have other reasons to worry. Finally, even a person who arrives without any preformulated views on the issues will form them soon enough after hearing a fair number of cases.

Personal ideology, therefore, will always be part of what an asylum adjudicator brings to the job or at least soon develops. Consequently, the objective should not be to avoid hiring anyone with a preexisting ideological bias, but simply to avoid affirmatively factoring a candidate's ideology into the hiring decision.

That conclusion might be less obvious than it seems. Since asylum has substantial policy implications, a politically accountable official might assert the legitimacy of hiring adjudicators who share his or her world view. There are two arguments for doing so. One is that the official is part of an administration that was elected or appointed through democratic processes and remains accountable to the people. Thus, the argument would run, the official has the right, if not the duty, to appoint people who will effectuate his or her policy goals. The second argument would be that only by appointing ideologically similar personnel can the official hope to achieve outcomes compatible with each other and with the policy decisions that that official makes in his or her rulemaking or other political capacities. Persuasive as those arguments would be with respect to the appointments of political subordinates, however, they seem unconvincing with respect to adjudicative positions, where the job duties consist of finding facts and interpreting law.

The authors of the Refugee Roulette study urge more rigorous hiring criteria and procedures.[86] They point out that between 2004 and 2007 the attorney general bypassed the formal competitive vetting procedures used by the chief immigration judge, instead hiring his own preferred candidates in "the overwhelming majority" of cases.[87] When political officials make the hiring decisions, the temptation to prize ideological and partisan political preferences over judicial aptitude and temperament becomes clear. In the final days of his tenure at the Justice Department, the attorney general told the Senate Judiciary Committee that he had instituted new hiring procedures by which "the initial vetting, evaluation, and interviewing functions have been placed within the Office of the Chief Immigration Judge and within the Executive Office for Immigration Review as a whole."[88] The qualifier "initial" leaves it open to the attorney general to appoint his or her preferred candidates for ideological or partisan reasons.

It does not have to be that way. Immigration judges could be made ALJs and appointed in the same way.

As for the appellate stage, the authors of the Refugee Roulette study, like several who have gone before them, recommend replacing the BIA with an Article I immigration court.[89] Some, including the authors of the Refugee Roulette study, have argued for appointment by the president and confirmation by the Senate, much like the process in place for the U.S. Parole Board.[90] Others prefer the current model of attorney general appointments.[91]

While the current model has the advantages of relative speed and philosophical compatibility between the attorney general and the adjudicators, I continue to believe that presidential appointment followed by Senate confirmation would make eminent sense for the BIA. The increased stature of a presidential appointment might help to attract the strongest candidates. The Senate confirmation process would increase the chance of exposing ideologues whose decisions can generate the very disparities that the Refugee Roulette study revealed.

7. PROFESSIONAL DEVELOPMENT

The earlier discussion of training illustrates the ways in which thoughtful professional development—both upon appointment and at regular intervals thereafter—can promote accuracy and consistency in adjudicative outcomes. For all those reasons, the authors of the Refugee Roulette study recommend more intensive training on asylum issues, particularly for immigration judges.[92] They also advocate regular meetings between adjudicators with unusually high asylum approval rates and those with unusually low rates, in the hope that some common ground can be located.[93] Both recommendations are sensible, and both have the potential to make modest inroads into the disparities in asylum approval rates.

8. DISSEMINATION OF ASYLUM APPROVAL RATES

The authors of the Refugee Roulette study were able to dig up large amounts of information on the asylum approval rates of asylum officers, immigration judges, and selected court of appeals judges, but they could not obtain analogous information on members of the BIA. They urged the BIA to begin compiling and publishing those data.[94]

There is a fine line between putting peer pressure on individual adjudicators to arrive at particular outcomes and simply alerting them to information that their decisional patterns are out of step with those of their colleagues. Both actions run the risk of compromising the adjudicators' independent judgment, but there are differences in degree. The latter action provides information that might be more welcome than threatening. If the adjudicators' job security is adequately safeguarded—a critical point discussed separately in part III.C.2 below—then it is hard to argue against providing adjudicators with information they might find helpful. The only concern would be that the peer pressure from one's colleagues upon receipt of this same information might induce some adjudicators to go against their better judgment in a certain number of asylum cases in order to bring their overall rates closer to the norm. That possibility seems difficult to eliminate entirely, but my view is that it does not outweigh the value of adjudicators being able to discover whether their decisional patterns are at a relative extreme. I therefore endorse the authors' suggestion that the BIA compile and regularly disseminate the asylum approval rates of each member. The Asylum Office and the Office of the Chief Immigration Judge might consider regularly scheduling similar disseminations.

9. EXPANDING THE BIA'S SCOPE OF REVIEW

Earlier discussion explained how appellate review can either increase or decrease the consistency of the outcomes, depending principally on whether the appellate authority has more or fewer decisional units than the original decision maker. The same discussion then observed that narrowing the scope of appellate review tempers the effect of the appellate review on consistency.[95] As also discussed earlier, the BIA reviews immigration judges' legal and discretionary decisions de novo but, since 2002, reviews their findings of fact only under the more deferential "clearly erroneous" standard.[96]

Even with its increased reliance on single-member decisions, the BIA has far fewer decisional units than the immigration judges. In theory, therefore, BIA review is a unifying force, promoting consistent outcomes. In practice, the narrow scope of review on fact questions lessens that positive effect for all the reasons given earlier. Thus, one way to promote consistency would be to restore de novo BIA review of immigration judges' findings of fact.

The main concern in doing so would probably relate to questions of witness credibility. Immigration judges, to be sure, have the advantage of face-to-face contact with any witnesses who appear at the hearings. They are therefore best positioned to observe the witnesses' demeanor. The BIA must rely on a cold transcript.

That difference, however, is easily exaggerated. Asylum hearings involve very few live witnesses other than the applicants themselves.[97] As to the applicant's testimony, Congress has recently laid out the specific factors on which the credibility determination may rest,[98] and the courts have insisted on tangible reasons before they will affirm the immigration judges' credibility judgments.[99] The requirement of concrete evidence makes it easier for the BIA to review credibility judgments. At any rate, myriad cultural signals can render demeanor evidence highly misleading.[100] My view is that any remaining marginal advantage of deferring to the immigration judges' opportunity to observe the witnesses' physical demeanor is outweighed by the BIA's ability to bring some measure of consistency to the now highly disparate immigration judge outcomes.

10. REASONED AND BINDING OPINIONS

As earlier discussion explained, regulations introduced by the attorney general in 2002 for the purpose of easing the BIA backlog greatly expanded the categories of cases in which the BIA is prohibited from giving reasons.[101] The attorney general's recent pledge to decrease the usage of these affirmances without opinion[102] is commendable, but the authors of the Refugee Roulette study would prescribe stronger medicine. Echoing a recommendation of the U.S. Commission on Religious Freedom, they argue that all BIA asylum cases accompanied by written briefs deserve reasoned dispositions that respond specifically to each of the arguments raised.[103] Put another way, the shift would be from an absolute prohibition on reasoned opinions to a positive obligation to provide them in the affected cases.

I fully concur. The ways in which written reasoned opinions promote consistency—both directly and by enhancing accuracy—have already been summarized.[104] Reasoned dispositions have side benefits too. They assure applicants, their counsel, and the general public that their arguments were actually heard and considered. Of course, depending on whether the extra work is accompanied by increased resources, there would presumably be either additional fiscal cost or a reduction in the speed with which the backlog is eliminated. But even from a purely fiscal standpoint, a requirement of written reasons might well pay for itself. As the authors of the Refugee Roulette study point out, counsel can use the opinions to decide whether it is worthwhile to seek review from a court of appeals and, as a result, might opt for fewer appeals.[105]

The attorney general has also said that the BIA would increasingly use its power to designate selected decisions as precedents, which are binding on immigration judges and all DHS employees, including asylum officers.[106] For the reasons given earlier, that step too should promote consistency.[107] The BIA can, and should, adopt a system analogous to that of the courts of appeals. A court of appeals panel is absolutely bound by a decision of a prior panel of the same court; only the full court sitting en banc, or the Supreme Court, may overrule the court's own precedent.[108] The BIA could similarly make its precedent decisions binding on single members and on three-member panels while allowing either limited en banc panels or the full BIA en banc to overrule precedents.

B. Possible Enhancements to Consistency but Bad Ideas Nonetheless

I. DEMOGRAPHIC HIRING CRITERIA

The Refugee Roulette study demonstrated that certain demographic and work-experience variables significantly correlate with adjudicators' asylum approval rates. Nevertheless, for reasons elaborated elsewhere,[109] the use of demographics to hire like-minded adjudicators as a strategy for enhancing consistency is not recommended.

2. MORE FREQUENT AGENCY HEAD REVIEW OF BIA DECISIONS

Though the power is not exercised often, the attorney general may review any BIA decision that he or she wishes to review.[110] This is not an unusual arrangement; Congress often authorizes agency heads to review adjudicative decisions that fall within their domains.[111] To reduce the approval-rate disparities identified in the Refugee Roulette study, one might be tempted to urge more frequent attorney general review of BIA decisions.

For reasons that are spelled out in greater detail elsewhere,[112] I hope that temptation will be resisted. There is little need for agency-head review. Interdecisional consistency can be achieved through a combination of en banc BIA review, legislative rules (including interim rules when necessary), and interpretative rules. Rulemaking and other powers can also preserve agency-policy primacy and agency-policy coherence. Moreover, agency-head review poses inherent dangers to the dispensation of justice, including especially the substitution of a political outcome for one based on an independent adjudicative tribunal's honest reading of the evidence and the law. All of these considerations have special force in the asylum context, where the stakes are high and the potential for inappropriate political and ideological influence has been amply demonstrated.

3. MORE RESTRICTIONS ON JUDICIAL REVIEW

As developed earlier,[113] judicial review of asylum decisions by the twelve general courts of appeals can be assumed to have some centrifugal effects, exacerbating the disparate outcomes arrived at by the BIA. The courts are already forbidden to review at least two important categories of asylum denials—those reached in expedited removal proceedings and those based on findings that failure to file the claim within the one-year deadline was not attributable to changed or extraordinary circumstances.[114] For the stated purpose of reducing asylum-approval-rate disparities, some might be tempted to advocate further restrictions on judicial review of asylum denials. Those restrictions could conceivably include barring judicial review of other selected subcategories of asylum cases, making judicial review discretionary, or narrowing the scope of review.[115]

There are other costs of judicial review of administrative decisions, but in my view the benefits of judicial review overwhelm the costs.[116] For reasons that are spelled out elsewhere, Congress should not only resist any further incursions into judicial review of asylum claims but should repeal the existing restrictions.[117]

4. TRANSFERRING JUDICIAL REVIEW TO A SPECIALIZED IMMIGRATION COURT

Earlier discussion described the ways in which specialized adjudicators can promote decisional consistency within the specialized subject area.[118] Some of the reasons fall under the heading of improved expertise, while others arise simply because specialization reduces the total number of different adjudicators who will be needed to handle a given caseload. Given these effects, some might advocate greater specialization as a way to address the sharp disparities revealed by the Refugee Roulette study. For reasons that go beyond the pursuit of consistency, several commentators over the years have advocated replacing the immigration judges or the BIA or both with a statutory, specialized immigration court.[119] The pros and cons of specialized justice, and the case attributes that influence the weights those pros and cons should command, are the subject of a separate book.[120] Here, it is enough to suggest that the advantages of specialized asylum adjudication, both in enhancing consistency and in achieving other goals, seem greater at the initial decision-making stages than at any appellate stages.

C. Potentially Dramatic Gains in Consistency but Especially Bad Ideas

1. QUOTAS OR OTHER DIRECT CONTROLS ON OUTCOMES

The authors of the Refugee Roulette study briefly consider, but rightly reject, the strategy of policymakers imposing acceptable ranges of asylum approval rates on asylum officers and immigration judges. I include this option in the interest of completeness, but numerical quotas would be pernicious for the reasons they give[121] and for some additional reasons.[122]

2. PUNISHING WAYWARD ADJUDICATORS

I have saved my most serious worry for last. Given the glaring disparities in the asylum approval rates from one adjudicator to another, one temptation might be to "rein them in." This could be done by taking wayward adjudicators aside, quietly "encouraging" them to increase or decrease their approval rates, and then, after a decent interval, terminating or reassigning those who remain recalcitrant. Performance reviews that take approval rates into account and serve as a criterion for retention or promotion might be another device for eliminating adjudicators who veer too far from the mean.[123]

Any of these strategies might well reduce the disparities in asylum approval rates. As discussed earlier, however, threats to adjudicators' job security inherently compromise their decisional independence.[124] As the same discussion explained, the actions of attorneys general over the past five years have already dangerously sapped the independence of the immigration judges and the BIA.

In a previous article I explored the implications of decisional independence more generally; here, they will be just briefly recounted. Decisional independence has costs that have to be acknowledged.[125] Probably the most controversial cost is that, by definition, decisional independence is the flip side of political accountability. When the decision has broader policy implications, as is especially likely when it is designated as binding precedent, that consequence can be viewed as a cost to the democratic process. It is a cost that we readily accept when courts interpret an entrenched Constitution, use judgment in interpreting ambiguous statutory language, or make common law. It is a cost nonetheless.

Some might feel that decisional independence erodes agency policy primacy. The earlier discussion on agency-head review of adjudicative decisions, however, showed how agency policy primacy can be maintained through rulemaking and other devices.[126] The admittedly substantial logistical constraints can be minimized. But whether or not one shares that assessment, the point here is that even a passionate advocate of agency-head review can applaud decisional independence. As the Administrative Conference report emphasizes, precisely that combination—adjudicator independence in reaching the decision but agency-head authority to reverse it—lies at the heart of the compromise philosophy enshrined in the Administrative Procedure Act.[127]

In the administrative context, a further cost, many would argue, is the kind of decisional inconsistency exposed by the Refugee Roulette study. Earlier discussion suggested that decisional independence might have mixed effects on interdecisional consistency, but let us assume arguendo that the net effect is negative.[128] There is also the related problem of assuring that adjudicative decisions cohere with formal rules and other expressions of agency policy.

Decisional independence might also impair good-faith measures to boost adjudicators' productivity. While there might be ways for agencies to impart productivity expectations to adjudicators without threatening their independence, the key variable is the consequence of failure to meet those expectations.[129] If the consequences are significant enough to alter the adjudicators' behavior—and communicating expectations would be useless if they are not—then they will necessarily give adjudicators an incentive to trade off care and quality for quantity. Only the latter can be statistically compiled. For that reason, independence and productivity will always be in tension.

In an adjudicative setting, however, my view is that decisional independence, despite these potential costs, is critical to the rule of law and to the dispensation of justice. The most familiar benefit of decisional independence is procedural fairness—minimizing adjudicative bias. An adjudicator should decide each case based on his or her honest reading of the evidence, interpretation of relevant legal sources, and exercise of any delegated discretion—not by choosing whichever outcome seems most likely to please the officials who will control his or her professional future. Decisional independence can also discourage what I have called "defensive judging"—playing it safe by avoiding rulings that might prove controversial.[130] Decisional independence can be a vital safeguard for unpopular individuals, minorities, and political viewpoints, and it is crucial to safeguarding constitutional rights against transient majoritarian preferences. Decisional independence is, moreover, integral to at least the U.S. version of separation of powers.[131]

Apart from those rationales, which I have argued all derive ultimately from fidelity to the rule of law, decisional independence has important side benefits.[132] They include maintaining public confidence in the integrity of the justice system, avoiding "reverse social Darwinism" in which the weakest adjudicators are the ones most likely to survive ideological purges, attracting and retaining adjudicator candidates, and facilitating the continuity of adjudicative outcomes from one administration to its successor.[133]

For all those reasons, further assaults on the decisional independence of the immigration judges and the members of the BIA would be regrettable. To the contrary, their prior decisional independence should be restored and further safeguarded despite any possible negative effects on either decisional consistency or agency policy coherence. There are several possible, non–mutually exclusive ways to protect decisional independence; these are outlined elsewhere.[134]

Conclusion

The hobgoblin of little minds it might well be, but consistency matters. The moral imperative of equal justice, the needs for certainty and predictability, the benefits of efficiency, and the objective of public acceptability all demand attention to consistency in any adjudicative framework. The Refugee Roulette study—the product of a prodigious and highly successful effort by Professors Ramji-Nogales, Schoenholtz, and Schrag—has brought home the extraordinary extent to which the outcome of an asylum claim hinges on the particular adjudicators who are assigned the case.

But the forces that generate inconsistent adjudicative outcomes are not easy to constrain, at least not without costly trade-offs. Among the determinants are the number of decisional units; the size of the decisional units; the total caseload; the criteria and procedures for appointing adjudicators; the training and policy guidance they receive; their degree of decisional independence; the amount of deference and the scope of review on appeal; the prevalence of written reasoned opinions and the accompanying use of stare decisis; the fiscal resources devoted to the process; the procedural resources; the degree of specialization; and such subject-matter attributes as the degrees of complexity, dynamism, emotional or ideological content, and determinacy.

In asylum cases, the unavoidable abstractness, complexity, and dynamism of the relevant legal language make it inevitable that the human adjudicators will bring their diverse emotions and personal values to bear on their decisions. Under those circumstances, we should not expect anything but the sorts of disparate outcomes that the Refugee Roulette study has documented.

There are ways to reduce the inconsistencies at the margins, to be sure. The strategies for doing so might include more detailed legal and policy guidance, more adjudicators, larger decisional units, bolstered support staffs, appointment of counsel for indigent asylum applicants, improved quality controls at the hiring stage, beefed-up training for adjudicators and other professional development, dissemination of asylum approval rates at all stages of the process, enlargement of the scope of the BIA's review of immigration judges' decisions, and increased use of reasoned and binding opinions.

But any strategies that would shrink the inconsistencies more dramatically—and some that would not do even that—have costs that I argue are unacceptably high. These include more frequent agency-head review of BIA decisions, additional restrictions on judicial review, and punishing wayward adjudicators. Each of those devices would either severely compromise decisional independence or impose other excessive costs.

In the end, we shall have to learn to live with some measure of unequal justice. It is not ideal, but, as they say, it beats the alternatives.

NOTES

1. Dr. Stephen H. Legomsky is the John S. Lehmann University Professor at the Washington University School of Law in St. Louis. An earlier version of this chapter appeared in 60 Stanford L. Rev. 413 (2007) and is reprinted by permission of the Board of Trustees of the Leland Stanford Junior University. I thank the Asia Research Institute of the National University of Singapore for hosting me while I was writing the paper from which this essay is excerpted, Ron Levin for his insightful early comments, the law faculties of Washington University and the University of Florida for their thoughtful feedback during faculty workshops, and Joanna Ruppel of the Department of Homeland Security for her useful data. I congratulate Jaya Ramji-Nogales, Andy Schoenholtz, and Philip Schrag for the groundbreaking Refugee Roulette study that inspired this project.

2. Introduction, chapters 1 through 6, and the Methodological Appendix of this book [hereinafter Refugee Roulette study].

3. Kenneth R. Feinberg, Special Master, September 11th Victim Compensation Fund, Lecture at the University of Alabama School of Law (Apr. 8, 2004), in 56 Ala. L. Rev. 543, 553 (2004).

4. Ralph Waldo Emerson, *Self-Reliance*, in The Complete Essays and Other Writings of Ralph Waldo Emerson 145, 152 (Brooks Atkinson ed., 1940).

5. Inconsistent procedures and inconsistent employment criteria for adjudicators were among the problems that inspired the Administrative Procedure Act. For an insightful description, see Jeffrey S. Lubbers, APA-Adjudication: Is the Quest for Uniformity Faltering?, 10 Admin. L.J. Am. U. 65, 65–68 (1996). These problems were also the focus of a superb consultants' report prepared for the Administrative Conference of the United States. Paul R. Verkuil et al., *Report for Recommendation 92–7: The Federal Administrative Judiciary*, in II Administrative Conference of the United States, Recommendations and Reports 777 (1992); see also Recommendations and Statements of the Administrative Conference, 57 Fed. Reg. 61,759 (Dec. 29, 1992) (codified at 1 C.F.R. pts. 305, 310) (recommending many of the reforms urged by the consultants' report) [hereinafter ACUS Recs.].

6. Immigration and Nationality Act, Pub. L. 82–414, 66 Stat. 163 (June 27, 1952), as amended [hereinafter INA], § 101(a)(42).

7. Id.

8. INA § 208.

9. INA § 240A(b)(1)(D).

10. See Introduction, page 1; see also Stephen H. Legomsky, Forum Choices for the Review of Agency Adjudication: A Study of the Immigration Process, 71 Iowa L. Rev. 1297, 1313–14 (1986) [hereinafter Legomsky, Forum Choices].

11. Introduction, page 1; see also Verkuil et al., supra note 5, at 991.

12. Legomsky, Forum Choices, supra note 10, at 1313.

13. Id.; see also Roger C. Cramton, Administrative Procedure Reform: The Effects of S. 1663 on the Conduct of Federal Rate Proceedings, 16 Admin. L. Rev. 108, 112 (1964).

14. Introduction, page 1.

15. See, e.g., Henry J. Friendly, Federal Jurisdiction: A General View 186–87 (1973); Samuel Estreicher & Richard I. Revesz, Nonacquiescence by Federal Administrative Agencies, 98 Yale L.J. 679, 736–37 (1989).

16. See infra part II.A.2.

17. See, e.g., Friendly, supra note 15, at 183 (suggesting that a national administrative court would improve uniformity); Peter J. Levinson, A Specialized Court for Immigration Hearings and Appeals, 56 Notre Dame Law. 644, 653 (1981); Maurice A. Roberts, Proposed: A Specialized Statutory Immigration Court, 18 San Diego L. Rev. 1, 13–14, 19–20 (1980).

18. See infra part III.B.4.

19. United States v. Smith, 354 F.3d 390 (5th Cir. 2003).

20. The specialization variable has other effects as well, both positive and negative. See infra parts II.E.1, III.B.4.

21. In order not to succeed, this applicant would have to draw both of the automatic deniers out of a panel of three. If the panel members are selected at random, the chance that the first pick will be an automatic denier is 2/6; if that happens, the chance that the second denier will be the one chosen from the remaining five will be 1/5; and thus the chance that the first two picks will be the two deniers will be 2/6 times 1/5, or 1/15. Since there are three ways in which those two members could be drawn (picks 1 and 2, picks 1 and 3, and picks 2 and 3), the probability of drawing both of them will be 3/15, or 1/5. Thus the probability of not drawing both of them will be 4/5.

22. Chapter 5, pages 77–81.

23. See supra part II.A.1.

24. See the sources summarized by the Refugee Roulette study in chapter 3, note 41, especially the classic work of Carol Gilligan, In a Different Voice: Psychological Theory and Women's Development (1982).

25. Chapter 3, page 47.

26. Id. at 49.

27. Id. at 50–51.

28. Chapter 5, pages 83–85. In the Third Circuit there was no appreciable difference. Id. at 82–183.

29. Verkuil et al., supra note 5, at 993–94.

30. Elsewhere I have attempted to flesh out more comprehensively the various theories of decisional independence and their application to immigration judges, the BIA, and court-stripping legislation. See Stephen H. Legomsky, Deportation and the War on Independence, 91 Cornell L. Rev. 369 (2006).

31. See supra part II.B.2, infra parts III.A.1, III.B.2.

32. See Legomsky, supra note 30, at 372–85.

33. Verkuil et al., supra note 5, at 992 & nn.1138–41.

34. Paul D. Carrington et al., Justice on Appeal 2–3 (1976); David P. Leonard, The Correctness Function of Appellate Decision-Making: Judicial Obligation in an Era of Fragmentation, 17 Loy. L.A. L. Rev. 299, 299–303 (1984).

35. See infra parts II.C.3, III.A.10.

36. 8 C.F.R. § 1003.1(d)(3) (2007).

37. 5 U.S.C. § 706(2)(A), (E) (2000).

38. Chevron, U.S.A., Inc. v. Natural Res. Def. Council, 467 U.S. 837 (1984).

39. 67 Fed. Reg. 54,878 (Aug. 26, 2002).

40. Oversight of the U.S. Department of Justice: Hearing before the S. Comm. on the Judiciary, 110th Cong. 22 (2007) (Statement of Attorney General Alberto R. Gonzales), available at http://lawprofessors.typepad.com/immigration/files/gonzales_testimony_72407.pdf.

41. 8 C.F.R. § 1003.1(g) (2007).

42. Oversight Hearing, supra note 40, at 22.

43. See supra part II.A.1.

44. See chapter 3, pages 45–46, and sources cited therein.

45. Id. at 45.

46. Chapter 5, pages 77–81.

47. Stephen H. Legomsky, Specialized Justice courts, Administrative Tribunals, and a Cross-National Theory of Specialization (Oxford Univ. Press, 1990), at 7–32.

48. See S. Rep. No. 97–275, at 5–6 (1981), as reprinted in 1982 U.S.C.C.A.N. 11, 15–16.

49. E.g., Levinson, supra note 17, at 653; Roberts, supra note 17.

50. Glen O. Robinson, On Reorganizing the Independent Regulatory Agencies, 57 Va. L. Rev. 947 (1971).

51. See David R. Woodward & Ronald M. Levin, In Defense of Deference: Judicial Review of Agency Action, 31 Admin. L. Rev. 320, 329, 332 (1979).

52. The expertise itself might also prove efficient, so that each adjudicator's caseload could increase and fewer than two would now be needed. The point made in this paragraph, however, will be true even without assuming added efficiency.

53. See 8 U.S.C. §§ 1101 et seq.

54. See 6 C.F.R. §§ 5.1-1000.11 (2007); 8 C.F.R. §§ 1.1-1337.10 (2007); 20 C.F.R. §§ 1.1-1005 (2007); 22 C.F.R. §§ 1.1-1701.999 (2007).

55. Stephen H. Legomsky, Immigration and Refugee Law and Policy 1 (4th ed. 2005).

56. Karl N. Llewellyn, The Common Law Tradition: Deciding Appeals 19–61 (1960).

57. See INA § 208(b)(1).

58. See INA § 101(a)(42).

59. See INA § 208(b)(1)(B)(ii)–(iii).

60. This prayer, modified by Alcoholics Anonymous, is generally attributed to Rheinhold Niebuhr. See The Origin of Our Serenity Prayer, http://www.aahistory.com/ prayer.html.

61. The authors of the Refugee Roulette study similarly attribute the disparities largely to the "officers' or judges' different degrees of skepticism about the veracity of applicants, or the adjudicators' different political philosophies or personal backgrounds." Chapter 6, page 99.

62. See, e.g., id.; see also T. Alexander Aleinikoff, The Meaning of "Persecution" in United States Asylum Law, 3 Int'l J. Refugee L. 5 (1991).

63. Arthur C. Helton, Persecution on Account of Membership in a Social Group as a Basis for Refugee Status, 15 Colum. Hum. Rts. L. Rev. 39, 45 (1983).

64. See 5 U.S.C. § 553(b)(3)(A) (2000).

65. INA § 101(a)(42).

66. Memorandum from Phyllis Coven, Office of Int'l Affairs, U.S. Dep't of Justice, to All INS Asylum Office/rs and HQASM Coordinators (May 26, 1995), reprinted in 72 Interpreter Releases 781 (1995).

67. Chapter 6, page 98.

68. See supra part II.A.1.

69. See chapter 6, pages 108–109.

70. See supra part II.A.2.

71. See Legomsky, Immigration and Refugee Law and Policy, supra note 55, at 717.

72. Id. The details appear in the consultants' report on which the Administrative Conference recommendations were based. See ibid. at 1370–74.

73. Executive Office for Immigration Review; Board of Immigration Appeals; Designation of Judges, 53 Fed. Reg. 15, 659, 15,660 (May 3, 1988) (codified at 1 C.F.R. pt. 3 (1988)).

74. See 67 Fed. Reg. 54,878 (Aug. 26, 2002).

75. Peter J. Levinson, The Façade of Quasi-Judicial Independence in Immigration Appellate Adjudications, 9 Bender's Immigration Bulletin 1154 (2004).

76. Chapter 6, page 115.

77. 8 C.F.R. § 1003.1(a)(5) (2007).

78. Pub. L. No. 95–486, § 6, 92 Stat. 1629, 1633 (1978); see also Fed. R. App. P. 35(a).

79. Chapter 6, page 109.

80. INA §§ 240(b)(4)(A), 292.

81. Chapter 3, pages 45–46; Andrew I. Schoenholtz & Jonathan Jacobs, The State of Asylum Representation: Ideas for Change, 16 Geo. Immigr. L.J. 739, 743–46 (2002).

82. See generally Legomsky, Immigration and Refugee Law and Policy, supra note 55, at 653–67.

83. Chapter 6, page 113–114.

84. Id.

85. See INA § 235(b)(1)(B)(ii), (iii), (v). Credible fear requires "a significant possibility . . . that the alien could establish eligibility for asylum." INA § 235(b)(1)(B)(v).

86. Chapter 6, pages 113–114.

87. Id. at 101–103.

88. Oversight Hearings, supra note 40, at 22 (emphasis added).

89. Chapter 6, pages 103–104; see also Levinson, supra note 17; Roberts, supra note 17.

90. See chapter 6, pages 103–104; see also Legomsky, Forum Choices, supra note 10, at 1378–80; Levinson, supra note 17, at 650–51; Maurice A. Roberts, The Board of Immigration Appeals: A Critical Appraisal, 15 San Diego L. Rev. 29, 44 (1977).

91. See the sources cited in Legomsky, Forum Choices, supra note 10, at 1379 n.483.

92. Chapter 6, pages 109–112.

93. Id. at 382.

94. Id. at 384.

95. See supra part II.C.2.

96. Id.

97. David A. Martin, Reforming Asylum Adjudication: On Navigating the Coast of Bohemia, 138 U. Pa. L. Rev. 1247, 1349 (1990).

98. See INA § 208(b)(1)(B)(iii).

99. See, e.g., Osorio v. INS, 99 F.3d 928, 931 (9th Cir. 1996).

100. See the classic article by Walter Kälin, Troubled Communication: Cross-Cultural Misunderstandings in the Asylum-Hearing, 20 Int'l Migration Rev. 230 (1986).

101. See supra part II.C.3.

102. Oversight Hearing, supra note 40, at 22.

103. Chapter 6, page 115.

104. See supra part II.C.3.

105. Chapter 6, pages 115.

106. 8 C.F.R. § 1003.1(g) (2007).

107. See supra part II.C.3.

108. See, e.g., United States v. Smith, 354 F.3d 390, 399 (5th Cir. 2003).

109. See Legomsky, supra note 1, at 457–58.

110. 8 C.F.R. § 1003.1(h)(1)(i) (2007).

111. Verkuil et al., supra note 5, at 1004; cf. 5 U.S.C. § 557 (2000) (authorizing agency member decisions).

112. Legomsky, supra note 1, at 458–62.

113. See supra parts II.C.2, III.A.9.

114. See INA §§ 208(a)(2)(B), (a)(2)(D), (a)(3), 242(a)(2)(A).

115. See Jill E. Family, Stripping Judicial Review during Immigration Reform: The Certificate of Reviewability, 8 Nevada L.J. 499 (2008).

116. The costs and benefits are analyzed in Stephen H. Legomsky, Political Asylum and the Theory of Judicial Review, 73 Minn. L. Rev. 1205, 1211–16 (1989).

117. Id.; Legomsky, supra note 1, at 462–64.

118. See supra part II.E.1.

119. For the earlier calls for such a structure, see Levinson, supra note 17, at 653; Roberts, supra note 17.

120. See Legomsky, Specialized Justice, supra note 47, at 33–42.

121. Chapter 6, pages 96–97.

122. Legomsky, supra note 1, at 468–69.

123. These are favored by several respected commentators. See, e.g., ACUS Recs., supra note 5; Jeffrey S. Lubbers, The Federal Administrative Judiciary: Establishing an Appropriate System of Performance Evaluation for ALJs, 7 Admin. L.J. Am. Univ. 589 (1993).

124. See supra part II.C.1.

125. Legomsky, supra note 30, at 385–401.

126. See supra part III.B.2.

127. See Verkuil et al., supra note 5, at 795–96, 986–87.

128. See supra part II.C.1.

129. Verkuil et al., supra note 5, at 1021–23.

130. Legomsky, supra note 30, at 396.

131. For elaboration of these benefits, see id. at 396–98.

132. Id. at 398–401.

133. Id. at 401.

134. See Legomsky, supra note 1, at 472–73.

13 The Counsel Conundrum

Effective Representation in Immigration Proceedings

M. Margaret McKeown and Allegra McLeod[1]

MARIA MORALES, a single mother of two native-born U.S.-citizen children, first came to the United States from Mexico as a young child. In 2000, Morales was charged with being "an alien present in the United States without admission or parole." Although Morales was represented by counsel at her hearing, her lawyer failed to introduce available documentary evidence and failed to elicit relevant testimony. Less than two weeks after Morales's hearing (at which she was denied relief), her lawyer was suspended from the practice of law. The California State Bar Court found that Morales's attorney handled more than 2,720 immigration cases during a two-year period in a manner that was "reckless and involved gross carelessness," and that while earning more than $250,000 annually, he failed to competently represent clients, accepted more cases than he could handle, routinely "placed his interests above those of his clients" by permitting nonlawyers to perform legal work, and "consistently demonstrated a profound lack of understanding of his duty of fidelity to his clients."[2]

KEVIN SCOTT moved to the United States from Jamaica when he was eight years old. He attended grade school, high school, and college in New York, where his mother, father, and two sisters also live. At an immigration hearing to show cause why he should not be deported, the judge stated his belief that Scott was eligible for discretionary relief from deportation. The judge instructed Scott's counsel to file an appropriate application for relief within one month. Scott's lawyer assured the court that he did not need more time; nonetheless, Scott's attorney never filed an application. Shortly after, Scott was taken into INS custody and deported. Scott might well have received relief had it not been for his counsel's ineffective assistance.[3]

These unfortunate stories represent the classic "good news, bad news" scenario: the good news is that the petitioners had a lawyer; the bad news is that the petitioners had a lawyer. On a positive note, individuals facing the potentially dire consequences of deportation managed to retain counsel to help them navigate the complicated U.S. immigration legal system. Ultimately, though, their lawyers failed to perform to the most minimal standards of professional competence.

Of the many insights afforded by the Refugee Roulette study, among the most striking conclusions is that "whether an asylum seeker is represented in court is the single most important factor affecting the outcome of her case."[4] According to the study's authors, asylum seekers without legal counsel had a success rate of 16.3 percent, as compared to a 45.6 percent grant rate for those with representation.[5] While attorneys appeared in only 35 percent of the 323,845 matters before immigration courts in 2006,[6] asylum seekers represented by a lawyer were roughly three times more likely to be granted relief than applicants without legal counsel.[7] But what these statistics obscure is that beyond the significance of the presence of legal counsel, the *quality* of representation in immigration litigation is of vital consequence. The authors of the Refugee Roulette study acknowledge that their analysis does not account for the relative effects of the quality of counsel on case outcomes.[8]

To begin to bridge this gap, this chapter examines federal appellate immigration case law addressing ineffective-assistance-of-counsel claims arising both in the asylum context and in other nonasylum immigration matters.[9] In a court system that commences at the trial level before an immigration judge (IJ) and proceeds to an appeal before the Board of Immigration Appeals (BIA), the federal courts of appeal are, effectively, the courts of last resort. In 2006–2008, the United States Supreme Court heard only four immigration cases.[10] In contrast, there were 9,123 immigration filings in the federal courts of appeal in 2007.[11] Federal appellate courts have a unique perspective on immigration proceedings: although only a select subset of cases is appealed (in virtually every case, the noncitizen party has lost at the administrative level and is challenging the result), the federal courts consider some of the most significant issues in immigration law.

Underrepresentation and poor quality of representation in immigration proceedings are but two of the trends noted frequently in federal appellate case law and showcased by the American Bar Association (ABA) at its 2008 program "The Immigration Crisis, the Courts, and the Rule of Law."[12] The crisis the program referenced is caused by a geometric rise in cases, the result of increased immigration enforcement and detention. By March 2002, the BIA struggled with a backlog of more than fifty-six thousand cases.[13] In response, and in accord with procedural changes put in place in 2002 by then-Attorney General John Ashcroft, the BIA began to rely increasingly on summary dismissals and affirmances without opinion,[14] escalating considerably the number of petitions for review filed in the federal circuit courts of appeals.[15] While between October 1999 and March 2002 there were 4,407 immigration appeals to circuit courts, between April 2002 and September 2006, 47,329 petitions for review were filed.[16] These numbers provide evidence of the stresses borne by the system and the pressures under which lawyers, judges, and administrators labor. The deluge of immigration filings—what one of this essay's authors has pointedly described as a "legal tsunami"—threatens to overwhelm the system.[17]

The impact of the growth in immigration appeals has fallen disproportionately on the Second and Ninth Circuits.[18] In the Ninth Circuit alone,[19] since 2001, the number and proportion of immigration filings has grown dramatically, comprising almost 40 percent of the court's docket by 2006, up from 10 percent in 2001.[20] Although the proportion of immigration cases in the Ninth Circuit has begun to fall slightly, as of 2007 immigration matters remained more than 35 percent of the court's docket.[21] In the Second Circuit,[22] immigration cases constitute 39 percent of the court's docket, up from 4 percent in 2001.[23] Particularly in those federal circuits most affected by the rise in immigration cases, the resulting opinions all too often bear witness to the downstream consequences of inadequate representation.

Attending to this body of law, we suggest in this chapter that when the competency of counsel in immigration proceedings is taken into consideration, the differential outcomes associated with the presence of effective counsel are likely to be even more pronounced than identified by the authors of Refugee Roulette. Sadly, however, these cases also underscore that some individuals may be better served without counsel than by the assistance of an incompetent attorney or unqualified nonlawyer "immigration specialist." As a consequence, efforts to improve the fairness and consistency of immigration adjudication must focus on improving the quality of immigration counsel, not simply the availability of such counsel alone.

There are, of course, many highly competent, dedicated, and often underpaid immigration lawyers who diligently represent individuals and families. We wish to make clear at the outset that this chapter is not meant to be an indictment of the immigration bar, but instead is an effort to highlight and extend the crucial work that competent immigration attorneys perform. The expansion of the ranks of skilled immigration representation would have salutary effects for the immigration legal system in terms of efficiency, uniformity, and fairness, and would not undermine decisional independence, as might other reforms intended to address the inconsistencies revealed in Refugee Roulette.[24] Toward the ends of improved fairness and efficiency in immigration adjudication, this chapter examines the benefits enabled by high-quality representation and explores existing programs devoted to the recruitment, support, and training of immigration counsel.

I. The Critical Role of Effective Counsel in Immigration Proceedings

The severe costs associated with deportation accentuate most evidently the importance of skilled counsel in immigration proceedings. In a 1948 opinion, the Supreme Court observed that "deportation is a drastic measure and at times the equivalent of banishment or exile."[25] At risk in immigration proceedings are aspects central to human life and dignity: the unity of family, the ability to work to support oneself and one's children, access to medical treatment and education, and sometimes the prospect of being returned to a country where one would face torture or persecution on account of race, religion, nationality, or political opinion. Indeed, "[t]he high stakes of a removal proceeding and the maze of immigration rules and regulations make evident the necessity of the right to counsel."[26]

Judge Robert A. Katzmann of the Second Circuit has also eloquently noted the not uncommon defenselessness of individuals facing removal or deportation from the United States.[27] In *Aris v. Mukasey*, Judge Katzmann wrote that immigrants are often members of "a vulnerable population who come to this country searching for a better life, and who often arrive unfamiliar with our language and culture, in economic deprivation and in fear."[28] Such barriers only exacerbate the difficulty of comprehending the notoriously complicated tangle of U.S. immigration statutes, regulations, and cases.[29] As one judge put it, "[w]ith only a small degree of hyperbole, the immigration laws have been termed 'second only to the Internal Revenue Code in complexity.'"[30] Frequently, without skilled legal counsel, a person will be unable to "thread the labyrinth."[31]

Apart from the importance of high-quality lawyering for individuals and their families, the administrative system itself would benefit considerably from more widespread availability of competent representation. Judge Juan Osuna, chair of the BIA, summarized the effect of legal representation on the system as follows: "Effective and robust legal representation is absolutely critical to the immigration court system. Good lawyers help immigrants navigate a complex process, so that those with potential relief from removal get the assistance they need. And the system overall benefits when good lawyers get involved. Effective and professional representation makes everything work more smoothly."[32]

At every stage of immigration proceedings, as in other areas of litigation and adjudication, the presence of competent counsel improves the efficiency of case processing and the administration of justice. At the outset, as a result of skilled advice, noncitizens may be diverted from the court system to other alternatives, such as nonjudicial relief, like family petitions, or they may decline to file for relief for which they are patently ineligible. Once the noncitizens are in the system, it is easier for immigration judges and administrative or judicial staff to deal with representatives who understand the procedural intricacies and substantive complexities of the system. The presence of competent counsel cuts down on administrative continuances and unnecessary schedule disruptions. Effective counsel also makes possible a flowing presentation of the facts coupled with an explanation of the law that benefits both the client and the judicial system. For these reasons, effectively counseled cases are likely to move more quickly through the courts.

Just outcomes are more likely as well when effective counsel is present, because the facts necessary to a fair determination of the case will be developed, presented, and tested in light of the relevant law. In contrast, without an attorney or with an ineffective attorney, individuals testifying are frequently unaware of how to impart even the most fundamental information relating to the case to be decided. In one disturbing immigration trial, the Baltazars, husband and wife, who had lived in the United States since 1989 and who were parents of a U.S.-citizen child, sought suspension of deportation.[33] The Baltazars were represented in the preliminary stages of their immigration proceedings by the same ineffective attorney at issue in Morales's case introduced in the epigraph to this chapter.[34] On the day of Mr. Baltazar's merits hearing, his attorney did not show up, so the IJ postponed the trial; ultimately, as it turned out, the Baltazars were forced to present their case without representation.[35] The main question before the court at the Baltazars' subsequent merits hearing involved what hardship would befall the couple and their U.S.-citizen child were the husband and wife to be deported. The IJ proceeded by simply asking the Baltazars whether it would cause them "hardship" to leave the United States.[36] In response, apparently not understanding, Mr. Baltazar responded, "No, that would be your decision." When asked again whether he had anything else he wished to contribute so that the IJ might be made aware of any grounds for a favorable hardship determination, Mr. Baltazar added, "No, I really believe it is your decision."[37] Unwittingly, the Baltazars abdicated their burden with respect to hardship, and the IJ denied the family relief. Without a lawyer to assist in the elaboration of the relevant equities, the Baltazars were effectively unable to articulate any ground upon which a hardship finding might be based, despite the facts that the couple had lived in the United States since they were teenagers, raised a U.S.-citizen child, and Mrs. Baltazar suffered from a disability. Competent counsel was necessary to a full consideration and proper determination of the Baltazars' case, and yet, as in numerous other immigration cases, effective counsel was absent, to the detriment of the administration of justice.

As retired California Supreme Court Justice Earl Johnson, Jr., explained,

> If a quarter century on the appellate bench has taught me anything, it is that the judge suffers more than anyone other than the parties when litigants lack counsel. Whether presiding over a jury trial or struggling to personally decide a case, the trial judge faces a daunting, too often impossible task. Moreover, it is bad enough

when both sides are unrepresented; it is much worse when an unrepresented litigant faces the lawyer retained by a "well-counseled" adversary. . . . [O]dds are the decision will be based on a skewed version of the law and facts. The result? Far too often, an erroneous decision. . . . The trial judges in those cases would have had to have felt . . . uncomfortable about the distinct possibility that they were delivering injustice, rather than justice in those cases.[38]

Another problem that arises routinely in uncounseled or poorly counseled cases involves the presentation to appeals courts of incomprehensible and incomplete transcripts of jumbled administrative trials.[39] Convoluted transcripts make it difficult for appellate courts to determine what occurred at the trial level, and thus make difficult efficient and accurate appellate adjudication. The order and organization that is brought to an administrative hearing by well-prepared counsel considerably reduces problems related to convolution in trial transcripts and poorly reasoned or unsubstantiated factual findings.

Additionally, advice from effective counsel would reduce frivolous appeals and the time some petitioners spend incarcerated pending resolution of their cases. The stops, starts, detours, and endless motions to reopen occasioned by ineffective counsel produce yet another costly pressure on the system. Where there is an appeal, competent counsel assists the administration of justice in terms of both efficiency and fairness by constructing a clearly organized and substantiated factual record and legal analysis for review.

II. The Right to Effective Assistance of Counsel under Current Law

Unlike in criminal proceedings, an individual in immigration proceedings has no right to appointed counsel.[40] Instead, there is a statutory entitlement to secure representation by counsel of one's choice, though "at no expense to the Government."[41]

In some instances, federal courts have recognized that in extraordinary circumstances there may be a potential due process right to appointed counsel in immigration proceedings. The Sixth Circuit was the first federal appellate court to recognize such a possible due process right: in 1975, Jesus Aguilera-Enriquez claimed that the denial of appointed counsel deprived him of his due process rights in his deportation proceeding. While holding that the absence of appointed counsel did not deprive Aguilera-Enriquez of "fundamental fairness," the Sixth Circuit determined that "[t]he test for whether due process requires the appointment of counsel for an indigent alien is whether, in a given case, the assistance of counsel would be necessary to provide 'fundamental fairness—the touchstone of due process.'"[42] Despite *Aguilera-Enriquez* and later decisions from other circuits holding out, under exceptional conditions, the possibility of a right to counsel, as a practical matter, appointment of counsel for an individual facing deportation has never been required under the fundamental fairness test.[43]

Nonetheless, many courts have recognized that certain constitutional due process rights obtain in immigration court, including some related to counsel.[44] Only several months after the Sixth Circuit decided *Aguilera-Enriquez*, the Fifth Circuit acknowledged in *Paul v. INS* the potential existence of a right to effective assistance of counsel in immigration proceedings.[45] In the intervening years, multiple other circuits have acknowledged such a right where ineffective assistance is the cause of the forfeiture of relief.[46]

In 1988, the BIA in *Matter of Lozada* articulated a set of criteria that must be satisfied to establish a claim of ineffective assistance of counsel in immigration court.[47] Federal appellate courts have mostly adopted the *Lozada* requirements,[48] and over the past decade and a half, courts have repeatedly reopened or remanded proceedings due to deficient performance of counsel.[49]

In the final weeks of the Bush administration in early 2009, former attorney general Michael Mukasey issued a decision to supersede *Lozada*.[50] In *Matter of Compean*, Mukasey wrote that there is no due process right or other right to effective assistance of counsel in immigration proceedings. Instead, under the *Compean* framework, it is a matter of immigration judge or Board of Immigration Appeals discretion to reopen removal proceedings in "extraordinary cases" due to egregious lawyer error.[51] As of mid-2009, Attorney General Holder withdrew the *Compean* decision and the issue is now slated for rulemaking. It is unclear whether ultimately the *Compean* or *Lozada* approach will control, but regardless of the governing legal framework, inadequate representation continues to impede the administration of justice in immigration proceedings.

III. The Consequences of Ineffective Immigration Lawyers

Ineffective assistance of counsel comes in many forms. Sometimes ineffectiveness is blatant and involves fraud and misrepresentation or failure to notify a client of proceedings. Oftentimes it is the result of irresponsibly missed deadlines; and on yet other occasions, only sheer ineptitude can explain the failure to cite the correct law, appear for a hearing, or respond to court orders.

The Department of Justice's Executive Office of Immigration Review (EOIR) has authority to impose sanctions on attorneys and accredited representatives who violate professional standards.[52] As of late 2008, well over two hundred immigration attorneys had been suspended or expelled through the EOIR disciplinary process from practice before the immigration courts, often following their suspension from a state bar.[53]

A brief review of the governing regulation brings to light the range of unethical conduct in question: repeated failure to appear for scheduled hearings, false statements, knowing false certification of a copy of a document, grossly excessive fees, improperly soliciting clients, and the list goes on.[54] Sadly, conduct of this ilk constitutes a "disturbing pattern of ineffectiveness" that occurs with "alarming frequency."[55]

One widespread problem involves the failure of counsel to assemble relevant documentation to support in-court testimony. For example, in *Yang v. Gonzales*,[56] the IJ found Yang not credible based on discrepancies between Yang's hearing testimony and the documentation gathered (and not gathered) by Yang's counsel, who, like the California immigration attorney described in the epigraph to this chapter, was sanctioned for professional misconduct related to his immigration practice.[57] In the New York lawyer's disbarment proceeding, the Appellate Division of New York noted that the conduct of Yang's attorney reflected "a 'truly shocking disregard for his clients' and constituted 'a danger to any client who might retain him.'"[58]

Immigration attorneys have even introduced affirmative falsehoods in some instances. In *Hamedi v. Gonzales*, Hamedi claimed his lawyer misrepresented multiple facts in documents presented to the court and then failed to meet with Hamedi so that he might discover these falsehoods.[59] The IJ based an adverse credibility finding in significant part on discrepancies between the documents filed by the attorney and Hamedi's testimony.[60]

Another familiar situation arises when the court notifies the attorney of a critical filing deadline, and the attorney fails to take action or to notify the client, in so doing forfeiting the client's opportunity to pursue the claim.[61] Some courts have held that the due process notice requirement is satisfied even if the client was never actually informed of receipt of relevant documents; hence relief from counsel's errors may not be available on due process or other grounds.[62] Had the client proceeded in such circumstances without counsel, at least she would have had access to basic information about her case.

Disregard of court deadlines is also not uncommon at the appellate level. *Singh v. Demore* provides a prime illustration. Singh, an Indian citizen seeking asylum on account of his claimed support of the Sikh independence movement, sought to appeal the denial of his asylum application to the Ninth Circuit. He retained an attorney, who promised to file a timely appeal.[63] As the filing deadline approached, Singh repeatedly attempted to contact his lawyer. Singh's final email, excerpted in the Ninth Circuit's opinion, urged his counsel to file the appeal as agreed: "I haven't got any response from you regarding appeal to 9th circuit court before August 9, 2002. Given how INS is treating immigrants like me these days, makes me very worried. Please let me know when you [sic] planning to file for appeal?"[64] The very day the appeal was due, the lawyer finally wrote to Singh: "It would be a waste of time, money and energy to file an Appeal with the 9th

Circuit. All that would do is have another court deny your case. However, there is another way we can help you. I will contact you over the weekend regarding what has to be done."[65] Despite continuing assurances from Singh's lawyer that his "case was being taken care of" and that Singh was not "at risk of deportation," he was ordered to surrender, which he did, and was taken into custody to await deportation. Ultimately, after Singh retained a different attorney, the Ninth Circuit remanded the case to the BIA to reconsider Singh's application in light of his ineffective-assistance-of-counsel claim.

The lawyers who are the subject of ineffectiveness challenges in the federal courts of appeals—such as those retained by Singh, Hamedi, and Yang—handle a large volume of immigration matters; as a result, the ineffective counsel opinions authored by federal appellate courts offer a window into a much broader problem than is presented in these individual cases. In *Morales Apolinar v. Mukasey*, for example, the Ninth Circuit observed that Morales's attorney had been repeatedly warned about his unacceptable comportment in other cases in immigration court.[66] Reflecting the widespread impact of such ineffectiveness, the opinion quotes a telling admonishment by an immigration judge: "[H]e's overbooked. Most attorneys have maybe one or two hearings set. He has anywhere from six to ten set each morning or afternoon, and he's all over this courthouse. The result is his clients are not represented in court."[67] In multiple cases, immigration judges elsewhere complained that every one of this attorney's cases "is a problem," that his pleadings were among the "shoddiest" submitted, that he was "taxing the system," and that he was exhibiting "complete irresponsibility."[68]

In *Yang v. Gonzales*, the Second Circuit took into account that Yang's attorney had been charged with "forty-three counts of professional misconduct related to his immigration law practice."[69] All forty-three counts were ultimately sustained in an opinion finding that this attorney had for five years "purported to specialize in representing illegal immigrants, chiefly from China, who seek political asylum in the United States."[70] With reference to a New York Appellate Division decision affirming Yang's attorney's disbarment, the Second Circuit recounted the arrangements underlying this lawyer's practice:

> [T]hese immigrants [the attorney's clients] are brought into the United States by a series of middlemen known as "snakeheads," who hand the immigrants over to an "agency" when they reach their destination in this country. The immigrant, lacking any knowledge of either the English language or the American legal system, then becomes completely dependent on his "agency," which provides him with a job, a place to sleep, translators, and legal representation in immigration matters. The non-lawyer "agency" generally performs the actual legal work, and retains an attorney to front for it in the Immigration Court. An attorney retained by an "agency" to represent an illegal immigrant client generally has little or no contact with the

client, exercises no control over the case, and serves at the pleasure of the "agency" which pays his fee. The Referee concluded that [Yang's attorney] lent himself to this "insidious system."[71]

In yet another case, which was remanded on the basis of an ineffective-assistance-of-counsel claim, the Ninth Circuit in *Tinoco-Aguilera v. INS* noted that the ineffective counsel "was the same attorney who was the subject of our opinion in *Castillo-Perez* and who resigned from the State Bar of California . . . with charges pending against him."[72] At the time of his resignation, the attorney faced seventy-one counts of misconduct relating to his work on immigration cases and had been recommended for disbarment.[73]

All indications are that such incompetence impacts hundreds if not thousands of individuals and leads, in repeated instances, to the forfeiture of avenues for relief as well as to the unnecessary multiplication of proceedings. Morales's ineffective attorney alone handled more than twenty-seven hundred immigration cases in a two-year period.

If such ineffective and sometimes exploitative counsel were somehow identifiable and segregable from the statistical analysis of counsel undertaken in *Refugee Roulette*, it is probable that the presence of *competent* counsel would affect outcomes even more dramatically than the study's analysis of the impact of counsel presently suggests. Lawyers differ markedly in the amount of time and money they are able to invest in a case, and particularly in the painstaking factual research required to corroborate a client's claims, often including obtaining affidavits and other documents from eyewitnesses in the respondent's home country.[74] Whether the grant rates for all competent counsel would be as high as that of Georgetown University Law School's asylum clinic, or for applicants represented pro bono by large law firms (roughly 90 percent) is unknown,[75] primarily because it is unclear how much some degree of selection bias explains these disproportionately higher grant rates, and how much the quality of lawyering is the driving causal force. Similarly, the inordinately low grant rate for those without legal counsel in the study (16.3 percent) may be partially explained by selection bias in the other direction (that is, some of these may be cases that, after assessing the merits, no pro bono or other counsel would pursue).

While defining and identifying precisely what constitutes competence on the part of counsel would be no simple undertaking, an examination of ineffectiveness cases such as those described here elucidates that at least some minimal level of competence of counsel rather than the presence of counsel alone makes the critical difference in immigration proceedings. In other words, these cases strongly suggest that the positive effects of high-quality counsel on outcomes are considerably in excess of those identified by the authors of the Refugee Roulette study; and the especially negative effects of representation by ineffective counsel importantly bear on immigration case outcomes, and more generally on the administration of justice.

It is worth acknowledging again that many immigration attorneys work carefully, zealously, and competently on their clients' behalf. Many others who may fall short of standards of professional competence probably mean well but are overwhelmed by the same structural factors that engulf the immigration courts and federal circuit courts. Calling attention to this systemic stress, perhaps inadvertently, one immigration attorney, a possibly well-intentioned though hapless lawyer who was threatened with discipline as a consequence of his careless work on immigration appeals, agreed with the criticisms of his deficiencies: "Some attorneys, including myself," he acknowledged, "do not spend enough time. We're not trained properly in terms of federal appeals. I ventured into an area I found later was very demanding. I was probably not qualified to do the job."[76] This lawyer's clients, whom he charged a flat fee of twenty-five hundred dollars for an appeal, are mostly poor and could not afford the more sizable fees charged by elite law firms. The attorney confessed that he felt "ashamed" and understood he had "no excuse": "[e]ven if you don't charge a lot of money, you have to do your job."[77]

Immigration attorneys working for the government are not without blame either when it comes to deficient performance in the face of heavy caseloads. One need not look far into federal appellate case law of recent years to find instances of government counsel being chastised for submitting legally inaccurate arguments and factually misleading information.[78] As is the case with some of the lawyers representing immigrants, these failings may be, in part, the consequence of a system stretched to the breaking point.

IV. Fraud and the Unauthorized Practice of Law

Adding to the problems posed by ineffective, though licensed, immigration lawyers, each year thousands of individuals are defrauded by disbarred attorneys, "notarios" or "immigration specialists,"[79] who mislead their clients to believe they are attorneys or who pretend to have special immigration expertise.[80] Trade in fraudulent documents and extortionist fees charged by so-called immigration specialists are recurring complaints. In *Aberin v. Gonzales*, the lead petitioner was told by Mendoza, a nonattorney pretending to be a lawyer, that lawful permanent residence status could be obtained for the entire family for twenty-eight thousand dollars.[81] After being paid, Mendoza gave the lead petitioner passports with I-55 stamps and informed him that the family need not appear at their hearing because they had all become lawful permanent residents. The stamps, as it turned out, were official government stamps, but had been procured through illegitimate means. The family was ordered deported in absentia.

In another illustrative case, *Ahmed v. Gonzales*, Ahmed's "counsel" promised to file "something," despite the thirty-day window for a motion to reopen having closed. Ahmed then retained another "counsel," who turned out not to be an attorney and who did nothing to advance the case and delayed in turning over Ahmed's file when the relationship terminated.[82] Only when his third counsel received Ahmed's file did he become aware of the "immigration specialists'" misrepresentations and misconduct.

Similarly, in *Fajardo v. INS*, Normita Fajardo, a native of the Philippines, hired an "immigration paralegal" to handle her case.[83] After receiving notice that Fajardo's application had been denied, the paralegal failed to inform Fajardo of her deportation hearing date. When Fajardo failed to appear for the hearing, she was ordered deported in absentia. Upon learning of her deportation order, Fajardo sought the assistance of another immigration specialist, who though not a lawyer indicated he could help her. She paid this second consultant one thousand dollars. When her untimely appeal was denied because her representative missed the filing deadline, she finally hired an attorney. Like Ahmed, only then did Fajardo become aware of the misconduct to which she had been subjected.[84]

Federal and state prosecutors have begun to pursue criminal charges against disbarred immigration attorneys, fraudulent lawyers, and "immigration specialists" who have committed crimes in the course of their "representation." For instance, Mendoza, the nonlawyer in *Aberin v. Gonzales*, was sentenced to nine years in prison.[85] In another case involving a disbarred attorney, a former San Jose, California, lawyer was charged with giving immigration advice and preparing legal documents without a license as well as four counts of grand theft.[86] The former attorney had a record of disciplinary measures challenging his competence and had resigned from the California Bar, but continued to charge clients fees for immigration legal counsel. Ultimately, he was arrested at his "law" office.

V. Programs Devoted to Improving Access to Quality Counsel

Although discipline may play a role in rooting out fraudulent and unethical representatives, these avenues do not address the broader need to enhance the availability of competent counsel. We now consider a range of programs that focus on training and attorney recruitment.[87] Our nonexhaustive account emphasizes initiatives engaged concurrently in training and mentoring alongside recruitment of new immigration counsel, with the simultaneous goals of expanding the number of counsel and enhancing their substantive expertise. While these various programs are relatively small-scale efforts that merely begin to address the large numbers of unrepresented cases in the system, these initiatives still constitute an important initial attempt to respond to the critical need for available and effective representation in immigration proceedings.

In response to the increasing number of immigration cases over the past decade, some of the circuit courts have become active in training immigration counsel. Enhanced training is a first step to address problems of both ethical violations and incompetent advice and practice. Even as ethics training is not a panacea for outright fraud and greed, the inclusion of an ethics module in every continuing legal education program on immigration would start to address the issue of ethical breaches. Training in substantive immigration law and practice likewise offers a means of tackling problems related to the quality and quantity of counsel.

For the past six years, the Ninth Circuit has been affirmatively involved in training counsel for both immigrant petitioners and the government. In conjunction with various bar groups, each year the court sponsors several sessions aimed at both new and experienced immigration counsel. One of the distinctive programs provides participants the opportunity to participate in small-group and individual meetings that include drafting a brief and obtaining constructive feedback from experienced counsel and judges. The program showcases model appellate arguments and briefs. The court's website includes a comprehensive immigration outline that is easily accessible to all practitioners.[88] The Ninth Circuit also administers a pro bono program that appoints counsel in immigration cases. In the last several years, counsel has been appointed in more than two hundred cases. In exchange for their service, participating attorneys are guaranteed an appellate argument.

In 2005, Judge Edward Becker of the Third Circuit, now deceased, created a training program in conjunction with the Pennsylvania Bar Institute, "Representing Asylum Seekers in the Circuit Courts." More recently, the New York Bar Council, in cooperation with Judge Katzmann, has begun to explore pro bono and training programs for the Second Circuit.

While the immigration trial courts do not sponsor any pro bono programs, some individual courts spearhead initiatives to address competence and representation concerns. The BIA coordinates a formal pro bono appeals program, the BIA Pro Bono Project, which has offered counsel in more than 550 appeals since 2001. In cooperation with the BIA Clerk's Office, the project identifies cases for possible pro bono representation in accord with criteria determined by partnering nongovernmental organizations (NGOs).[89] Attorney "screeners" drawn from various NGOs then review the cases to determine which are most suitable for available pro bono counsel; these cases are then distributed to pro bono representatives throughout the country.[90] Those who ultimately accept cases through the project receive copies of the court record, and in most instances, additional time to file appeal briefs.[91] The BIA reports that legal representation in these cases has had a marked positive impact: an internal evaluation in 2004 concluded that the project met its original goals of increasing the level and quality of pro bono representation before the Board.[92]

Since 2000, the Department of Justice, through its Legal Orientation and Pro Bono Program, "has worked to improve access to legal information and counseling and increase rates of representation for immigrants appearing before the Immigration Courts and the . . . BIA."[93] The Legal Orientation Program provides group and individual sessions to detained individuals in various jurisdictions. EOIR also sponsors a "Model Hearing Program," which aims to improve the quality of advocacy in the immigration courts through small-scale mock-trial training involving immigration judges and experienced counsel.

These judicial efforts have been enhanced by dialogue between the judges of the immigration courts and the circuit courts. In one notable instance, the Federal Judicial Center, in conjunction with Georgetown University Law Center, sponsored a program in 2006, "Immigration Law for Judges of the U.S. Court of Appeals," that brought together immigration judges, BIA members, circuit judges, and immigration law experts.

Another set of programs focused both on training and attorney recruitment is managed by the ABA. The ABA coordinates three organizational efforts in South Texas, Seattle, and San Diego dedicated to enlisting the cooperation of significant numbers of pro bono immigration counsel and training and mentoring immigration lawyers.

The ABA's South Texas Pro Bono Asylum Representation Project (ProBAR) is a "national effort to provide pro bono legal services to asylum seekers detained in South Texas" and to this end the "project recruits, trains and coordinates the activities of volunteer attorneys, law students and legal assistants."[94] The Seattle program, the Volunteer Advocates for Immigrant Justice, "offers free legal services to detained immigrants seeking asylum or other forms of legal relief before the immigration courts."[95]

The Immigration Justice Project (IJP) of San Diego, created in 2007, is the ABA's newest project.

> The mission of the IJP is to promote due process and access to justice at all levels of the immigration and appellate court system, through the provision of high-quality pro bono legal services for those in immigration proceedings in San Diego. Partnering in the project are several ABA entities,[] the Executive Office for Immigration Review (EOIR), the federal courts, Georgetown University Law Center's Institute for the Study of International Migration (ISIM), the American Immigration Lawyers Association, and the private bar. The IJP serves both detained and non-detained individuals, and recruits, trains, and mentors volunteer

attorneys and law students representing clients. Through funding from the EOIR, the IJP also implements a Legal Orientation Program for adult immigration detainees.[96]

The IJP operates by screening unrepresented immigration cases at the San Diego district detention facility and following nondetained Master Calendar hearings at the immigration court. These cases are then assigned to volunteer attorneys predominantly from major law firms. The volunteer attorneys are trained in the applicable immigration law and are paired with experienced immigration attorney mentors to whom volunteers can address questions about their assigned cases. The San Diego project includes a unique academic study as well: during the first two years of the project, Georgetown University social scientists will evaluate the impact of quality representation on individual case outcomes, the immigration court, and the appellate process.[97]

As a supplement to these initiatives, the ABA Commission on Immigration has recently created, through an organizational partnership, an "Immigration Advocates Network," which "is a collaborative effort of leading national immigration advocacy organizations designed to increase access to justice for low-income immigrants." In particular, the network "provides free, easily accessible and comprehensive online resources on a password-protected website for non-profit immigration advocates, organizers, and service providers."[98] Further, the ABA and the American Law Institute provide, at minimal cost, video resources for immigration training available to law firms, bar associations, public interest lawyers, and not-for-profit service organizations.[99]

The American Immigration Lawyers Association (AILA) administers a series of initiatives as well, invested simultaneously in enhancing the quantity and quality of available immigration counsel. AILA has created a pro bono coordinator position in its chapters around the country to facilitate various opportunities for qualified lawyers to work on a pro bono basis on a range of matters for indigent noncitizens in immigration proceedings.[100] AILA also directs, in association with the American Immigration Law Foundation, the Legal Action Center, staffed by experienced immigration litigators and other practitioners who produce practice advisories on a number of topics, offer individualized nationwide advice and technical assistance to immigration counsel, and conduct impact litigation to promote fairness for immigrants, their families, and their employers.[101]

Alone, pro bono, legal-resources, and training programs such as these and others do not provide a solution to the severe problems of underrepresentation and poor-quality representation in immigration proceedings. Particularly at the trial level, very little has been done to address problems in the quality of representation. Sadly, many failures at the trial level are incapable of being corrected on appeal, because few immigrants can afford an appeal and even in those matters that are appealed, the record has been made and the evidence of ineffectiveness warranting a remand and opportunity to supplement the record may be scarce.

Conclusion

Ultimately, the primary challenge in expanding training, pro bono, and other immigration-counseling programs is the limited availability of resources. As these programs continue to produce demonstrated improvements, both for individual immigrants and in the administration of justice for the immigration legal system, we expect that the significance of competent representation will become ever more apparent.

Of the many issues identified in the Refugee Roulette study—inconsistent adjudication, risk of error, prolonged detention in sometimes inhumane conditions, and ambiguous and complicated laws—effective representation for individual immigrants provides only a partial solution. Still, increasingly widespread high-quality representation will probably incrementally and indirectly exert a positive influence on each of these problems, as well as contribute to improved fairness and efficiency in immigration litigation.

NOTES

1. M. Margaret McKeown serves as U.S. Circuit Judge on the United States Court of Appeals for the Ninth Circuit. Allegra McLeod, an Arthur Liman Fellow at the American Bar Association's Immigration Justice Project in San Diego, served as a law clerk to Judge McKeown, 2006–2007, and earned her J.D. at Yale Law School, 2006, and Ph.D. at Stanford University, 2008. The views expressed in this essay are personal to the authors and do not reflect the position of the United States Court of Appeals for the Ninth Circuit; nor do the authors necessarily endorse the analysis, conclusions, and policy prescriptions presented by the principal authors of this book or by other contributors.

2. See Morales Apolinar v. Mukasey, 514 F.3d 893, 894–98 & n.4 (9th Cir. 2008) (quoting In re Valinoti, No. 96-O-08095, 2002 WL 31907316 (Cal. Bar Ct. Dec. 31, 2002)).

3. See United States v. Scott, 394 F.3d 111, 113–21 (2d Cir. 2005).

4. See chapter 3, page 45 (confirming earlier studies reporting the strong correlation between the retention of legal representation and favorable immigration court outcomes for asylum seekers); see also Donald Kerwin, Revisiting the Need for Appointed Counsel, in Insight (Migration Policy Inst., Washington D.C.) Apr. 2005, No. 4, at 1, available at http://www.migrationpolicy.org/insight/Insight_Kerwin.pdf.

5. See chapter 3, page 45.

6. See U.S. Department of Justice, Executive Office for Immigration Review, FY 2006 Statistical Year Book, Feb. 2007, at G1, available at http://www.usdoj.gov/eoir/statspub/fy06syb.pdf.

7. See Andrew I. Schoenholtz & Hamutal Bernstein, Improving Immigration Adjudications through Competent Counsel, 21 Geo J. Legal Ethics 55 (2008).

8. See chapter 3, page 45 ("[T]he data do not take into account the quality of representation.").

9. Whereas the principal authors *have* focused exclusively on asylum cases, our analysis addresses immigration litigation more generally.

10. *See* Dada v. Mukasey, 128 S.Ct. 2307 (2008) (holding that an alien may withdraw a petition for voluntary departure before expiration of the departure period); Gonzales v. Duenas-Alvarez, 549 U.S. 183 (2007) (regarding the removal of an alien for a "theft offense" under 8 U.S.C. § 1101(a)(43)(G)); United States v. Resendiz-Ponce, 549 U.S. 102 (2007) (addressing specificity required in an allegation of illegal reentry under 8 U.S.C. § 1326(a)); Lopez v. Gonzales, 549 U.S. 47 (2006) (defining an "aggravated felony" sufficient to trigger removal under 8 U.S.C §1101(a)(43)(B)).

11. *See* Administrative Office of the U.S. Courts, 2007 Annual Report of the Director: Judicial Business of the United States Courts 98 (2008), *available at* http://www.uscourts.gov/ judbus2007/JudicialBusinesspdfversion.pdf [hereinafter 2007 Judicial Business].

12. *See* American Bar Association Annual Meeting, Presidential Showcase CLE Program, Aug. 10, 2008, New York City.

13. *See* Robert A. Katzmann, The Legal Profession and the Unmet Needs of the Immigrant Poor, 21 Geo. J. Legal Ethics 3, 5 (2008) (citing Donald Kerwin, Charitable Legal Programs for Immigrants: What They Do, Why They Matter, and How They Can Be Expanded, Immigration Briefings 1 (2004)).

14. Simultaneous to the upsurge in cases, the number of BIA judges was reduced from twenty-three to eleven. On December 7, 2006, the number of BIA judges was increased to fifteen. *See* 8 C.F.R. § 1003.1(a)(1) (2006). The Department of Justice explained that the increase was necessary to handle an "extremely burdensome" and potentially "overwhelming" caseload. *See* BIA: Composition of Board and Temporary Board Members, 71 Fed. Reg. 70,855 (2006) (finalized by 73 Fed. Reg. 33,875 (2008)) (stating that the number of filings with the Board increased from 35,000 appeals and motions in 2002 to 42,700 in 2005). As of September 2008, thirteen members have been appointed to the Board. *See* Press Release, EOIR, Fact Sheet: BIA Biographical Information (September 2008), *available at* http://www.usdoj.gov/eoir/fs/biabios.htm (listing thirteen members).

15. *See, e.g.,* Carolyn Kolker, *Swamped with Asylum Cases, Federal Appeals Judges Take Aim at Immigration Courts,* American Lawyer, Feb. 2006, at 72–73.

16. *See* Andrew I. Schoenholtz & Hamutal Bernstein, Improving Immigration Adjudications through Competent Counsel, 21 Geo J. Legal Ethics 55, 57–58 (2008) (citing Administrative Office of the U.S. Courts, Judicial Business of the U.S. Courts 2006, at 115 tbl.B-3 (2006), *available at* http://www.uscourts.gov/judbus2006/appendices/b3.pdf.

17. *See* Tony Mauro, *Circuit Judges Decry Immigration Case Tsunami,* Legal Times, Aug. 12, 2008 (quoting Judge McKeown).

18. From 2003 to 2007, the circuit courts received 53,028 appeals from the Board of Immigration Appeals. *See* 2007 Judicial Business, *supra* note 11, at 98. Of these, the Second Circuit received 12,080 (approximately 23%), and the Ninth Circuit 26,299 (approximately 50%). *Id.* at 99, 112.

19. The Ninth Circuit encompasses nine western states, Guam, and the Northern Mariana Islands, has international borders with Mexico and Canada, and has a vast maritime border.

20. *Compare* 2007 Judicial Business, *supra* note 11, at 102 (chart showing appeals from Board of Immigrations Appeals constituting 5,862 of 14,636 total appeals in 2006) *with* Administrative Office of the U.S. Courts, 2004 Annual Report of the Director: Judicial Business of the United States Courts 92 (2005), *available at* http://www.uscourts.gov/judbus2004/appendices/b3.pdf [hereinafter 2004 Judicial Business] (chart showing that total appeals from administrative agencies to Ninth Circuit, which includes immigration appeals, comprising just 1,063 of 10,342 total appeals in 2001).

21. *See* 2007 Judicial Business, *supra* note 11, at 102.

22. The Second Circuit's territory borders Canada and is comprised of the states of Connecticut, New York, and Vermont.

23. *Compare* 2004 Judicial Business, *supra* note 20, at 89 (chart showing appeals from all administrative agencies, including immigration appeals, comprising 184 of 4,519 total appeals to the Second Circuit in 2001) *with* 2007 Judicial Business, *supra* note 11, at 99 (chart showing appeals from Board of Immigration Appeals comprising 2,177 of 6,334 total appeals to the Second Circuit in 2007).

24. *Cf.* Stephen H. Legomsky, *Learning to Live with Unequal Justice: Asylum and the Limits to Consistency*, chapter 12, page 251 ("[M]ore dramatic inroads into adjudicative inconsistency bear costs that . . . are socially unacceptable. The major cost is the erosion of decisional independence, but there are others as well.").

25. *See* Fong Haw Tan v. Phelan, 333 U.S. 6, 10 (1948).

26. *See* Biwot v. Gonzales, 403 F.3d 1094, 1098 (9th Cir. 2005).

27. *See* Katzmann, *supra* note 13.

28. *See* Aris v. Mukasey, 517 F.3d 595, 600 (2d Cir. 2008). We recognize also, as Daniel M. Kowalski has noted, that while many noncitizens in the United States have little material wealth or education, hundreds of thousands of noncitizens "who visit, study, work and live in the U.S. . . . are fluent in English and other languages as well, . . . are highly educated, cultured, and sophisticated, and . . . well-traveled and economically self-sufficient if not prosperous or even wealthy." *See* Kowalski, Things to Do While Waiting for the Revolution, 21 Geo. J. Legal Ethics 37, 37 n.4 (2008) (citing John Buchanan, *Lost in the Shadows: the Remarkable Untold Story of America's Affluent Illegal Immigrants*, Aventura, Oct. 2007, at 129).

29. *See, e.g.,* Iturribarria v. INS, 321 F.3d 889, 901 (9th Cir. 2003) ("One reason that aliens . . . retain legal assistance in the first place is because they assume that an attorney will know how to comply with the procedural details that make immigration proceedings so complicated.").

30. *See* Castro-O'Ryan v. INS, 847 F.2d 1307, 1312 (9th Cir. 1987) (quoting Elizabeth Hull, Without Justice for All: The Constitutional Rights of Aliens 107 (1985)).

31. *See* Castro-O'Ryan, 847 F.2d at 1312.

32. *See* email from Judge Juan Osuna to Judge M. Margaret McKeown (Sept. 8, 2008) (on file with authors).

33. *See* Baltazar-Alcazar v. INS, 386 F.3d 940, 948 (9th Cir. 2004).

34. *See id.* at 942, 946.

35. *See id.* at 943–44.

36. *See id.* at 948.

37. *See id.*

38. *See* Justice Earl Johnson, Jr., "And Justice For All": When Will the Pledge Be Fulfilled?, 47 Judges' Journal 5, 5 (Summer 2008).

39. *See, e.g.,* Recinos de Leon v. Gonzales, 400 F.3d 1185, 1193 (9th Cir. 2005) ("The IJ's opinion— which appears to be an unedited version of a badly transcribed, rambling set of oral observations—is incoherent regarding both the findings made and the legal standards applied.").

40. *Cf.* Gideon v. Wainwright, 372 U.S. 335, 342 (1963) (holding that the Sixth Amendment right to counsel during initial criminal trial proceedings is so fundamental that the Fourteenth Amendment incorporated it against the states); Douglas v. California, 372 U.S. 353, 357–58 (1963) (holding that the Fourteenth Amendment requires states that guarantee criminal appellate review to provide counsel in such proceedings).

41. *See* 8 U.S.C. § 1362 (2000). The right to choose counsel, though it may sound hollow, does mean something: individuals in immigration proceedings must be permitted to proceed with any licensed attorney that they elect to retain. *See* Baltazar-Alcazar v. I.N.S., 386 F.3d 940, 949 (9th Cir. 2004) (holding that "the summary disqualification of an entire law firm violates the statutory right to counsel of choice").

42. *See* 516 F.2d 565, 568 (6th Cir. 1975) (quoting Gagnon v. Scarpelli, 411 U.S. 778, 790 (1973)).

43. *See* Note, A Second Chance: The Right to Effective Assistance of Counsel in Immigration Removal Proceedings, 120 Harv. L. Rev. 1544, 1549 (2007).

44. *See, e.g.*, Mustata v. U.S. Dep't of Justice, 179 F.3d 1017, 1022 n.6 (6th Cir. 1999); Castaneda-Suarez v. INS, 993 F.2d 142, 144 (7th Cir. 1993); Magallanes-Damian v. INS, 783 F.2d 931, 933 (9th Cir. 1986).

45. *See* 521 F.2d 194, 198–99 (5th Cir. 1975) (recognizing potential right to effective assistance of counsel and reopening of proceedings, but concluding that the petitioners had not alleged facts sufficient to permit the inference that competent counsel would have resulted in a different outcome).

46. *See, e.g.*, Chmakov v. Blackman, 266 F.3d 210, 215–16 (3d Cir. 2001); Huicochea-Gomez v. INS, 237 F.3d 696, 699 (6th Cir. 2001); Akinwunmi v. INS, 194 F.3d 1340, 1341 (10th Cir. 1999) (per curiam); Mejia Rodriguez v. Reno, 178 F.3d 1139, 1146 (11th Cir. 1999); Mojsilovic v. INS, 156 F.3d 743, 748 (7th Cir. 1998); Saleh v. Dep't of Justice, 962 F.2d 234, 241 (2d Cir. 1992); Figeroa v. INS, 886 F.2d 76, 78–81 (4th Cir. 1989); Lozada v. INS, 857 F.2d 10, 13–14 (1st Cir. 1988); Magallanes-Damian v. INS, 783 F.2d 931, 933–34 (9th Cir. 1986).

47. *See* 19 I. & N. Dec. 637 (B.I.A. 1988). These requirements include the filing of an affidavit describing the agreement between the client and attorney as well as the specific manner in which the attorney's performance was deficient. The client is to inform the attorney of the complaint and provide the attorney an opportunity to respond; in addition, if the attorney is alleged to have committed ethical or legal violations, the client must either file a complaint with the appropriate disciplinary body or explain why he or she has not done so. In the federal courts of appeal, "[t]hese factors are not rigidly applied, especially when the record shows a clear and obvious case of ineffective assistance." *See* Rodriguez-Lariz v. INS, 282 F.3d 1218, 1227 (9th Cir. 2002).

48. *See, e.g.*, Lara v. Trominski, 216 F.3d 487, 498 (5th Cir. 2000); Lata v. INS, 204 F.3d 1241, 1246 (9th Cir. 2000); Esposito v. INS, 987 F.2d 108, 110 (2d Cir. 1993).

49. *See, e.g.*, Calderon-Huerte v. Ashcroft, 107 Fed. Appx. 82, 83 (9th Cir. 2004) (ineffective assistance of counsel reopening on grounds of attorney's failure to inform client that appeal had been dismissed and subsequent abandonment of case); Rabiu v. INS, 41 F.3d 879, 883 (2d Cir. 1994) (ineffective assistance of counsel reopening due to attorney's failure to file for discretionary relief for which client was eligible).

50. *See* Matter of Compean, 24 I. & N. Dec. 710 (A.G. 2009).

51. See *id.* at 727, 732. In order to warrant a favorable exercise of discretion under *Compean*, a petitioner must establish (1) that the attorney's failings were egregious; (2) that the petitioner exercised "due diligence" in attempting to address the alleged deficient performance; and (3) that "but for" the attorney's deficient performance "it is more likely than not that the [petitioner] would have been entitled to the ultimate relief he was seeking." *Id.* at 733–34.

52. 8 C.F.R. §§ 1003.1(d)(2)(iii), 1003.1(d)(5); 1003.101–106, 1292.3.

53. *See* U.S. Dep't of Justice, Executive Office for Immigration Review, List of Currently Disciplined Practitioners, *available at* http://www.usdoj.gov/eoir/profcond/chart.htm.

54. 8 C.F.R. § 1003.102.

55. *See* Aris v. Mukasey, 517 F.3d 595, 600 (2d Cir. 2008).

56. 478 F.3d 133 (2d Cir. 2007).

57. *Id.* at 143. Incidentally, Yang's lawyer is one of the main protagonists in Professor Richard L. Abel's article on immigration lawyers' neglect of clients and related misconduct. *See* Richard L. Abel, Practicing Immigration Law in Filene's Basement, 84 N.C. L. Rev. 1449, 1452–76 (2006).

58. 478 F.3d at 142.

59. 247 Fed. Appx. 874, 875 (9th Cir. 2007). The reader may notice that we cite unpublished cases in this essay, and the Refugee Roulette study's statistics on U.S. courts of appeals cases also included unpublished decisions. Published opinions generally address significant or novel legal issues, whereas unpublished decisions routinely address the application of settled law to a variety of factual situations. In the immigration context, unpublished federal appellate cases are valuable resources for policy and scholarly research because they reveal patterns that arise repeatedly, but may otherwise go unnoticed because they do not necessarily involve precedential legal issues.

60. *See id.*

61. *See, e.g.,* Tinoco-Aguilera v. INS, 73 Fed. Appx. 946 (9th Cir. 2003) (petitioners hired attorney who then failed to file timely application for suspension of deportation and attorney was later disbarred for seventy-one counts of similar misconduct in other immigration cases).

62. *See, e.g.,* Anin v. Reno, 188 F.3d 1273, 1277 (11th Cir. 1999) (holding that the due process notice requirement and all statutory rules are satisfied by an attorney's receipt of notice through certified mail, even if the immigrant client never receives actual notice).

63. *See* 150 Fed. Appx. 639, 640 (9th Cir. 2005).

64. *See id.* at 640.

65. *See id.*

66. *See* 514 F.3d 893, 897 n.5 (9th Cir. 2008).

67. *Id.*

68. *Id.*

69. 478 F.3d at 138.

70. *Id.* at 138–39.

71. 478 F.3d at 139 (quoting In re Muto, 291 A.D.2d 188, 739 N.Y.S.2d 67, 69 (N.Y. App. Div. 2002)).

72. 73 Fed. Appx. 946, 947 (9th Cir. 2003) (internal citations omitted).

73. *Id.*

74. For qualitative descriptions of two very different models of representation, compare the descriptions of the overcommitted attorneys who represented Morales and Yang, with the work of the law student representatives described in David Ngaruri Kenney & Philip G. Schrag, Asylum Denied: A Refugee's Struggle for Safety in America (2008), pages 95–161.

75. *See* chapter 3, pages 45–46.

76. *See* Adam Liptak, *The Verge of Expulsion, the Fringe of Justice*, New York Times, Sidebar, April 15, 2008.

77. *See id.*

78. *See, e.g.,* Yi-Tu Lian v. Ashcroft, 379 F.3d 457, 459–60 (7th Cir. 2004) (noting misstatements and "disingenuous" legal arguments presented by immigration lawyers for the government).

79. Such "specialists," who are not authorized to practice in immigration court, should be distinguished from "accredited representatives," who are employed by nonprofit organizations and "approved by the Board of Immigration Appeals to represent aliens before the Board, the Immigration Courts, and the Department of Homeland Security." *See* Executive Office for Immigration Review, Immigration Court Practice Manual Ch. 2.4 (2008); *see also* 8 C.F.R. §1292.1(a)(4), 1292.2(d).

80. *See, e.g.,* Andrew F. Moore, Fraud, the Unauthorized Practice of Law, and Unmet Needs: A Look at State Laws Regulating Immigration Assistants, 19 Geo. Immigr. L. J. 1, 2–3 (2004).

81. 170 Fed. Appx. 890 (9th Cir. 2006).

82. 223 Fed. Appx. 633, 634 (9th Cir. 2007).

83. 300 F.3d 1018, 1018 (9th Cir. 2002).

84. *Id.* at 1019.

85. *See* David Rosenzweig, *Sellers of False Residency Permits Sentenced to Prison,* Los Angeles Times, June 22, 1999, at B-2; *see also* Press Release, U.S. Dep't of Justice, Hartford Immigration Lawyer Pleads Guilty to Federal Document Fraud Charges (May 9, 2008) (announcing plea of Hartford immigration attorney to document fraud).

86. *See* Jessie Mangaliman, *Disbarred Lawyer Arrested,* San Jose Mercury News, July 19, 2008 (Local Crime News Section).

87. *See* Katzmann, *supra* note 13, at 10–19 (describing programs that seek to increase the numbers of attorneys available to represent indigent immigrants facing removal from the United States).

88. *See* Ninth Circuit Immigration Outline, *available at* http://www.ca9.uscourts.gov/ca9/Documents.nsf (click on download by topic (order by subject), then scroll to and click on Immigration Outline).

89. *See* U.S. Dep't of Justice, EOIR Legal Orientation and Pro Bono Program, http://www.usdoj.gov/eoir/probono/ MajorInitiatives.htm.

90. *See id.*

91. *See id.*

92. *See* Board of Immigration Appeals, The BIA Pro Bono Project is Successful (2004), http://www.usdoj. gov/eoir/reports/BIAProBonoProjectEvaluation.pdf.

93. *See* U.S. Dep't of Justice, EOIR Legal Orientation and Pro Bono Program, http://www.usdoj.gov /eoir/probono/probono.htm.

94. ProBar is also sponsored by the State Bar of Texas and the American Immigration Lawyers Association. *See* ABA, South Texas Pro Bono Asylum Representation Project (ProBAR), http://www.abanet.org/publicserv/immigration/probar.shtml.

95. *See* ABA, Volunteer Advocates for Immigrant Justice (VAIJ), http://www.abanet.org/publicserv/immigration/vaij.shtml.

96. *See* ABA Commission on Immigration, The ABA Launches the Immigration Justice Projects (IJP) of San Diego.

97. *See id.*

98. *See* ABA Commission on Immigration, Launch of the Immigration Advocates Network, *available at* http://www.abanet.org/publicserv/immigration/home.html; *see also* Immigration Advocates Network, Welcome to the Immigration Advocates Network, http://www.immigrationadvocates.org.

99. *See* ALI-ABA, Best Practices in Representing Asylum-Seekers: A Video Resource for Pro Bono Attorneys, *available at* http://www.ali-aba.org/aliaba/rdvd01.asp.

100. *See, e.g.,* AILA Chicago Chapter, Chapter Pro Bono Programs, http://www.aila.org/content/default.aspx?docid=20441.

101. *See* American Immigration Law Foundation, AILF Legal Action Center, http://www.ailf.org/ lac/lac_index.shtml.

Methodological Appendix

I. Benchmarks for Counting and Comparing the Number of Outlying Adjudicators

In order to evaluate consistency within an adjudication body, we needed to select a benchmark for counting the number of adjudicators (asylum officers, immigration judges, or appellate judges) who deviated significantly from the mean. To begin, we had to decide whether to measure deviation in terms of the difference from the national mean or the mean for the office in which the adjudicator worked. We decided on the latter standard; therefore, unless otherwise indicated, we measured deviation from a mean for asylum officers only in terms of the mean of the regional office in which the asylum officer works, and deviation from a mean by immigration judges only by measuring their grant rates against the mean grant rate for the judges in the city in which they sit. (In a small number of instances, we compared regions or cities, but these are clearly indicated in the text.) We believe that making local comparisons is appropriate because the national origin of the population of asylum seekers varies considerably from region to region. For example, Haitians and Colombians apply for asylum in much larger proportions in Miami than in other cities. Even when we considered only asylum seekers from one country, those who migrate to one U.S. city may be significantly different from those who migrate to another city (for example, asylum seekers from one province may tend to flee to the East Coast of the United States while those from another province may flee via a different route and end up on the West Coast).

To compute mean regional or city grant rates, we included all cases from the time period of the study. For regional asylum office grant rates, we multiplied each adjudicator's grant rate by the number of cases decided by that adjudicator; the product represented the total of that adjudicator's grants. For immigration court grant rates by city, the data provided by the government included numbers of cases granted. In both cases, we added total adjudicator grants, and then divided that sum by the total number of cases decided on their merits by all adjudicators in the region or city. We reported and evaluated the grant rates of only those adjudicators who decided at least the threshold number of cases reported in the text (one hundred cases in most instances, fifty in others, and twenty-five in two instances: studies of decisions of asylum officers deciding cases from China and remands by federal courts of appeals). We were concerned that grant rates of adjudicators who decided fewer than twenty-five cases might not accurately represent the grant rates of those adjudicators if they had decided more cases.[1] That is, an adjudicator who decided only five cases might have been assigned five weak or five strong cases by chance.

We also had to decide how to count the number of adjudicators who are "outliers" in a particular region or court. Any benchmark is necessarily arbitrary, but we selected one that we thought was relatively conservative and that many people would agree represented a measure of significant deviation from the norm. By our measure, an adjudicator is an outlier if that adjudicator's grant rate was more than 50% higher or lower than the regional or city mean. Thus for a region or city with a 30% mean grant rate for the type of case under consideration, an adjudicator is not an outlier for our purposes unless his or her grant rate is lower than 15% or higher than 45%. Many people might think that a deviation of 50% above and below the mean is too large a range and that our study therefore understates the degree of disparity in asylum grant rates. Others might think that we were too intolerant of differences in perspective among adjudicators. Since we are publishing our raw data on a website[2] in Microsoft Access and Excel formats, others may easily count the number of outliers using benchmarks of their own choosing, such as deviations of 30% or 70% rather than 50%.

In most of the studies reported in this book, the mean grant rate falls in a relatively narrow range, between 25% and 50%. However, there are a few studies (relating to particular asylum applicant populations) in which the mean grant rate is particularly low (e.g., 15%) or high (e.g., 73%). When the mean grant rate falls significantly, the range of percentages in which an adjudicator is not deviant becomes smaller. For example, when the mean is only 15%, the nondeviant range runs from 7.5% to 22.5%, a difference of only fifteen percentage points rather than forty percentage points, and when the mean is 70%, the nondeviant range is 35% to 100%, a range of sixty-five percentage points.

For this reason, we also considered defining outliers as those who deviated from the local mean by more than a fixed number of percentage points. We seriously considered an alternative definition of outliers as those adjudicators whose grant rates were more than fifteen percentage points higher or lower than the regional mean. However, this computation also had its problems. For a study in which the regional grant rate was 15% or less, by definition there could be no outliers on the low side. In our view, the fact that a region's mean grant rate is as low as 15% does not exclude the possibility of outlying adjudicators; for example, an adjudicator with a 3% grant rate in such a region seems out of step with the norm. Therefore, we believe that our chosen method is a more accurate representation of deviance. By contrast, a fixed-percentage-point method tends to understate low-side deviations and overstate high-side deviations in a study with low regional means, and it tends to understate high-side deviations and overstate low-side deviations in studies with high regional means. Of course, any reader who wants to examine the adjudicators' deviations by using a measure based on a fixed percentage point spread rather than by measuring the percentage of deviation from the mean may do so by working with the raw data on the website.

II. The Asylum Office

The Asylum Office of the U.S. Department of Homeland Security provided us with data on all asylum applications decided by its asylum officers from FY 1999 through FY 2005. For each of the 928 officers who served during this period, the office provided us with the number of cases decided by that officer, the officer's approximate grant rate, and the region in which the officer worked. In addition, for the 884 officers who decided cases from the fifteen APCs, the Asylum Office provided us with the number of cases the officer decided from each country, the identity of the country in question, the officer's approximate grant rate for nationals from that country, the region in which the officer worked, and the officer's gender.[3] Our analysis of adjudications by asylum officers included only asylum applications because those officers do not have authority to grant withholding of removal,[4] and Convention against Torture cases are rare.

All the data exclude Mexican asylum applicants. According to the Asylum Office, Mexican nationals voluntarily entered the affirmative asylum system in large numbers during this period principally in order to be placed into immigration court proceedings where they could seek relief other than asylum. Since they were generally not seeking asylum, they are not included in the analysis articulated in this book.[5]

For privacy and security reasons, the Asylum Office data did not reveal the identity of either the individual officer or the regional office. Numbers were assigned randomly to each of the asylum officers on a nationwide basis. Letters A through H were assigned randomly to each of the eight asylum offices.

The grant rates for each officer were provided to us in ranges of 5%: that is, 1–5%, 6–10%, 11–15%, etc. We took the middle of the range in computing and graphing our analysis. For example, an 11–15% range is calculated as 13%. We assume that because our APC data cover such a large number of officers and cases, this rounding off of some rates higher than the midpoint and some rates lower than the midpoint averages out in the analysis.

This study focuses on merits decisions only. Grants and denials are clearly merits decisions, as are referrals to immigration courts based on interviews where the asylum officers did not regard the merits as strong enough for grants. We also treat rejections based on failure to meet the one-year filing deadline or an exception to it as merits decisions, as filing on time is a criterion for eligibility.[6]

Accordingly, our grant rate calculation divides the number of grants by the number of cases decided on the merits. Cases decided on the merits include grants; denials of applications filed by aliens in valid immigration statuses; referrals of out-of-status aliens to immigration court because the applicants failed, after interviews, to prove eligibility for asylum; and referrals of out-of-status aliens to immigration court because the applicants did not prove either that they had met the one-year application deadline or that they had a suitable explanation for late filing.

To compare each office to office, and officer to officer, and account for nationality differences in caseloads, we based comparisons on grant rates regarding nationals from countries that, as noted above, we call Asylee Producing Countries (APCs). To make this list, at least five hundred asylum seekers from such a country must have presented claims before the Asylum Office or immigration court in FY 2004, and asylum seekers from that country must have garnered a national grant rate of at least 30%, before either the Asylum Office or immigration courts. These criteria ensure, first, that the database includes a statistically significant number of applicants and grantees. Second, the minimal grant rate requirement provides for a set of decisions where asylum officers or immigration judges as a group have reached a reasonable degree of consensus in concluding that many applicants from these countries are bona fide. Fifteen countries met these criteria: Albania, Armenia, Cameroon, China, Colombia, Ethiopia, Guinea, Haiti, India, Liberia, Mauritania, Pakistan, Russia, Togo, and Venezuela. Countries that generated low grant rates, such as El Salvador and Guatemala, are not on this list.

With regard to the Asylum Office data, we refined the set of APC countries to ensure that there were enough data on individual asylum officers at enough offices to compare certain nationalities fairly. For four nationalities, that was not the case. From the list of fifteen APC countries used for the national and regional data analysis, we could not use data concerning Guinea, Mauritania, Togo, and Venezuela. For example, only one office decided the vast majority of Venezuelan cases. So the analysis of individual decision making at the Asylum Office consists of decisions regarding asylum seekers from the eleven remaining APC countries. In our APC analyses, we included all officers who had adjudicated at least fifty cases. Our Asylum Office APC data analysis, then, concerns 126,504 cases decided by the 527 asylum officers.

In a second approach, we looked for a way to correct for differences in the particular mix of APC countries in a region's pool of cases adjudicated in a particular region that might affect that region's grant rate and explain at least some of the APC grant rate disparity between offices. To accomplish this, we looked at whether regional office grant rates continued to vary when we narrowed our focus to applicants from a single country. To obtain enough data on cases from particular countries that were adjudicated by an individual officer, however, we had to reduce to twenty-five the minimum number of cases decided by an asylum officer.

We computed mean grant rates for the group of applicants in question by including all decisions for each office by all asylum officers in that office during the period of analysis, even though we report the grant and deviation rates only for officers who decided at least a certain threshold number of cases.

III. The Immigration Courts

The immigration court data were analyzed in two separate ways. First, we examined grant rate data on their own. Second, we conducted a cross-tabulation analysis of grant rate data in conjunction with biographical data and certain data about the cases. Each section of analysis merits its own subpart in this methodology, as different methods were used for each.

A. Grant Rate Data Analysis

There are ample data on the asylum grant rates of particular immigration courts and immigration judges; for this we are indebted to asylumlaw.org,[7] which filed a Freedom of Information Act request with the Executive Office of Immigration Review to obtain this information.[8] This book focuses on asylum cases decided in immigration court between January 1, 2000, and August 31, 2004, the period covered by that request.[9]

The available data are vast, including 140,428 decisions on the merits. We focused on significant comparisons between immigration courts and between immigration judges on the same court. First, we looked only at immigration courts that decided at least fifteen hundred asylum cases during the relevant time frame. We use the term "high-volume immigration courts," or "HVCs," to refer to these seventeen courts. The seventeen high-volume courts are located in Arlington, Atlanta, Baltimore, Boston, Chicago, Dallas, Detroit, Houston, Los Angeles, Memphis, Miami, Newark, New York City, Orlando, Philadelphia, San Diego, and San Francisco. Then, to keep the countries of origin constant, we limited our analysis to applications for asylum by nationals of the fifteen APCs.[10] The term "national averages" includes only the cases from APC countries decided by high-volume courts.

We excluded detained cases from the data as best we could. This allowed us to better compare decision making regarding the affirmative asylum cases at the Asylum Offices with decision making at immigration courts. The Elizabeth Immigration Court would have been among the top eighteen courts by volume of cases (having heard over fifteen hundred cases during this time period), but we excluded Elizabeth from the study because this court hears almost exclusively the cases of detained asylum seekers. We also excluded the cases heard by the judges assigned to Miami's Krome Detention Center and those heard by the judges assigned to New York's Varick Street Detention Center; again, the judges in question were not assigned cases randomly. They were, instead, assigned almost exclusively the cases of detained respondents. Such respondents request asylum as a defense to removal and face much greater obstacles to obtaining representation and corroborating evidence; both of these factors could contribute to significantly lower grant rates. The cases of some detained asylum seekers who are seeking asylum defensively remain in the data, but we have removed from the study the judges who hear claims from detained persons almost exclusively.[11]

We also applied minimum case decision requirements in the following ways. When analyzing grant rates in individual courts on asylum claims from individual APCs, we examined only HVCs that had decided at least one hundred applications by nationals of that country during the period in question. Similarly, in comparing decisions by immigration judges in the same court on asylum claims from all APCs, we looked only at judges who had decided at least one hundred asylum claims from APCs. In comparing decisions by immigration judges in the same court on asylum claims from a particular APC, we looked only at judges who had decided at least fifty cases involving the country in question and excluded decisions by immigration judges detailed to the court in question.[12] For judges who switched courts during the time frame studied, we placed them on the court in which the judge practiced the longest; if there was a tie, we placed the judge on the court in which she sat between 2000 and 2002.

B. Cross-Tabulation Analysis

In addition to the simple grant rate analysis, we conducted a cross-tabulation analysis to describe the effects of independent variables drawn from biographical data and other asylum seeker data on asylum grant rates. While we used the same grant rate data on which we relied for the simple grant rate analysis, we approached the data differently, thus requiring a separate methodology subpart for the cross-tabulation analysis.

We used immigration judges' biographical data, provided by the Executive Office of Immigration Review, in conjunction with the grant rate data described above to run this cross-tabulation analysis, as well as the regression analyses to confirm the initial results. Again, we worked only with asylum cases, and did not examine withholding of removal and Convention against Torture claims. The database includes 269,756 decisions. For the cross-tabulation and regression analysis, we examined only grants and denials, and eliminated cases that were abandoned, withdrawn, or disposed of in some other way.[13] This step excluded 129,328 cases, leaving 140,428 cases in the database.

We also looked only at primary cases, excluding the cases of dependents. Primary cases were identified in the following way: where the database contained identical entries for more than one decision in all of the column variables (date, court, nationality, decision, representation, type of claim), we determined that these decisions came from the same "family." This method may be overinclusive in some instances but is the most effective method available using the data provided to us.[14] From this "family," we selected a "primary case" and eliminated all the others as "dependent cases." This step excluded 26,572 cases, leaving 113,856 cases in the database.

Additionally, we removed defensive cases from the data. We did this because defensive cases are a good proxy for detained cases; we know that 94.5% of detained cases in the full database (excluding Mexican cases) were defensive.[15] The defensive or affirmative nature of the case was determined by the "C_ASY_TYPE" column in the data; an entry of "E" represented a defensive case and an entry of "I" represented an affirmative case.[16] This method excluded 46,042 cases (including 191 missing observations), leaving 67,814 cases in the database.

Finally, we removed Mexican cases from the data, for reasons explained in part 2 of this Methodological Appendix. This was easily accomplished as the database included the country of origin for each asylum seeker. This step excluded 1,371 cases (including fourteen missing observations), leaving 66,443 cases in the database.[17]

We used cross-tabulations to examine the impact of nine independent variables on the dependent variable, grant rate. These variables, further explained below, include how many dependents the asylum seeker had in the United States; whether the asylum seeker was represented by an attorney or other accredited representative; gender of the judge; and previous work experience: for the Immigration and Naturalization Service or Department of Homeland Security, for the government, in the military, in a nongovernmental organization, in private practice, or in academia.

We determined the independent variables concerning asylum seekers from the data provided in response to asylumlaw.org's FOIA request. Specifically, dependents could be discerned through the method described above.[18] Representation was determined by EOIR's "ALIEN_ATTY_CODE" column; cells in this column including a code were interpreted to mean that the asylum seeker was represented and blank cells to mean that the asylum seeker was unrepresented.

We determined the independent variables concerning immigration judges largely through biographical data from the Executive Office of Immigration Review. Some biographies were available on the EOIR website, and others could be found at the very helpful Transactional Records Access Clearinghouse (TRAC) website.[19] For four judges, we obtained biographical information from news articles. Of 249 immigration judges whose decisions were analyzed, we were unable to obtain biographical data for two: Richard Knuck and Terry Christian. Moreover, there were some time gaps as to employment before appointment in some of the biographical information provided by EOIR. The gaps are as follows: twenty-three biographies with imprecise employment information; ten biographies with one to two years of employment information missing; twenty-two biographies with three to five years of employment information missing; ten biographies with six to nine years of employment information missing; and fifteen biographies with ten or more years of employment information missing. We requested assistance in filling in these holes from the Office of the Chief Immigration Judge, who sought but was unable to provide us with further information. We mailed individual questionnaires to each of the eighty immigration judges whose biographies were missing information; we received responses from eight of these judges. We made educated guesses concerning the biographies with imprecise information, but could not do so for the other holes in the biographies.

We pulled seven variables from the immigration judges' biographies. The simplest to determine was gender. The most complicated biographical information concerned employment history. We analyzed only post–law school experience prior to appointment as an immigration judge. We broke this out into six categories: government, INS or DHS, military, nongovernmental organization, private practice, and academia. Government included all nonmilitary employment in federal, state, or local government, but excluded prior INS or DHS experience. INS or DHS comprised all employment in a role adversarial to immigrants (including trial attorney, Office of Immigration Litigation, special assistant United States attorney, border patrol, etc.). Military experience included all post–law school service; work in the Reserves did not count but work as a military judge did count. We categorized as nongovernmental organization experience all work for nonprofit organizations that involved the provision of legal assistance to indigent or marginalized populations, including legal services and public defender organizations. Private practice included all for-profit legal or nonlegal work, including the World Bank, Wells Fargo, and independent contract work for different law firms. Finally, we included in the academia category only full-time law school teaching jobs, whether they were clinical or classroom positions. Adjunct positions were not counted. For periods in which the judge had two jobs, we looked only at the judge's primary job—for example, we excluded time spent in the Reserves, in the National Guard, or as an adjunct professor.

We ran a simple cross-tabulation analysis of grant rates by each of the nine variables. We checked the statistical significance of these results using chi-square tests and found that all variables were statistically significant.[20] This analysis produced the results that are discussed in chapter 3 of this book.[21] The theories underlying the inclusion of each variable follow.

Number of dependents. We were interested in examining the number of dependents that each asylum seeker had with him in the United States to determine the impact that the welfare of additional family members might have on the immigration judge's decision. The Immigration and Nationality Act limits the definition of dependents to the asylum seeker's spouse and unmarried children under the age of twenty-one. Our hypothesis was that an asylum seeker who brings his family with him to the United States might be more credible than either a single asylum seeker or one who leaves his family behind in his home country.

Representation. We were interested in knowing whether asylum seekers were represented in immigration court by an attorney or other accredited representative. As discussed above, several studies have found that representation is a very important factor in winning asylum.[22]

Gender of the judge. We had no reason to think that male and female judges might grant asylum at different rates. We included this variable in our analysis, however, because we were able to determine the gender of the judge easily from the pronouns used in the biographical data. When the cross-tabulation revealed significant differences, we retained the variable in our study.

Government experience. We wondered whether judges who had previously worked for the government would be more or less supportive of the government trial attorney's position in asylum cases.

INS/DHS experience. We wanted to know whether the data supported our hypothesis that many years of work enforcing immigration laws against noncitizens influenced the judge's approach to asylum cases.

Military experience. We wanted to know what kind of impact military experience had on grant rates. On the one hand, patriotism and affinity with the government might make these judges less likely to grant asylum claims. On the other hand, the military justice system includes thorough training for its judges and attorneys, and those judges who worked in the military after law school may have had experience in this system and thus be more likely to decide cases based on the merits rather than based on preexisting biases.

NGO experience. We suspected that judges who had worked for nongovernmental organizations or in a defense capacity would both be more sympathetic to asylum seekers and have a greater understanding of how difficult it is to present a successful asylum claims. As a result, we thought these judges would be more likely to grant asylum claims.

Private practice experience. We were interested to learn whether employment in the private sector had any impact on judges' decision-making process. Judges who represented plaintiffs in private practice would understand the difficulties posed in presenting any type of case and might be more sympathetic to asylum seekers.

Academic experience. We wondered whether immigration judges who had taught full-time would be more open to seeing all sides of every issue and therefore less likely to dismiss novel claims or those that alleged types of persecution as to which State Department human rights reports were silent.

We ran three regression analyses to test for the general robustness of the bivariate findings. These analyses select one variable at a time and equalize all of the other variables in the database. They report the likelihood of a grant of asylum if the selected variable is altered. We added seven variables to the regression analyses to increase accuracy of our models: age of the judge, president whose attorney general appointed the judge, caseload of the judge, caseload of the judge's court, national freedom ranking for the asylum seeker's country of origin, weekly earnings in the state in which the judge's court sits, and years on the bench.

To determine age, we used the year of graduation from college and assumed each judge was age twenty-two when she graduated from college. For judges who obtained their first law degree in a foreign country and did not have a college graduation date, we used the date of the first law degree and added twenty-two because in many countries, a law degree is a college degree. Age was calculated to the date of each case. The country of origin of the asylum seeker was determined by the "NAT_NAME" column in the data. We used national freedom rankings from Freedom House to categorize these countries as free, partially free, or not free.[23] We determined weekly earnings in the state in which the judge's court was located by tabulating Current Population Survey microdata.[24] We used the date of the first appointment to determine the political party of the appointing president. Cases decided by each immigration judge and by each court on which those judges sat were determined using the data provided in response to asylumlaw.org's FOIA request. Finally, we calculated years on the bench by looking at date of initial appointment, and, where relevant, dates of termination of employment and reappointment. The theories underlying the inclusion of these variables follow.

Age of the judge. We were interested in learning whether a judge's age impacted grant rate. There could be many reasons for this: older judges might be more jaded and cynical about asylum cases, having presumably seen more fraudulent cases than the younger judges. Older judges might see only certain kinds of claims (e.g., political cases) from certain regions (e.g., Communist countries) as worthy of asylum, and may not have adapted to changes in asylum law. On the other hand, as grandparents and parents, older judges might be more sympathetic and protective towards asylum seekers.

Appointing president. We wondered whether the political leanings of the president in office when the attorney general appointed the judge would impact the judge's rulings in asylum cases. This question goes back to the Edwards-Revesz debate described in the introduction to this book—do judges vote their political convictions or do they decide cases based on the law? We were interested in the answer to this question.

Caseload and cases per court. These two variables, the first being the number of cases that the judge in question decided during the period studied and the second being the number of cases that the immigration court in which the judge in question sat during the period studied, could impact decision making in several ways. A judge who hears many cases might be likely to hear and decide cases quickly, which might lead to a lower grant rate. Particularly if the immigration court on which she sits hears a high volume of cases, the judges might be under pressure to move their docket by denying many cases. On the other hand, such a judge and her colleagues might become more familiar with country conditions in certain countries after seeing particularly well-prepared asylum cases from that country, and might be more likely to grant these cases.

Local weekly earnings. We wondered whether local affluence would impact judges' grant rates.

National freedom ranking. We investigated whether an asylum seeker's country of origin impacts the possibility of being granted asylum. In a system based on the merits of the cases, one might expect that asylum seekers from countries with poor human rights records (i.e., partially free or not free countries) would be regarded by judges as more likely to win asylum than asylum seekers from countries viewed as free in this index. It is possible that the stronger cases from the not free or partially free countries are granted in the asylum office (especially given that our database includes only affirmative cases); either way, this variable is of interest.

Years on the bench. We wondered whether the number of years a judge had served on the immigration bench might impact her grant rate, independent of her age. A judge with more years on the bench might understand the law more thoroughly and decide cases more impartially, or may become jaded by the process and skeptical of all asylum claims before her.

The first regression, using the logistic model, confirmed the results of the cross-tabulation.[25] We next ran a logistic regression with fixed effects for court. Five variables were less than 95% likely to be statistically significant: caseload of the judge, years the judge had sat on the immigration bench, appointment under

President Reagan, prior military experience, and prior private practice experience. Prior military experience was found to be slightly positively correlated with grant rate. Otherwise, the regression confirmed the results of the cross-tabulation analysis. We also ran a hierarchical linear regression, which confirmed the results of our cross-tabulations. The results of these regression analyses are reported at http://www.law.georgetown.edu/ humanrightsinstitute/refugeeroulette.htm.

IV. The Board of Immigration Appeals

We requested data from the Board regarding asylum determinations for fiscal years 1998–2005. We specifically asked for statistics that would enable us to examine individual member decision making on the merits of claims for asylum. We also requested data regarding the mode of decision making (i.e., panel, single-member short opinions, or affirmances without opinion). Finally, we asked for information on nationality and representation.[26]

The Board provided us with data on nationality and representation, as well as on mode of decision making. Two important problems surfaced, however, with regard to the data that the Board collects and the way it does so. First, the Board knows the period of service of every Board member, and it knows the outcome of each Board decision, but it does not keep records from which it can ascertain which members made or participated in which decisions, or from which it could calculate the rate at which individual members rendered decisions (asylum grants or remands) that benefited asylum applicants. Therefore, we were not able to perform an analysis of disparities in the decisions from one member to the next, as we were able to do for asylum officers and immigration judges. Nor could we explore the possible effect of the genders or prior experiences of the adjudicators. Second, for fiscal years 2001 and 2002, the Board did not have reliable data on the mode of decision making—whether particular decisions were rendered by a single member or by a three-member panel. The coding of the decision modes changed during that period. Unfortunately, the very helpful EOIR staff responsible for statistical reports did not have the information needed to decipher the meaning of the codes used in those years.

The BIA provided us with a set of decision and disposition codes that it uses to describe the full range of its procedural and substantive determinations.[27] As discussed above, our study focused on asylum merits decisions only. Accordingly, we analyzed only those asylum decisions in which a merits decision was favorable either to the noncitizen or to the government. Our analysis excluded immigration appeals that did not involve asylum, as well as asylum cases that the Board coded as outcomes that it could not determine to be either favorable or unfavorable to the applicant.

Most of the BIA analyses included all nationalities. In certain instances, we examined only APC merits decisions. In those analyses, we include decisions on all fifteen APC countries. In one analysis, we report the individual APC grant rates for individual countries. Where we were not examining the mode of decision making, we included the data for all the fiscal years provided. Any of our analyses that specifically examine three-member panel decisions, single-member short opinions, or single-member affirmances without opinion only included fiscal years 1998–2000 and 2003–2005, for the reason discussed above.

Despite the limits on the data set, we were able to measure the degree of change that occurred once the BIA implemented the major streamlining reforms proposed in February 2002. We compared changes in the rates of decisions favorable to asylum applicants for the three decision modes individually, comparatively, and combined.

V. The United States Courts of Appeals

The U.S. courts of appeals do not keep separate statistics showing their dispositions of cases involving asylum, withholding, or the Convention against Torture. We therefore had to construct a database containing all of these decisions over a representative period of time. We chose the calendar years 2004 and 2005 as the period for our consideration.[28]

Most asylum decisions are unpublished, nonprecedential decisions, so we could not obtain the necessary data from printed reports. However, six circuits (the First Circuit through the Sixth Circuit) have searchable websites on which they have posted the full texts of all of their calendar year 2004 and 2005 precedential and nonprecedential decisions. For these circuits, we began by searching for all cases in which one of the parties was identified as "Ashcroft" (for 2004), "Gonzales" (for 2005) or "Attorney General."[29] We inspected these cases individually, rejecting from the database those that were not appeals from the Board of Immigration Appeals.[30] From this preliminary database, we excluded all cases that did not involve appeals from denials of asylum, withholding of removal, or claims under the Convention against Torture.[31] We also excluded cases that involved only procedural issues rather than any consideration of the merits. Specifically, we excluded those in which the court decided that a motion to reopen or a motion to reconsider had not been timely filed, or other procedural prerequisites (such as filing a promised brief) had not been met, and those in which the foreign national claimed only that the process of adjudication itself (e.g., the summary affirmance procedure of the Board) violated due process.[32] Cases in which the court characterized its decision as either an "affirmance" of the Board's decision or a "denial" or "dismissal" of the appeal (or "petition for review") were regarded as losses for the foreign national; any remand of the case to the Board, in whole or in part, was considered a success for the foreign national.[33]

The courts' official websites for the Seventh through the Eleventh Circuits were not as complete in that they did not include all of the unpublished decisions for the two years in question. For the Seventh, Eighth, and Tenth Circuits, we relied on a Westlaw search to collect the preliminary database and to exclude decisions that were merely procedural.[34] We restricted the database by applying the same criteria that we used in the first six circuits, again examining each decision individually to characterize it as a denial or a remand.

The Ninth and Eleventh Circuits presented special challenges. Until April 2005, the Eleventh Circuit neither posted its unpublished decisions on its website nor supplied them to Westlaw. However, Westlaw did post the briefs for the Eleventh Circuit cases during this period in its CTA11 database. Because the dates on the briefs predated the dates of the corresponding opinions, we expanded the search dates for 2004 to begin with March 1, 2003, and to end with October 31, 2004.[35] This search produced 253 hits. We examined both the briefs and the docket sheets[36] in these cases and found that eighty-nine cases were appeals from the Board involving the merits of asylum, withholding of removal, or the torture convention.[37]

The Westlaw search of Ninth Circuit cases revealed 1,229 cases in calendar year 2004 that qualified for our preliminary database, a much larger volume of decided cases than in any of the other circuits. The volume in 2005 was only slightly smaller (877 cases). We could not examine so many cases individually to determine whether the outcome was an affirmance or a remand. Instead, beginning with the 1,229 and 877 cases, we searched for the term "remand." That search yielded 291 cases for 2004 and 235 cases for 2005, which we examined individually. We found that 225 of the 291 cases in 2004 were actually remands; the rest mentioned the word "remand" somewhere in the opinion but affirmed the Board's denial of relief. For 2005, the comparable number was 183 actual remands. Therefore, we computed the remand rate for the Ninth Circuit in 2004 as 18.3% (225 actual remands out of 1,229 asylum cases). For 2005, the remand rate was 20.9% (183 remands out of 877 cases).

For our analysis of remand rates from the fifteen APC countries, we had to determine the nationality of each appellant. For cases in circuits other than the Ninth Circuit, we obtained the nationality of the applicant by examining the decisions (or for the Eleventh Circuit, the briefs). To find the approximate number of APC cases in the Ninth Circuit, we did a string search in the Westlaw database for that circuit, using the same criteria as those described above but limiting the search further by requiring the name of one of the fifteen countries. This search yielded 552 cases, too many to examine individually, so there are undoubtedly a few "false positives," such as decisions that mentioned flight through one of the listed countries rather than specifying the country in question as that of the applicant's nationality. We then added the term "remand" to the string and then examined all of the resulting cases individually to eliminate those that were not true remands. This process showed 243 remands, again a slight overstatement because some of those cases named countries that were not the country of the applicant's nationality. We encourage other researchers to do a more careful study of the Ninth Circuit's remand rate by examining each published and unpublished case individually rather than relying on the searching method that we had to use because our resources were limited.

For our analysis of remand rates from China, we used the same search string we used for APC decisions, but limited the search to decisions that used the word "China." We then manually eliminated cases that were not actually asylum appeals by nationals of China (e.g., cases in which asylum seekers from other nations had traveled in China).

We analyzed only the Third and Sixth Circuits for internal consistency. As noted in the text, the judges of the Fourth, Fifth, and Eleventh Circuits did not vote to remand very often, so although consistency was quite high in these circuits, there were not enough votes for us to study the effect of appointments by different presidential administrations. The total number of cases in the First and Tenth Circuits was not large enough for analysis. Evaluation of the Second Circuit was complicated by the fact that because of the docket explosion described in the text, many of its more difficult cases were held for 2006. We chose not to evaluate consistency in the Seventh Circuit because it was not typical, in that it had an unusually high remand rate. The Ninth Circuit had too many cases for us to count individual votes of judges. That left only the Third, Sixth, and Eighth Circuits, and of those circuits, we evaluated consistency in the two circuits with the largest numbers of asylum cases.

NOTES

1. In one instance (our study of the votes of judges in the Sixth Circuit during 2004 and 2005), we dropped the threshold to twenty-three, which added two more judges to the sample.

2. See http://www.law.georgetown.edu/humanrightsinstitute/ refugeeroulette.htm.

3. See Letter from Andrew Schoenholtz to Joseph Langlois (Jan. 5, 2006) (on file with authors). For further explanation of the term Asylee Producing Country, see chapter 2.

4. 8 C.F.R. § 208.16(a) (2007).

5. For a full explanation, see Andrew I. Schoenholtz, Refugee Protection in the United States Post-September 11, 36 Colum. Hum. Rts. L. Rev. 323, (2005), at 338 n.62.

6. For more information about the one-year filing deadline, see chapter 1 and its notes.

7. These data can be found on the asylumlaw.org website. U.S. Immigration Judge Decisions in Asylum Cases, Jan. 2000 to Aug. 2004, http://www.asylumlaw.org/legal_tools/ index. cfm?fuseaction=showJudges2004.

8. The FOIA request sought the following information on decisions by immigration judges on requests for asylum, withholding of removal, and claims for relief under the Convention against Torture: "the country of origin or asserted citizenship of each applicant; the number of subsidiary applicants, if any; the immigration judge's name; the location (city) in which the immigration court is located; the date of the hearing; the date of the decision; and the decision, with respect to each form of relief requested." It also sought information on whether the asylum seeker was represented, and whether her case was referred from the Asylum Office. Letter from David Berten, President, asylumlaw.org, to Charles Adkins-Blanch, Gen. Counsel, Executive Office for Immigration Review, Dep't of Justice (Aug. 3, 2004) (on file with authors).

9. This database includes only asylum decisions, and does not include decisions on claims of withholding of removal or protection under the Convention against Torture. Telephone conversation with David Berten, Asylumlaw.org (Nov. 16, 2007). Denials resulting from legal bars—such as for missing the one-year filing deadline—are included in these statistics as denials.

10. *See supra* Methodological Appendix, part 1 (listing the criteria by which we selected these fifteen countries).

11. Due to resource constraints, we were not able to use the more reliable method of removing defensive cases from the data, which would eliminate 95 percent of the detained cases.

12. In order to address caseload imbalances, EOIR solicits volunteers from among the immigration judges to work on a different immigration court for a short period of time. This process is known as "detailing." For further explanation of the process of and reasons for detailing immigration judges to different courts, see U.S. Gov't Accountability Office, Executive Office for Immigration Review: Caseload Performance Reporting Needs Improvement (2006), at 18.

13. Grants included conditional grants of asylum, which were awarded to individuals granted asylum statutorily under the coercive population control provision of the Immigration and Nationality Act. 8 U.S.C. § 1101(a)(42)(B) (2000). This provision awards asylum to individuals persecuted through or on account of coercive population control measures, but because there was a cap of one thousand grants of asylum each year under this measure during the time frame of the study, asylum was granted conditionally until a final approval could be awarded. *See* Executive Office for Immigration Review, U.S. Dep't of Justice, Fact Sheet: Conditional Grants of Asylum Based on Coercive Population Control Policies (Dec. 16, 2004), *available at* http://www.usdoj. gov/eoir/press/04/ CPCAsylumFactSheetDec04.htm.

14. For example, we identified one such "family" with twenty-five members, which may imply that at least this categorization was overbroad. However, such large "families" were not common in the database.

15. *See* E-mail from Executive Office of Immigration Review to Jaya Ramji-Nogales (Jan. 25, 2007) (on file with authors).

16. E-mail from Executive Office of Immigration Review to Jaya Ramji-Nogales (Jan. 22, 2007) (on file with authors).

17. For some independent variables, there were additional missing observations that decreased the number of cases included in the analysis.

18. *See supra* note 14 and accompanying text.

19. TRAC Immigration, Immigration Judge Reports—Asylum, http://trac.syr.edu/ immigration/reports/judgereports.

20. The chi-square test examines the relationship between two variables, assessing the difference between a situation in which no relationship exists between two variables and the actual relationship between the variables being analyzed. Where the chi-square outcome is statistically significant, a causal relationship between the variables may exist.

21. The full cross-tabulation results are reported at http://www.law.georgetown.edu/human-rightsinstitute/ refugeeroulette.htm.

22. *See* Donald Kerwin, *Revisiting the Need for Appointed Counsel, in* INSIGHT, at 1 (Migration Policy Inst., No. 4, 2005), *available at* http://www.migrationpolicy.org/insight/ Insight_Kerwin. pdf; Charles H. Kuck, *Legal Assistance for Asylum Seekers in Expedited Removal: A Survey of Alternative Practices, in* II Report on Asylum Seekers in Expedited Removal (2005), *available at* http://www.uscirf.gov/countries/global/asylum_refugees/2005/february/index.html at 674; Andrew I. Schoenholtz & Jonathan Jacobs, The State of Asylum Representation: Ideas for Change, 16 Geo. Immigr. L.J. 739, 742 (2002).

23. The freedom rating scores created by Freedom House and Freedom House's description of its methodology are available through Freedom House, Freedom in the World, http://www. freedomhouse.org/template.cfm?page=15.

24. *See* U.S. Census Bureau, Current Population Survey (CPS), http://www.census.gov/cps.

25. The appointment under President Reagan variable, which was not part of the cross-tabulation analysis, was less than 95% likely to be statistically significant.

26. *See* Letter from Andrew Schoenholtz to Lori Scialabba, Chairman, Bd. of Immigration Appeals (Jan. 30, 2006) (on file with authors).

27. Board of Immigration Appeals, Board of Immigration Appeals Decision and Disposition Codes (June 2005) (unpublished code sheet, on file with the authors).

28. In retrospect, it might have been better to have used FY 2004 and 2005 (October 1, 2003, through September 30, 2005) as the database, for purposes of better comparison with federal statistics, which are usually kept by fiscal year. However, by the time we realized this, we had already compiled the calendar year 2004 database. We do not know of any reason why our use of a time frame that starts and ends three months later than the fiscal year would appreciably change any of the statistical information. The database of cases in most courts of appeals is relatively small, so in our study of decisions of these courts, we searched for remands after denials by the Board of Convention against Torture cases as well as remands after denials of asylum. Asylum cases are, however, the vast majority of the cases in our database. We did not specifically search for appeals involving denials of withholding of removal because foreign nationals who appeal from denials of withholding also appeal from denials of their applications for asylum.

29. All appeals from Board decisions to the U.S. courts of appeals are taken by foreign nationals; the United States does not appeal decisions rendered by its own Department of Justice. *See* John R. B. Palmer, Stephen W. Yale-Loehr & Elizabeth Cronin, Why Are So Many People Challenging Board of Immigration Appeals Decisions in Federal Court? An Empirical Analysis of the Recent Surge in Petitions for Review, 20 Geo. Immigr. L.J. 1, 38 n.3 (2005). All asylum appeals considered by the courts in 2004 appeared to have been filed against John Ashcroft in his capacity as attorney general. Appeals from decisions of his predecessor Janet Reno, who left office in January 2001, had been resolved or had been renamed to reflect the appointment of Attorney General Ashcroft. Alberto R. Gonzales became attorney general on January 3, 2005. Nine First Circuit cases from early 2004 were denominated as cases against the Immigration and Naturalization Service, or INS, an agency within the Department of Justice whose functions were transferred to the Department of Homeland Security in 2003, but these nine cases were located and included in the database. The Department of Homeland Security is not the named respondent in these cases because the appeals are technically Petitions for Review of a decision of the attorney general.

30. In some cases, aliens in detention sought writs of habeas corpus from the district courts and appealed denials to the court of appeals. These cases were excluded from the database.

31. The texts of a small number of nonprecedential Fifth Circuit decisions were so summary that we could not even tell whether these cases involved asylum. We excluded these cases from the database.

32. However, we included such a case if the foreign national also challenged the merits of the Board's individualized decision and the court considered those merits. In a few cases, a foreign national appealed both the denial of an asylum claim and the denial of a motion to reopen. These cases were included in the database if the court of appeals evaluated the merits of the asylum claim or the fairness of the immigration judge hearing in connection with either appeal, even if it dismissed the other appeal without reaching its merits.

33. The statistics for the Second Circuit understate both the number of asylum appeals disposed of by that circuit and the number of cases remanded. In most circuits, the Office of Immigration Litigation (OIL) of the Department of Justice represents the government in immigration appeals, including asylum cases. Except in very rare instances, OIL lawyers have not negotiated with lawyers representing foreign nationals or agreed to stipulate for remands. For historical reasons, however, the U.S. Attorney's Office (USAO) for the Southern District of New York, rather than OIL, has represented the government in Second Circuit immigration cases. USAO has been willing to discuss cases with foreign nationals' lawyers and to stipulate to remands when it appears that the Board of Immigration Appeals has affirmed an erroneous or doubtful immigration court decision. These negotiated remands do not show up in any searchable database of court opinions. Along with stipulated withdrawals of appeals, they do show up in the PACER records of Second Circuit cases, but unfortunately, although the docket sheets show that the case was resolved without a decision by the court, those docket sheets do not usually reveal whether the disposition was a voluntary withdrawal, a negotiated withdrawal, or a negotiated remand. USAO does not keep statistics on the disposition of asylum cases in which it engaged in discussion or negotiation before the case was removed from the docket of the circuit. It may seem surprising that the Second Circuit decided only about thirty-six asylum cases during 2004, although it disposed of 421 such cases during 2005. During 2004, the Second Circuit received more than two thousand appeals from BIA decisions. *See* Palmer et al., *supra* note 29, at 54 tbl.1 (showing 945 appeals from the BIA to the Second Circuit from June through September 2004). However, the USAO and the court were so unprepared for the sudden increase in caseload that most cases were simply put into a backlog, which built up to about five thousand cases before the Second Circuit decided, in August 2005, to adopt a "nonargument calendar" to dispose of most BIA appeals without oral argument. Judge Jon O. Newman, The Second Circuit's Expedited Adjudication of Asylum Cases: A Case Study of a Judicial Response to an Unprecedented Problem of Caseload Management, 74 Brooklyn L. Rev. 429 (2009).

34. For 2004 cases, we used the following search string for each circuit: (asylum torture & ashcroft "attorney general") & da(aft 12/31/2003 & bef 1/1/2005) % bg(habeas "motion to reopen" "motion to reconsider" "cancellation of removal" "adjustment of status" "suspension of deportation"). For 2005 cases the search string sought cases in which Gonzales rather than Ashcroft was a party and substituted dates in 2005. The searches excluded appeals from the BIA that may have mentioned asylum in passing but were actually claims of erroneous denial of other forms of relief from removal. It also excluded habeas corpus appeals and appeals from motions to reopen.

35. We assume that all Eleventh Circuit appeals that were briefed before March 2003 were decided in 2003, not 2004, and that no case in which the foreign national's brief was filed in November or December 2004 would have resulted in an opinion during the calendar year 2004. In the CTA11 database for 2004 decisions, we used the following search string to expand the search: (asylum torture) & (Ashcroft "attorney general") & da(aft 3/1/2003 & bef 10/31/2004) % bg (habeas "motion to reopen").

36. The docket sheets may be inspected for a fee on the government's PACER system, PACER Service Center, http://pacer.psc.uscourts.gov.

37. Seven other cases may have qualified by our criteria, but the court had not posted the docket sheet or opinion, so we could not tell the result. We excluded those seven cases from our analysis.

Ninth Circuit Appendix

PROFESSOR DAVID LAW studied the votes in asylum cases in the Ninth Circuit between 1992 and 2001. His primary focus was a study of whether judges made strategic use of publication rules to shape the development of case law.[1] He concluded, among other things, that "to some extent, judges vote strategically and bargain amongst themselves so as to maximize the amount of 'good law' and minimize the amount of 'bad law' that will appear in the pages of the *Federal Reporter* and bind their colleagues in subsequent cases."[2]

Professor Law was kind enough to share with us his data on how each judge voted in the nearly two thousand cases in his study.[3] The method by which he selected cases was similar to ours, with these exceptions: (a) he included affirmances of habeas corpus denials in his study, whereas we excluded them, and he reports that there were not many such decisions; (b) he included both grants of asylum and remands to the Board as decisions favorable to asylum applicant, while in our study, there were virtually no grants, because the Supreme Court in *Ventura* had directed the appellate courts to affirm or remand in nearly all cases.[4]

From his data set, we excluded all judges who cast fewer than twenty-five votes during the period in question.

Figure A.1 shows the grant rates of the Ninth Circuit judges.

FIGURE A.1

Rate of Votes of Ninth Circuit Judges Favorable to Asylum Applicants, by Judge

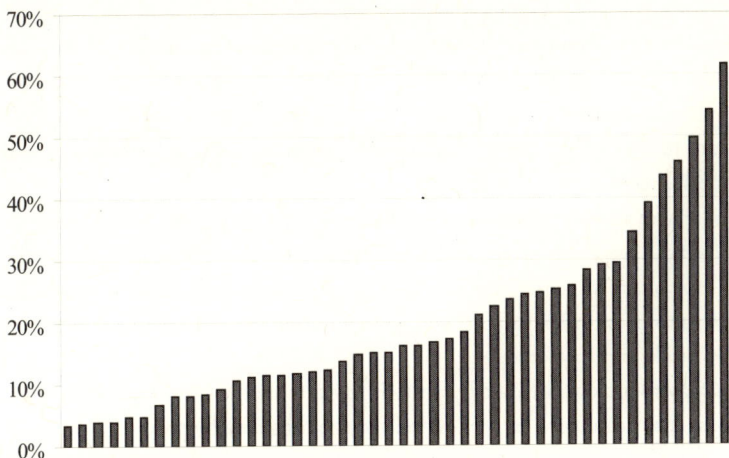

FIGURE A.2

Disparities in Ninth Circuit Voting

Note: The black bars indicate those judges who deviated from the mean by more than 50%.

Figure A.2 shows that twenty of the forty-four judges (45%) voted for the applicant at a rate that was more than 50% higher or lower than the 17.9% mean rate at which judges in the Ninth Circuit voted in favor of the asylum applicant on the merits.

Figure A.3 shows that as in the Sixth Circuit, judges appointed by Democrats voted for asylum applicants at a rate much higher than those appointed by Republicans.

This visual representation may actually understate the degree of the differences among the parties' appointees. In fact Democrats voted, in the aggregate, to support the applicant 24.0% of the time, while Republicans voted to support the applicant 10.9% of the time, less than half as often. Looking at the effect of voting on panels, Professor Law concluded,

> With an all-Republican panel, the likelihood that an unpublished decision will favor the asylum seeker is just 4%. The addition of one Democrat to the panel triples that probability to 12%. With two Democrats on the panel, the probability increases again to just over 20%, and with an all-Democrat panel, the asylum seeker's chances top 30%.[5]

A final way to look at the data by party is to examine the extent to which disparities from the mean were on the low side or the high side by party (figure A.4):

Grant Rates by Party of Appointing President

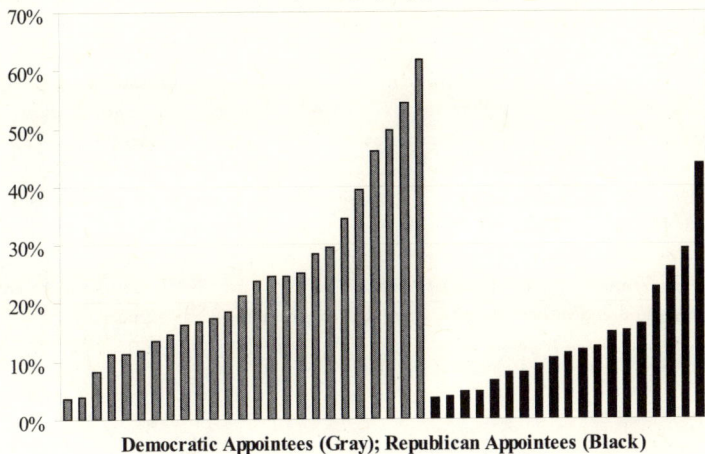

Democratic Appointees (Gray); Republican Appointees (Black)

Disparities by Party

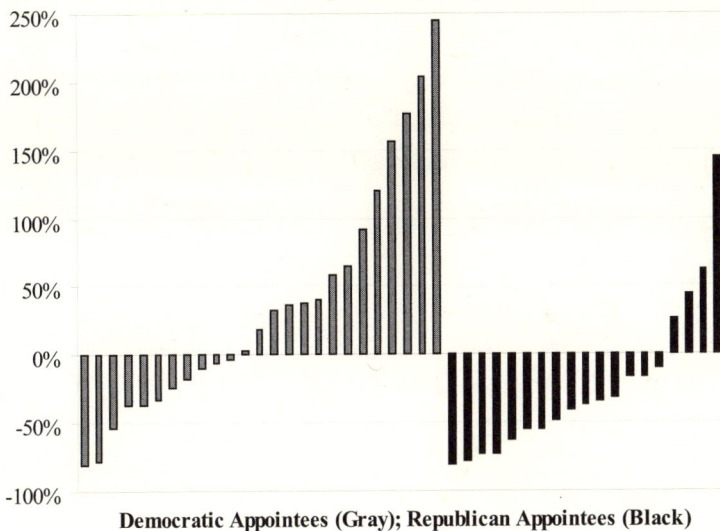

Democratic Appointees (Gray); Republican Appointees (Black)

This graph shows that of the nine Republican judges who voted lower or higher than the mean by more than 50%, seven were on the low side, whereas of the eleven Democrats who so voted, eight were on the high side. This is yet another way of saying that political party seems to matter, even when judges are applying a federal refugee statute.

1. His study appears as David S. Law, Strategic Judicial Lawmaking: Ideology, Publication, and Asylum Law in the Ninth Circuit, 73 U. Cin. L. Rev. 817, 819 (2005).

2. *Id.* at 864.

3. Like us, Professor Law had to create the data set by examining each published and unpublished decision that mentioned asylum; the U.S. courts do not code asylum decisions of the courts of appeals as such. He did so with the financial support of the National Science Foundation. We also received help from Professor Joshua Fischman, who has written an article based on Prof. Law's data. See Joshua B. Fischman, Decision-Making under a Norm of Consensus: A Structural Analysis of Three-Judge Panels (Amer. Law & Econ. Ass'n Working Paper Series, Paper No. 58, 2007), available at http://papers.ssrn.com/sol3/papers.cfm?abstract_id=912299.

4. See INS v. Ventura, 537 U.S. 12 (2002). Professor Law separately coded decisions that were merely procedural, and we have excluded those decisions from the data we report here.

5. Law, *supra* note 1, at 847–48.

Index

consistency: factors affecting, 255–267; public perceptions, 1; reasons for, 1, 89, 251–255

counsel. *See* representation

credibility determinations, 188–193; and cultural differences, 195; in United Kingdom, 169–173

Creppy, Michael, 124n66

Department of Homeland Security (DHS): asylum office interviews, 12; disparities among regions, 91–92; grant rate variation within regional offices, 18–31, 90–91; quality control, 17, 116; regional offices, 12; role in asylum adjudication, 11, 17–18; training of officers, 17, 29–30, 112. *See also* policy recommendations

Department of Justice: Legal Orientation Program, 299. *See also* Board of Immigration Appeals; immigration courts

dependents, in immigration courts, 46

disparities among courts, causes, 255–267

Edwards, Harry, 1–2

Einhorn, Bruce, 187–201

Environmental Protection Agency (EPA), 2

European Community Qualification Directive, 172

Executive Office for Immigration Review (EOIR), 230. *See also* Board of Immigration Appeals; immigration courts

Federal Judicial Center, 117

Fischman, Joshua, 330n3

Frist, Bill, 117

gender: in immigration films, 216; theories to explain differences in judging, 210–218. *See also* immigration courts

Georgetown University, 45, 58n33

Gilligan, Carol, 203–204, 210–211

Gonzales, Alberto: implementation of proposed reforms, 125n80, 126n92; political hiring of immigration judges, 101–103; proposed budget increase rejected, 108; reforms proposed, 122n42, 127n95, 237, xvii

Goodling, Monica, 102

Government Accountability Office (GAO), 5, 55n16, 56n25, 57n27, 75n34, 75n35

Guthrie, Chris, 108, 111

Haitian nationals, 72

Human Rights First, 45–46; critique of Board of Immigration Appeals, 63

immigration courts, 13–14; Asylee-Producing Countries (APCs), 38–41; corroborating evidence, 131n130; *de novo* review, 33; decisions by politically appointed judges, 121n44; detailing, 322; disparities among courts, 35–37, 55n15, 92; disparities within courts, 38–44, 90; documentation of corroborating evidence, 46; effect of combined variables, 51–53; effect of dependents, 46; effect of judge's gender, 47–53, 202–219; effect of judge's prior work experience, 48–53; effect of representation, 45–46; hiring standards for judges, 123n62, 124n66; Miami, xv; New York, xv; political tests used in selection of judges, 101–103; reporting poor quality of adjudication, 130n121; structure, 33; training of judges, 110, 196; variables affecting judges' decisions, 44–53; variables affecting judges decisions, 92–93. *See also* policy recommendations

ineffective assistance of counsel. *See* representation

INS v. Benslimane, 105

INS v. Ventura, 86n6, 330n4

inspector general, Department of Justice (DOJ), xvii

Ireland, 165

Jackson, Robert H., 89

Jury of Her Peers, A (Glaspell), 215

Katzmann, Robert A., 289

Kerwin, Donald, 114

Kohlberg, Lawrence, 203

Law, Anna, 105

Law, David, 6, 87n12, 327–328

Legomsky, Stephen, 71, 95, 250–285

Levinson, Peter, 71, 73n5, 74n17

About the Authors

JAYA RAMJI-NOGALES is an assistant professor of law at Temple University's Beasley School of Law. She received her B.A. with highest honors and distinction from the University of California at Berkeley; her J.D. from the Yale Law School; and her LL.M. with distinction from the Georgetown University Law Center. She has authored several articles on immigration and refugee law, including *A Global Approach to Secret Evidence: How Human Rights Law Can Reform Our Immigration System* in the Columbia Human Rights Law Review and *Legislating Away International Law: The Refugee Provisions of the Illegal Immigration Reform and Immigrant Responsibility Act* in the Stanford Journal of International Law. In 1999, she was awarded the Robert L. Bernstein Fellowship in International Human Rights to create a refugee law clinic at the University of Witwatersrand in Johannesburg, South Africa.

ANDREW I. SCHOENHOLTZ, a visiting professor of law at Georgetown University, teaches courses on refugee and immigration law and policy, codirects Georgetown's Certificate in Refugees and Humanitarian Emergencies, and serves as Deputy Director of the Institute for the Study of International Migration at the School of Foreign Service. He is the author of numerous publications on refugee and immigration matters. Before coming to Georgetown, he served as Deputy Director of the U.S. Commission on Immigration Reform and practiced immigration, asylum, and international law with the Washington, D.C., law firm of Covington & Burling. Schoenholtz holds a J.D. from Harvard Law School and a Ph.D. from Brown University.

PHILIP G. SCHRAG, a graduate of Harvard College and Yale Law School, is the Delaney Family Professor of Public Interest Law at Georgetown University and director of the Center for Applied Legal Studies, in which students, working under faculty guidance, learn to become effective advocates by representing asylum applicants in federal immigration court. He began his career as Assistant Counsel at the NAACP Legal Defense Fund, and before joining the Georgetown faculty he served as the first Consumer Advocate of the City of New York and as the Deputy General Counsel of the United States Arms Control and Disarmament Agency. He is the author of dozens of articles and fourteen books, including *Asylum Denied: A Refugee's Struggle for Safety in America* (with David Ngaruri Kenney).